**Finally, from Phil Rosenthal, beloved host of the hit Emmy-nominated Netflix series *Somebody Feed Phil*, comes a brand-new cookbook that brings fans on a heartwarming and delicious journey—inviting you into Phil's kitchen to experience the flavors and stories that have shaped his life with comfort food recipes you can make at home.**

Phil believes eating is a way to expand your circle of family and friends. That's why *Phil's Favorites* is more than just a cookbook; it's a celebration of food and relationships. With contributions from his wife, actress Monica Horan; his daughter, Lily, and son, Ben; and his brother, Richard, as well as friends like Judy Gold and Anna Romano—plus beloved dishes from past seasons and homey favorites from chefs who have become like family—the book is filled with touching stories and mouthwatering meals. Savor Monica's Chicken Corn Soup, Judy Gold's Carrot Kugel, and Lily's Chocolate Chip–Streusel Banana Bread, or make Phil's very own classic Tuna Sandwich. Delight your family with comfort food from renowned chefs and iconic restaurants worldwide, such as Pizzeria Beddia in Philadelphia, Daddy's Dogs in Nashville, and the Bombay Canteen in Mumbai.

*Phil's Favorites* encourages you to gather, cook, and savor the simple joy of sharing a meal. As Phil reminds us, food is the ultimate connector, and laughter is the glue that holds it all together. With cheerful photography celebrating food, family, and Phil's special brand of joy, this book beautifully captures the warmth of coming together around the table.

# Phil's Favorites

**Recipes from Friends and Family to Make at Home**

## Phil Rosenthal

# Phil's Favorites

**Recipes from Friends and Family to Make at Home**

## Phil Rosenthal
and **Jenn Garbee**

*Photography by*
**Andrea D'Agosto**

*Location Photography by*
**Richard Rosenthal**

Simon Element

New York   Amsterdam/Antwerp   London   Toronto   Sydney/Melbourne   New Delhi

An Imprint of Simon & Schuster, LLC
1230 Avenue of the Americas
New York, NY 10020

For more than 100 years, Simon & Schuster has championed authors and the stories they create. By respecting the copyright of an author's intellectual property, you enable Simon & Schuster and the author to continue publishing exceptional books for years to come. We thank you for supporting the author's copyright by purchasing an authorized edition of this book.

No amount of this book may be reproduced or stored in any format, nor may it be uploaded to any website, database, language-learning model, or other repository, retrieval, or artificial intelligence system without express permission. All rights reserved. Inquiries may be directed to Simon & Schuster, 1230 Avenue of the Americas, New York, NY 10020 or permissions@simonandschuster.com.

Copyright © 2025 by Phil Rosenthal
Photography Copyright © 2025
by Andrea D'Agosto
Location Photography Copyright © 2025
by Richard Rosenthal

All rights reserved, including the right to reproduce this book or portions thereof in any form whatsoever. For information, address Simon Element Subsidiary Rights Department, 1230 Avenue of the Americas, New York, NY 10020.

First Simon Element hardcover edition
November 2025

SIMON ELEMENT is a trademark
of Simon & Schuster, LLC

Simon & Schuster strongly believes in freedom of expression and stands against censorship in all its forms. For more information, visit BooksBelong.com.

For information about special discounts for bulk purchases, please contact Simon & Schuster Special Sales at 1-866-506-1949 or business@simonandschuster.com.

The Simon & Schuster Speakers Bureau can bring authors to your live event. For more information or to book an event, contact the Simon & Schuster Speakers Bureau at 1-866-248-3049 or visit our website at www.simonspeakers.com.

Interior design by Casalino Design
Food styling by Caroline Hwang
Prop styling by Alicia Buszczak

Manufactured in China

10 9 8 7 6 5 4 3 2 1

Library of Congress Cataloging-in-Publication Data has been applied for.

ISBN 978-1-6680-3555-9
ISBN 978-1-6680-3556-6 (ebook)

Steve Nathan's Vanilla Pancakes (page 47) from *Huckleberry: Stories, Secrets, and Recipes from Our Kitchen* by Zoe Nathan with Josh Loeb and Laurel Almerinda, Copyright © 2014 by Zoe Nathan, Chronicle Books.

*This book is for my growing family,
which includes Monica, Ben, Lily,
and now DeLaney and Mason,
and all of you.*

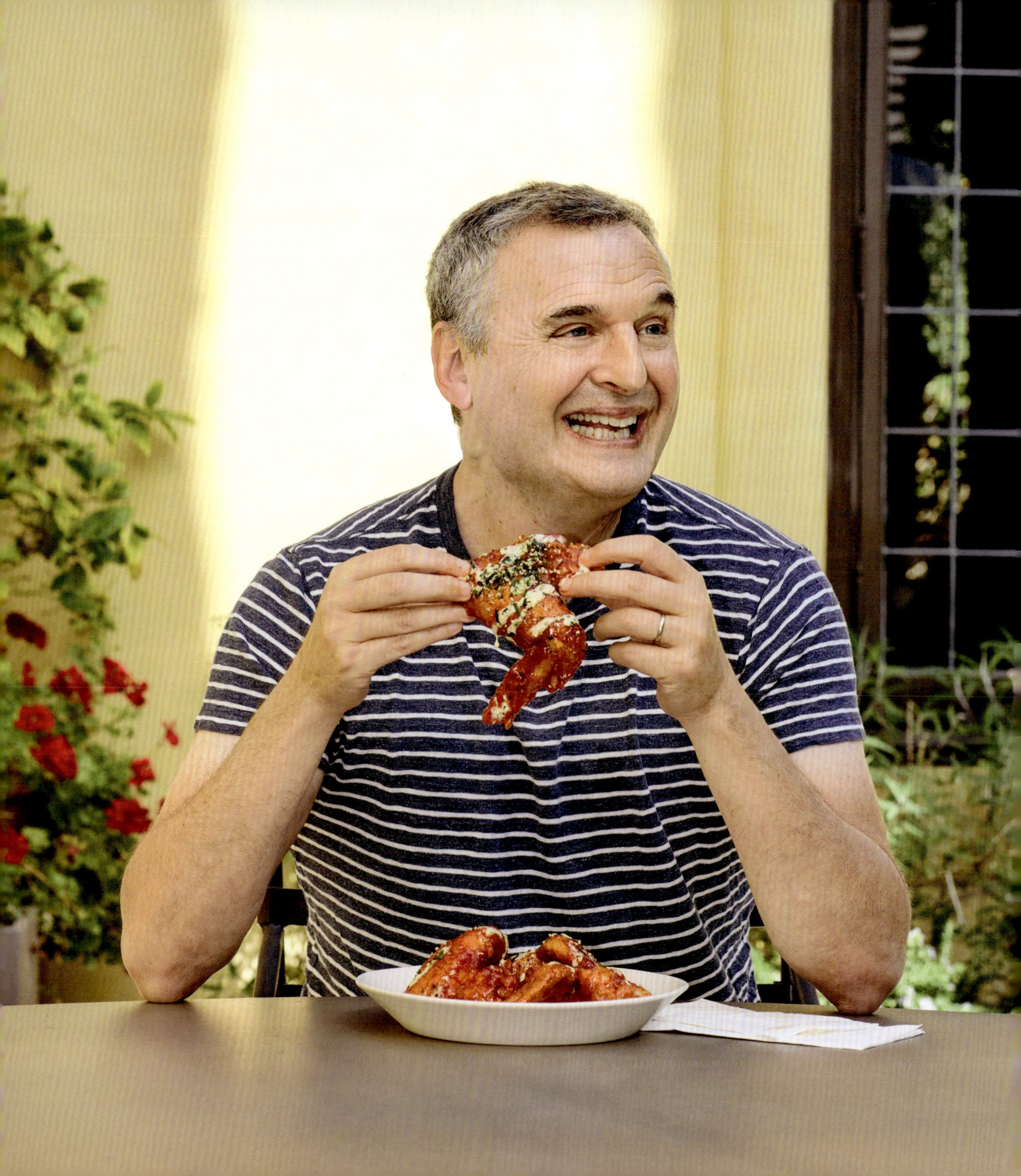

# Contents

**Foreword by Monica Horan Rosenthal**
..................................................................15

**Introduction**
..................................................................17

## When I Get Up

GGET's Iced Almond-Macadamia Latte
(The "New York"), Go Get Em Tiger, Los Angeles
..................................................................23

Wife & Husband's Honey Cheese Toast, Kyoto
..................................................................25

Ludo Lefebvre's French Omelette,
Petit Trois, Los Angeles
..................................................................29

Max's Fluffy Eggs with Slab Bacon and Toast,
Max & Helen's, Los Angeles
..................................................................35

The Yolko Ono (Fried Egg, Sausage,
and Basil Pesto on Sourdough),
Fried Egg I'm In Love, Portland
..................................................................39

Jimmy Shaw's Huevos Rancheros
with Salsa de Chile Morita and Frijoles Negros,
Lotería Grill, Los Angeles
..................................................................43

Steve Nathan's Vanilla Pancakes,
Huckleberry, Santa Monica
..................................................................47

Siggi Hilmarsson's Geothermal Lava Bread,
Laugarvatn Fontana, Iceland
..................................................................49

Lily's Chocolate Chip–Streusel Banana Bread
..................................................................55

Homeboy Bakery's Cinnamon Coffee Cake,
Los Angeles
..................................................................57

Brauð & Co.'s Cinnamon Rolls, Reykjavík
..................................................................61

## The Best Invention in the World: The Sandwich

Chad Conley and Greg Mitchell's Tuna Melt, Palace Diner, Biddeford ...................69

Joe Beddia's Tuna and Smoked Sardine Hoagie, Pizzeria Beddia, Philadelphia ...................73

My Tuna Sandwich ...................77

Marc Vetri's Mortadella and Ricotta Sandwich, Fiorella, Philadelphia/LA Loves Alex's Lemonade, Los Angeles ...................79

Bill Miller's Turkey-Brie Sandwich (aka "The Phil"), Malibu Kitchen ...................81

Ajay Sahgal's Peanut Butter and Pickle Sandwich ...................85

Bite into Maine's Curry Lobster Roll, Fort Williams Park, Cape Elizabeth ...................87

The Best Classic Maine Lobster Roll, Red's Eats, Wiscasset ...................89

The SPACCA Burger, Chi SPACCA, Los Angeles ...................93

Orfali Bros' Cheeseburger, Dubai ...................95

The Crustburger, Joyland, Nashville ...................99

Big Daddy's Hot Dogs (The Big Daddy, The Music City, and The Carolina), Daddy's Dogs, Nashville ...................101

## Soups, Stews, and Curries

Carolina Bazán's White Gazpacho, Ambrosia Bistró, Santiago ...................109

Monica's Chicken Corn Soup ...................113

The Only Way Ray Will Eat Broccoli (Anna Romano's Sicilian Broccoli-Pasta Soup) ...................119

Saw Naing's Pe Hainn (Coconut Chickpea Curry with Greens), The Dutchess, Ojai ...................121

Roseleaf's Cullen Skink (Scottish Smoked Fish Chowder), Roseleaf, Edinburgh ...................125

Jasper Pääkkönen's Lohikeitto (Finnish Smoked Fish Soup), Löyly, Helsinki ...................129

Thalía Barrios García's Mushroom-Tomatillo Soup, La Cocina de Humo at Levadura de Olla, Oaxaca ...................133

## Things to Share

La Casa del Abuelo's Gambas al Ajillo
(Garlic Shrimp), Madrid
..................................................................139

Angel Barreto's Korean Fried Chikin Wings,
Anju, Washington, DC
..................................................................141

Ibérico Ham, Barcelona
..................................................................145

Jennifer Heftler's Chopped Liver
..................................................................147

Steve Horan's Fried Chicken Livers
..................................................................151

The Bombay Canteen's Butter Garlic Crab
Kulcha, Mumbai
..................................................................153

San Xi Lou's Sichuan Spicy Chicken, Hong Kong
..................................................................157

Mohamad Orfali's Charred Eggplant Bayildi,
Orfali Bros, Dubai
..................................................................163

Sieger Bayer's Golden Beets with Tofu Crema
and Verjus, Here's Looking At You, Los Angeles
..................................................................167

Judy Gold's Carrot Kugel
..................................................................173

## An Entire Chapter for Richard

Richard's Staten Island
..................................................................179

## The Reason I Pace Myself

Daniele Uditi's Spaghetti alla Puttanesca,
Pizzana, Los Angeles
..................................................................183

Tracy Malachek's Cavatelli with Tomatoes,
Anchovies, and Garlic Bread Crumbs,
Birdie's, Austin
..................................................................187

Mason Royal's Lemony Chicken
with Garlic-Anchovy Sauce
..................................................................191

Shola Olunloyo's Charred Steak
with Olive Oil, Philadelphia
..................................................................197

Yamuel Bigio's Puerto Rican Porchetta,
Crocante, Orlando
..................................................................201

Seng Luangrath's Moak Paa
(Steamed Fish in Sticky Rice Marinade),
Thip Khao, Washington, DC
..................................................................205

Oma's Stuffed Cabbage Rolls
..................................................................211

Chintan Pandya's Lucknow Dum Biryani, Adda, Queens ..................................................215

Bonnie Morales's Duck Plov, Kachka, Portland ..................................................221

Salam Dakkak's Fatet Muskhan, Bait Maryam, Dubai ..................................................229

Mike Solomonov and Andrew Henshaw's Lamb and Beef Koobideh, Laser Wolf, Philadelphia ..................................................235

Ben and Jeremy's Seafood Boil ..................................................239

Debra Barone's Braciole, "Debra Makes Something Good," Season 4, Episode 18 of *Everybody Loves Raymond* ..................................................247

Gverović-Orsan's Black Risotto, Dubrovnik ..................................................251

## The Best Part of the Day

Dario Landi and Dania Nuti's Cavallucci Cookies, Antico Forno Giglio, Florence ..................................................257

DeLaney Harter Rosenthal's One-Bowl Black Brownies ..................................................261

Bob Champion's Chocolate Peanut Butter Triple Layer Bars ..................................................265

Scott Linder's Flourless Chocolate Cake, Matū, Beverly Hills ..................................................269

Rob Weiner's Poppy Seed Cake ..................................................275

The Pie Guy's Marionberry Pie, North Plains ..................................................277

Buckwheat Blossom Farm's Wild Blueberry Pie, Wiscasset ..................................................283

Sweet T's Sweet Potato Pie, Philadelphia ..................................................285

Marie Mercado's Halo Halo with Vegan Halaya, Sampaguita, Orlando ..................................................289

Somebody Scoop Phil, Caffè Panna, New York ..................................................291

## Other Things You Want to Have Around

### Condiments and Sandwich Spreads

Chad's Bread-and-Butter Pickle Chips,
Palace Diner, Biddeford
.................................................................298

Mohamad's Brown Butter Caramelized Onions,
Orfali Bros, Dubai
.................................................................299

Nancy's Ultimate Hamburger Onions,
Chi SPACCA, Los Angeles
.................................................................301

Nancy's Calabrian Chili–Mint Aioli,
Chi SPACCA, Los Angeles
.................................................................302

Joe's Anchovy-Caper Aioli,
Pizzeria Beddia, Philadelphia
.................................................................303

Jace's Basil Pesto Sandwich Spread,
Fried Egg I'm In Love, Portland
.................................................................304

Sean's Fancy Burger Sauce, Joyland, Nashville
.................................................................309

### Dressings, Salsas, and Sauces

Ludo's Dijon Vinaigrette,
Petit Trois, Los Angeles
.................................................................310

Sieger's Vegan Soya Crema,
Here's Looking At You, Los Angeles
.................................................................311

Angel's Gochujang Wing Sauce,
Anju, Washington, DC
.................................................................312

Angel's White Barbecue Sauce,
Anju, Washington, DC
.................................................................313

Everyday Garlic-Ginger Paste
.................................................................314

Hussain's Butter-Garlic Sauce,
The Bombay Canteen, Mumbai
.................................................................316

Jimmy's Salsa de Chile Morita,
Lotería Grill, Los Angeles
.................................................................318

Big Daddy's Slaw Sauwce,
Daddy's Dogs, Nashville
.................................................................321

Mohamad's Tarator, Orfali Bros, Dubai
.................................................................322

Salam's Fatet (Fatteh) Sauce, Bait Maryam, Dubai
.................................................................323

CONTENTS • 11

## Breads and Sweet Things

**Bombay Canteen Kulcha, Mumbai** ..................324

**GGET's Toasted Almond-Macadamia Milk, Go Get Em Tiger, Los Angeles** ..................327

**Sampaguita's Vegan Halaya, Orlando** ..................332

**Hallie's Vanilla Bean Ice Cream, Caffé Panna, New York** ..................334

**The Pie Guy's Pie Crust, North Plains** ..................336

## Acknowledgments
..................340

## Index
..................344

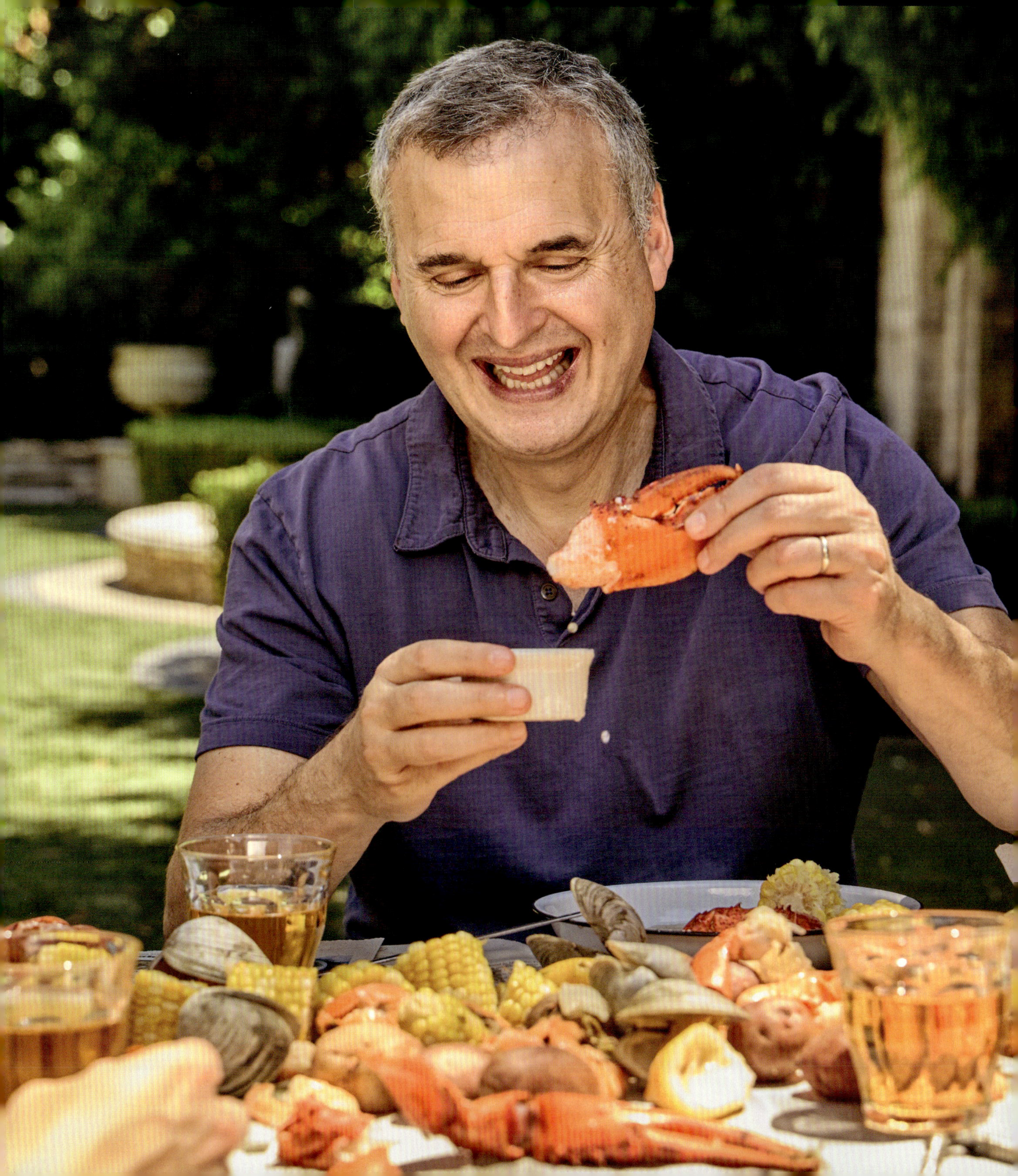

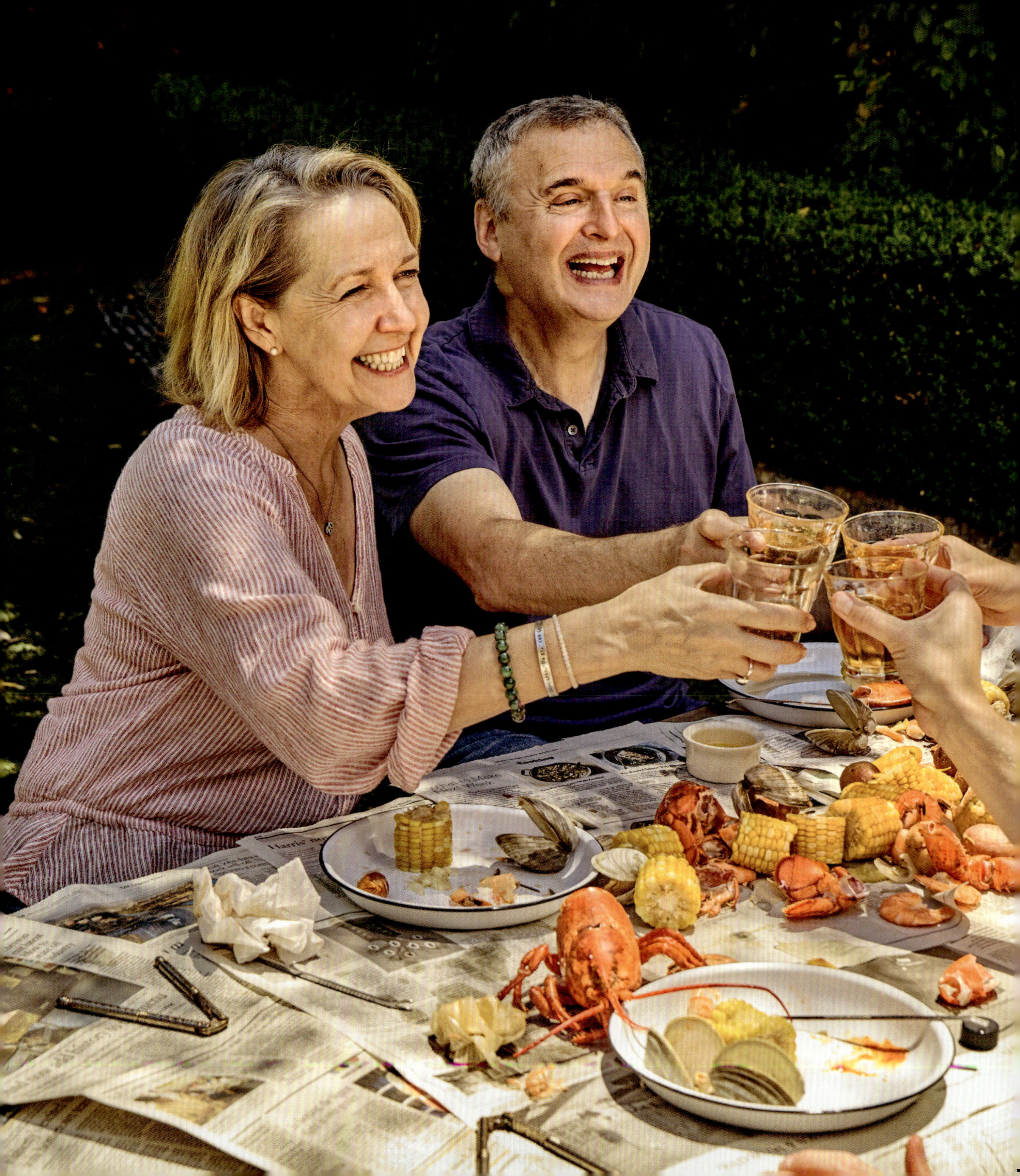

# Foreword

The first time I laid eyes on Phil Rosenthal in person was in New York City at the Ninth Avenue Food Fair in 1986. He was wearing a Joe Jackson *Jumpin' Jive* T-shirt and had a rib in his hand. I say "in person" because in some ways he was a celebrity to my twenty-three-year-old self, as I'd been hearing about him since my first days as a drama major at Hofstra University on Long Island. (Phil Rosenthal was the reason my new pal Lori Gunty chose Hofstra in the first place. If it was good enough for the star of *Little Me* at Clarkstown North, it was good enough for her!) When friends and I put on a very-far-off-Broadway play earlier that year, word quickly made it backstage that Phil Rosenthal had seen the play and thought I was funny! And now there he was, being introduced to me by old college pals, so darn cute that I didn't think it was disgusting at all that he had a giant piece of meat in one hand as he shook my hand with the other and said, "I'm a fan of yours." I almost died.

A few weeks later, I found myself in a rehearsal with *the* Phil Rosenthal. It was for the workshop of a new play directed by his pal Rob Weiner and actor friends Tom McGowan and Susan Varon at Columbia University. I had a small part and Phil was a lead, but we had scenes together, and I had plenty of time to fall in love with this hilarious, talented, and handsome young man whose face reminded me of a statue—though I couldn't quite place it. (I realized on my first trip to Florence that the statue was Michelangelo's David. Phil's face turns red every time I tell that story, so how could I resist putting it in print?)

On our first date, Phil told me about his travels. Mind you, we were starving artists; it was back in the days when you could live in NYC and pursue your dreams while getting by with very, very little money. "How can you possibly manage to travel?" I asked. Within months, I had my own passport and was meeting Phil in Zurich, Switzerland, where we would take trains to Paris, Rome, Florence (where I met our good friends Dania and Dario for the first time—you have to bake their cookies on page 257!), and then back to Zurich. Phil and his friends had found a way to travel to Europe for free, as DHL couriers, and he signed me up. Without internet and the Zero Point Zero dream team (the production team for *I'll Have What Phil's Having* and *Somebody Feed Phil* ), Phil was a one-man show, researching cities, restaurants, accommodations, every detail . . . and I was the one-person audience.

It's impossible to put into words how beautifully my life changed as I traveled with Phil and shared in his joy, enthusiasm, curiosity, and good will toward all. Fortunately, I don't have to—it's something everyone who knows him, loves him, and watches him on *Somebody Feed Phil* knows all too well. And I'm only too happy to share him with you all. As Phil says, "It's only good if you can share it!"

—**MONICA HORAN ROSENTHAL**

# Introduction

We're back. It's been three years since *Somebody Feed Phil the Book* was released, and here I am again, with the great Jenn Garbee and our second book, *Phil's Favorites*. I remember Richard, the team, and I were in Thailand filming the very first episode of *Somebody Feed Phil*. It had been two years since *I'll Have What Phil's Having* aired on PBS, and I was on a tiny seat in a tiny boat navigating the fantastic floating market in Bangkok. Richard and the crew were shooting what would become the very first scene in that first episode, and he turned to our director, John Bedolis, and said, "We're back." I was just as excited then, to be doing the show again, as I am now to be sharing another book with you. This time it's not only the stories and recipes from my favorite chefs and places from three more seasons of the show (seasons five through seven) but further travels, on and off camera. I even want to share my favorite dishes from the very special people in my everyday life.

My travel life has expanded since (and because of) the show. I now do live speaking engagements around the world, and as always, the best part of this life is meeting all of you very sweet and amazing people. The food is secondary. I realize that may not be the best message to start with in a cookbook, but why do we cook? I know. To eat. But to me, eating has always been about sharing the food, the stories, the laughs, connecting to family and friends, and expanding the circle of friends and family. It's a simple message as we share a meal: You're included.

Food is the great connector, and laughs are the cement.

There are a lot of recipes and people we couldn't include in this book because there wasn't room, their recipe had already run in another book, or some other reason. And even today, it can be hard to get in touch with some people when you are thousands of miles away. (Another good reason to travel.) One of those recipes is the scallion pancake from the "Taipei" episode in season seven of the show. It's some of the best street food I've ever had, anywhere. I could have that scallion pancake every day, any time of day, and be happy. But I can't. We just stumbled upon that cart and didn't get the contact information of the woman who made it for us. I blame Richard. Maybe you can help me. There are a lot of street vendors selling their own versions of scallion pancakes all over Taipei. I'm looking for the one run by the very nice lady who fries up an egg in the hot oil in her wok while she cooks the pancake, then she folds up the egg inside the pancake, so it becomes this crispy scallion breakfast wrap. It's not just delicious but a very good example of how many different types of sandwiches there are around the world. If you go to the episode, about halfway through you can see her white cart with some red writing on it and a blue umbrella. She's got two kinds of homemade sauces you can put on the pancake, but it doesn't need a thing. When you find her, please tell her I love her.

*Me and Jenn!*

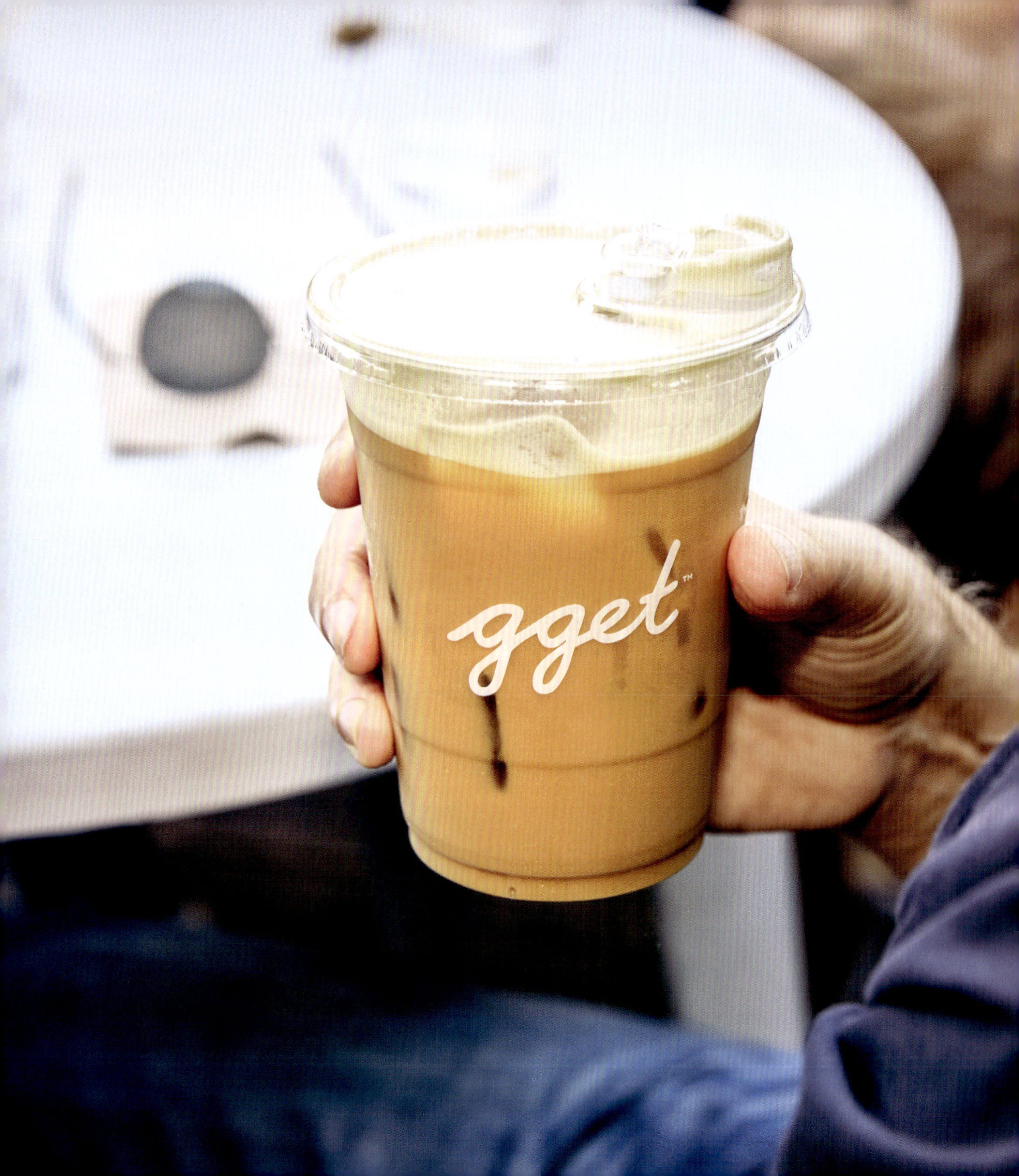
ggetTM

# WHEN I GET UP

I start planning what I'm going to eat as soon as I wake up. If I'm meeting somebody for lunch, I'm not going to have a big breakfast. Or if Monica and I have a special dinner, that's when I'll go to one of my favorite neighborhood breakfast spots and get something that might last me till dinner. (I love Great White in Larchmont. Go there and get the breakfast burrito. Ask for it with avocado and, this is very important, light on the potatoes. It comes cut in half, so it's perfect to share, and you'll have room for something else.)

It doesn't matter what I'm doing the rest of the day; every single day I can, I take Murray on a morning walk to my favorite neighborhood coffee place to meet our friends (their iced latte is the very first recipe in this book). When I'm home on weekends, I never miss going out to breakfast with family and friends. (My rule: go early, before the crowds.) It's one of the things I look most forward to every week. Beyond the great food, nobody's in a hurry, so you can spend as much time together as you want. When I'm traveling, I'll get some eggs or a fresh pastry or some bread from the local bakery. It's a great way to get to know the local food scene without being too full for lunch.

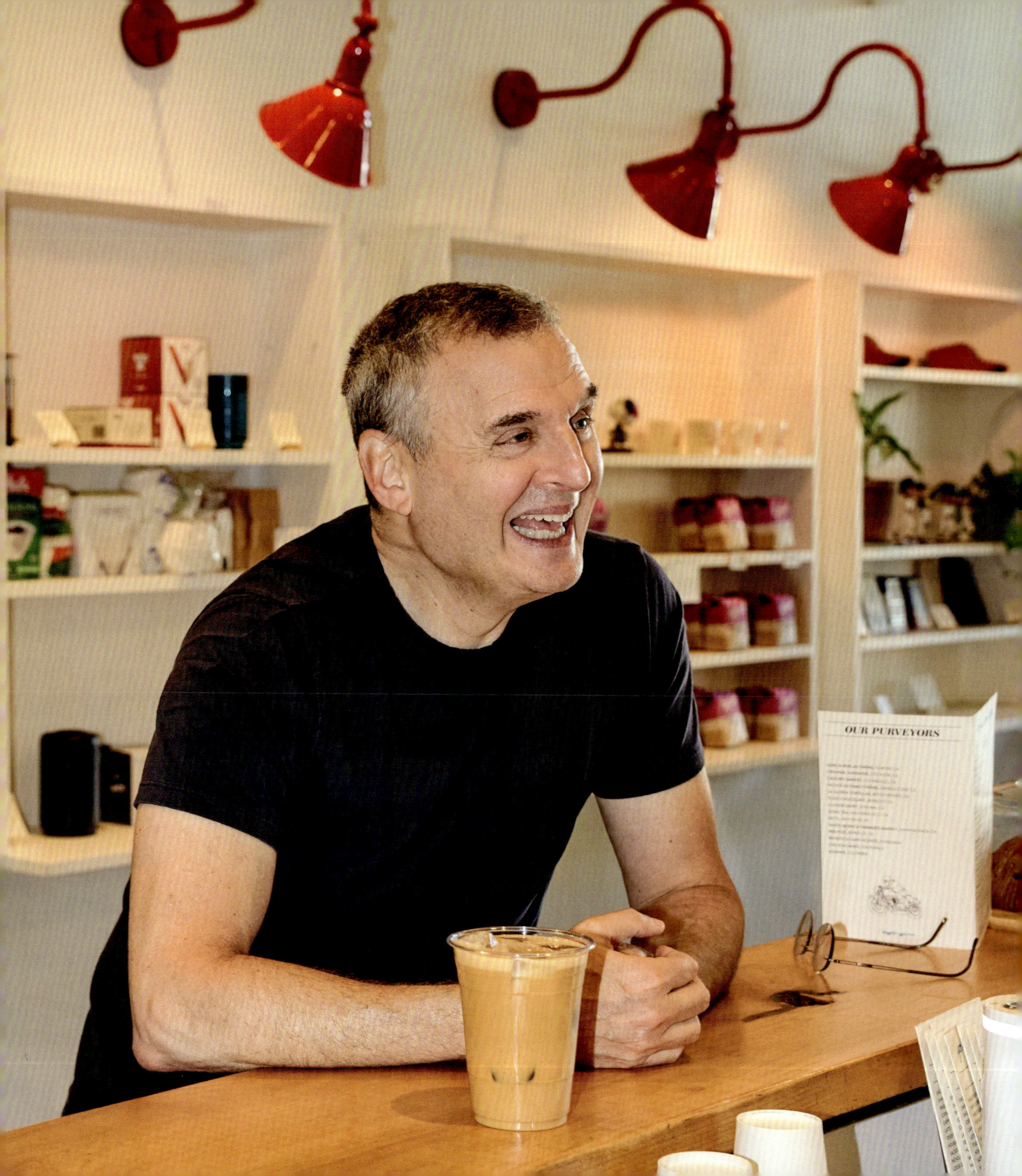
OUR PURVEYORS

# GGET's Iced Almond-Macadamia Latte (The "New York")

📍 *Go Get Em Tiger, Los Angeles*

Go Get Em Tiger, which goes by GGET, is my neighborhood coffee shop, and I'm there every single morning that I'm in town. I walk Murray there—a lot of people take their dogs—and we've made so many friends who have joined our little group. Some mornings the group is as big as fifteen people. The coffee shop has almost replaced the diner in this country as the community hub, so I see it as a very good retirement plan. Our friendships have started over one basic thing we have in common: we all like this coffee. (There are four other coffee shops on the same street.) I usually get my coffee black, and GGET's house espresso blend is the best I've ever had. (I've learned the difference between good and not-so-good coffee: when it's good, it doesn't need anything in it.) This one is not as dark as most or at all bitter. (I buy their beans for the coffee I make at home.) When I do want something a little sweeter than my usual, this iced latte is what I get. *The New York Times* named it the best iced latte in all of America, and after the article came out, customers gave it the nickname the "New York." The secret to their nut milk is they make it with both almonds and macadamia nuts. If you don't have an espresso machine, Kyle Glanville, one of the cofounders, says you can use a good double-strength cold brew concentrate or even a good coffee capsule. Try it, and I think you'll agree: the New York in LA wins.

**MAKES 1 ICED LATTE**

⅔ cup (165ml) GGET's Toasted Almond-Macadamia Milk (page 327)

1 2-ounce (60ml) double shot medium roast espresso (GGET's Minor Monuments) or 5 to 6 ounces (150 to 180ml) Cold Brew Concentrate (recipe follows)

---

*For the espresso, we recommend a standard double shot, which for us means 20 grams of ground coffee in and 40 grams of extracted liquid out (in about 25 to 30 seconds) using a traditional home or commercial espresso machine. Make sure you use an excellent quality, medium(ish) roasted coffee for this. Our espresso blend is our darkest roast, but it's still on the lighter end of the spectrum and far more balanced compared to much of what is out there.* —**KYLE**

**TIP**

*For the cold brew concentrate, ask your local coffee roaster for a medium-coarse grind. To use a retail store's bulk grinder, go with the "French Press" setting.*

Fill a large glass with 4 to 5 ice cubes and a cocktail shaker with 2 ice cubes.

Before measuring, stir the nut milk well and add it to the cocktail shaker. Add the espresso or 5 ounces (150ml) cold brew concentrate, cover the shaker, and shake vigorously until the milk is frothy, 15 to 20 seconds. If using cold brew concentrate, taste and add a splash more, if needed.

Strain the latte into the glass and serve.

## COLD BREW CONCENTRATE

*Whether you're using a cold brew concentrate as a stand-in for espresso in the iced latte or to make coffee, it's important to keep the water-to-coffee ratio consistent. In this case, that's eight parts water to one part coffee. Always use filtered water and a good roast coffee.* —**KYLE**

**MAKES ABOUT 16 OUNCES (480ML), ENOUGH FOR 3 ICED LATTES**

**1 cup plus 1 tablespoon (75g) medium roast coffee (GGET's Minor Monuments), medium-coarse grind**

**20 ounces (600ml) filtered water**

In a large pitcher, combine the coffee and filtered water, cover, and refrigerate for 24 hours.

Strain the coffee through a fine-mesh strainer into a container or bowl; scrape all the coffee solids into the strainer to fully strain the brew. (Discard the solids.) Strain the coffee concentrate a second time to remove any fine sediment.

Cover and refrigerate the concentrate for up to 1 week.

**For espresso:** Use the cold brew concentrate at full strength.

**For cold brew coffee:** Dilute the concentrate with equal parts filtered water.

# Wife & Husband's Honey Cheese Toast

📍 *Kyoto*

I've never been to a place where I felt such serenity, peace, and incredible beauty as Kyoto. It's hard now for me to imagine my life before I went there for the first time when we were filming season seven of the show. It's the most exquisite place I think I've ever been to and the quietest city, and of course that beauty can be felt in the food and people.

One thing that takes me back to Kyoto is this cheese toast from Wife & Husband, one of the best coffee shops in the city. Ikumi (the "wife") and Kyoichi (the "husband") Yoshida not just live but work together, and they're doing it exceptionally well. (They might have the secret of life.) Their daughter was working the counter the day we went, and their younger son also helps out, so it's a true family effort. It's a beautiful relationship, and we all benefit from the beautiful things to eat and drink that come from it. Like many places in Japan, the shop is tiny and specializes in only a few things—coffee, tea, two kinds of toast, maybe a slice of cake—so each is perfected. At anyplace else people might look at the menu, wonder why there isn't more to order, and never walk inside. And if you did that, you'd miss one of the simplest and most perfect pieces of toast.

> *We are very honored to share our toast recipe with the world. As the base, we chose mild, shredded mozzarella cheese, which has no peculiarities and is moderately salty, so that the flavor of blue cheese is accented. We coat the bread with unsalted butter so the pure flavor of the butter can be felt without additional saltiness. For toasting, we recommend using a toaster with a steam function (like a Balmuda), as it keeps the interior of the bread moist. If you don't have one, you can achieve a similar effect by lightly misting the bread with water before you put it in a regular toaster oven.* **—KYOICHI AND IKUMI**

**FEEDS 1**

1 very thick (1-inch/2.5cm) slice shokupan (Japanese milk bread) or loaf-style brioche (Texas toast)

1 smear (about ½ tablespoon) unsalted butter, room temperature

Small handful (about 3 tablespoons/20g) grated mozzarella, loosely packed

Small spoonful (about ½ tablespoon/3g) crumbled Danish blue cheese (Castello Extra Creamy; see Tips)

Mild honey, for drizzling

Extra-virgin olive oil, for drizzling

Freshly ground black pepper

**TO SERVE**

A very good cup of coffee

### TIPS

*The mild flavor of Danish blue cheese ("Danablu"), available at most well-stocked grocery stores, doesn't overwhelm its more subtle mozzarella background. Kyoichi and Ikumi prefer Castello's Extra Creamy Danish blue, but Castello's traditional Danish blue is also great.*

*Oven toasting: To mimic the steam effect of a Japanese steam oven in a conventional oven, put a rack within a few inches of the broiler. Lay a baking rack over a rimmed sheet pan, put it in the oven, and preheat the oven to 375°F (190°C). When the oven is preheated, pour a little cold water into the sheet pan and put the cheese bread on the baking rack. Bake the bread just until the cheese has melted and the bottom starts to crisp up, 3 to 4 minutes; the bread will only be lightly toasted instead of golden brown (don't leave it in too long or it will dry out). Turn off the oven and broil the bread just until the cheese caramelizes in spots.*

**Prep:** Prepare a Japanese steam toaster for toasting the sandwich bread (level 4 on a Balmuda). Or use a regular toaster oven.

**Make the toast:** Lightly coat one side of the bread with the butter. Scatter enough mozzarella on top to evenly cover the bread in a single layer; be sure to go all the way to the edges.

Finely crumble any larger pieces of blue cheese and evenly disperse little bits of the cheese; the mozzarella should like it has blue cheese freckles.

If not using a steam oven, use a spray bottle to very lightly mist the bottom of the bread with water.

Put the bread directly on the toaster oven rack and toast until the cheese is golden brown in spots; watch the bread closely once the cheese begins to brown so it doesn't burn. The time will vary depending on the toaster.

Generously drizzle the honey (about ½ tablespoon) evenly over the toast in a crisscross pattern, followed by a splash of olive oil and a sprinkle of black pepper.

**Serve:** Enjoy the cheese toast warm, with the coffee.

In Kyoto,
hearing the cuckoo,
I long for Kyoto.
—Matsuo Bashō, seventeenth century

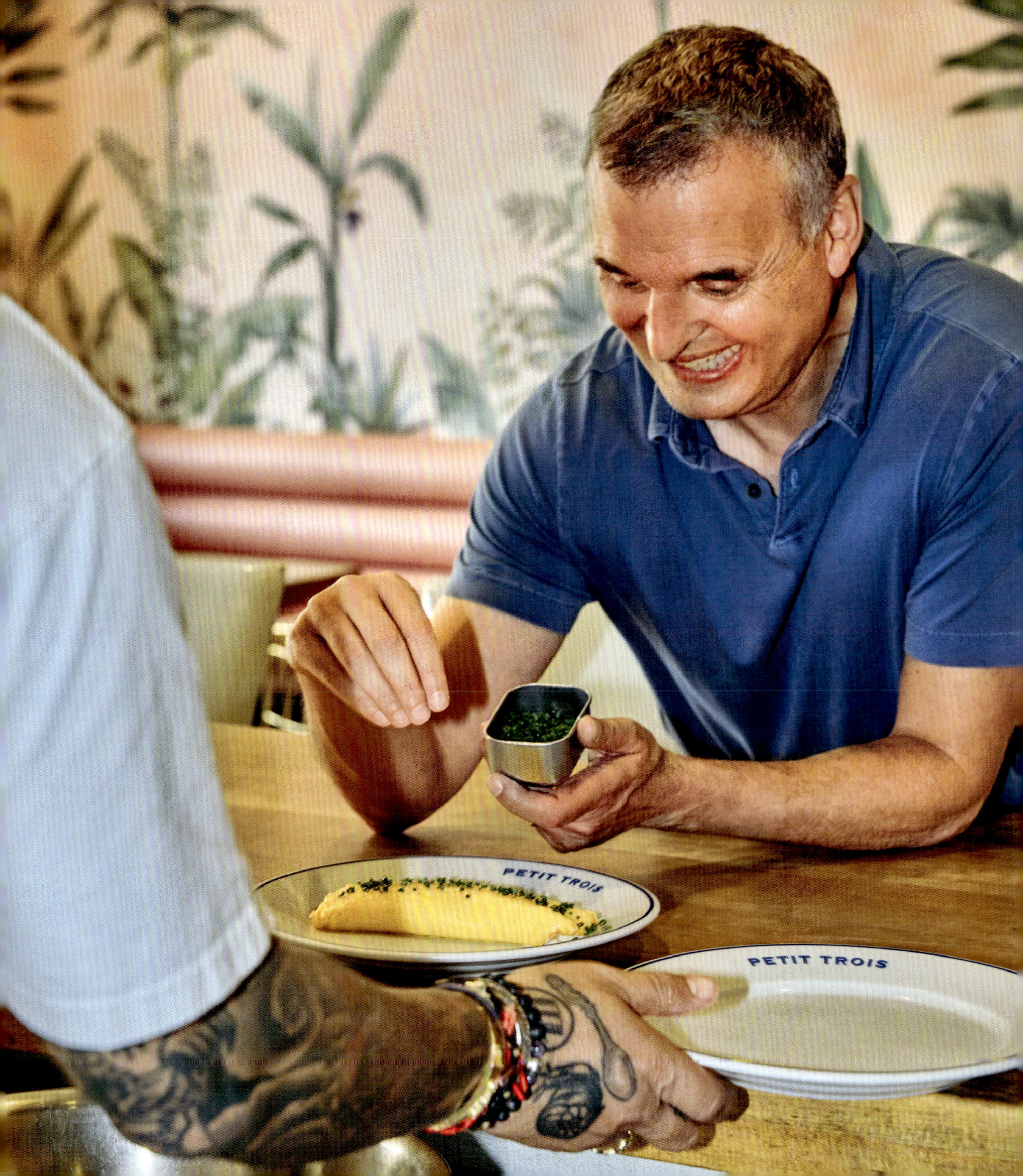
PETIT TROIS
PETIT TROIS

# Ludo Lefebvre's French Omelette

📍 *Petit Trois, Los Angeles*

In *Somebody Feed Phil the Book*, I told you that an omelet like the one at Camellia Grill in New Orleans is one of the things I really do make for myself at home. That's because it's a great omelet, but also because even somebody like me can make it. (You can get the recipe in that book.) All you have to do is blend up the eggs in a blender, cook them in some butter, put some grated cheese in the middle, and fold it up when it's ready. It's a delicious, classic dinner-style omelet, very fluffy and light, but the best omelet I've ever had is the one that my friend the chef Ludo Lefebvre serves at Petit Trois, one of his California-French restaurants in LA.

I actually know how to make this omelet, too, because we did a scene in the "Los Angeles" episode of *I'll Have What Phil's Having* where Ludo taught me how to make it. Like so much French cuisine, you have to get the very best ingredients and pay attention to how you make it. The eggs, which Ludo gets at the farmers' market, are so creamy and buttery, almost silky. To cook the omelet, you've got to use really good French butter from Normandy, and you're also going to need Boursin cheese, which Ludo calls the "French Velveeta." (You want the black pepper flavor in the brown-and-white package, not the garlic and herb one in the green-and-white package.) The cheese almost melts into the eggs, so together the two become the creamiest thing you can imagine.

> *The most important thing when cooking this omelette is to be gentle (cook the eggs over low heat), and every ingredient counts. Get good, fresh eggs from the farmers' market. The yolks are so much richer; you will notice the flavor. The black pepper in the Boursin is the only black pepper; you need to use white pepper in the omelette so you don't overwhelm the flavors of the eggs and butter. The butter at the end has to be the very best (Bordier from Normandy is my favorite), but as you cook the omelette, you can use a different good butter (it must be French, like Rodolphe le Meunier or Isigny Sainte Mère). Rubbing the surface of the omelette with a little butter at the end makes it shiny, so the omelette looks nice. We serve it with a salad with our Dijon vinaigrette (page 310).* —LUDO

**FEEDS 1**

3 large
good-quality eggs
(from the farmers' market)

Fleur de sel

Freshly ground
white pepper

2 tablespoons (28g)
good-quality salted
artisan French butter
(Le Beurre Bordier),
divided

2 packed tablespoons (28g)
Cracked Black Pepper
Boursin cheese

**TO SERVE**

1 tablespoon
finely chopped chives

**Prep:** In a small bowl, use a fork (not a whisk) to vigorously whisk the eggs, a generous pinch of fleur de sel, and 2 pinches of white pepper until you can't see any visible egg whites at all, about 1 minute.

**Make the omelet:** Put 1 tablespoon of the butter in a cold 9-inch (23cm) nonstick skillet. (If you don't have one that size, go with a larger, not smaller, nonstick skillet; see Tips.) Slowly melt the butter over medium heat; swirl the butter around so it covers the bottom of the skillet as it melts. Pour the beaten eggs into the skillet and use a large rubber spatula to constantly stir the eggs in a circular pattern; don't lift the spatula off the bottom of the skillet as you stir. After 1 to 1½ minutes, the eggs will begin to firm up and look like undercooked scrambled eggs (they will still look very "wet"). Use the spatula to spread out the eggs so they cover the bottom of the pan in a single layer without any gaps. If you are using a nonstick skillet larger than 9 inches, spread out the eggs into a roughly 8-inch (20cm) circle.

Crumble the Boursin cheese in a straight line down one side of the omelet, closest to the handle side of the pan. Use the spatula to gently lift up one edge of the omelet; it should hold together. If it starts to break apart, let the eggs cook a few seconds longer. Use the spatula to roll up about a third of the omelet toward the center.

Cut the remaining 1 tablespoon of butter in half. Put half of the butter in the now exposed part of the skillet and use the rubber spatula to gently rub the butter as it melts on the sides and top of the omelet section that you just rolled up. Keep rolling up the omelet until the cheese is fully enclosed, then shake the skillet or use the spatula to move the omelet to the other side of the skillet so the eggs absorb all the butter that's left in the pan.

**Serve:** Carefully slide the omelet out onto a serving plate. Rub the top of the omelet with the remaining ½ tablespoon of butter, scatter the chives on top, and finish the omelet with a pinch of fleur de sel. Don't think about doing anything else but eating the omelet right away.

### TIPS

*The omelet is as much about the technique and recipe portions (if you try to increase the serving size, you'll end up with a frittata; even the skillet size matters) as it is about the very best ingredients.*

*A nonstick skillet is essential, ideally one that's 9 inches (23cm). Even with a classic, slightly smaller 8-inch (20cm) "omelet pan," you'll end up with that frittata. To use a larger nonstick skillet, when the eggs begin to set up, make a slightly smaller circle of eggs in the middle of the skillet so your omelet isn't too thin.*

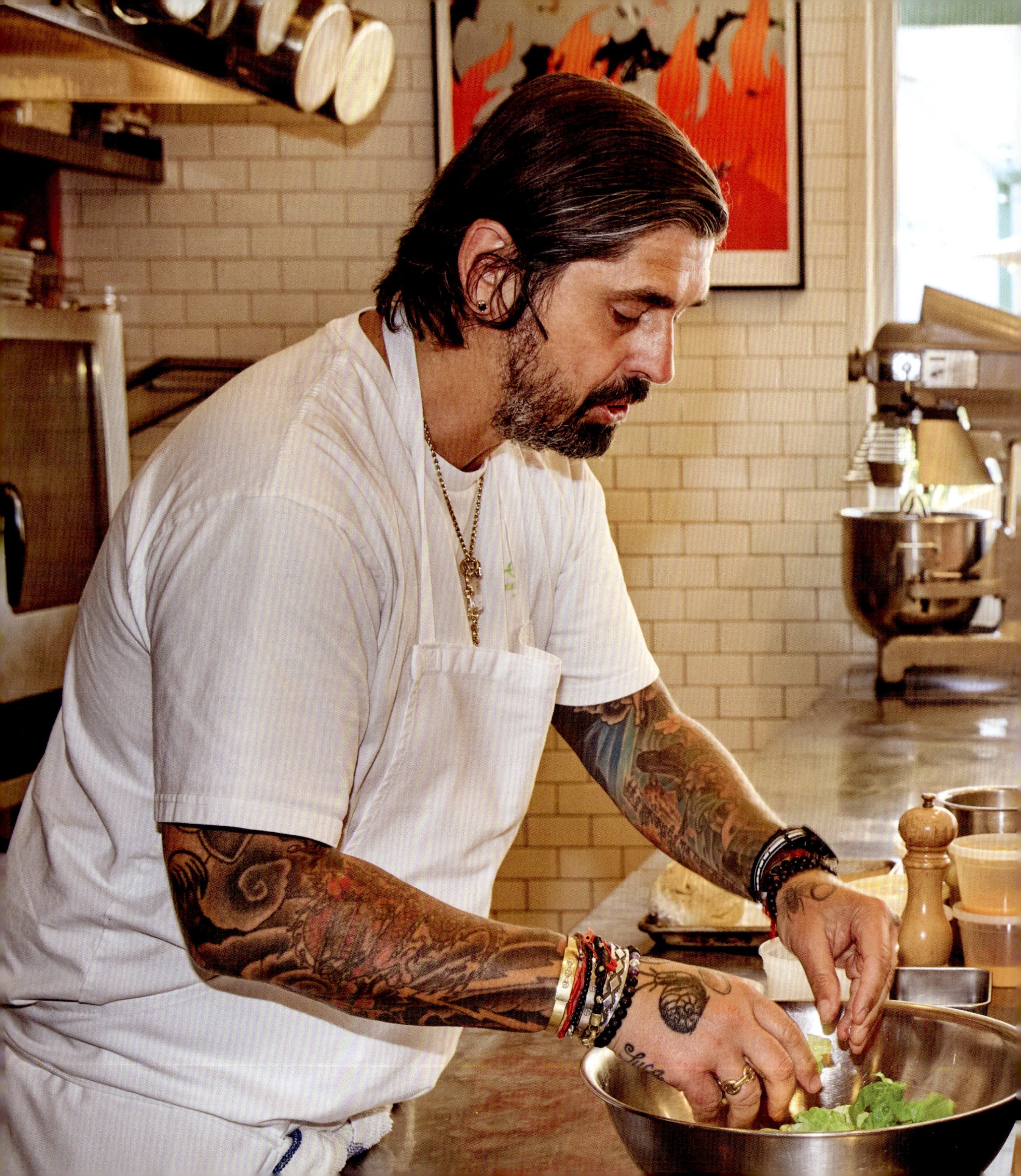

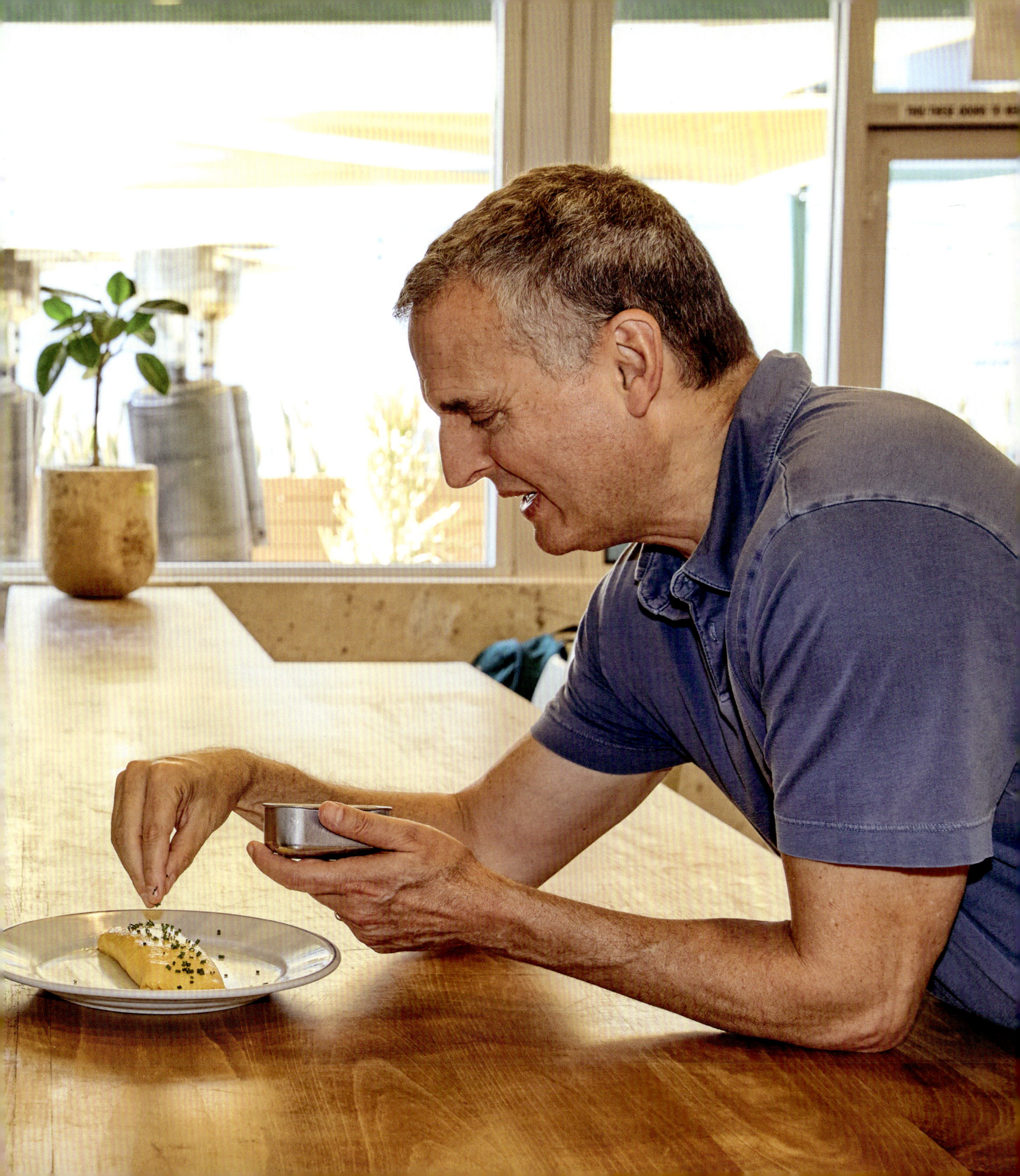

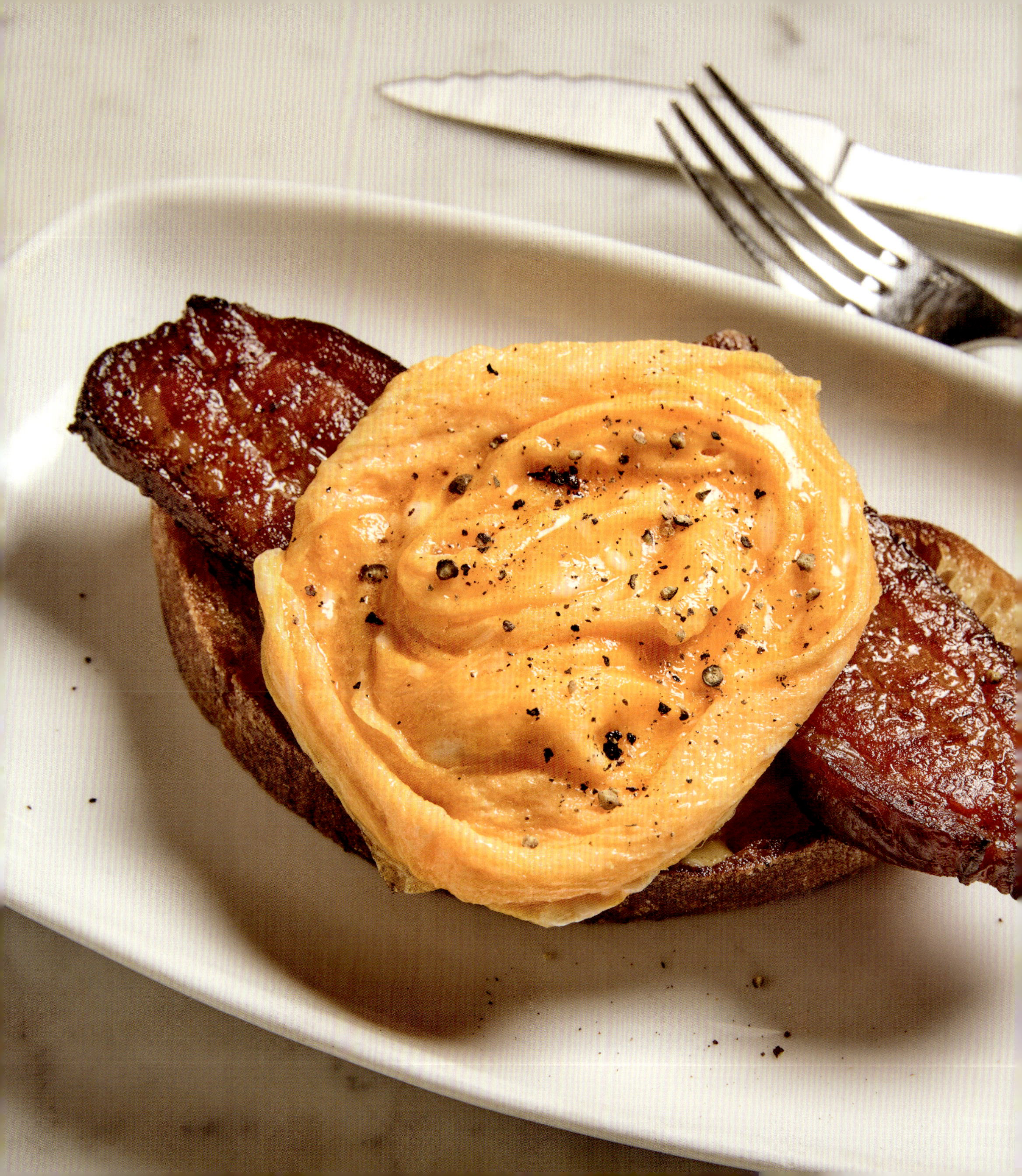

# Max's Fluffy Eggs with Slab Bacon and Toast

📍 *Max & Helen's, Los Angeles*

We now have Max & Helen's in Larchmont (which I'll be frequenting by the time this book comes out).

I think if I had to pin down Dad's great loves in his life, it would be his family and soft scrambled eggs every morning, and I'm not sure if this is in the right order.

Eggs every day? Every day. Through the cholesterol scares of the eighties, back around to when eggs were declared "the perfect food" by scientists who had even deeper nutritional knowledge than Dad.

"Are my eggs fluffy?" he would ask Mom every day as she cooked them for him.

"Max, I've been cooking your eggs for sixty years; do you think I know how to do them yet?" she'd reply.

"I'm just checking," he'd say. And then, "I like them fluffy."

It's a miracle he never got hit with a frying pan.

If we went to a diner, it was all we could do to keep him from going back into the kitchen and telling the chef who might be overcooking his eggs, "That's enough."

Fluffy eggs. That was his thing. For Mom it was listening to the opera.

There's a lesson here for me: This little thing gave him such pleasure every day. If we could find such pleasure in a simple little thing like this every day, wouldn't we be happy every day?

Dad lived to ninety-six (with a little help from Lipitor), and it actually says on his tombstone, "Are my eggs fluffy?"

And on Mom's right next to him it reads, "I'm listening to the opera."

Put on *La Traviata* and enjoy this recipe.

---

*Pushing the eggs through a sieve to strain them thoroughly mixes the eggs so they are fully combined without adding additional air. Be sure to plate each egg spiral as it is ready.*
—NANCY SILVERTON

WHEN I GET UP • 35

**FEEDS 2**

2 8-inch (20cm) slices slab applewood smoked bacon (sliced ½-inch [12mm] thick)

3 tablespoons (42g) unsalted butter, divided

2 slices good-quality crusty white bread, sourdough or similar (sliced roughly ¾-inch [2cm] thick)

4 extra-large or 5 large eggs

Kosher or coarse sea salt and freshly ground black pepper

**Cook the bacon and toast the bread:** Preheat the oven to 350°F (175°C).

Arrange the bacon slices in a single layer on a sheet pan and bake, rotating the pan front to back halfway through, until completely cooked but not crispy, 30 to 35 minutes. (Check the bacon after 20 to 25 minutes if you're using thick-cut instead of slab.) If the underside is not cooked, flip the bacon and bake for about 5 minutes longer. Transfer the bacon to a baking rack, or paper bags or towels, to drain.

Meanwhile, heat a large sauté pan over medium heat. Add 1 tablespoon of the butter and, when melted, add the slices of bread to the pan. Rub the bread into the melted butter to evenly coat one side, immediately flip the slices, and toast the unbuttered sides until nicely golden brown, about 4 minutes. Flip the bread again to the buttered side and toast another 4 minutes, or until golden brown.

Arrange the toast on two serving plates, and lay a slice of bacon in the center of each.

**Make the eggs:** Lay a fine-mesh sieve over a medium bowl. Crack the eggs into the sieve and use your fingers to push the eggs through. Occasionally wipe off the underside of the sieve to loosen the strained eggs clinging to bottom, if needed. (With the finest-mesh sieves, it takes some patience to fully strain the eggs.) Transfer the eggs to a measuring cup, add ½ teaspoon salt, and gently stir to evenly distribute the salt.

Have a large rubber spatula nearby and heat a medium 8- or 9-inch (20 to 23cm) nonstick sauté pan over medium heat until hot, 1 to 2 minutes. (A larger pan will distribute the eggs too much and you'll end up with more of a crepe.) Add 1 tablespoon of the butter and swirl the pan to evenly melt; it should sizzle but not brown quickly. (If it browns, the pan is too hot; start over.)

Pour half the eggs (about ½ cup/120ml) into the pan and shake the pan back and forth gently and continuously to prevent the eggs from sticking to the pan, cooking until the outer edges are set, 30 to 45 seconds; the eggs will look like a crepe that hasn't finished cooking, as the center should still be very wet. Remove the pan from the heat.

With the pan off the heat, stand the rubber spatula upright in the center of the eggs and gently pull the eggs toward you in a straight line toward the edge of the pan, creating several folds. (With a smaller spatula, you may need to do this a few times.) The folds should be very loose because of the wet eggs in the center, but if the eggs are too wet to make any folds, return the pan to the heat for a few seconds to slightly firm up the eggs. Create the next fold by cutting into the eggs on the right side of the pan and pushing them clockwise toward you (and toward the middle of the first fold), forming the center of your spiral. Now start at the top of the pan and push all the remaining eggs counterclockwise, along the outer edges of the pan, toward the egg spiral. Tidy up the eggs by slightly folding up the edges to create a roughly 5-inch (12.5cm) egg round. Now tilt the pan toward you so any excess uncooked egg liquid runs down into the eggs; if needed, return the pan to the stove over low heat and cover it with a lid for 15 to 30 seconds to let the steam cook off any remaining liquid-y eggs. Be careful not to overcook the eggs at this point; the folds should be very moist and glossy in the center.

**Assemble and serve:** Slide the egg round onto a slice of bacon-topped toast and finish with a pinch of kosher salt and freshly ground black pepper. Serve the first batch of egg toast right away to whoever will be enjoying it, then wipe out the sauté pan and repeat the cooking process with the remaining 1 tablespoon of butter and the eggs.

### TIP

*Like Ludo's omelette, it's best to plate each serving of eggs as you make them. The process of making multiple folds in a very loosely set, crepe-like egg mixture takes some attention, but after mastering the first batch the eggs are not difficult to make. And, because the "folds" are made with the pan off the heat, unlike most stovetop eggs, you can take your time without worrying about overcooking them.*

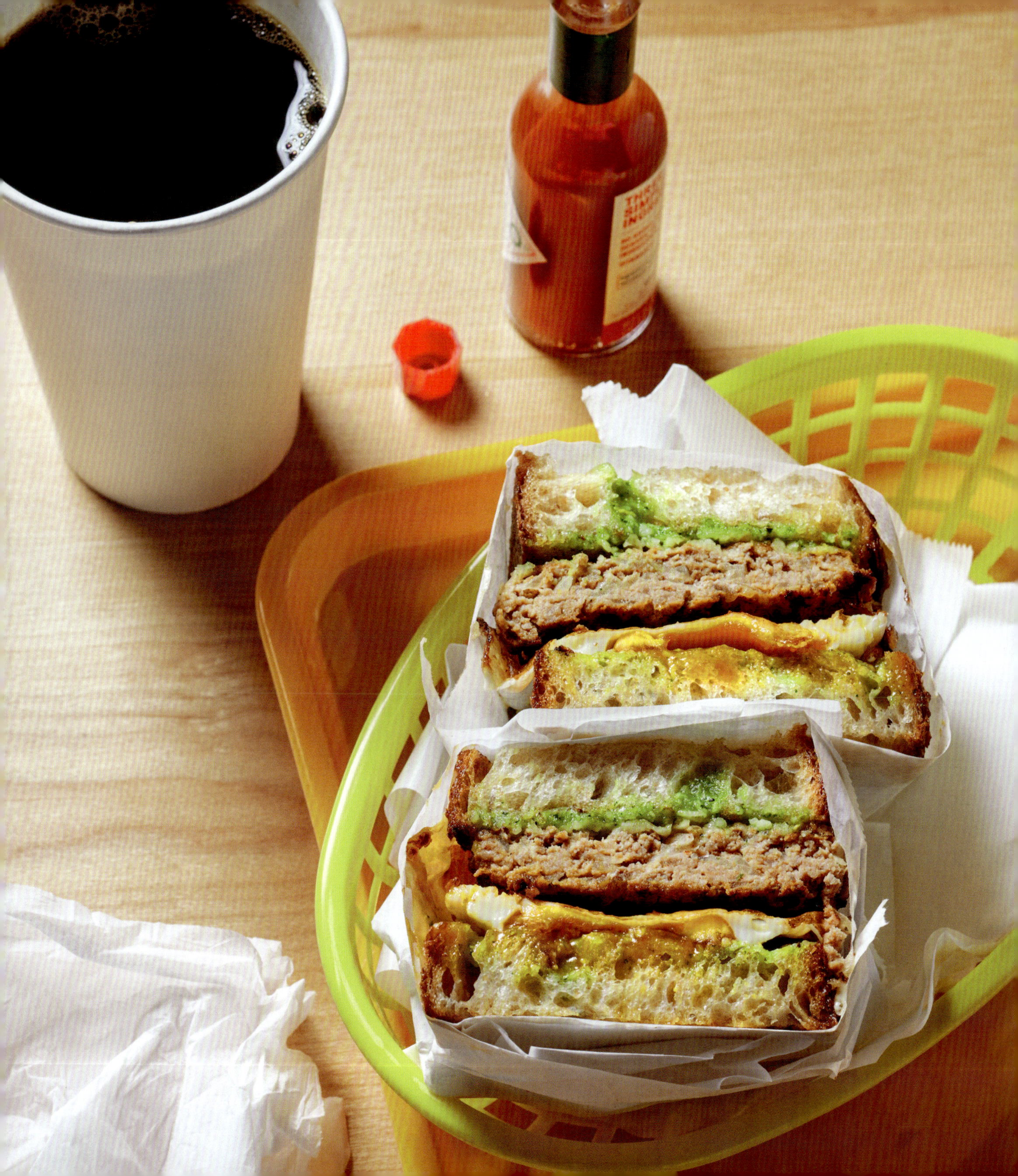

# The Yolko Ono
## (Fried Egg, Sausage, and Basil Pesto on Sourdough)

📍 *Fried Egg I'm In Love, Portland (Oregon)*

I love street food. It's casual, it's convenient and affordable, and it's delicious. (You can't put a price on delicious.) I've been to the best cities in the world for street food, like Marrakesh, Rio, and Bangkok, and I live in LA, home of the taco truck. But I'd never been to Portland, what people say is the best street-food city in all of the US. It's only a two-hour flight from my house. How had I never been? I'm so glad I finally went for season five of the show. I loved all of the young, creative people I met there.

One of those people is Jace Krause. He set up his first food cart in 2012, after the last recession, when city governments streamlined regulations to make it easier for food carts and other outdoor dining places to set up shop. (I think we can all agree that's something our governments did well.) Mike Russell, who writes about the food pods all over Portland (a food pod is like a food court, only with a curated collection of food trucks), took me to one of his favorites, Prost Marketplace, where Jace has his truck, Fried Egg I'm In Love. Everything I ate at that pod was great. There was an Indian place called Desi PDX run by Deepak Saxema with cardamom tea–brined chicken and really good lamb (it closed, but Deepak has a couple of other places in town you can go to). We also went to Matt's BBQ, where Matt Vicedomini brought out a huge platter of barbecue (including my favorite, turkey legs), and then there was Jace's fried egg sandwich with sausage and a really garlicky basil pesto. A lot of times you get an egg sandwich that's got scrambled eggs. This egg was perfectly fried up by a nice young woman named Madison. I love a fried egg sandwich because you get extra sauce when you bite into the sandwich; all this delicious yolk comes out. This is what dry cleaners are for.

> *Your skillet shouldn't be too hot when you add the egg. When the egg hits the pan, we carefully "swirl" the stiffer whites that directly surround and are beneath the yolk (when you crack an egg, it looks like the yolk is sitting on top of an egg-white pillow). It gives those whites closest to the yolk a creamier texture that contrasts with the fried, crispy brown edges and allows you to move the yolk back to the center of the whites (good for a sandwich). We cook our eggs "over medium" so they're no longer super jiggly and have an oozy, lava-like consistency. Tap the yolk with your finger. It should move a little, but not too much.* —JACE

**FEEDS 6**

¾ cup (1½ sticks/170g) unsalted butter, divided

6 large slices loaf sourdough bread, cut in half, or 12 smaller slices

Jace's Basil Pesto Sandwich Spread (page 304)

About ¾ cup (75g) grated parmesan cheese

6 Spiced Breakfast Sausage patties (recipe follows)

6 large eggs

Cayenne pepper

Freshly ground black pepper

**Toast the bread and partly assemble the sandwiches:** Melt half the butter (6 tablespoons) in a cast iron skillet over medium heat. Brush the melted butter on both sides of the bread. Increase the heat to medium-high and toast the bread, 1 or 2 slices at a time, until lightly toasted on both sides.

Spread about 2 tablespoons of the pesto sandwich spread on each slice of toasted bread, going all the way to the edges. Scatter about 2 tablespoons of parmesan over each bottom slice of bread and set aside.

**Fry the sausages:** Increase the heat to medium-high, and when the skillet is very hot, add 2 sausage patties. Use a large metal spatula to flatten the sausages to roughly the size of the bread; if the sausage sticks to the spatula, you can scrape it off at this point and reshape it. Fry until dark golden brown on the bottom, about 2 minutes. Flip and cook until golden brown and cooked through, about 2 minutes more. Transfer the sausages to a plate and cover to keep warm while you fry the remaining sausages.

**Cook the eggs, one at a time:** In a large nonstick skillet, melt 1 tablespoon of the butter over medium-low heat. Firmly double tap 1 egg on the flat surface of the pan to crack it directly over the butter. The egg should sizzle when it hits the pan; adjust the heat as needed. If the egg yolk isn't in the center of the whites, gently guide it back the center, then use a corner of the spatula to move the stiffest whites directly surrounding the yolk in a circle around the yolk a few times; the whites should "follow" the spatula around the yolk. Sprinkle a pinch each of cayenne pepper and black pepper over the egg. When the whites are only translucent in the very center near the yolk, about 2 minutes, loosen the egg all around the edges with the spatula. Flip and cook just until the yolk is no longer super jiggly when gently tapped, about 1½ minutes.

**Assemble and serve:** Lay 1 sausage patty on top of a piece of toast and finish with the fried egg. Gently lay another slice of toast on top (don't press down) and serve the sandwich right away.

Wipe out the skillet before continuing to fry the eggs.

## SPICED BREAKFAST SAUSAGE

*Get a basic country-style breakfast sausage, nothing too herb-y or sage-y that will overpower the eggs or basil pesto.* —JACE

**MAKES ABOUT 1¼ POUNDS (570G), ENOUGH FOR 6 SANDWICHES**

1 medium yellow onion

1 garlic clove, minced

1 teaspoon yellow mustard

½ teaspoon sweet paprika

Generous pinch dried oregano

Kosher or coarse sea salt and finely ground black pepper

1 pound (455g) ground pork breakfast sausage

Cut the onion in half vertically from the root to stem, then peel. Hold one half by the root end and coarsely grate the onion over a large bowl. (Save the second onion half for another use.) Add the garlic, mustard, paprika, oregano, and a generous pinch each of salt and pepper and toss to combine.

Break the sausage into small chunks over the bowl, and use your hands to massage the spices into the sausage until the sausage is almost paste-like. Divide the sausage into 6 large meatballs (about 3 ounces/85g each), and shape each into a firm ball in the palms of your hands. Be sure the balls are very compact, as it helps the sausage stay together when smashed on the griddle.

If not using right away, cover the sausage balls with plastic wrap and refrigerate for up to 2 days, or freeze for up to 3 months.

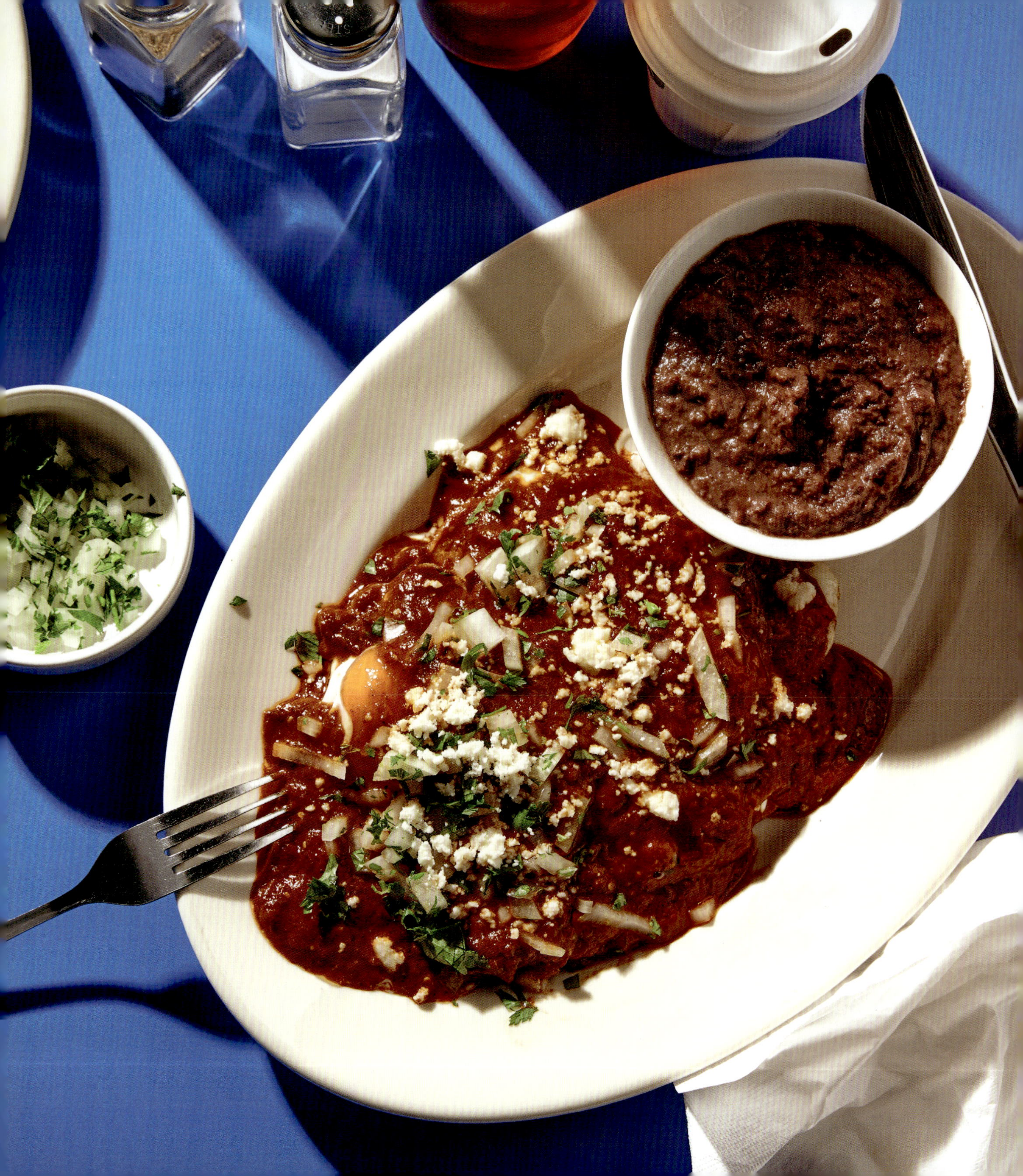

# Jimmy Shaw's Huevos Rancheros

## with Salsa de Chile Morita and Frijoles Negros

📍 *Lotería Grill, Los Angeles*

Monica and I have been going to the Original Farmers Market at Third and Fairfax since we first moved to LA. We were still dating, and I wooed her with the most beautiful California fruits and vegetables, ice cream, and other delicious things. The last episode of *I'll Have What Phil's Having* was all about Los Angeles, so of course we had to go there. Monica and I met two of our dearest friends, Ray and Anna Romano, at the market one morning. (Anna's got a recipe in this book on page 119.) We had breakfast at Lotería Grill, which is owned by another longtime friend, the great chef Jimmy Shaw. (His Farmers Market restaurant is no longer there, but Jimmy has several other LA locations you can go to.)

Jimmy's huevos rancheros is different from any I've had. The tortillas and fried eggs are covered in a dark, smoky chipotle sauce that's so delicious—and spicy. Ray doesn't like anything very spicy, so he took the tiniest bit of sauce from my plate. You could barely hear him, but before he took a bite he said, "I don't know if I wanna do it." You want to do it.

> *I don't know a better breakfast than huevos rancheros with black beans. With the spicy chile morita salsa (page 318), it really does wake you up! This recipe calls for one to two tortillas per plate. At my grandmother's house, it was always two tortillas. My mother served huevos rancheros with one tortilla.* —JIMMY

**FEEDS 6**

Vegetable oil, for frying

6 or 12 corn tortillas

Jimmy's Salsa de Chile Morita (full recipe; page 318)

Frijoles Negros (recipe follows)

12 large eggs

About ⅔ cup (160ml) Mexican crema (see Tip)

**TO SERVE**

½ cup (60g) queso fresco

1 medium white onion, finely chopped

¼ bunch cilantro, tender top stems and leaves chopped

WHEN I GET UP • 43

> **TIP**
>
> *If you don't have Mexican crema, whisk just enough heavy cream into crème fraîche or sour cream to make it easier to drizzle with a spoon; it should still be fairly thick.*

**Fry the tortillas:** Line a plate or pan with paper towels. In a skillet wide enough to fit the tortillas, heat about ½ inch (12mm) of the vegetable oil over medium heat.

When the oil is very hot, fry the tortillas, one at a time, for about 10 seconds. Use tongs to flip the tortilla by lifting up the end farthest from you (this directs any hot oil splashes away from you), and fry until the edges are crispy but the middle is still soft, about 5 seconds. Transfer the tortilla to the plate and blot off any excess oil. Fry the remaining tortillas, stacking them on top of one another after they are fried. (Leave the frying oil in the pan.)

**Warm the salsa and beans:** In a saucepan or pot, warm the salsa over medium heat, stirring often to prevent the salsa from sticking, until darkened in color and reduced to the consistency of a thin gravy, about 5 minutes; the cooking time will vary depending on the amount of salsa. (Do not boil.)

With the tongs, fully submerge each crispy tortilla, one or two at a time, in the warm salsa and transfer to serving plates. If using 2 tortillas per serving, slightly overlap them.

Turn off the heat and cover the pan to keep the salsa warm.

In another saucepan, rewarm the Frijoles Negros over medium heat, stirring occasionally.

**Fry the eggs:** Pour off all but a thin layer of oil from the skillet and reheat over medium heat. Fry half the eggs until the whites are only translucent in the very center near the yolk, about 1½ minutes. Use a large metal spatula to flip the eggs and cook until the whites are fully set but the yolk is still runny, about 15 seconds. Transfer the first batch of fried eggs to a large plate while you fry the rest. (The warm salsa will rewarm the eggs when they're ready to be served.)

**Assemble and serve:** Drizzle a little of the Mexican crema over each serving of tortillas and lay 2 fried eggs on top. Make sure the salsa is very hot before you pour it over the eggs; they should be completely covered by the salsa. Scatter the crumbled queso fresco, chopped onion, and cilantro on top and serve the huevos rancheros with the warm Frijoles Negros.

## FRIJOLES NEGROS

*These black beans are so good with the huevos rancheros. Throw in one or two small dried avocado leaves (not too many), if you have some. You'll like it.* —JIMMY

In a stock pot, heat a thin layer of vegetable oil over medium heat and add the onion, garlic, tomato, thyme, and epazote. Cook, stirring, until the onion softens, about 5 minutes. Add the chicken stock and black beans. Cover the beans with water by about 2 inches (5cm).

Add the dried avocado leaves, bring to a boil, reduce to a simmer, and cover the pot. Cook the beans, stirring occasionally so they don't burn (add a little more water if needed), until very creamy and beginning to burst apart, 2 to 3 hours.

Scoop out the avocado leaves and season with salt and pepper.

**FEEDS 6 TO 8**

Vegetable oil

½ white or yellow onion, chopped

3 to 4 garlic cloves, minced

1 or 2 Roma tomatoes, chopped

3 leafy sprigs fresh thyme or 2 teaspoons dried thyme

2 teaspoons dried epazote or oregano

1 quart (about 1L) chicken or vegetable stock

16 ounces (about 450g) dried black (turtle) beans

1 or 2 small dried avocado leaves or bay leaves

Kosher or coarse sea salt and freshly ground black pepper

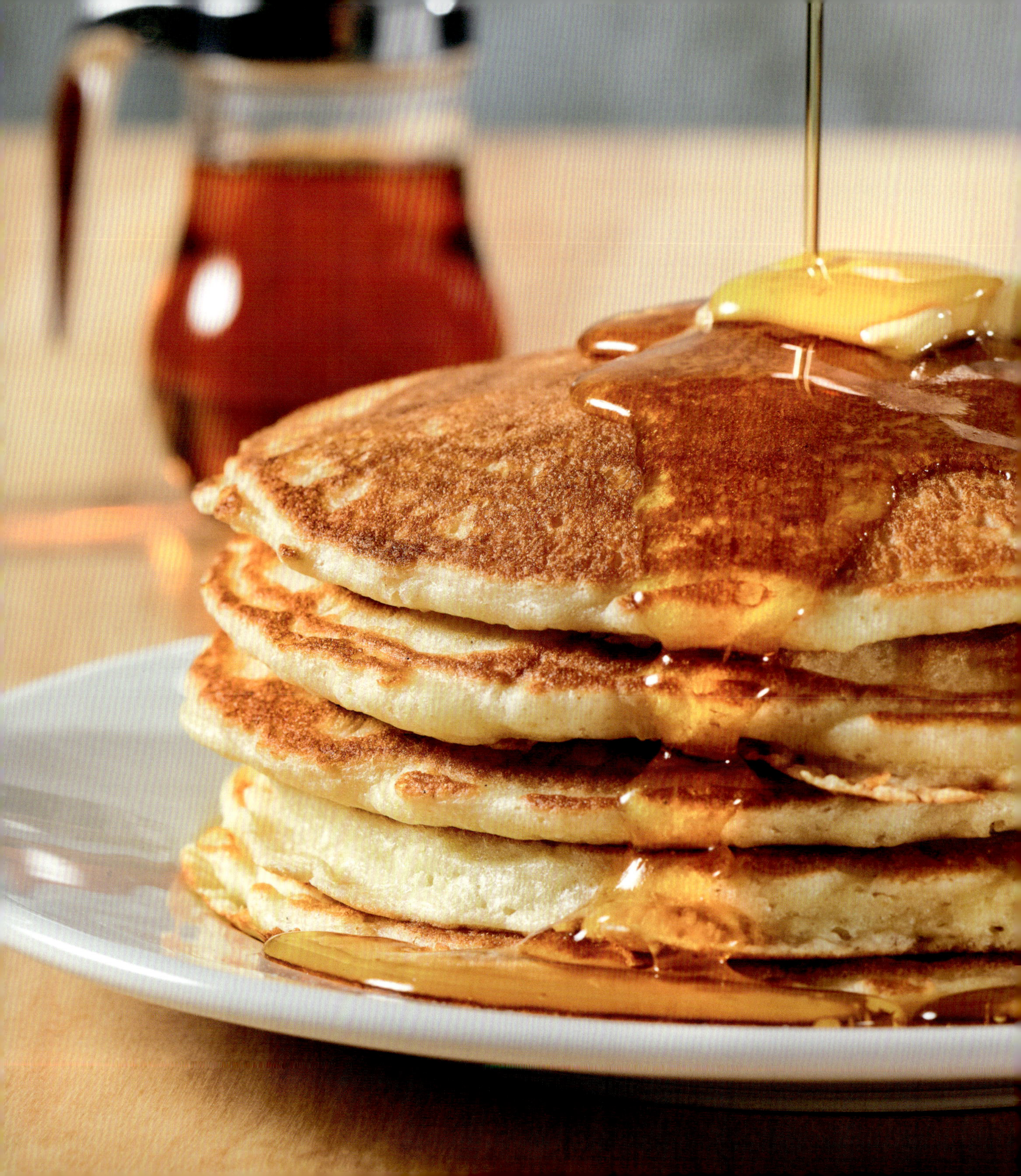

# Steve Nathan's Vanilla Pancakes

📍 *Huckleberry, Santa Monica*

Steve Nathan and I have been friends for nearly thirty years. We first worked together when he was a writer on *Raymond*, then he went on to run this other show you might know called *Bones*. One day I was reading about this great new bakery in Santa Monica called Huckleberry (this was back in 2015), and so I had to go there for the "Los Angeles" episode of *I'll Have What Phil's Having*. I get there, and there's Steve, up to his elbows in turkey meatballs. His daughter happens to be Zoe Nathan, the owner and a fantastic pastry chef. Steve hands me an apron and says I have to work for my breakfast, so we made these pancakes, which are actually based on his recipe that he used to make at home when his kids were growing up.

I learned from Steve that it's best to crack the eggs with your hands and let the whites slip through your fingers. (I don't do that. It's disgusting. I crack my eggs on the counter and hope for the best.) The other thing that's important is how you whip the egg whites and fold them into the batter to make the pancakes lighter. In the episode, Steve and I thought we got an actual pancake order, and so after my ten-minute internship, I became a professional line cook. Zoe was bluffing and rang the order bell just so we wouldn't feel bad, so we found some people to share the pancakes with, and they loved them, or at least they said they did. My career as a chef ended when Zoe taught me to make kouign-amann, which is a cross between a puff pastry and a croissant. Mine were "Phil's Smushballs."

**FEEDS 5 TO 6; MAKES 12 PANCAKES**

1 vanilla bean or 1 tablespoon vanilla bean paste

2 cups (480ml) whole milk

2 cups (240g) all-purpose flour

1 tablespoon baking powder

1 tablespoon plus 1 teaspoon granulated sugar

Kosher or coarse sea salt

1 cup (2 sticks/225g) unsalted butter, melted and cooled, plus more for the pan

4 large eggs, separated

**TO SERVE**

Plenty of room-temperature butter and maple syrup

---

*My father used to make these almost every weekend when I was growing up. They're so simple and the perfect example of why we say color is flavor. If these pancakes aren't done on a super-hot griddle and don't get that deep brown color, they become an entirely different, sadder animal. So please, cook these properly and make my dad proud.* —ZOE

**Prep:** If using a vanilla bean, split it lengthwise, scrape the seeds into the milk, and add the pod. Bring to a boil, whisking occasionally to help break up the vanilla bean. Refrigerate the infused milk until completely cool or, better still, overnight.

**Make the batter:** In a large bowl, mix together the flour, baking powder, sugar, and 1¼ teaspoons salt. Add the melted butter, egg yolks, and vanilla bean–infused milk (discard the pod) or milk and vanilla bean paste and whisk to combine. The mixture should be slightly lumpy.

In a stand mixer fitted with a whisk attachment (or with a hand mixer), whip the egg whites on medium-high speed to soft peaks, 3 to 4 minutes. Use a rubber spatula or large spoon to gently fold the whites into the batter until just combined; don't overmix.

**Cook the pancakes:** Lightly butter a large skillet and heat over medium-high heat until very hot, about 5 minutes. A few droplets of water should sizzle and dance across the surface. Drop about ½ cup (120ml) of batter into the skillet and cook until bubbles set on the surface and the bottom is golden brown, about 1 minute. Use a large metal spatula to flip the pancakes and cook until fully set, about 1 minute.

**Serve:** Serve the pancakes as soon as they come off the griddle with the butter and maple syrup. Lightly butter and reheat the pan before cooking the remaining pancakes.

# Siggi Hilmarsson's Geothermal Lava Bread

*Laugarvatn Fontana, Iceland*

Talk about a transporting dish. I can taste this bread that Monica and I had when we went out to Laugarvatn, which is about an hour outside of Reykjavík, as I write this. The drive is worth it for the scenery alone; this traditional Icelandic bread at the bakery at Laugarvatn Fontana (a spa that's fueled by geothermal springs) is another reason to go. Siggi Hilmarsson, the general manager, took us out to the lake to show us how he makes it. (It's his family's recipe.) You dig a hole, put the pot in the hole, cover it up with the bubbling black volcanic sand, and walk away. That's it. Twenty-four hours later, you dig up the pot and inside is this sweet rye bread that tastes almost like gingerbread even though it doesn't have a single spice. (If you don't have a geothermal spring in your backyard, you can make it in your oven.) You eat the bread warm with the very best local butter and smoked trout that they also make there, which is closer in color and flavor to smoked salmon because of the type of trout, along with eggs that are boiled right in the hot springs. The recipe makes a very large loaf, so I recommend doing what Siggi's grandmother did whenever she made this bread: invite friends over so you can share.

*This is my grandmother's recipe for the traditional lava bread (Hverabrauð) that we serve at our geothermal bakery. Whenever the family was expecting guests from Reykjavík, she would pop up a nice warm rye bread from the hot spring. It's a very simple recipe; my kids love to make it. Everyone has their own formula. It's really the slow cooking process that gives the bread its unique taste. When the bread is cooked in the hot volcanic sand, twenty-four hours is the magic number. A few hours less and it doesn't bake all the way in the middle; longer and the bread starts to dry out. This recipe has been adjusted so you can bake the bread for half that time in an oven (a little baking soda also helps it rise more quickly). We use a sturdy stainless steel pot to bake the bread, but people use all kinds of things, even empty Mackintosh's chocolate tins. Whatever you use, it should be about 20 centimeters (7½ to 8 in) wide. If it's too big, the bread will be flat.* —SIGGI

**MAKES 1 EXTRA-LARGE LOAF; FEEDS A SMALL CROWD (18 TO 20) OR CAN BE FROZEN FOR LATER**

Unsalted or salted butter, for the pot

4 cups (480g) medium- or fine-grind (not coarse) dark rye flour (Bob's Red Mill Organic Dark Rye)

2 cups (240g) all-purpose flour

2 cups (400g) granulated sugar

1 tablespoon plus 1 teaspoon baking powder

1 teaspoon baking soda

Kosher or coarse sea salt

4¼ cups (34 ounces/1L) whole milk

**TO SERVE**

Good-quality salted butter

Good-quality smoked trout or salmon, sliced (optional)

6 to 8 hard-boiled eggs, sliced (optional)

**Prep:** Put a rack in the lower half of the oven and remove the top rack. Preheat the oven to 325°F (165°C).

Generously butter the bottom and about halfway up the sides of an enameled Dutch oven (aluminum or nonstick, not cast iron) or other oven-safe stockpot that is 7 to 8 inches (about 20cm) in diameter. Line the bottom of the pot with parchment paper and butter the paper.

**Make the batter and bake the bread:** In a very large bowl, combine the rye flour, all-purpose flour, sugar, baking powder, baking soda (if the baking soda is clumpy, break it up with your fingers as you add it to the bowl), and 1 teaspoon salt, and mix the dry ingredients together with a large spoon. Add the milk and stir to combine, then switch to a whisk to get out any large lumps. The consistency will be like a thin pancake batter with some small lumps.

Scrape the batter into the pot and cover the pot snugly with two to three layers of plastic wrap (this traps steam as the bread bakes). Seal the pot with one layer of aluminum foil and pinch the foil snugly around the rim.

Bake the bread for 30 minutes. Reduce the temperature to 225°F (110°C) and bake for 11 hours, rotating the pot front to back roughly halfway through. Don't remove the foil to peek at the bread during the baking process; it will tear the plastic wrap seal.

Remove the pot from the oven and carefully peel away the foil and plastic wrap (the steam will be very hot). Let the bread partly cool in the pot for about 15 minutes.

**Serve:** Cut the bread into quarters, then cut each quarter into slices (only slice as much bread as you plan to serve right away). Slather the warm bread with plenty of butter and serve with the smoked fish and sliced hard-boiled eggs, if you'd like.

Wrap any leftover bread tightly and store at room temperature for up to 3 days, or freeze for up to 3 months.

### TIP

*This is a very simple recipe, but it doesn't do well with any fiddling. Even using a larger or smaller pot can completely change the texture of the bread (it bakes up too wet or very dry). And if you do happen to have a geothermal spring nearby, leave the baking soda out, wrap the entire pot snugly with plastic film so no liquid from the hot springs seeps in (instead of just covering the top of the pot), and bury the bread for a full 24 hours.*

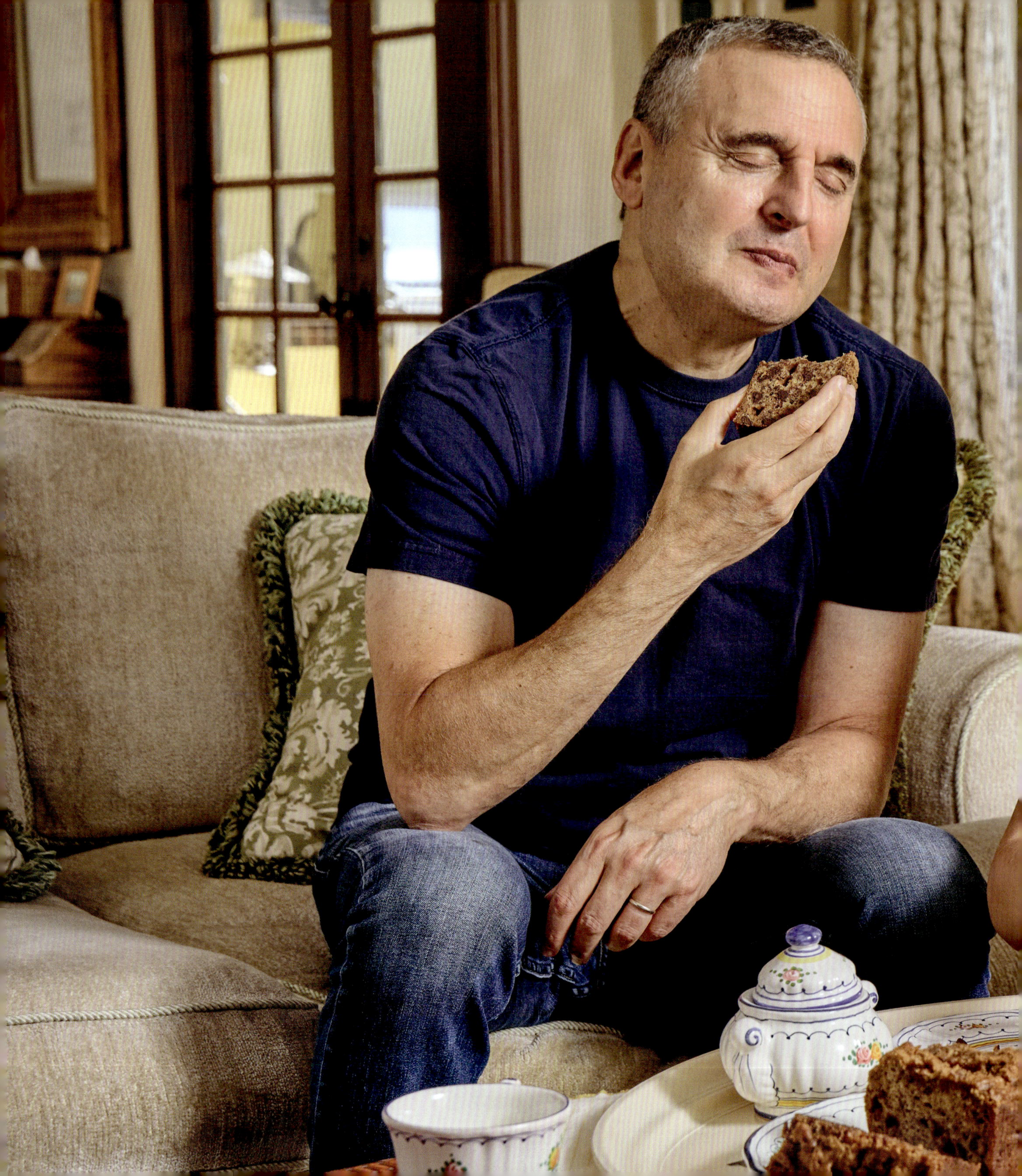

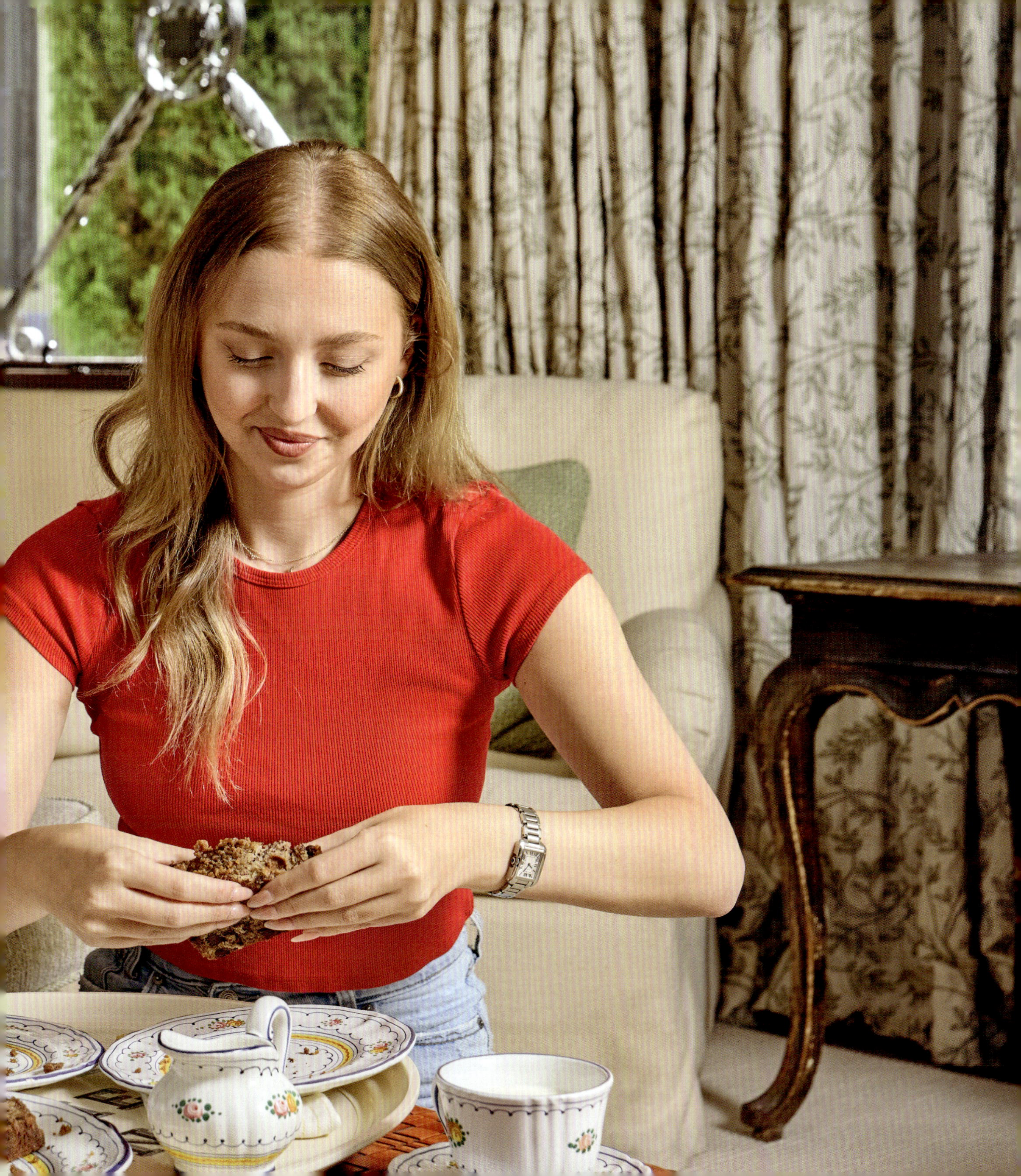

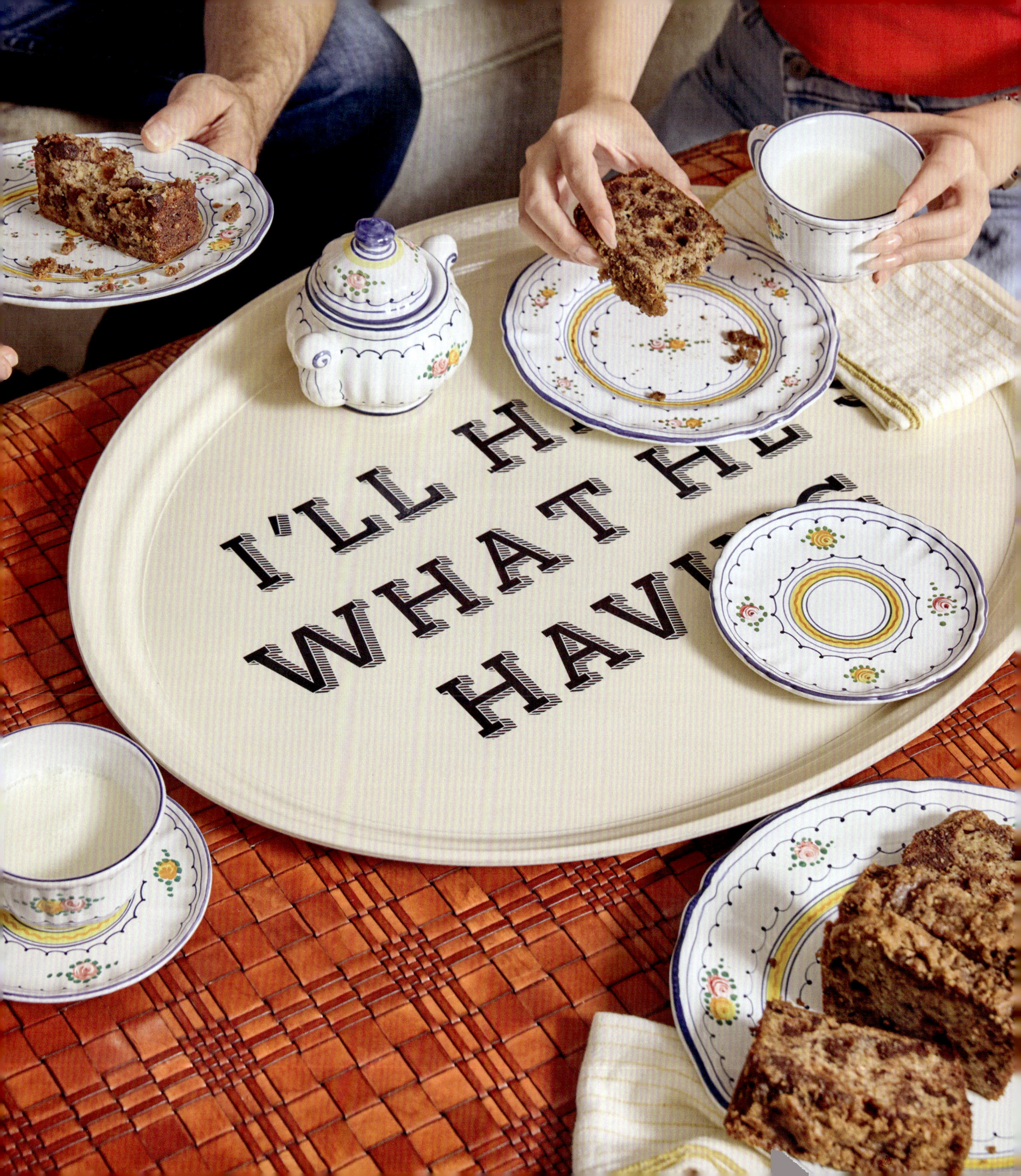
I'LL H
WHAT HE
HAV

# Lily's Chocolate Chip–Streusel Banana Bread

Lily has always loved food. No idea where she gets this from. She always had great taste, and she was, honestly, not very much like the Lily in the children's book we wrote together called *Just Try It!* Total transparency: I was the very picky eater when I was a kid. Really. My mother couldn't believe I got so into food later in life. "You never ate anything as a child." My father would then say, "Maybe it was the chef." He was funny. Lately, Lily's gotten into baking. She has talent! Her banana bread is my absolute favorite because it's so flavorful and moist, and has chocolate.

> *There was a TikTok trend for a while where everyone was posting recipes for banana bread. I tried a couple of different ones and combined the best parts of my favorites. One that stood out had streusel on top—incredible! We all like chocolate in our family, so I put enough so there's a bunch in each piece. If you've got a picky eater at home, I recommend calling it chocolate chip cookie bread!* —LILY

**Prep:** Preheat the oven to 350°F (175°C). Put a rack in the middle of the oven and a second rack in the lower third of the oven. Put a baking sheet on the lower rack to catch any buttery drippings from the streusel topping.

Lightly coat a metal or glass loaf pan with butter or cooking spray.

**Make the streusel:** In a small bowl, mix together the brown sugar, flour, and cinnamon. Cut the butter into small pieces and use your fingers to rub the butter into the brown sugar mixture.

---

**MAKES 1 LOAF; FEEDS 6 TO 8**

Butter or cooking spray for the baking pan

**STREUSEL**

½ cup (105g) packed dark brown sugar

3 tablespoons all-purpose flour

⅛ teaspoon ground cinnamon

3 tablespoons (42g) salted butter, or unsalted butter plus a pinch salt

**BANANA BREAD**

5 tablespoons (2½ ounces/70g) salted butter, or unsalted butter plus 2 pinches salt

4 large, overly ripe bananas (about 1¼ pounds/570g), peeled

*(ingredients continue)*

WHEN I GET UP • 55

¾ cup (150g) granulated sugar

1 large egg

1 teaspoon vanilla extract

1 teaspoon baking soda

1½ cups (180g) all-purpose flour

2 large handfuls (about 1 cup; 6 ounces/170g) dark or bittersweet chocolate chips

**Make the banana bread:** In a small saucepan (or in the microwave), melt the butter.

In a large bowl, use the back of a fork (or your hands) to mash the bananas really well; you should have about 2 cups (450g) mashed bananas. Add the melted butter and granulated sugar and mix well. Stir in the egg and vanilla extract.

Sprinkle the baking soda over the batter; if clumpy, break it up with your fingers first. Add the flour and mix until well combined, then fold in the chocolate chips. Scrape the batter into the prepared loaf pan and scatter the streusel evenly on top.

**Bake the bread:** Put the banana bread on the middle rack and bake, rotating the pan front to back halfway through, until the edges of the streusel are dark brown, the center of the bread is firm, and a knife or skewer inserted in the center is covered in melted chocolate but not batter, 55 to 65 minutes, depending on the size and type of loaf pan.

Run a knife around the edges of the pan to loosen the topping from the sides, and let the banana bread cool for about 15 minutes.

**Serve:** Turn out the bread onto a cutting board, slice, and serve warm. Store any leftover banana bread, tightly wrapped, at room temperature for up to 5 days, or freeze for up to 3 months. Enjoy!

# Homeboy Bakery's Cinnamon Coffee Cake

*Homeboy Bakery, Los Angeles*

Homeboy Bakery, just outside of Chinatown, has been a Los Angeles institution since 1992, when it was started by Father Greg Boyle. Monica and I have supported the nonprofit for a long time, and we ended the final episode of *I'll Have What Phil's Having* there. The bakery (and its sister location, Homegirl Café) is a place where kids and adults who've been in gangs and other difficult situations get to come together to bake bread and make other delicious things. But what they really get is a chance to change their lives. Homeboy Industries offers these men and women all sorts of opportunities, from educational and medical services to job placement and legal assistance. And this isn't just a nonprofit offering support to people who might not get it otherwise. What they make is top quality. Some of the best restaurants in town use their breads, and when you taste this cinnamon coffee cake, you'll understand why it's their most popular breakfast pastry. The cake is so light, and the streusel has just the right amount of cinnamon.

When we filmed that episode back in 2015, I got to make challah with one of Homeboy's best bakers, Vidal Martinez, who had been in and out of prison his whole life before he ended up at Homeboy. Vidal shared how when he got out of prison and was trying to get a job just to feed his family like everybody else, people would see his tattoos all over his body and on his face, recognize them, and he wouldn't get the job. (One of the things that Father Boyle has at the program is tattoo removal to help these people.) At Homeboy, Vidal worked his way up, first doing maintenance, then making the muffins and learning how to make every single thing they bake, until eventually he became the second in command of the bakery operations. When we were rolling out the challah dough, I asked about his family. Vidal said he has three kids, and I asked how they're doing, and he looked at me and said, "My girl's going to college."

By the way, Vidal is still at Homeboy. His daughter graduated from college and works in a law office. She got married—so did his other daughter—and Vidal is a grandfather now. He spends every day off with his son, who was twelve when we were working on this book, taking him to baseball practice and games.

And Father Boyle just received the Presidential Medal of Freedom.

*This is a really easy recipe to make because instead of doing a separate mix for the topping, we mix all the dry stuff and then pull out a few pounds of it (we're making a lot of coffee cakes) for the topping. You set that aside and make your batter with what's left.* —VIDAL

**Prep:** Put a baking rack in the middle of the oven and preheat the oven to 375°F (190°C). Lightly grease the bottom and sides of an 8x8-inch (20cm) square cake pan and line the bottom with parchment paper.

**Make the streusel and batter:** In a stand mixer fitted with a paddle attachment (or in a large bowl with a hand mixer), combine the flour, brown sugar, superfine sugar, cinnamon, nutmeg, and salt, and mix on low speed until combined.

With the mixer running, slowly add the vegetable oil and mix until crumbly. Set aside 1 loosely packed cup (160g) of the mixture for the topping.

To the stand mixer bowl, add the baking powder and baking soda and mix for a few seconds. Increase the speed to medium and, with the mixer running, add the buttermilk, then the egg, and mix for 1 minute. Use a rubber spatula to scrape any batter off the sides and the very bottom of the bowl, then mix the batter until very smooth, about 30 seconds.

**Bake the cake:** Scrape the batter into the cake pan, lightly smooth out the top, and gently squeeze the streusel topping into soft crumbs as you scatter it evenly over the batter. Bake the cake for 10 minutes. Reduce the oven to 350°F (175°C), rotate the pan from front to back, and bake until a cake tester inserted in the middle comes out with just a few crumbs on it, 25 to 30 minutes.

Transfer the coffee cake to a baking rack or stovetop grate and let it cool for about 15 minutes.

**Serve:** Run a knife along the edges of the baking pan, cut the cake into squares, and serve.

Cover the pan tightly with plastic wrap or store the pieces in a zip-top food storage bag (put a piece of parchment or a paper towel in the bag to soak up any excess moisture) at room temperature for up to 3 days.

---

**MAKES 1 CAKE; FEEDS 8**

Cooking spray, butter, or neutral vegetable oil for the baking pan

3 cups (360g) all-purpose flour

1 packed cup (210g) brown sugar, preferably a mix of light and dark

½ cup plus 1 tablespoon superfine (caster) or 2 tablespoons granulated sugar (125g)

1 teaspoon ground cinnamon

1 teaspoon ground or freshly grated nutmeg

1 teaspoon fine salt

⅔ cup (160ml) vegetable oil

1 teaspoon baking powder

1 teaspoon baking soda

1 cup (240ml) buttermilk

1 large egg

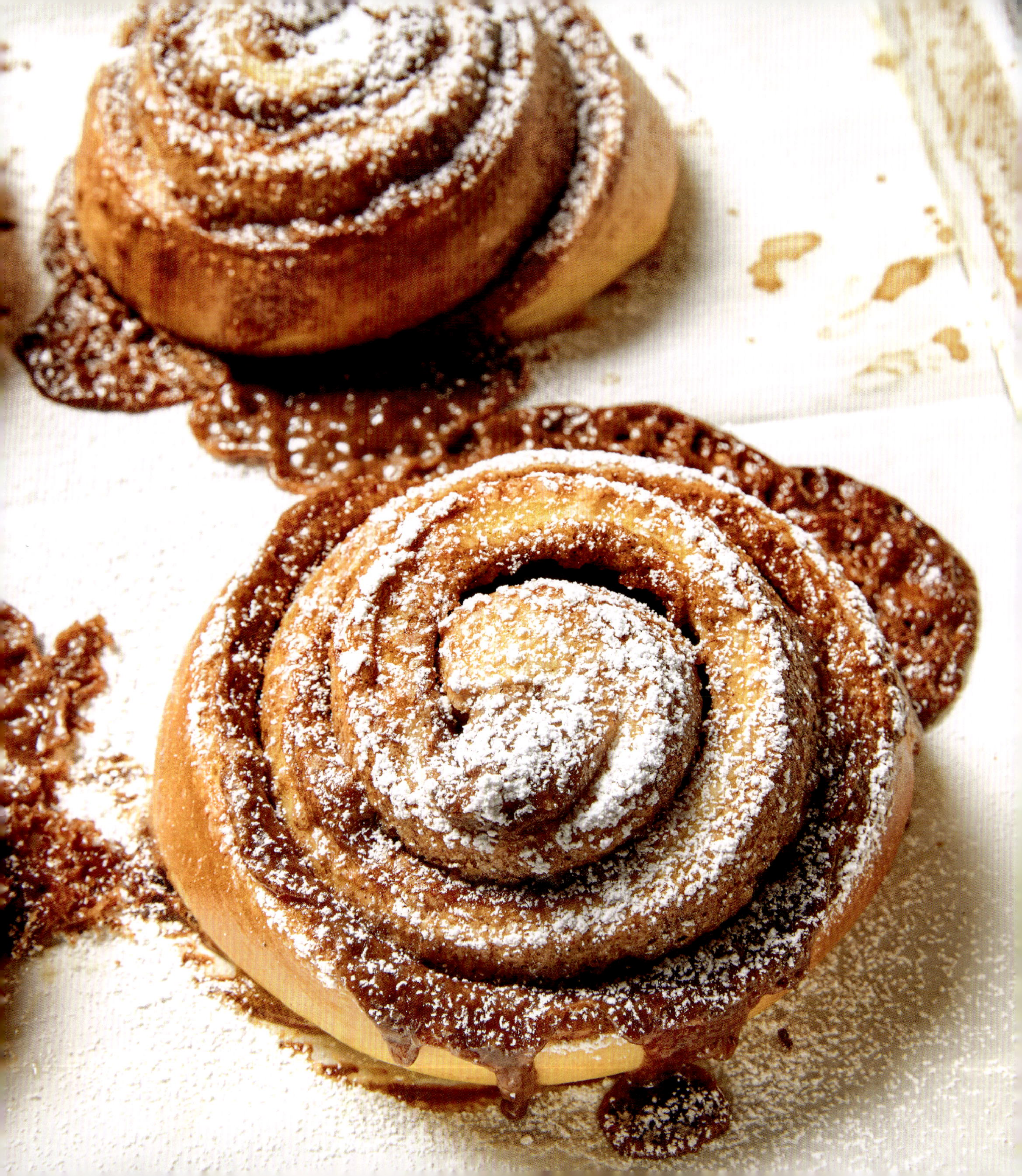

# Brauð & Co.'s Cinnamon Rolls

📍 *Reykjavík, Iceland*

I wasn't expecting Iceland to be a place with great breads and pastries, but between Siggi Hilmarrson's Geothermal Lava Bread (page 49) and these cinnamon rolls from Brauð & Co. in Reykjavík, the baked goods I had on that trip were some of the best I've had anywhere. These aren't like American cinnamon rolls. They're what happens when you take a Danish or almond croissant filling, add cinnamon, and stuff it into a giant bun. At the bakery, they've got a machine that rolls out the dough very thin, but two of their best cinnamon roll bakers, Joanna Akimowicz and Jón Anton Bergsson, helped put this recipe together that you can make at home.

> *We use 00 flour, which is 11 to 13 percent protein, about the same as bread flour. For the filling, the butter must be very soft before you mix it into the marzipan, and you need to add it slowly or the marzipan can get lumpy.* —JÓN

> *I recommend using the oven as a proofer. It really helps proof the buns fully and retain the dough's moisture, especially in the cold weather and with the dry air that we have in Iceland. I set mine to 35°C (95°F), then when it reaches that temperature, I turn the oven off and leave the light on to keep it a little warmer. If your oven doesn't go that low, heat it fully up, turn off the heat, and let the buns proof on top of the warm stovetop.* —JOANNA

### TIPS

*This home version of Brauð & Co.'s cinnamon buns requires some advance planning (take the time to read through the full recipe before making them), but it's well worth the effort. You won't get the perfectly uniform spirals like those at the bakery (you need a professional dough sheeter for such a stiff dough), but the flavor and texture of this more rustic version are just as fantastic and impressive.*

*The leftover marzipan can be wrapped tightly in plastic wrap and refrigerated for up to 2 weeks or frozen for a second batch of cinnamon rolls.*

**MAKES 8 EXTRA-LARGE CINNAMON ROLLS**

**CINNAMON-MARZIPAN FILLING**

3½ ounces (100g) marzipan (Odense; half a 7-ounce/200g tube), at room temperature

½ cup (100g) granulated sugar

7 tablespoons (100g) unsalted butter, cubed, at warm room temperature (very soft but not melted)

3½ tablespoons ground cinnamon

Fine salt

**DOUGH**

2 teaspoons instant or active dry yeast

6 tablespoons (85g) unsalted butter, at room temperature

5 cups (600g) 00 or bread flour

½ cup (100g) granulated sugar

1 large egg

Fine salt

### DAY 1

**Make the cinnamon-marzipan filling:** In a stand mixer fitted with the paddle attachment, combine the marzipan and sugar and mix on low speed until the marzipan is broken into small pieces, about 1 minute. Slowly add the butter, a few cubes at a time, mixing each addition until fully incorporated before adding more butter. Increase the speed to medium-low and mix until creamy. Add the cinnamon and ¼ teaspoon fine salt and mix until the cinnamon is fully incorporated and the filling is very smooth.

Scrape the filling into a small bowl, press a piece of plastic wrap on the surface, and leave at room temperature overnight. (Don't refrigerate.)

**Make the dough:** Wipe the stand mixer bowl and paddle attachment clean. Add the yeast and 1 cup (240ml) room-temperature water. If using active dry yeast, set aside for 5 minutes to bloom the yeast; with instant yeast, there's no need to wait.

Add the butter, 00 flour, sugar, egg, and 1¼ teaspoons fine salt and mix on low speed until a shaggy dough forms.

Increase the speed to medium and mix the dough for 4 minutes. If the dough partly rises above the paddle the first minute or two, stop the mixer and push it back down; it will cling to the dough hook the longer it is mixed. Shape the dough into a round, let rest for 1 to 2 minutes, and press it with your finger. The indentation should spring back slowly (if not, mix for another minute). Put the dough in a medium bowl, cover with plastic wrap, and refrigerate overnight or for up to 18 hours.

**DAY 2**

**Shape the cinnamon rolls:** The cinnamon-marzipan filling should be easily spreadable. If the room is cold, set the filling in a warm spot until softened (turn on the oven for a few minutes, turn it off, and lay the marzipan on top of the stovetop; be sure it doesn't melt).

Line two baking sheets with silicone baking mats or parchment paper.

Very lightly flour a very large (at least 2 feet/62cm long) and flat work surface. Flatten out the cold dough and shape it into a narrow rectangle; arrange the rectangle vertically, if your workspace allows. If you have a small workspace, cut the dough into two equal halves.

Roll out the dough into a large rectangle 20 to 22 inches (50 to 55cm) long and 12 inches (30.5cm) wide (or two smaller rectangles roughly half those dimensions). The dough is very stiff, so you need to really press down on the rolling pin. If the rectangle becomes too wide, simply pat in the sides before re-rolling; if the dough becomes difficult to roll, lift it up and stretch it out with your hands into a larger rectangle and, if needed, lightly dust the work surface with flour. Don't leave the dough on the countertop too long as you roll it out or it will start to warm up and rise, causing the buns to split apart as they bake.

Trim off the sides of the rectangle to make straight edges, then dollop the cinnamon-marzipan filling evenly over the dough. Use an offset spatula or the back of a large spoon to spread the filling out to the edges; reserve a spoonful of the filling for any dough scraps.

**TOPPING**

**1 egg**

**Spoonful (1 tablespoon) heavy cream or milk**

**Powdered (confectioner's) sugar, for dusting**

Starting at one of the shorter sides (the bottom of the rectangle, if it's arranged vertically on your work surface), roll up the dough very snugly, like a cigar; if the dough sticks to the counter as you roll it, slide a pastry cutter or blunt knife underneath as you roll.

Use a serrated knife to gently saw back and forth and trim off the two ends of the log; don't press straight down on the knife or it will compact the dough. If you have one large log, cut it in half. Score four evenly spaced notches in each log, then cut each log into 4 pieces to make 8 buns.

Arrange the cinnamon buns on the prepared baking sheets at least 2 inches (5cm) apart; put any smaller-size buns and the end scraps toward the middle of the baking sheets.

Lift up each bun, pull out the very end of the dough spiral, and tuck it fully underneath the bun. Use the palm of your hand to firmly smash the buns as flat as possible (they will partly spring back), wiping any excess filling off your hand as you go.

Loosely cover the baking sheets with plastic wrap and let the buns rise in a warm spot or in the oven on the proofer setting until puffy and almost double their smashed height, 1 to 1½ hours; each should be about 4 inches (10cm) wide.

**Bake the cinnamon rolls:** About 15 minutes before the rolls have finished rising, put a rack in the top third and another rack in the bottom third of the oven. Preheat the oven to 400°F (205°C).

In a small dish, whisk together the egg and cream. Use a pastry brush or your fingers to lightly brush the tops and sides of the buns with the egg wash. Just before baking, use a sieve to quickly dust each bun generously with powdered sugar. (Wait until the oven has preheated or the powdered sugar will melt into the wash.)

Immediately put the buns in the oven and bake, rotating the pans top to bottom and front to back halfway through, until golden brown on the edges and lightly toasted on the bottom, 10 to 12 minutes.

**Serve:** Let the cinnamon buns cool on the baking sheet for about 10 minutes. Dust the buns with more powdered sugar, if you like, and serve warm or at room temperature. The cinnamon rolls are best eaten the day they are made.

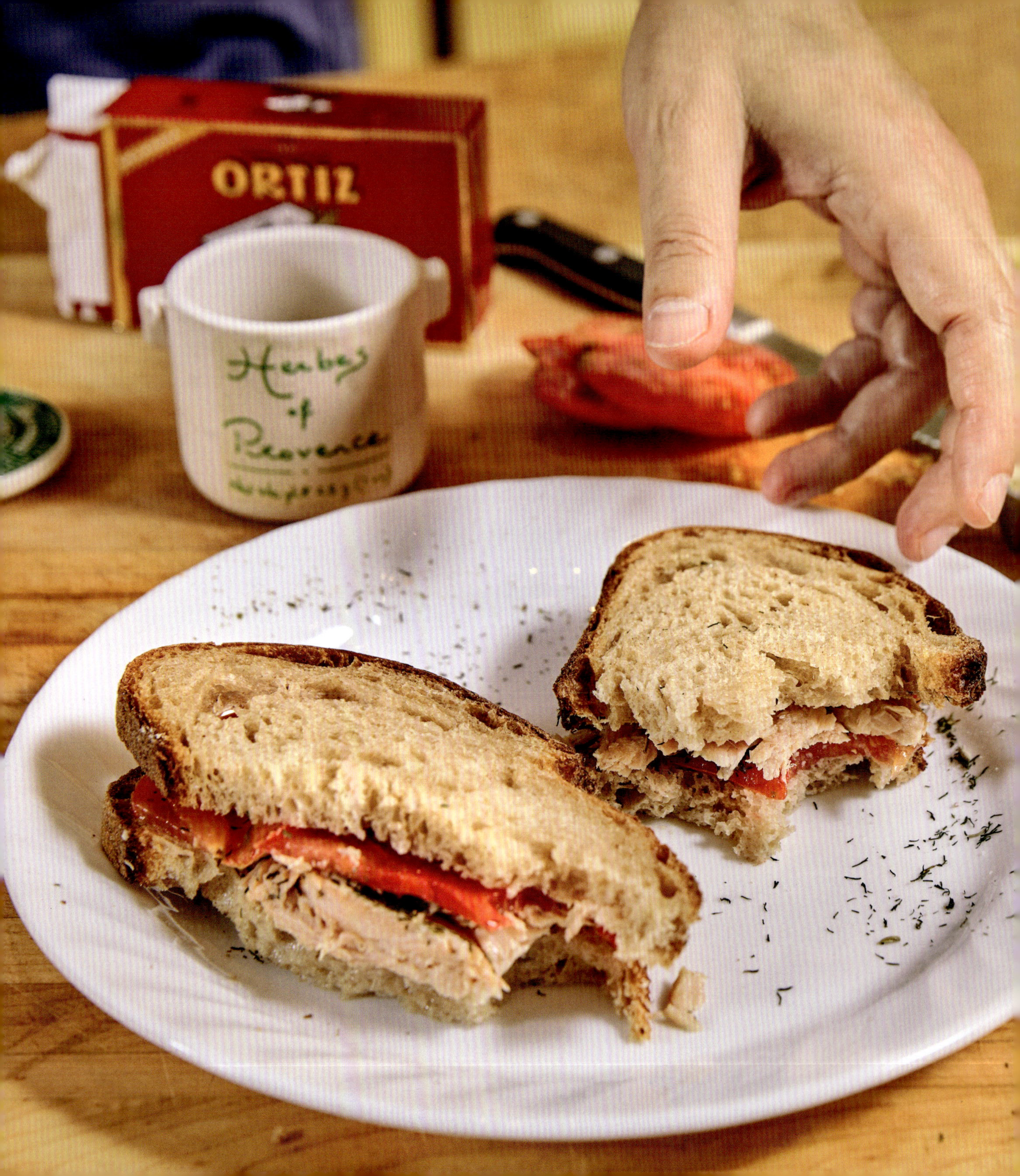
ORTIZ
Herbes
of
Provence

# THE BEST INVENTION IN THE WORLD: THE SANDWICH

I could do a whole book on sandwiches. They're convenient, affordable, portable, and every culture has some kind of bread, tortilla, pancake, or wrap that's filled with something delicious. A sandwich is probably the easiest thing for anybody to make at home, and Monica and I do like to make them sometimes, but I'm always going to go out for one if I have the chance. Doesn't matter if it's an old neighborhood diner that's been around for decades, a new sandwich place from a young chef, or a really good bakery that slices up their just-baked bread and fills it with something great. (If you're in LA, Bub and Grandma's bakery in Glassell Park is one of my favorites.) I'm going to find something I want to try, even if it's a sandwich that I've had hundreds of times. Burgers are a very good example of that. (Yes, a burger is technically a sandwich—so's a hot dog—we just never call them that.) There's always a new burger that somebody's doing, which is why I've got three burgers from three chefs in this chapter (plus two more in my first book), and even that isn't enough. When I went to Gotham Burger Social Club in New York for the first time, it was too late to get their burger recipe for you, and by the time this book goes to print, I know I'll have others I want to share. You can't go wrong with a good sandwich.

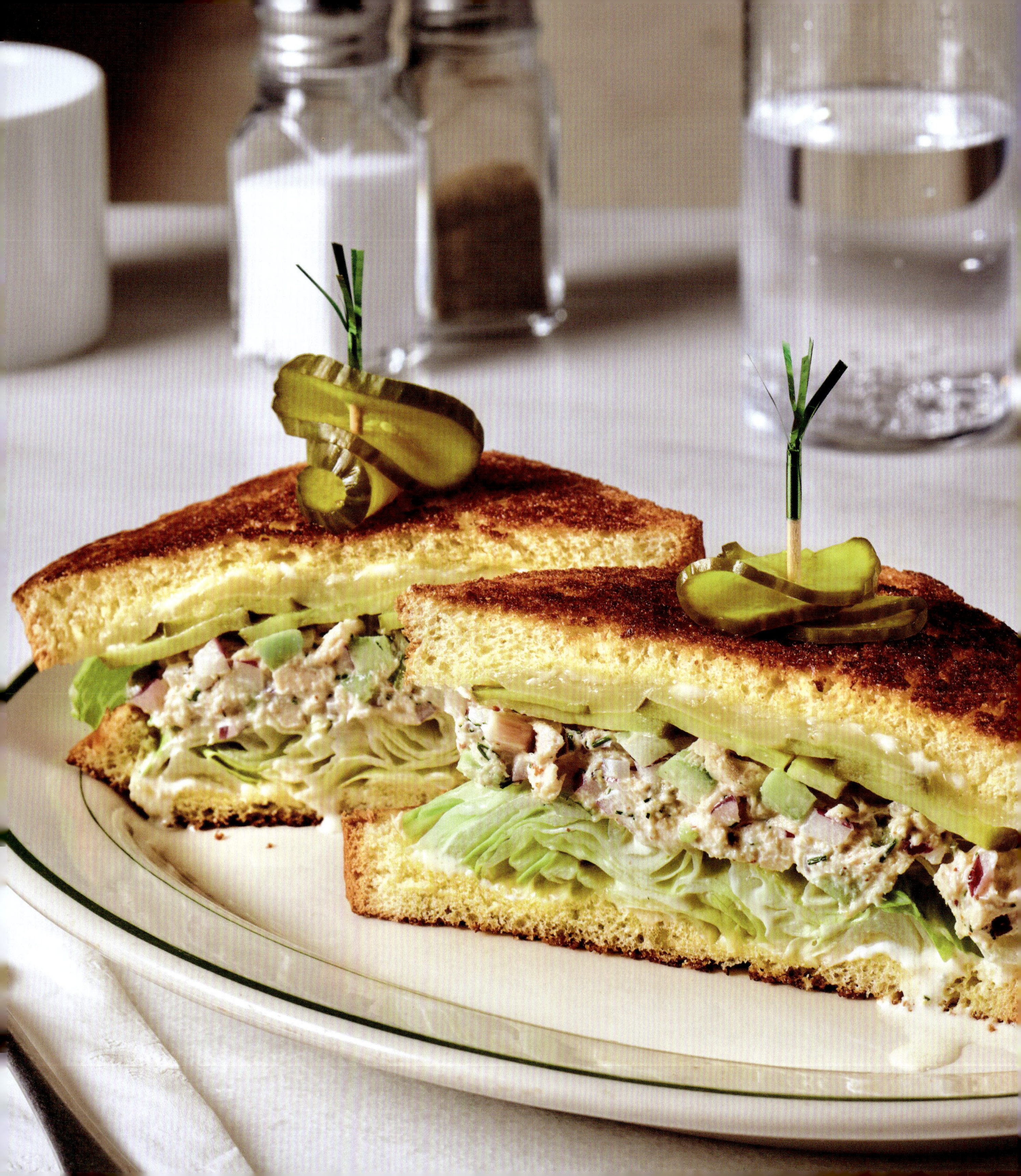

# Chad Conley and Greg Mitchell's Tuna Melt

*Palace Diner, Biddeford*

Chad Conley and Greg Mitchell are longtime friends and the chefs behind Palace Diner, a tiny dining car in Biddeford, Maine (about half an hour south of Portland), that's been around since 1927. They're comfort food perfectionists in the best possible way. I could eat anything they serve—an omelet, flapjacks, their burger or fried chicken sandwich—anytime. I loved going there so much in the "Maine" episode of season five that it was the inspiration behind Max & Helen's diner (see page 35).

This tuna melt is the grandest expression of a tuna sandwich I've ever had. Their homemade pickles are spicy and just sweet enough, their tuna salad is light and not at all dry, and the iceberg is cut a certain way so you get one thick crunchy piece that completely covers the bread. Even the mustard they use is special, so if you want the sandwich to be just like they make it, order some mustard from Raye's in Eastport, which is about a four-hour drive up the coast. It's the last stone-ground mustard mill still operating in the United States. They get the big, soft challah loaves for the sandwich fresh from Big Sky Bread in Portland, but you can get good challah at your local bakery.

> *You need a really large head of iceberg so you can slice it into very thick "steaks," which helps the lettuce stay in one piece on the sandwich.* —**CHAD**

**FEEDS 6**

6 tablespoons (85g) salted or unsalted butter

12 thick (1-inch/2.5cm) slices brioche sandwich bread or large loaf-style challah

About ¾ cup (180ml) mayonnaise

6 Iceberg Steaks (from 1½ large, heavy heads iceberg lettuce; technique follows)

The Palace Diner's Tuna Salad (about 3 cups/550g; recipe follows)

Chad's Bread-and-Butter Pickle Chips (about ¾ recipe; page 298), drained

2 cups (about 10 ounces/280g) grated sharp white cheddar cheese

**TO SERVE**

6 Pickle Skewers (technique follows; optional)

**Prep:** In a large sauté pan, melt the butter over medium-low heat.

Lay one side of each bread slice in the melted butter. Toast the bread in batches, buttered side facing down, pressing down to gently smash the bread as it toasts, until golden brown on the bottom.

**Assemble and serve:** Spread mayonnaise generously on the untoasted sides of each slice.

Lay 1 Iceberg Steak on each bottom slice of bread and arrange the tuna salad on top (about ½ cup/90g per sandwich), then "shingle" 10 to 12 pickle chips like roof tiles over the tuna so the pickles are tightly overlapping.

Cover the remaining slices of bread with the white cheddar.

In a toaster oven or beneath the broiler, lightly toast the cheese-topped slices of bread just until the cheese has melted. Close the sandwiches with slices of cheese toast and cut them in half diagonally.

Insert 1 Pickle Skewer into each sandwich half, if you'd like, and serve.

## THE PALACE DINER'S TUNA SALAD

In a medium bowl, mix together the mayonnaise, olive oil, mustard, lemon juice, celery salt, and hot sauce. Break up any large chunks of tuna with your fingers as you add it to the bowl. Mix the tuna into the mayonnaise, then stir in the cucumber, celery, red onion, chives, and dill. Season the tuna salad with salt, pepper, and more hot sauce, if you like. Cover and refrigerate the tuna salad for at least 2 hours or up to 2 days.

## ICEBERG STEAKS

**MAKES 4 TO 5 ICEBERG STEAKS PER HEAD OF LETTUCE**

Remove any loose outer leaves from a large, heavy head of iceberg lettuce (the leaves on lightweight heads tend to fall apart when sliced). Slice off the very bottom of the lettuce so you can stand it upright and make 4 or 5 parallel slices about 1 inch (2.5 cm) thick. Trim the core out of any of the slices. If not using right away, wrap the lettuce in a damp kitchen towel and refrigerate in the crisper drawer overnight. Save any leftover bits of lettuce for salads.

## PICKLE SKEWERS

Per skewer: Stack 2 Bread-and-Butter Pickle Chips, fold the stacked pickles in half, then spear the pickles with a toothpick. Flip the toothpicks upright, so the pickles will be near the top of the skewer when inserted into the sandwich.

---

**MAKES ABOUT 3 CUPS (550g), ENOUGH FOR 6 SANDWICHES**

Generous ⅓ cup (80ml) mayonnaise

3 tablespoons extra-virgin olive oil

1½ tablespoons spicy brown mustard (Raye's Old World Gourmet)

1½ tablespoons freshly squeezed lemon juice

½ teaspoon celery salt

4 to 5 dashes of vinegar-based hot sauce (Tabasco)

3 5-ounce (140g) cans water-packed solid white tuna, drained

½ large cucumber, peeled and chopped

1 large stalk celery, chopped

¼ red onion, finely chopped

1½ tablespoons finely chopped chives

1½ tablespoon finely chopped dill

Kosher salt and freshly ground black pepper

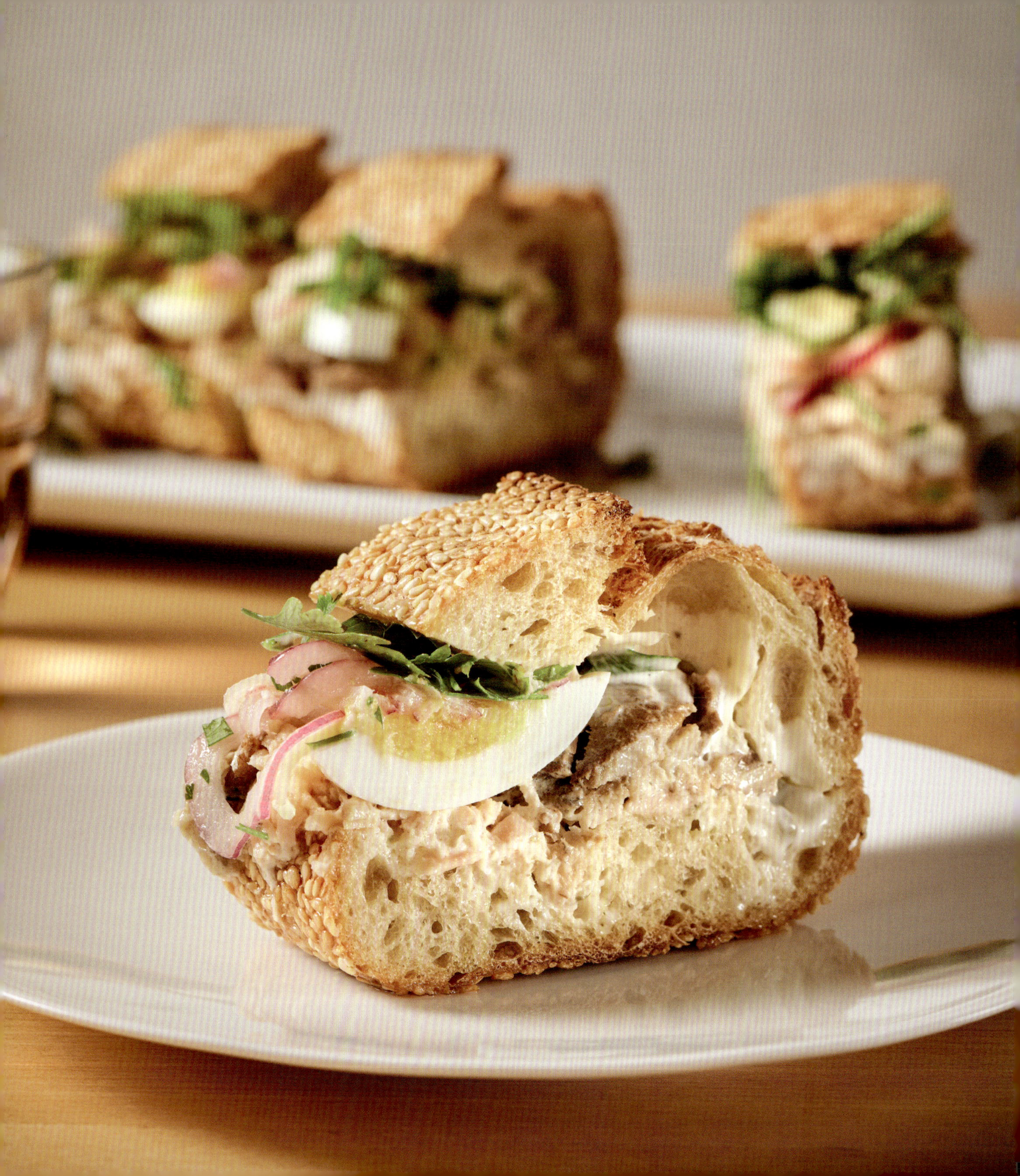

# Joe Beddia's Tuna and Smoked Sardine Hoagie

📍 *Pizzeria Beddia, Philadelphia*

Like the Palace Diner's tuna sandwich on the page before this, this tuna and smoked sardine hoagie is what happens when you have a great chef breaking down every component of a classic sandwich to make it the very best it can be. Joe Beddia is the chef and owner of Pizzeria Beddia, the number one pizza place in Philadelphia. So why is the chef behind a great pizza place making hoagies? And he's not just making hoagies, he's got an entire private Hoagie Omakase tasting room in the back of the restaurant. (If you're not familiar with the Japanese word, *omakase* means "chef's choice," and I'm pretty sure this is the first time it's been applied to hoagies.) Part of the reason is because of John Walker, Joe's good friend and the hoagie room manager, who was the guy you saw making the sandwiches when we were there filming the episode for season six of the show. Like everybody in Philly, John's a hoagie fanatic, and so he and Joe figured they might as well make them. These aren't your average hoagies. They're what happens when the hoagie is turned into an art form.

I always say a sandwich is only as good as the bread, and Joe starts with the very best. That's because he uses his own pizza dough to make the hoagie rolls. They're crusty on the outside, not doughy like some, and have an incredible flavor. If you want this sandwich to be exactly like the one Joe makes, you need to get his cookbook, *Pizza Camp*, so you can make the sesame bread. Or get a good sesame baguette. If you're in LA, we used the big sesame semolina baguettes from Bub and Grandma's in Glassell Park for the sandwich photo. You can also get them at most of Cookbook's locations (they're in Larchmont, Highland Park, and Echo Park). The sandwich was perfect.

> *I'm not trying to reinvent anything when I use ingredients like extra-virgin olive oil and really good tuna to make a hoagie. They follow the path, but I can make something my own. For the bread, you want the crusty outside and just a little of the soft interior (take out the extra) so you can build the sandwich correctly and in the right proportions. I like Ortiz tuna (the one in the yellow can), but there are so many other flavors going on here, you don't need to use expensive tuna. It's all of the components together that make this a great sandwich.* —JOE

**FEEDS 6; MORE AS PART OF AN OMAKASE TASTING**

**6 sesame seed demi baguettes (about 8 inches/20cm) or 3 full baguettes, cut in half**

**6 4- to 5-ounce (about 130g) cans good-quality tuna in olive oil (Ortiz or similar), chilled**

**½ cup (120ml) extra-virgin olive oil**

**3 6.7-ounce (190g) tins Bar Harbor smoked sardines, or 6 smaller tins (4 ounces/120g each) of your favorite brand, well chilled**

**Joe's Anchovy-Caper Aioli (about 1¼ cups/290g; page 303)**

**Coarse sea salt and freshly ground black pepper**

**6 Soft-Boiled Pickled Eggs, sliced (recipe follows)**

**Red Onion–Fennel Salad (about 2½ cups/300g; recipe follows)**

**2 medium bunches Italian parsley, tender stems roughly chopped and leaves left whole**

**Prep:** Preheat the oven to 400°F (205°C).

Bake the demi baguettes for 2 to 3 minutes to refresh the bread without toasting it.

Slice each demi baguette partly in half lengthwise; don't slice all the way through the bread. Pick out and discard about half of the fluffy, doughy center.

Meanwhile, drain the tuna well. In a small bowl, use your hands to toss together the tuna and olive oil and set the tuna aside to hydrate for at least 15 minutes.

Drain the sardines and break them up into large chunks, checking for any large bones.

**Assemble and serve:** Open up each demi baguette like a book and spread 2 to 3 spoonfuls (about 3 tablespoons) of the Anchovy-Caper Aioli all over the inside. Arrange the tuna on the bottom half of the bread, season lightly with salt and pepper, then arrange a single layer of sardines over the tuna. Top each sandwich with the pickled egg slices and 1 handful Red Onion–Fennel Salad. Stuff a generous handful of parsley in the split top of each sandwich, close the hoagie, slice in half, and serve.

## RED ONION–FENNEL SALAD

If the olives are whole, smash them lightly (the bottom of a bowl or mug works well) and remove the pits. Break up the flesh into large pieces with your fingers.

In a medium bowl, combine the olives, red onion, fennel, grated zest of ½ the lemon, and about ¾ of the lemon juice and toss to combine. Sprinkle 2 to 3 generous pinches of salt and a few pinches of pepper on top and toss again. Season the salad with more lemon juice and salt, if needed; it should be tangy.

If not using the salad within a few hours, cover and refrigerate overnight.

**MAKES ABOUT 2½ CUPS (300g), ENOUGH FOR 6 HOAGIES**

2 large handfuls (about ⅔ cup) drained Castelvetrano olives, whole or pitted

½ medium red onion, shaved on a mandoline or very thinly sliced

½ medium fennel bulb, core removed and shaved or very thinly sliced

1 large lemon

Kosher or coarse sea salt and freshly ground black pepper

## SOFT-BOILED PICKLED EGGS

**Make the brine:** In a small saucepan, combine the vinegar, sugar, salt, garlic, bay leaf, and ½ cup (120ml) water. Bring to a simmer and stir to dissolve the sugar. Remove the pan from the heat and let cool while you boil the eggs.

**Soft boil the eggs:** In a medium bowl, prepare an ice water bath for the eggs.

Fill a pot that will fit the eggs in a single layer with enough water to cover the eggs by at least ½ inch (12mm). Bring the water to a boil, use a ladle or spoon to gently lower each egg into the pot, and set a timer for 8 minutes.

As the eggs cook, adjust the heat as needed to keep the water simmering; it shouldn't vigorously boil. After 8 minutes, use a ladle

**MAKES 6 PICKLED EGGS, ENOUGH FOR 6 HOAGIES**

½ cup (120ml) white wine vinegar

1 tablespoon granulated sugar

1 tablespoon kosher or coarse sea salt

1 garlic clove

1 bay leaf

6 large eggs, chilled

> **TIP**
>
> *To serve smaller portions for a party, after assembling the sandwiches, you can slice them into tasting-size portions. For picnic-friendly hoagies, layer up the tuna and sardines on the bread and pack the Red Onion–Fennel Salad and parsley separately to assemble before serving.*

or spoon to gently transfer the eggs to the ice water bath. (Don't strain the eggs, as the shells will break.) Let the eggs cool for at least 5 minutes.

Peel the eggs. They should feel a bit soft, not completely firm like a hard-boiled egg.

**Cure the eggs:** Pack the eggs into a large jar or glass measuring cup that fits them snugly with some room at the top for the brine (a 4-cup or 1L jar works well). Pour the brine over the eggs, cover, and refrigerate overnight or up to 20 hours.

Strain off the brine and refrigerate the pickled eggs for at least 4 hours or up to 1 week.

# My Tuna Sandwich

This is my favorite sandwich to make at home. First, you need to get really good sourdough bread from a local bakery. And you need excellent tuna. My favorite is from Spain, the "Ventresca in Olive Oil" from Ortiz that comes in the red box with gold writing. The olive oil that the tuna is packed in is so good, you don't need mayonnaise. It's not cheap, but it's worth it when you want a really special sandwich. Another more affordable one that I really like is the smoked albacore by Fishwife, an American company that makes beautiful tinned fish. (It was cofounded by a young woman in her twenties, Becca Millstein, after she went on a trip to Lisbon, got home, and missed all the local food. Travel really does change your life.) I also put some herbes de Provence and a little dried dill weed from my spice rack and a slice or two of good tomato on the sandwich. That's it. You can add any salt, but I started using some of the herb sea salt blend that my friend the great Tuscan butcher Dario Cecchini makes. (You can get it at his butcher shop, Antica Macelleria Cecchini, in Panzano or order the salt online. It's called Profumo del Chianti.) It's a great sandwich. I think you'll be very happy.

**FEEDS 1**

1 tin really good olive oil–packed tuna (Ortiz Ventresca Bonito del Norte or Fishwife Smoked Albacore)

2 slices really good crusty bread

Herbes de Provence

Dried dill weed

Good sea salt

2 to 3 slices heirloom tomato

Open the tin of tuna and pour the olive oil over the bread. Sprinkle some herbes de Provence and dill over the bread (not too much), and pile the tuna on top of the bread. Sprinkle the sea salt over everything, then lay the tomatoes and the other slice of bread on top. Eat and be happy.

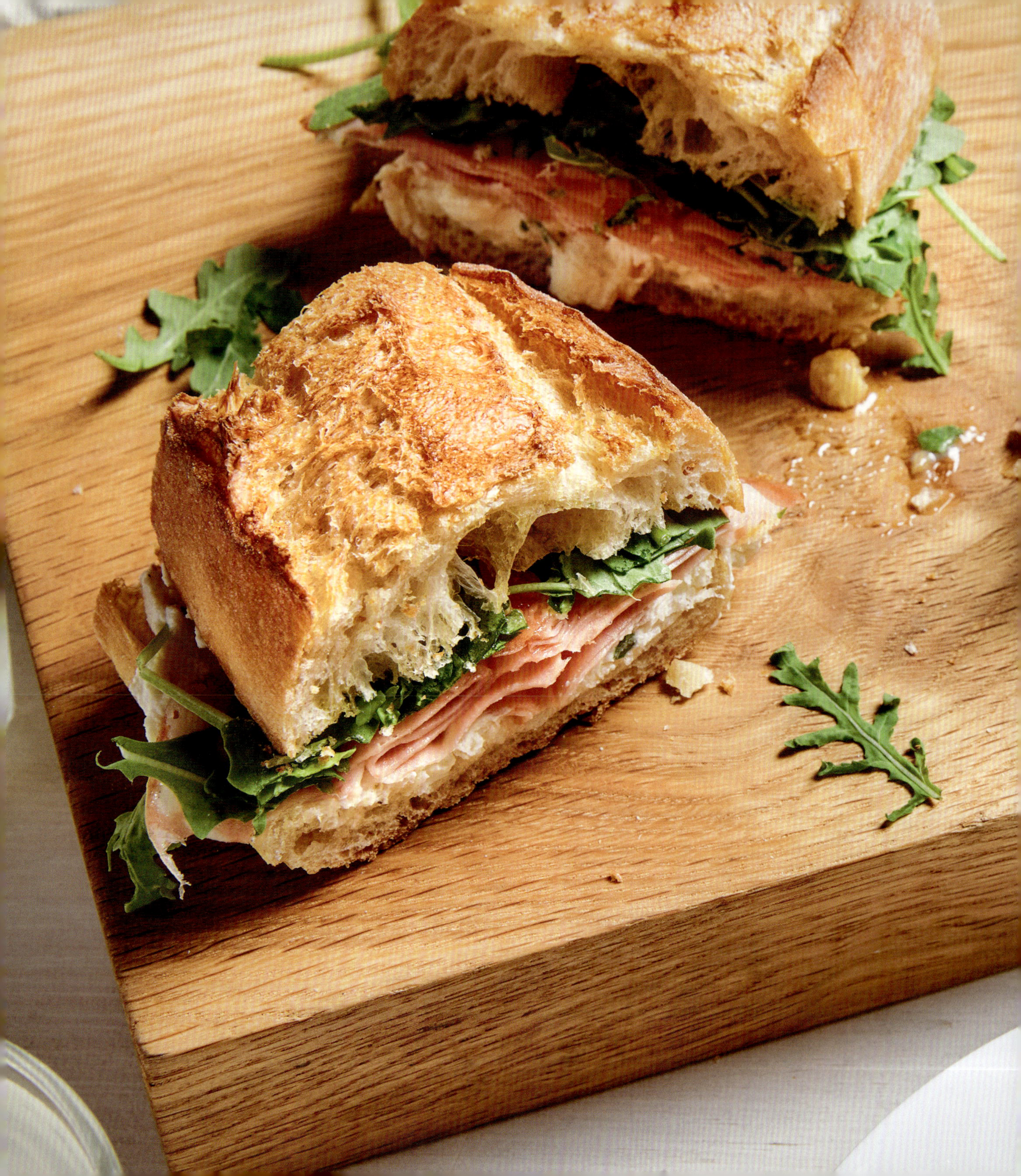

# Marc Vetri's Mortadella and Ricotta Sandwich

*Fiorella, Philadelphia/LA Loves Alex's Lemonade, Los Angeles*

Philadelphia is a place I've been to a lot, partly because a pretty lady I happen to know well grew up there. When I'm in town, I don't ever miss going to one of my friend Marc Vetri's restaurants. My current favorite is Fiorella, where we went in season six. You sit at the counter and watch the chefs make pasta, and it's not just a show. It's some of the best pasta I've had anywhere.

For as long as I can remember, Marc has been involved with a local nonprofit that's also important to Monica and me called Alex's Lemonade Stand Foundation for Childhood Cancer. For years they've had fundraising events in Philadelphia and LA where you get to go and taste food from some of the best chefs, and all the money raised goes toward pediatric cancer research. It's not only delicious but a great way to get to know some of the chefs behind these restaurants, who are usually there handing out their food themselves. In Philly, it's called the Great Chefs Event and happens in the early summer; in LA, it's called LA Loves Alex's Lemonade and takes place in the fall. (If you want to go, you can get the information at alexslemonade.org.) When we were doing the "Los Angeles" episode of *I'll Have What Phil's Having*, it happened to be the same time the event was happening at UCLA, and Marc also happened to be there making these mortadella sandwiches. Like everything he does, it's pretty spectacular.

> *My business partner, Jeff Benjamin, and I have been hosting the Great Chefs Event since we started it to support Alex's Lemonade Stand Foundation. We were making these giant mortadella as a way to get people excited about the event, and one year we had a seven-footer that took eight hours just to stuff the meat into the casing because we made the whole thing by hand. It was so heavy we had to use a forklift to get it into the fermentation tank at the local brewery, where we were cooking it in a pilsner bath for two days. It took five of us, including a guy inside the tank, to get it out. We couldn't do that in LA, so we made these sandwiches with store-bought mortadella and fresh ricotta.* —MARC

**FEEDS 6, MORE AS PART OF A TASTING MENU**

6 demi baguettes (about 8 inches/20cm) or 3 full baguettes, cut in half

⅓ cup (80ml) extra-virgin olive oil, plus more for toasting the baguettes

2 tablespoons finely chopped hazelnuts

⅓ cup plus 1 tablespoon (90ml) honey

3 cups (720g) hand-dipped ricotta (Calabro) or other good-quality whole-milk ricotta

Coarse sea salt and freshly ground black pepper

1 pound (about 500g) sliced mortadella (about 36 slices)

2 to 3 small bunches (6 ounces/170g) baby arugula leaves

**Prep:** Preheat the oven to 400°F (205°C). Slice the demi baguettes (or halved baguettes) fully in half lengthwise, and drizzle olive oil generously over both halves. Lightly toast the baguettes, cut sides facing up, until light golden brown on the cut surface, 6 to 8 minutes.

Meanwhile, put the hazelnuts in a small oven-proof dish and toast for 3 to 4 minutes; watch the nuts carefully so they don't burn. Scrape the honey into the dish.

In a small bowl, combine the ricotta, ⅓ cup (80ml) extra-virgin olive oil, a pinch or two of salt, and 2 to 3 grinds of pepper, and use a rubber spatula to whip the oil into the ricotta until smooth.

**Assemble and serve:** Spread about ½ cup (120g) ricotta on the bottom half of each toasted baguette. Shingle about 6 mortadella slices over the ricotta, drizzle the honey-hazelnut mixture on top, and finish with the arugula. Close the sandwich and cut in half or thirds, and serve.

### TIP

*Hand-dipped ricotta refers to the process of scooping up the cheese by hand to give it a lighter texture. It's typically a regional product (look for "hand-dipped" on the label); beyond Calabro, Bellwether Farms in California, Lioni Latticini in New York, and many regional creameries make good versions of the style.*

# Bill Miller's Turkey-Brie Sandwich (aka "The Phil")

📍 *Malibu Kitchen*

Anytime the family and I made the trip out to Malibu together, we would always stop at my old friend Bill Miller's place, Malibu Kitchen, for sandwiches. Bill was the tour manager for performers like Elvis, Led Zeppelin, Kiss, Sinatra, and the Moody Blues, and when he would travel overseas, he'd collect the menus from the best restaurants he ate at around the world. When he retired from the road trip life (not a bad way to travel and see the world), he opened Malibu Kitchen in 2000 in the Malibu Country Mart along the Pacific Coast Highway.

Everybody went there, from people driving in to the beach for the day to locals who lived in Malibu, and over the years it became the place to stop along the PCH for vintage car collectors. It was also a place I regularly took my mom and dad when they were in town because for us, beyond getting to see Bill, the main attraction was always the food. My favorite thing there was this turkey and Brie sandwich. Bill roasted a fresh turkey every day, so the turkey was never dry, and the tangy cranberry sauce with the Brie was perfect. After more than twenty years, Bill closed the Malibu Kitchen at the end of 2022. (It may reopen nearby, and I can't wait.) I went there on the last day it was open and ordered my favorite turkey sandwich by the sea.

**FEEDS 6**

2 to 2¼ pounds (1kg) leftover roasted turkey breast, sliced about ¼-inch (6mm) thick

6 medium ciabatta or rustica sandwich rolls

1½ to 2 wheels (7 to 8 ounces/200 to 225g each) double cream Brie (60% Tour de Marze)

About 1½ cups (180ml) Bill's Red Onion Cranberry Sauce (recipe follows)

6 handfuls (6 ounces/170g) mixed baby greens or arugula

---

*We made this turkey and Brie sandwich for years before Phil discovered it, only we'd been using deli turkey. He preferred fresh turkey breast, so we started roasting our own whenever he was coming in; it was so good, we made it a permanent change. Later, customers started asking for "the sandwich Phil eats" or just "the Phil." You can use leftover holiday turkey or the freshly roasted sliced turkey that a lot of grocery store deli counters cook up today. I reheat the sliced turkey in the oven in a little water so it steams the meat and doesn't dry out . . . a good trick, especially with leftover turkey breast.* —BILL

> *Ocean Spray cranberry juice and sauce really is the best... and you can get it all year.* —BILL

### TIPS

*Beyond Tour de Marze, even a basic Brie from the grocery store is delicious in this sandwich.*

*Reheating the turkey breast in a small amount of water keeps the meat moist, and does wonders for a somewhat dry, overcooked holiday turkey.*

**MAKES ABOUT 2 CUPS (480ML)**

2 tablespoons extra-virgin olive oil

1 small red onion, thinly sliced

¼ cup (60ml) cranberry juice (Ocean Spray)

1 14-ounce (400g) can whole berry cranberry sauce

**Prep:** Preheat the oven to 400°F (205°C).

Arrange the sliced turkey snugly in a single layer in a small baking dish. Add just enough water to come about halfway up the sides of the turkey, loosely cover the dish with foil, and bake until warm throughout (the water should be steaming), 8 to 10 minutes.

At the same time, bake the ciabatta for 2 to 3 minutes.

Slice off the rind from the edges of the Brie, and for a milder flavor, the top and bottom as well (optional). Slice the Brie into roughly ¼-inch (6mm) slices.

When the turkey is hot, use tongs to transfer the slices to a small sheet pan or a dry baking dish and lay the Brie on top. Bake, uncovered, just until the Brie begins to soften and melt, 1 to 2 minutes; the cheese will look shiny on the surface but shouldn't be runny.

In a small saucepan over low heat, gently rewarm the cranberry sauce, stirring occasionally.

**Assemble and serve:** Generously spread cranberry sauce on the top and bottom halves of the sandwich rolls (about 2 tablespoons per half). Arrange 1 to 2 generous scoops of the Brie-topped turkey on the bottom halves of the rolls and top the sandwiches with the baby greens or arugula. Close the sandwiches, gently press down to lightly smash the bread, cut in half, and serve warm.

## BILL'S RED ONION CRANBERRY SAUCE

In a large sauté pan, heat the oil over medium-high heat. Add the onion and cook, stirring occasionally, until the onion just begins to soften, 2 to 3 minutes. Stir in the cranberry juice and continue to cook until the onion is translucent but not brown, 8 to 10 minutes. Add the cranberry sauce and break up with a spoon until incorporated.

Cover and refrigerate the cooled sauce for up to 1 week.

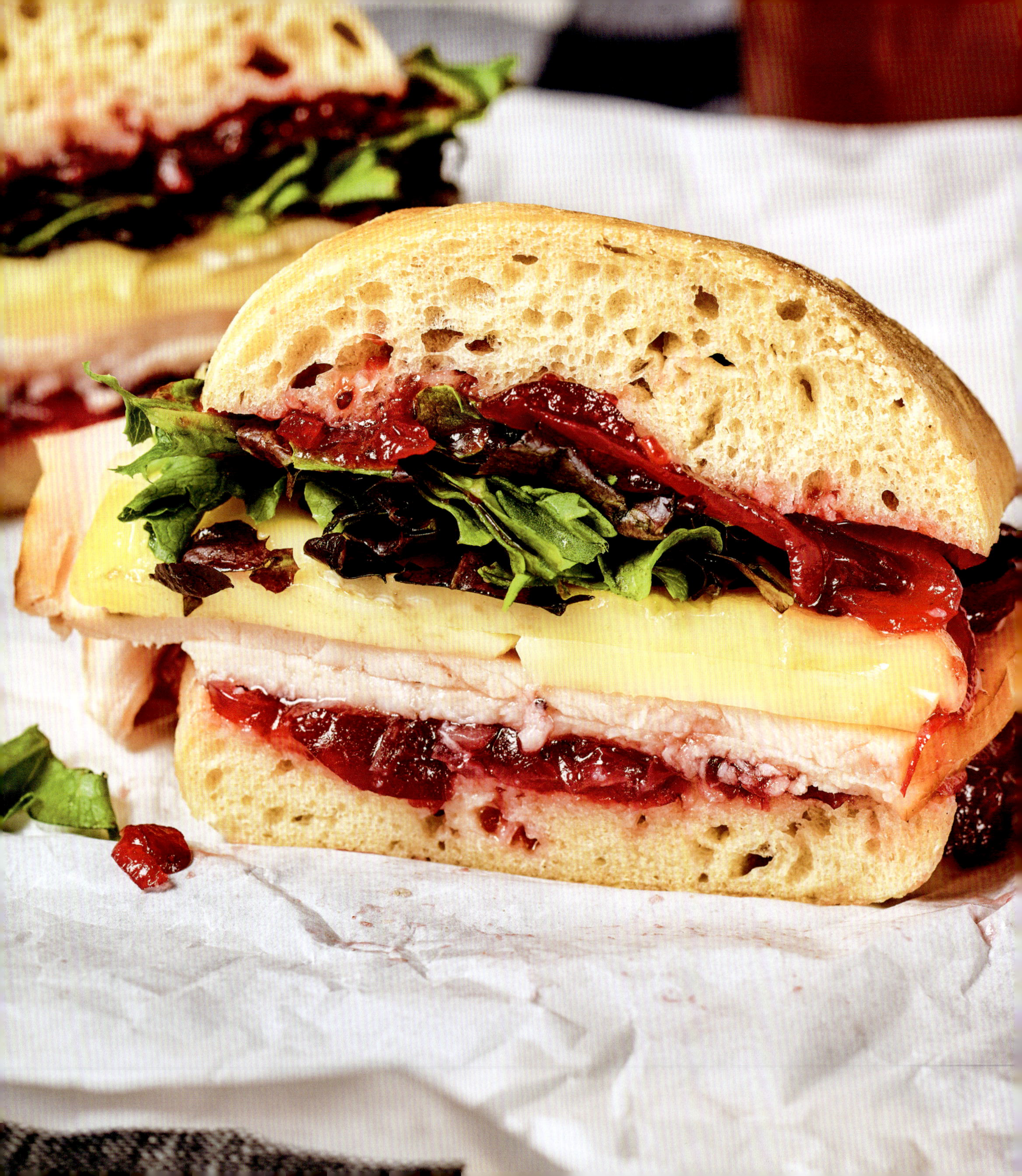

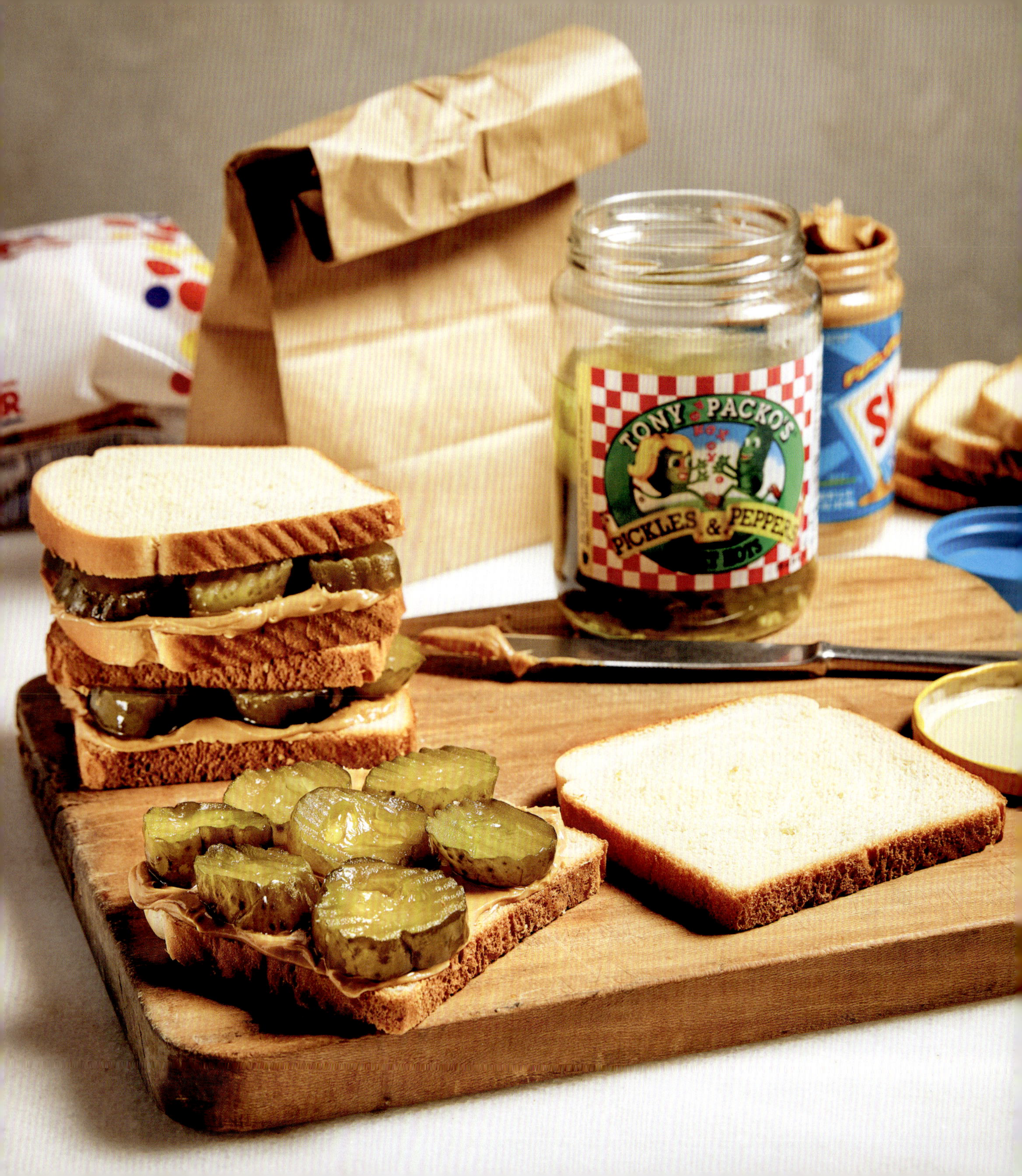
TONY PACKO'S
PICKLES & PEPPERS

# Ajay Sahgal's Peanut Butter and Pickle Sandwich

This sandwich is proof that peanut butter goes with anything. The first time I met my friend Ajay Sahgal was on the picket line at the first Writers Guild strike in 2008. The conversations on the picket line usually involved food, especially around lunchtime. I would bring snacks and sandwiches to share with everybody, and Ajay asked if I'd ever had a peanut butter and pickle sandwich. I had not. So, the next day he brings me one, and it was incredible.

The pickles Ajay uses aren't like most bread-and-butter pickles. These are spicy and sweet and three times as thick as most. They're actually from a nearly one-hundred-year-old Hungarian restaurant in Toledo, Ohio, called Tony Packo's that's known for its chili dogs, which come with their famous Sweet Hots pickles on the side. (It's the same place that was mentioned in several episodes of M*A*S*H because Jamie Farr, who played Corporal Maxwell Klinger, was from Toledo.) I haven't tried their chili dogs, but I can tell you their pickles, which you can order online, make the best peanut butter and pickle sandwich I've ever had.

**FEEDS AS MANY PEOPLE AS YOU WANT**

White sandwich bread (Wonder)

Creamy peanut butter (Skippy or Jif)

Tony Packo's Sweet Hots pickle slices

**TIP**

*You can find Tony Packo's Sweet Hots, very thickly sliced (1/2-inch/ 12mm) spicy bread-and-butter pickles, at the restaurant's online store (tonypacko.com) and some specialty markets and regional grocery stores.*

---

*You want to use smooth peanut butter in this sandwich (the spread, not natural peanut butter). The pickles provide all the texture you need. The softer the white bread the better (on the strike line I made the sandwiches with Wonder bread), and don't toast it. That's it.* —AJAY

---

Spread a generous layer of peanut butter on 1 slice of bread and top it with a single layer of Sweet Hots pickles and another slice of bread. Hand over the sandwich to whoever is around to eat it.

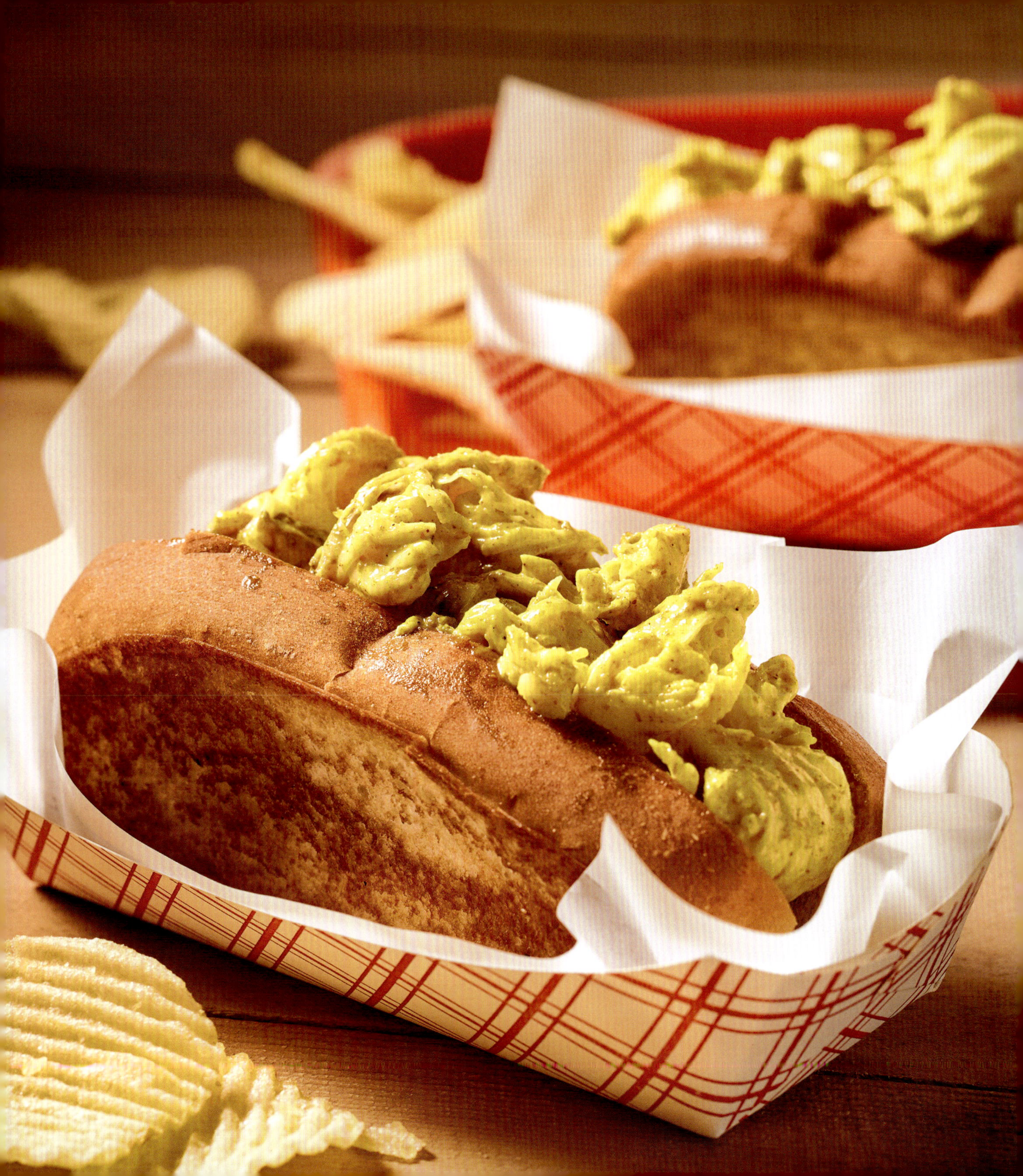

# Bite into Maine's Curry Lobster Roll

*Fort Williams Park, Cape Elizabeth*

When you go to Portland, Maine, I want you to drive about half an hour to Fort Williams Park, Cape Elizabeth, to see one of the world's greatest lighthouses in America. If you haven't been there, you will probably recognize it from photos. The park around the lighthouse is another reason to go. The park is not only gorgeous but you can see the Maine coastline, which is one of the most beautiful coastlines in the world. Here's another reason why you should go: in the warmer months, there's a food truck in the parking lot called Bite into Maine. (They close for the winter but have a couple other food truck and brick-and-mortar locations open year-round.)

Everybody said it's the place to get "gourmet" lobster rolls, so of course we had to go when we were shooting the "Maine" episode. The owner, Sarah Sutton, and her husband, Karl, take a classic Maine lobster roll and mix up the mayonnaise with things like wasabi, chipotle, and—my favorite—curry powder. There's probably a very good reason you don't usually see curry on a lobster roll in Maine or lobster at an Indian restaurant. I may not be able to say the word correctly, but I can write it down: this curry lobster roll is trans-for-ma-tive.

**FEEDS 6**

2 to 2¼ pounds (1kg; about 6 cups) cooked lobster meat

Zesty Curry Mayo (about ⅔ cup/160ml; recipe follows)

4 tablespoons (½ stick/55g) unsalted butter

6 large New England–style split-top brioche rolls or buns, or brioche hot dog buns

---

*These are best with fresh Maine lobster and a view of the ocean! If you don't want to boil your own lobsters, you can buy precooked lobster meat (freshly boiled and chilled) from your seafood market or online, which makes these quick and easy. (If you have any claw meat, leave it whole.) We use fresh-baked brioche rolls from a local bakery. Be sure to enjoy them while the roll is still warm.* —SARAH

---

**Prep:** If the lobster is packaged, remove it from the packaging and strain the juices from the meat. Don't rinse the lobster meat.

## TIPS

*If you're feeding a lot of people, you can butter and toast the buns in a sauté pan an hour or two ahead and rewarm the rolls in a low-temperature oven for a few minutes (arrange the buns in a casserole dish and cover tightly with foil).*

*The extra-large split-top buns used for lobster rolls can be tricky to find outside the Northeast. You can use any good hot dog bun or hoagie roll (even a hamburger bun), as long as it's brioche; the buttery flavor and soft texture are the perfect partner for the lobster. If the buns are on the small side, you can reduce the amount of filling (and serve more people).*

**MAKES ABOUT 2/3 CUP (160ML), ENOUGH FOR 6 LOBSTER ROLLS**

2 tablespoons yellow curry powder

1 tablespoon freshly squeezed lime juice

2/3 cup (160ml) mayonnaise, divided

Use your hands, not a knife, to break up the lobster tail meat into large bite-size pieces; if you have any claw meat, leave it whole. Transfer the lobster meat to a small bowl, cover, and refrigerate until well chilled or up to 8 hours.

**Make the lobster rolls:** Use a rubber spatula to gently stir a generous ½ cup (120ml) Zesty Curry Mayonnaise into the lobster meat until well incorporated. Taste and add a little more mayonnaise, if needed; it should not overwhelm the flavor of the lobster.

In large sauté pan, melt the butter over medium heat. Coat the outside of the rolls in the melted butter, then toast each side (don't open up the rolls) until golden brown, about 1 minute per side.

**Assemble and serve:** Lay each toasted roll, seam side facing up, on a plate and gently open it like a book; be careful not to break it in half. Arrange the lobster meat evenly down the length of the roll (about 1 cup/140g per sandwich) and serve.

## ZESTY CURRY MAYONNAISE

In a small bowl, combine the curry powder and lime juice and smash the two together with the back of a spoon, scraping against the sides of the bowl, until the mixture looks like coarse, wet sand. Use some muscle to scrape the sides vigorously and fully incorporate the spice powder into such a small amount of juice. (Don't add more lime juice; the citrusy flavor is intentionally subtle to not overpower the lobster.)

Add about half the mayonnaise, and keep stirring and scraping the side of the bowl until the curry paste is fully incorporated and the mayonnaise is smooth. Stir in the rest of the mayonnaise.

Refrigerate the curry mayonnaise for at least 30 minutes to allow the flavors to meld, or cover and refrigerate for up to 3 days.

# The Best Classic Maine Lobster Roll

📍 *Red's Eats, Wiscasset*

Here's another lobster roll place you should go to when you're in Maine. Monica and I go to Red's Eats, a seafood shack on Route 1, whenever we're in Wiscasset visiting family in the summertime. You're going to have to stand in line and wait, and I've done this sometimes for an hour and a half. It's worth it. The one time I got to butt the line was when we were there to film the "Maine" episode, so if it's raining, take an umbrella.

These are lobster rolls with the meat of a whole other lobster roll on top of them, and it's no secret how they make them. When we were there to film the episode, Debbie Gagnon, the co-owner, said, "I do not measure. We just pile it high." You can order it with melted butter or mayonnaise on the side. We always get butter.

**FEEDS AS MANY PEOPLE AS YOU WANT**

Tear more freshly cooked (steamed or boiled) Maine lobster than you think anybody can eat into large chunks with your fingers. Melt a lot of good local butter (they use Kate's of Maine). Put some of the butter in a pan and toast up the outside of a couple fresh-baked lobster roll buns (split-top brioche). Pile more lobster into the roll than you think will fit. Now add more lobster.

Put the hot melted butter in a teakettle and pour it into little cups for everybody.

Pour the butter over the lobster meat or dip the roll into the butter. And if your name is Richard, when you're done with your lobster roll, you can toss back any leftover butter in your cup like a shot of tequila.

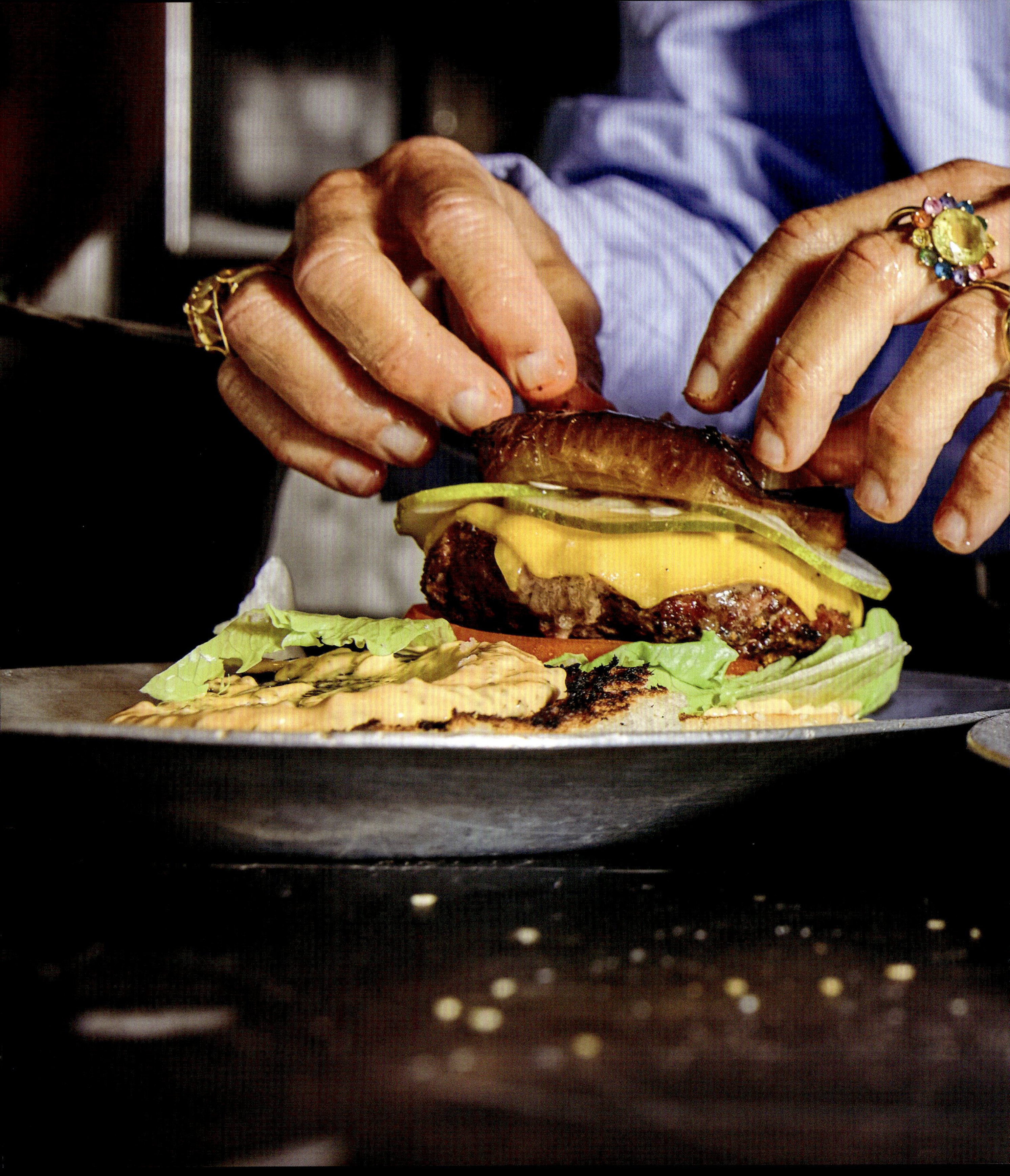

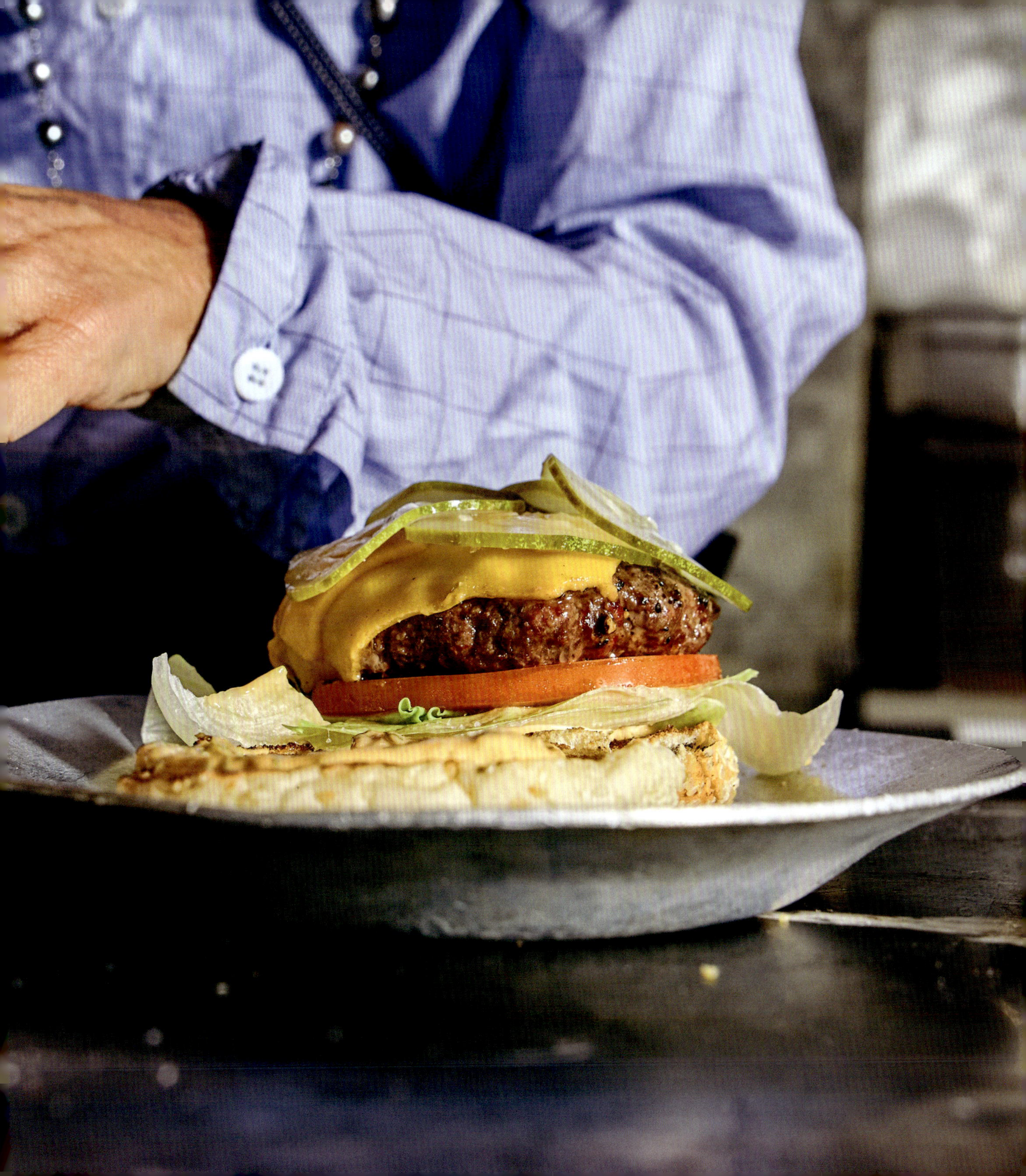

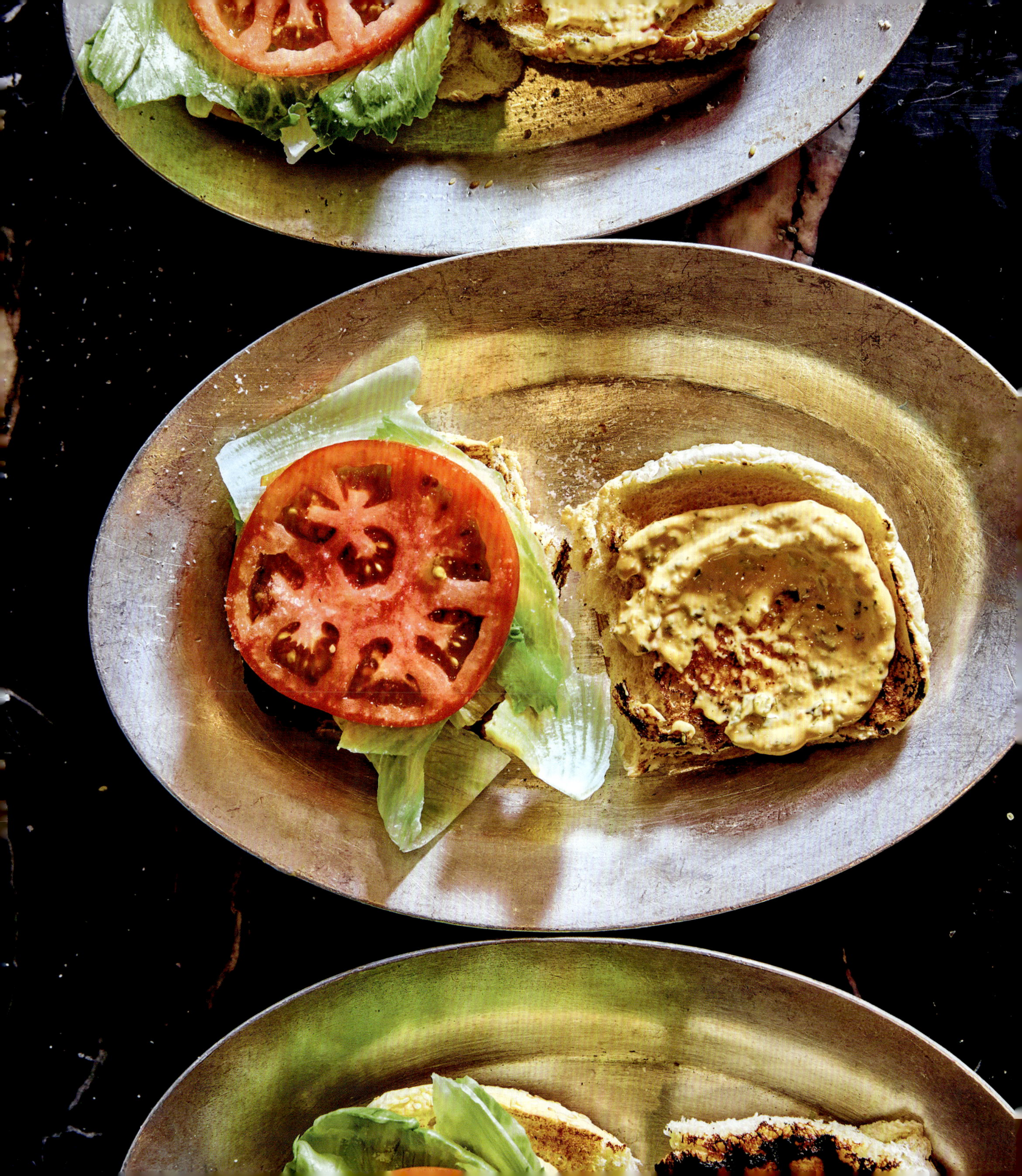

# The SPACCA Burger

📍 *Chi SPACCA, Los Angeles*

There's nothing my longtime friend and one of the greatest American chefs Nancy Silverton does that isn't brilliant. She's been, and still is, the chef behind some of LA's best restaurants for decades, she's written more than ten cookbooks, she travels the world doing fundraisers and other events, and she's one of my favorite people to spend time with. It's the reason I wanted her to be my partner and executive chef at Max & Helen's (see page 35).

Here, Nancy takes classic burger components—a beef patty, onions, pickles, cheddar cheese, and a special sauce—and completely reinvents them. It's proof that there is always something new waiting to be invented by the most creative chefs. My one piece of advice is to do what Nancy says and get ground beef from your butcher with a little dry-aged fat, if they have it, and the sesame seed buns she uses—they're the best. The onion recipe looks like it has way too much salt (it's perfect), and the spicy Calabrian chili mayonnaise has mint, something you don't normally see on a burger. When you put everything together, you'll understand.

> *One of the stars of this burger is the blend of ground beef. If possible, ask your butcher to coarsely grind 1½ pounds of brisket and 1½ pounds of beef chuck, plus ½ pound of dry-aged beef fat. You're looking for a ratio of 70 percent meat to 30 percent fat from the dry-aged trimmings to create the perfect burger blend. If you can't get it, the burger will still be great with pre-ground beef; get a 70/30 coarsely ground blend from your butcher. Seasoning your patties properly, both evenly and attentively, will ensure you get a good crust on the burgers when grilling them.* **—NANCY**

### FEEDS 6

**PATTIES**

**3 pounds (1.4kg) Nancy's beef blend: 1½ pounds (680g) brisket, 1½ pounds chuck, 8 ounces (225g) dry-aged beef fat, or 3 pounds (1.4kg) coarsely ground beef (70/30)**

**Kosher or coarse salt and fresh coarsely ground black pepper**

**BURGER ASSEMBLY**

**6 large sesame seed potato buns (Martin's "Big Marty's")**

**4 tablespoons (½ stick/55g) unsalted butter, melted**

**6 extra-large slices (6 ounces/170g) sharp cheddar cheese (Tillamook Farmstyle)**

**Flaky sea salt (Maldon)**

**About 1⅔ cups (400ml) Nancy's Calabrian Chili–Mint Aioli (page 302)**

*(ingredients continue)*

½ large head iceberg lettuce, cut into quarters and leaves separated

2 to 3 large tomatoes (Beefsteak), cut into 6 ½-inch (12mm) thick center slices, seasoned lightly with salt

2 to 3 large Kosher pickles (Dietz & Watson), thinly sliced into 36 ⅛-inch (3mm) rounds

6 Nancy's Ultimate Hamburger Onions (page 301), warmed

### TIPS

*Even without the dry-aged beef fat, these burgers are fantastic with any good ground beef.*

*These hefty, half-pound burgers need a large, sturdy bun; the average hamburger bun will fall apart. If Nancy's favorite, Martin's "Big Marty's" sesame-potato buns (shop.potatorolls.com), aren't available where you live, any large potato buns work well.*

**Prep:** Prepare a grill for direct cooking over high heat.

**Make the patties:** Divide the ground beef into 6 loosely packed meatballs (8 ounces/225g each) and shape each into a patty the size of the buns; be careful not to overly compact the meat. Lay the patties on a baking sheet and sprinkle 1 tablespoon kosher salt and 1 teaspoon pepper evenly over each. Flip the patties and repeat with the same amount of kosher salt and pepper.

**Make the burgers:** Brush the inside of each bun with the melted butter. Grill the buns, cut side facing down, until lightly toasted, about 1 minute, and set aside.

Put the seasoned burger patties on the grill and sear until they have a nice char, or crust, and can be flipped without sticking to the grate, about 4 minutes. Flip and sear the opposite side until the burgers are medium rare, 4 to 5 minutes.

About 1 minute before the patties are ready, lay 1 cheese slice in the center of each patty so that the edges of the cheese completely cover the patty as it melts.

Transfer the patties to a plate and sprinkle on a pinch of flaky sea salt.

**Serve:** Generously spread Nancy's Calabrian Chili–Mint Aioli on both the top and bottom halves of the toasted buns (about 2 tablespoons per side).

Building each burger from the bottom up, top each bottom bun with 1 to 2 iceberg lettuce leaves; there should be a generous amount of lettuce. Lay 1 tomato slice on the lettuce, then a burger patty, 5 to 6 pickle slices, and 1 whole Ultimate Hamburger Onion ring. Close the burgers (don't smash down on the bun) and serve.

# Orfali Bros' Cheeseburger

*Orfali Bros, Dubai*

Mohamad Orfali's cheeseburger is reason alone to go to Dubai. He ruined burgers for me.

> *A burger is my favorite comfort food. Isn't it everybody's favorite comfort food?* —**MOHAMAD**

**Cure the meat and make the patties:** Break the beef into chunks, spread it out in a single layer on a plate or cutting board, and sprinkle salt generously all over the top. Refrigerate, uncovered, overnight or up to 24 hours; the ground beef will slightly darken in color. Cover with plastic wrap until ready to use, up to another 24 hours.

Divide the ground beef into 6 loosely packed meatballs (about 5½ ounces/155g each) and shape each into a patty the size of the buns; be careful not to overly compact the meat.

**Make the burgers:** Preheat a griddle to 400°F (205°C) or a large cast iron skillet over medium-high heat until almost smoking, 2 to 3 minutes. Sear the patties in batches (don't crowd the pan) until golden brown and a crust develops on the bottom, 3 to 4 minutes. Flip the patties and sear the opposite side until medium rare, 2 to 3 minutes. Season the patties with salt and pepper and shingle 2 slices of cheese on top of each, then transfer to a plate, loosely cover with foil, and set aside for 5 minutes to rest.

While the patties rest, brush the inside of each bun with some of the meat fat from the skillet, then toast the buns in batches until golden brown on the cut side, about 1 minute. Transfer the buns to a plate.

---

**FEEDS 6**

**PATTIES**

2 to 2¼ pounds (1kg) coarsely ground Wagyu beef, preferably 40% fat (see Tip)

Kosher or coarse sea salt

**BURGER ASSEMBLY**

Fresh coarsely ground black pepper

12 slices (8 ounces/225g) American cheese

6 large, good-quality brioche buns

About 1½ cups (375g) Mohamad's Brown Butter Caramelized Onions (page 299)

About 1 cup (240ml) Secret Sauce, at room temperature (recipe follows)

> **TIP**
>
> *Mohamad cures seasoned chunks of Wagyu beef overnight, like a refrigerator-cured steak, before coarsely grinding the meat. The result is a more deeply flavored beef blend with the high fat content of Wagyu. Ask your butcher to coarsely grind Wagyu, or get good pre-ground Wagyu (the grass-fed Wagyu from First Light Farms is a Phil favorite) and use the same quick overnight curing technique. The meat won't have as high a fat content but it will make an excellent patty.*

Add Mohamad's Brown Butter Caramelized Onions to the skillet and stir a few times until warm.

**Assemble and serve:** Spread a spoonful of Secret Sauce on the top and bottom halves of the toasted buns (about 1 tablespoon per side). Lay a beef patty on each bottom bun and divide Mohamad's Brown Butter Caramelized Onions (3 to 4 tablespoons each) among the patties. Close the burgers (don't smash down on the bun) and serve.

## SECRET SAUCE

**MAKES ABOUT 1 CUP (240ML), ENOUGH FOR 6 BURGERS**

½ cup (120ml) mayonnaise

¼ cup (60ml) ketchup

2 tablespoons Dijon mustard

2 tablespoons finely chopped crunchy baby dill pickles (gherkins)

In a small bowl, mix the mayonnaise, ketchup, mustard, and pickles until smooth. Cover and refrigerate the sauce for up to 1 week; use at room temperature.

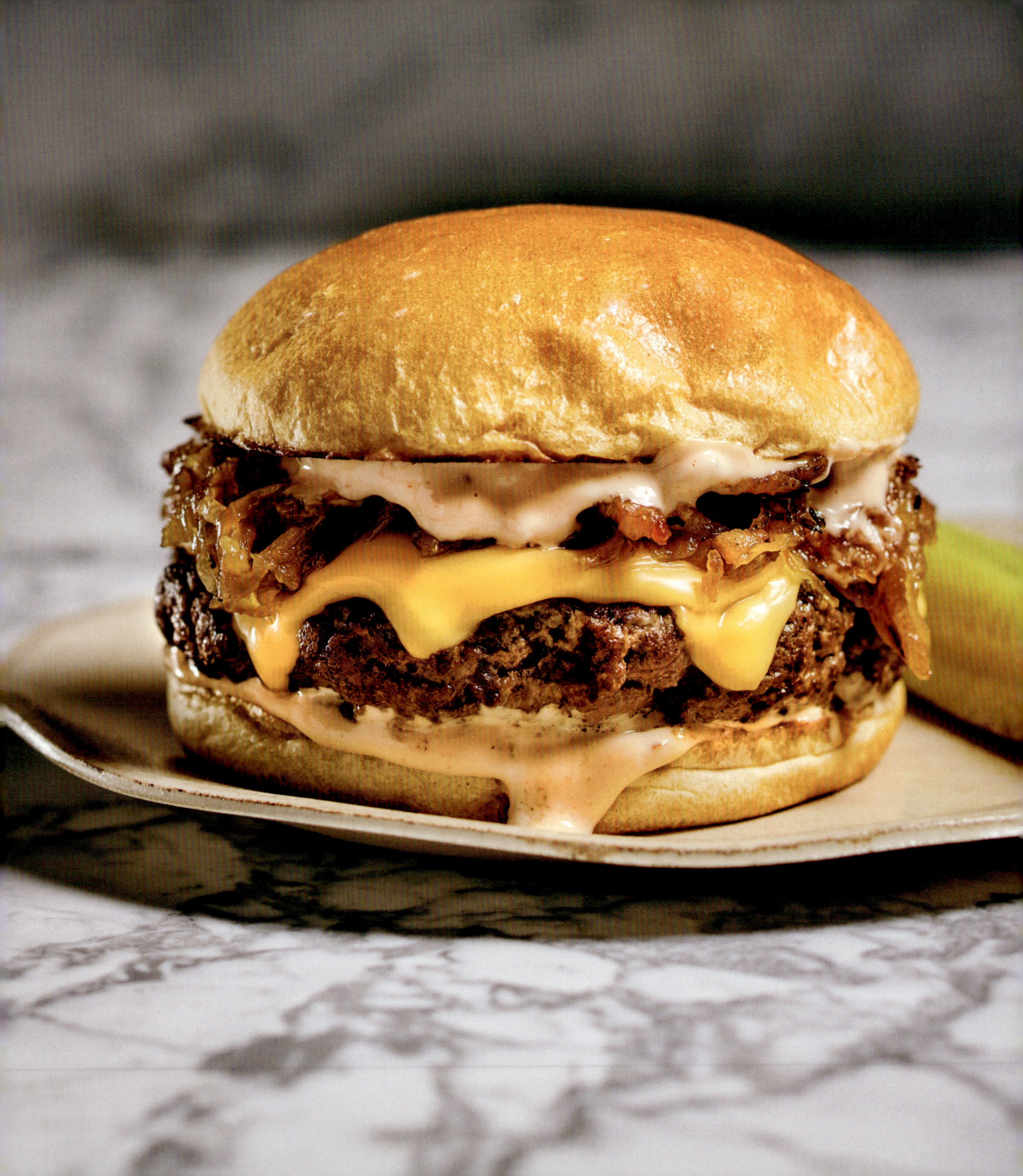

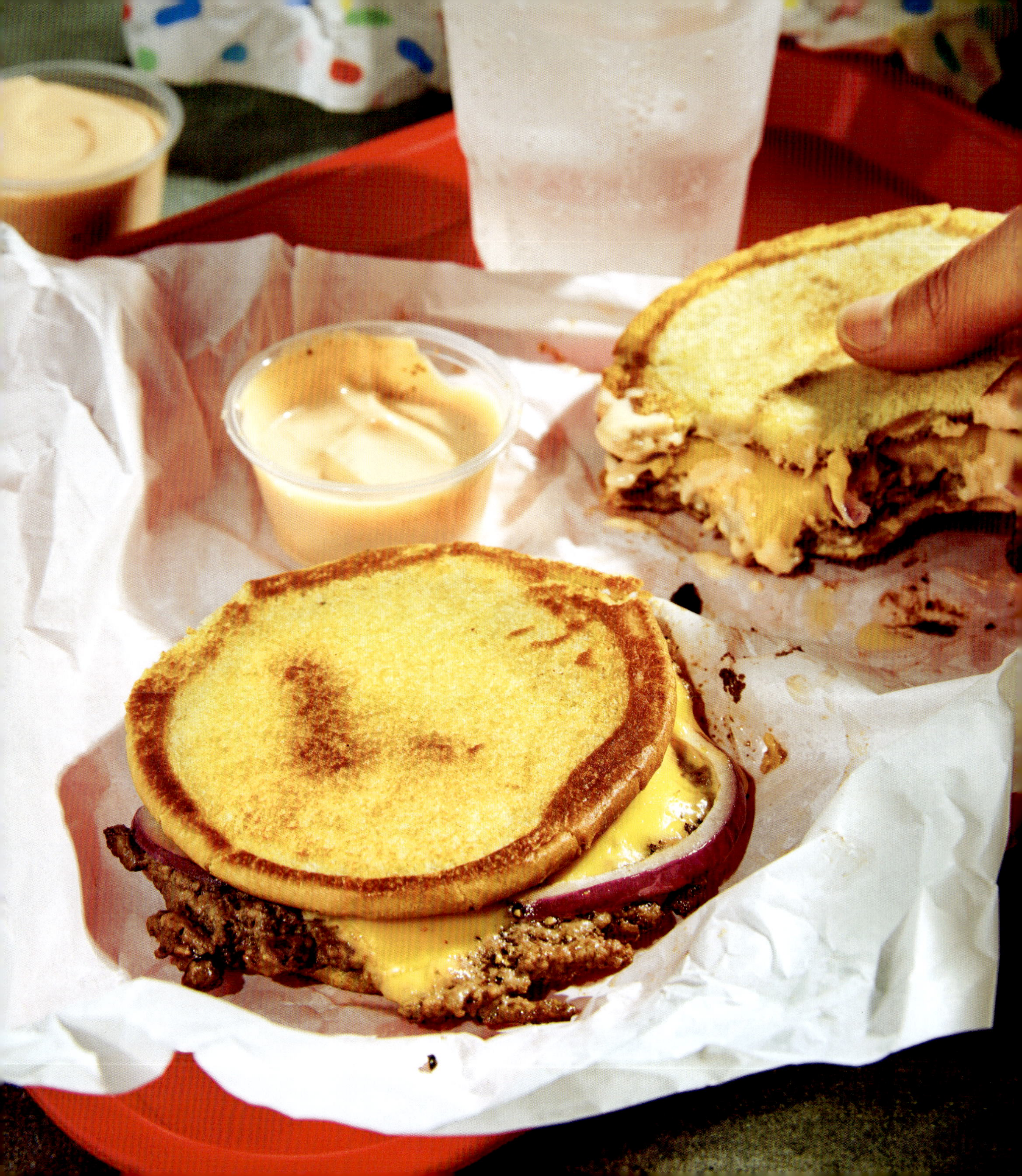

# The Crustburger

📍 *Joyland, Nashville*

Here's another reinvention of a classic burger. I first tasted it when I was in Nashville to shoot season six, and I took my friend Brad Paisley, a true superstar of country music, to Joyland, a restaurant by the local chef superstar Sean Brock. Everything on the menu is an ode to fast food the way it used to be, only made with the kind of perfection a great chef like Sean brings to the table. Every time I'm in Nashville I go there, and not just for the Crustburger but for the milkshakes and fries, the fried chicken on a stick like you get at gas stations in Mississippi, and the incredible soft serve. Sean's cheeseburger is a thin griddle patty like the ones you get at fast-food places, only it's made entirely of those seared bits that are usually only on the edges of a drive-thru burger. He puts the patty on a toasted bun that's been completely smashed (it's actually inside out) so it looks like you're eating the hamburger between two really small, flat pancakes. The man is a Jedi.

> *These need to cook at high heat (if the smoke alarm goes off, you're probably good), and you need to use a heavy-duty burger press to smash the beef. Then really get in there and move the press in a circular motion to flatten the patty out even more. Be sure to use a large, wide spatula (an extra-wide grill or burger spatula) to flip the burgers so the patty stays together.* —**SEAN**

**Make the patties:** Shape the beef into 6 meatballs, about 2½ ounces (70g) each.

**Toast and smash the buns:** Preheat a griddle to 400°F (205°C) or a large cast iron griddle pan or comal over medium-high heat. (Don't use an iron skillet with sides; you won't be able to remove the burgers easily from the pan.) As the griddle or pan begins to

---

**FEEDS 6**

**PATTIES**

16 ounces (about 500g) coarsely ground beef, preferably 30% fat

**BURGER ASSEMBLY**

6 tablespoons (85g) unsalted butter, plus more for the burger press

6 classic small white hamburger buns (Wonder, Ball Park, or similar)

Kosher or coarse sea salt and freshly ground black pepper

1 medium red onion, thinly sliced into ⅛-inch (3mm) thick rings

6 slices (6 ounces/170g) American cheese (Tillamook or similar)

**TO SERVE**

Sean's Fancy Burger Sauce (page 309), at room temperature

## TIPS

*These burgers are best cooked in smaller batches and served "to order," like at a fast-food restaurant. Cook each burger over very high heat; without the brown, crusty bits, it's just an ordinary burger.*

*The technique of smashing the patties isn't difficult, but if you've never tried it, get a little extra beef to try a "test" patty.*

*Skip the artisan buns here; small, classic white burger buns (1½ ounces/40g each) are the perfect size and texture for the patties.*

*Like other burger recipes in the book, Sean uses coarsely ground beef (ask your butcher), but any good ground beef works.*

warm up, add the butter, let it melt, and butter both the interior and outside of each bun.

In batches, toast the buns, cut side facing down. When they hit the pan, use a burger press to smash each bun utterly flat and toast until golden brown, about 30 seconds. Flip and smash each bun again, and lightly toast the top of the buns, about 20 seconds. Wipe any crumbs out of the griddle or pan.

**Make the first burger:** Rub a stainless steel (not plastic) burger press or the bottom of a large bowl lightly with butter.

Reheat the griddle or pan until very hot. Add 1 beef ball and use the burger press or bowl to firmly press the meat as flat as possible, then "smear" the meat by moving the press in a circular motion; it should be about ½ inch (2.5cm) larger than the flattened buns. It's fine if the meat tears in a few places.

Season the patty generously with salt and pepper, lay 2 to 3 red onion rings on top, then 1 slice of American cheese. Sear the patties until the meat on the edges is no longer pink and the cheese has melted, about 45 seconds.

Use a large, wide metal spatula to scrape up the patty; make sure to get all the crusty bits sticking to the pan. If the patty sticks to the cooking surface, move the spatula back and forth a few times to loosen it. Lay the patty between a flattened bun—with the *inside* of the bun facing out—and return the assembled burger to the griddle or pan to toast for about 30 seconds on each side.

**Cook the remaining burgers:** Scrape off any brown bits stuck to the griddle or pan. If the first patty wasn't very crusty, increase the heat. Sear the remaining patties in batches; be sure to leave at least 5 inches (12cm) between the beef balls so you can flatten each completely.

**Serve:** Serve the burgers with Sean's Fancy Burger Sauce on the side for dipping.

# Big Daddy's Hot Dogs

*Daddy's Dogs, Nashville*

In Nashville, the place to go for hot dogs is Daddy's Dogs, where Sean Porter (Sean's the actual "Big Daddy") serves up giant hot dogs with all kinds of toppings, including some I'd never think of putting on a hot dog. Sean started selling hot dogs out of a cart and now has several locations all over the city, but we went down to his restaurant in Printer's Alley, where the city's newspapers and publishers used to be. It's a great place to experience a piece of the city's early music history. There were a lot of saloons in the area that turned into speakeasies during Prohibition and, later, nightclubs, where some of the city's most famous musicians got their start. When you've worked up an appetite, find the Daddy's Dogs walk-up window or carts and get a bunch of Sean's hot dogs to share. The "Big Daddy," with bacon, grilled onions, pickles, Sean's secret sauce, and cream cheese, was probably the most surprising of all I tried, and it ended up being my favorite. This is why I always try something new wherever I go. And since you're in Nashville, be sure to say the word sauce right: it's *sauwce*, with a *w*.

**SERVES 1**

1 extra-large all-beef wiener (Daddy's Dog or Kirkland Signature; see Tip)

1 large New England–style split-top bun, preferably not brioche, or good-quality hoagie roll

Vegetable oil, for searing the bun

**TO SERVE**

Condiments and toppings for The Big Daddy, The Music City, or The Carolina (recipes follow)

> *To make a good hot dog, start with good buns; that's half your dog. Charpier's, a wholesale bakery in Nashville, bakes extra-wide, lobster roll–style split-top buns for us that can handle everything that goes into our dogs. We toast up the outside of the buns in a hot pan for a few seconds, then put them seam side down on the griddle to get some good char marks. Our Daddy's Dogs are an all-beef blend that have a super-rich beefy flavor the minute you bite into them, with the perfect amount of snap . . . and they're extra-large. Size matters!* —SEAN

**Prep:** Heat about ½ inch (12mm) water in a pot or skillet with a lid that's wide enough to fit the wiener just until simmering. Reduce the heat to low, add the wiener, cover, and let the wiener steam for a few minutes while you toast up the bun.

## TIPS

*If you can't get a Daddy's Dog wiener (he plans to sell them and his spicy mayo online), Sean recommends Costco's extra-large, all-beef store-brand wieners, Kirkland Signature.*

*A thick, classic barbecue sauce like Sweet Baby Ray's Original is a good stand-in for Sean's sauce.*

Slice off the very top of the split-top bun (where it closes) to remove the top crust (leave the hoagie roll untrimmed). Heat a splash or two of vegetable oil in a grill pan or cast iron skillet over medium-high heat until hot. Lightly sear the outside of the bun or roll until very lightly toasted, about 15 seconds per side. Toast the top of the bun or roll until you get good char marks.

Transfer the steamed wiener to the grill pan or skillet to sear until it just begins to brown, about 30 seconds; don't leave the wiener too long or it will start to dry out.

**Assemble and serve:** Open up the toasted bun or roll like a book; be careful not to break it in half. Layer up your hot dog, starting with any sauces or spreads on the bun, then lay the steamed dog in the center. Finish with your toppings and serve warm.

1 generous schmear (2 to 3 tablespoons) cream cheese, at room temperature

2 to 3 slices fried bacon

3 to 4 pickled jalapeño slices

1 dill pickle spear (¼ a large dill pickle)

1 small handful (about ⅓ cup) Big Daddy's Grilled Onions (recipe follows)

2 generous spoonfuls (2 to 3 tablespoons) Big Daddy's Slaw Sauwce (page 321) or Spicy Mayo (recipe follows)

## THE BIG DADDY

Spread the cream cheese all over the top half of the toasted bun. Lay the steamed wiener in the bun and tuck the fried bacon along both sides. Arrange the jalapeño slices on one side of the wiener and the dill pickle spear on the opposite side. Scatter Big Daddy's Grilled Onions on top and spoon Big Daddy's Slaw Sauwce or Spicy Mayo all over the everything.

## BIG DADDY'S GRILLED ONIONS

Slice sweet onions (Vidalia) into thin rings (count on half an onion per hot dog). Heat up a little vegetable oil in a skillet and cook the onions over medium heat, stirring occasionally, until golden brown and caramelized, 10 to 12 minutes.

## THE MUSIC CITY

Scatter about half the cheese all over the inside of the toasted hoagie roll. Lay the steamed wiener in the bun and tuck the fried bacon along both sides. Scatter the rest of the cheddar cheese over the hot dog, then the onions, and drizzle the barbecue sauce all over everything.

1 generous handful (about ½ cup/2 ounces/55g) grated sharp cheddar cheese, divided

2 to 3 slices fried bacon

Small handful (2 to 3 tablespoons) chopped sweet onions (Vidalia)

Good drizzle (2 to 3 teaspoons) barbecue sauce

## THE CAROLINA

Spread out Big Daddy's Slaw all over the top half of the toasted bun. Lay the steamed wiener in the bun and tuck the fried bacon along both sides. Spoon Big Daddy's Spicy Mayo all over everything, then drizzle barbecue sauce lightly on top.

Generous handful (about ½ cup/85g) Big Daddy's Slaw (recipe follows)

2 to 3 slices fried bacon

2 generous spoonfuls (2 to 3 tablespoons) Big Daddy's Spicy Mayo (recipe follows)

Good drizzle (2 to 3 teaspoons) barbecue sauce

## BIG DADDY'S SPICY MAYO

**MAKES ENOUGH FOR 6 HOT DOGS**

¾ cup (180ml) mayonnaise

1 teaspoon chili powder

¼ teaspoon garlic powder

Sriracha (as much as you can handle)

> *This is all I'm gonna tell ya, so get a bottle and figure it out yourself!* —SEAN

Mix together the mayonnaise, chili powder, garlic powder, and sriracha. Cover and refrigerate for up to 1 week.

## BIG DADDY'S SLAW

**FEEDS 6 TO 8 AS A SIDE (4 PACKED CUPS/680G), OR ENOUGH FOR 8 HOT DOGS**

½ large green cabbage (2 to 2½ pounds/about 1kg), core removed and finely chopped

1 large carrot, peeled and grated

About 1 cup (240ml) Big Daddy's Slaw Sauwce (page 321), as needed

In a large bowl, combine the cabbage and carrot, add about ¾ cup of Big Daddy's Slaw Sauwce, and stir well. Taste and adjust the amount of dressing; the slaw should be very tangy.

Cover and refrigerate the slaw at least 2 hours before serving (if you like a crunchy slaw) or, for a softer texture, up to 2 days.

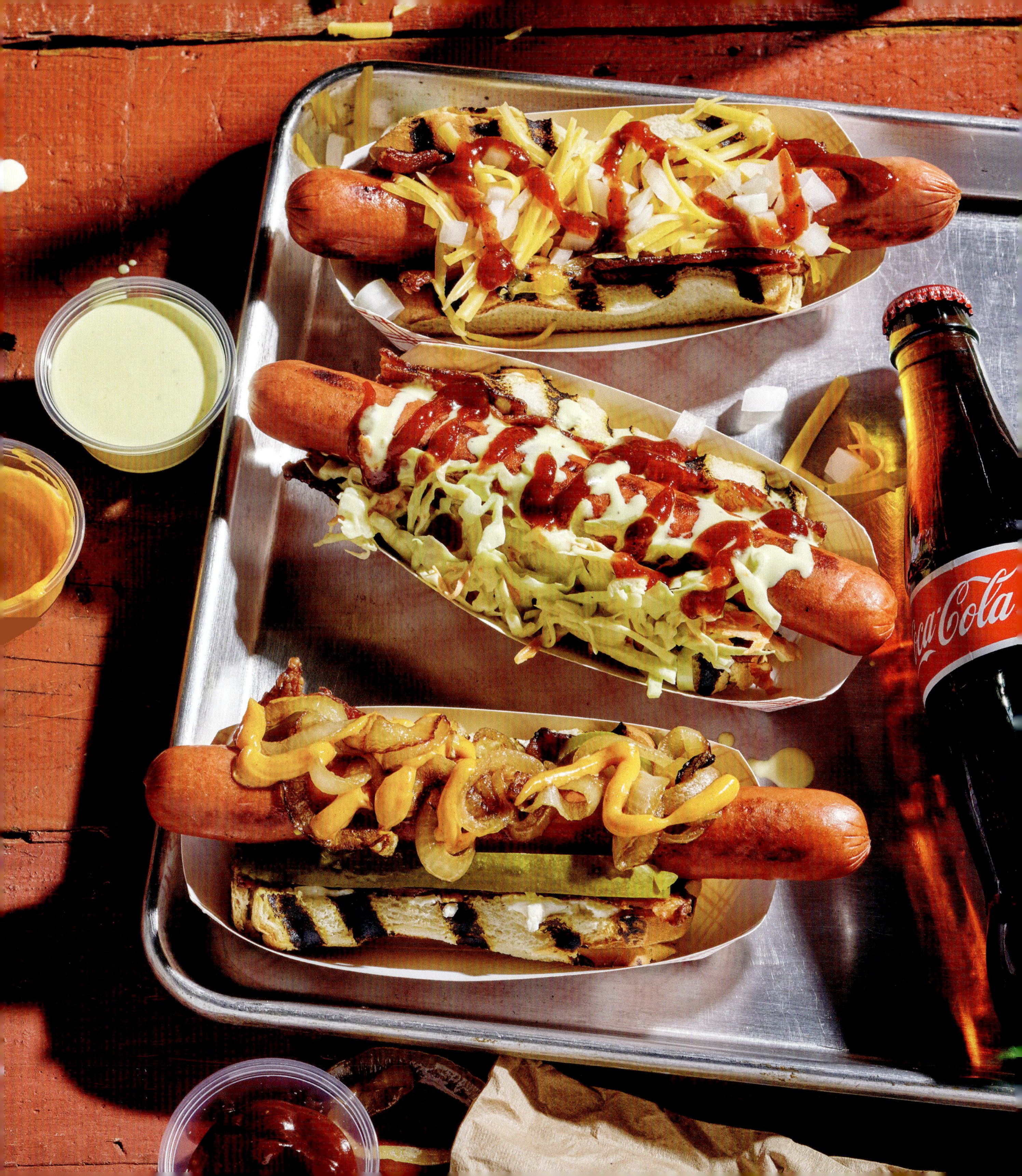

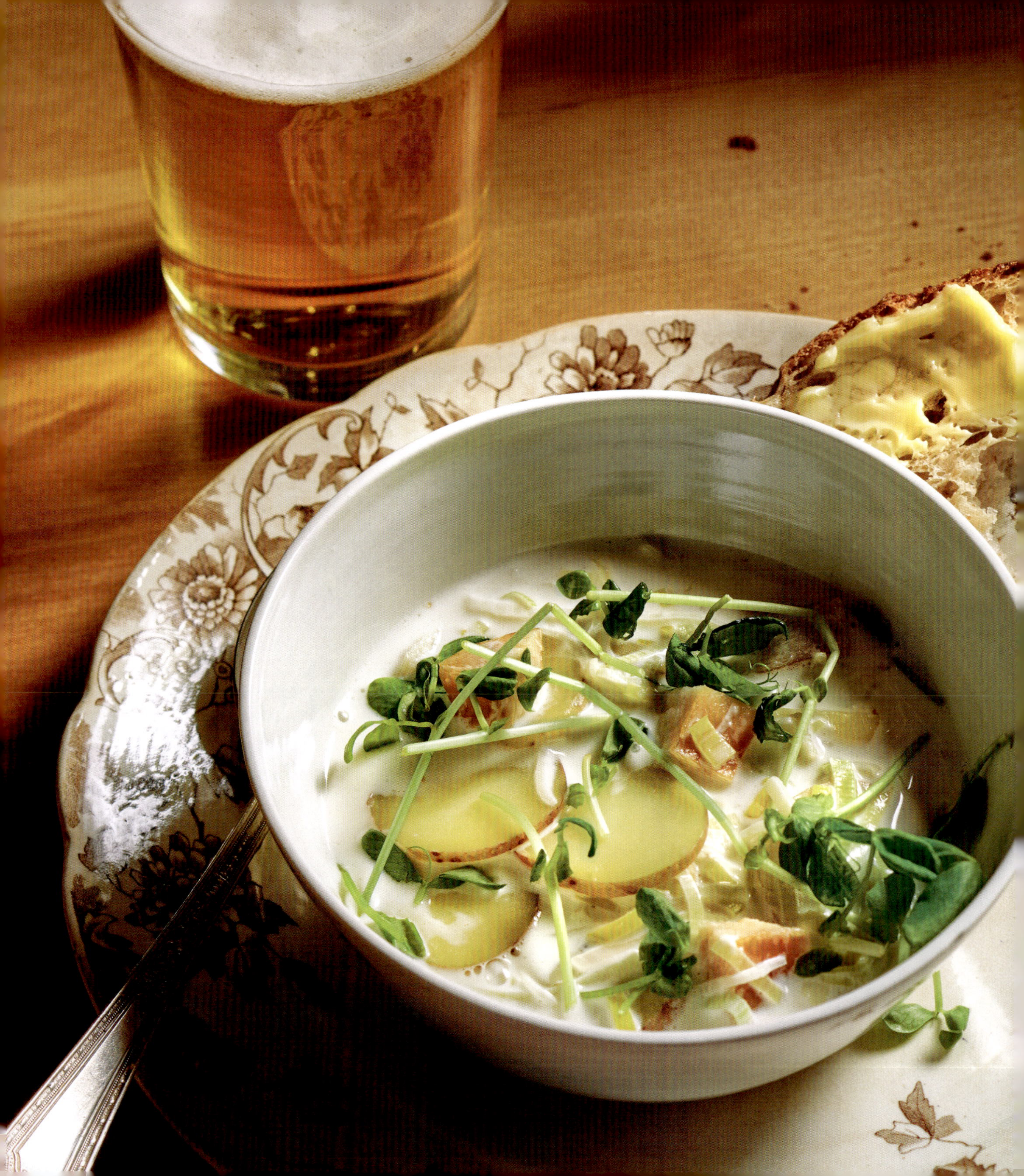

# SOUPS, STEWS, AND CURRIES

I love soup. And I came up with a tagline while in Vietnam that the Soup People can feel free to use: "Soup: Not Just for Old People Anymore."

Soups are one of my favorite things to order when I'm at a restaurant. They're delicious, and you can have a bowl and not be too full to try other things. They also tell you a lot about the local culture. Every place I've been around the world has a stew, curry, hot pot, gazpacho, phở, gumbo, or some other specialty. My mom's matzoh ball soup was her specialty and will always be the last thing I want to eat on this earth, but until then, I could have any of these and be very happy.

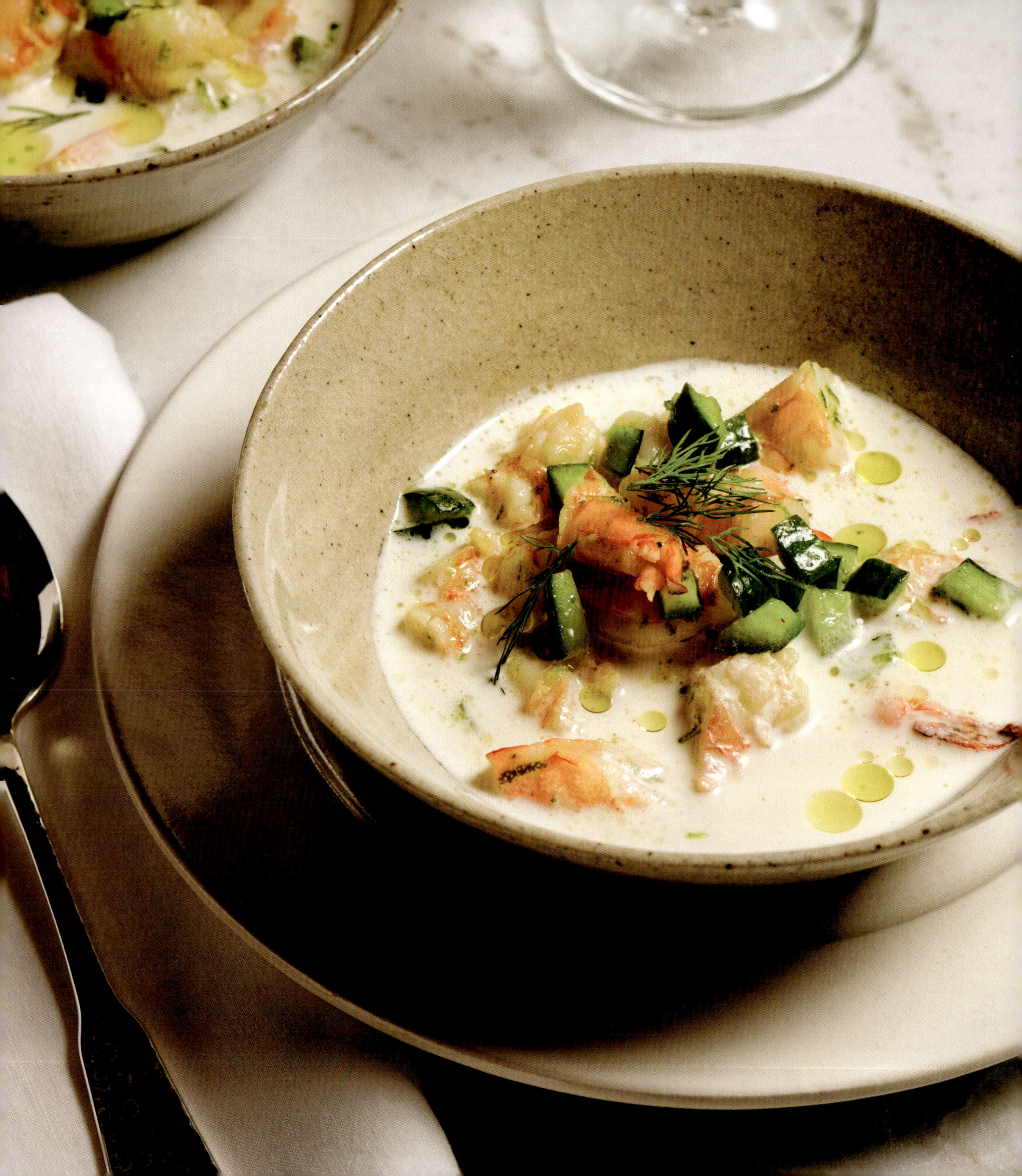

# Carolina Bazán's White Gazpacho

*Ambrosía Bistro, Santiago*

When I went to Santiago when we were filming the fifth and sixth seasons of the show, I didn't know what to expect. I'd never been and, until then, I hadn't had a lot of Chilean food. One of the people I'd heard a lot about was the chef Carolina Bazán, who had recently been named Latin America's best female chef. We went to Ambrosía Bistro, her more casual restaurant, which is centered around an open kitchen, one of my favorite restaurant designs when it's done well. When you sit at a counter (it doesn't matter if it's at a diner or a more formal restaurant), you get to be a part of the show, and, with any luck, it forces the nice people around you to be social. One of those nice people was Rosario Onetto, Carolina's partner in business and life who is the restaurant's sommelier and manager.

The first thing Carolina served us was a shot glass filled with a brothy soup and the local seafood delicacy, piure. I don't ever want to disparage the local culture, and what do I really know about what tastes good? Something might be delicious to me and somebody else absolutely hates it, but I think some of you who have tasted piure will agree that this sea creature is in a whole other category of "food." If you watched the episode, you know that before I went to Ambrosía Bistro, I had tasted piure earlier on my trip, in the experimental laboratory where Rodolfo Guzmán, another incredibly talented Santiago chef, develops dishes for his restaurant, Boragó. It looks like some kind of diseased lump of slimy coral and tastes like nothing I've ever had in my life. (Maybe because I never drank a bottle of iodine.) Rodolfo sliced up this thing and handed over what looked like the whole beating heart and, stupidly, I popped the whole thing in my mouth. I always say I'll try anything once, and I did. I also said after that scene with Rodolfo that I would never eat piure again. I did actually try Carolina's seafood soup, and it wasn't nearly as bad as eating the live sea monster, but this book is called *Phil's Favorites*. That isn't one of them. Instead, I asked Carolina if she would share the recipe for her white gazpacho with local white shrimp, because it was fantastic. It's her version of the chilled Spanish soup ajo blanco ("white garlic"), which is made with ground almonds, garlic, and usually some bread to thicken it up. Carolina calls it white gazpacho on the menu because she says a lot of Chileans don't think they like garlic, so they wouldn't order it otherwise. Now I understand why piure is considered the local delicacy.

*This is a great recipe for a hot summer day, and it's easy to make for a party because you need to make everything ahead. Chilean white shrimp are very special; they're sweeter than regular shrimp and taste more like langoustines or lobsters. You could also use crab legs.* —CAROLINA

**FEEDS 6**

**SHELLFISH**

3 pounds (1.4kg) shell-on jumbo shrimp, preferably sweet white, or about 2 pounds (910g; 4 to 5 medium) uncooked lobster tails

**PICKLED CUCUMBER SALAD**

2 tablespoons granulated sugar

Kosher or coarse sea salt

2 Persian cucumbers, peeled and finely diced, chilled

Small spoonful (about 1 tablespoon) extra-virgin olive oil

Grated zest of 2 limes

Finely ground white pepper

White Gazpacho, well-chilled (recipe follows)

**TO SERVE**

2 to 3 leafy sprigs dill

Extra-virgin olive oil

**Blanch the shellfish:** Fill a large bowl about halfway with ice water.

Fill a large pot with enough water to submerge the shrimp or lobster tails. Bring to a boil, add the shellfish, and cook until the flesh is firm, 1½ to 2 minutes for the shrimp and 4 to 5 minutes for the lobster tails. Strain and transfer to the ice water bath.

Peel and devein the shrimp and rinse under cold water. For the lobster tails, pull off the fins at the end of the tail and cut cleanly down the underside of the shell, then pull the shell open like a book. Remove the meat and the vein running down the top of the tail, if still intact. Slice each tail into large bite-size chunks. Cover and refrigerate the shellfish meat for at least 4 hours or overnight.

**Make the pickled cucumber-shellfish salad:** In a small bowl, mix together the sugar and 1 tablespoon salt. Add the cucumber, toss well, and set aside for 10 minutes. Strain the cucumbers and rinse well under cold running water.

In a medium bowl, combine the pickled cucumbers, chilled shellfish meat, olive oil, lime zest, and a pinch or two of white pepper. Use your fingers to gently toss the shellfish and cucumbers together. Cover and refrigerate the salad for at least 30 minutes or up to 4 hours.

**Serve:** Drain off any excess liquid from the seafood salad.

Mound the salad in the center of six large, shallow serving bowls. Stir the White Gazpacho well (it separates when refrigerated) and pour about ½ cup (120ml) around the seafood. Scatter 3 to 4 dill fronds over the gazpacho, followed by a drizzle of finishing olive oil.

# WHITE GAZPACHO

*There's no bread, so this is very light and almost like an almond milk soup. Make sure to blend the hell out of the almonds so they get really finely ground (also why it's always better to soak them a day in advance), and really squeeze the solids so you get out every last drop of liquid.*
—CAROLINA

### DAY 1

**Soak the almonds:** In a 1½-quart (1.4L) or larger container, combine the blanched almonds and 5 cups (1.2L) of cold water. Cover and refrigerate overnight or up to 24 hours. (Do not strain the soaked nuts.)

### DAY 2

**Blanch the garlic:** Slice off the root end from the garlic cloves and peel them with your fingers without smashing the cloves. Put the cloves in a small saucepan, cover with cold water, bring the water to a boil over high heat, and immediately strain. Rinse the garlic cloves under cold running water and repeat the blanching process two more times.

**Finish the gazpacho:** Strain the soaked nuts and reserve the soaking water.

In a blender, combine the almonds, garlic, 1 teaspoon salt, and 2 cups (480ml) of the reserved almond soaking water. Blend on high speed until the almonds are finely ground and the mixture starts to thicken, 1 to 1½ minutes; keep blending for the full time. Add the white balsamic vinegar and 1 cup (240ml) of the almond soaking water and blend for another 1 to 1½ minutes; the mixture should be almost silky smooth. Reduce the speed to low, slowly pour in the olive oil, and blend until combined.

---

**MAKES ABOUT 3 CUPS (720ML)**

8 ounces (225g) whole raw almonds (1⅔ cups), blanched (technique follows), or 2 cups blanched slivered almonds

3 medium very fresh garlic cloves

Kosher or coarse sea salt

1 tablespoon white balsamic vinegar or 1 tablespoon white wine vinegar mixed with ½ teaspoon honey

1½ tablespoons extra-virgin olive oil

**TIPS**

*The garlic needs to be very fresh; those with yellowing cloves or that have sprouted will give the soup a bitter flavor. The same goes for the nuts. Make sure they are fresh.*

*White balsamic vinegar is milder and fruitier than traditional balsamic vinegar and the light golden color doesn't darken the soup.*

Strain the gazpacho through a nut milk bag into a large bowl and squeeze and massage the bag firmly to get out every last drop of the liquid. Or line a fine-mesh strainer with two pieces of cheesecloth; they should be large enough so the overhanging fabric can be gathered together at the top. In batches, pour the nut milk into the cheesecloth and use the back of a spoon to push down on the solids to release the excess liquid. Gather up the edges of the cheesecloth to enclose the nut solids and very firmly squeeze out all the milk. (Discard the solids.)

Refrigerate the gazpacho for at least 4 hours or up to 3 days.

# Monica's Chicken Corn Soup

I think Monica would say that she is not really a chef. (And I would never agree, because I enjoy a nice marriage.) But you know many psychiatrists hypothesize that men marry their mothers …

I do love this soup and Monica makes it great—as she does my whole life.

> *This classic Pennsylvania Dutch soup recipe was passed on to me by my mom, Selma, as it was passed on to her by her mom, Violet. I loved this soup so much as a child, and whenever I came home from college and then after I'd moved away from home, I'd ask my mom to make it. When Phil and I got married in April 1990, we were both working; I was acting in a play and Phil was writing on a television show. We didn't have a lot of money or time off for our wedding, so we nixed the rehearsal dinner part of the festivities. Instead, my mom invited my college friends, who had come from out of town, over to the house for my favorite "chicken corn soup." It was the perfect way to spend my last night as a single lady, in the house I grew up in, laughing and sharing memories while sitting around the dining room table over giant bowls of this soup. I can't give the soup all the credit, but the wedding was a blast! The marriage, too. :)* —MONICA

**FEEDS A BIG FAMILY (ABOUT 8)**

1 4- to 5-pound (1.8 to 2.3kg) whole chicken

3 medium carrots, peeled

3 medium celery ribs

1 large yellow onion, peeled and halved through the root end

2 sprigs parsley

2½ to 3 tablespoons Better than Bouillon Roasted Chicken Base

8 large ears fresh corn, shucked

Kosher or coarse sea salt

6 to 8 hard-boiled eggs, peeled

**TO SERVE**

Small handful of finely chopped parsley leaves (optional)

**Make the chicken stock:** In a large Dutch oven or stockpot, combine the chicken, carrots, celery, onion, parsley, bouillon base (start with 2½ tablespoons if you prefer a less salty soup), and enough water to cover the chicken by about 2 inches (5cm). Cover the pot,

*Mom and Grandmom were way better home cooks than I will ever be, but this recipe is so forgiving that no matter how distracted I may get during the cooking process, it always comes out great and everybody loves it! I always use fresh corn in the summer, and even though my mom used frozen corn in the offseason, I prefer to go with the pre-shucked packaged fresh corn you can get at the grocery store most of the year. And don't leave out the Better Than Bouillon. It's the secret ingredient that gives the soup such a great flavor!* —**MONICA**

### TIP

*Better Than Bouillon Roasted Chicken Base, a concentrated paste enriched with roasted chicken and vegetable flavors, has a more complex flavor than dried chicken bouillon (cubes or powdered), but any bouillon can be used. Adjust the quantity to taste.*

bring the water to a boil, and skim off and discard the foam as it rises to the top. Reduce the heat to a simmer and cook the chicken, uncovered, until fall-apart tender, 1 to 1½ hours. Adjust the seasonings with bouillon base or salt.

Pick out the chicken and carrots from the broth and transfer them to a large bowl; have the bowl close to the pot, as the chicken will break apart as you move it. Set the chicken aside until cool enough to handle.

Pick out the celery, onion, and parsley from the broth and discard. Roughly chop or slice the carrots into medallions and return them to the pot. Pick off the chicken meat, shred it into bite-size pieces, and return it to the soup. You can finish the soup now or set everything aside for up to 1 hour.

**Finish the soup:** Over a bowl, slice the corn kernels off the cobs, then scrape the cobs with the knife to remove the last of the kernels and milky juice.

Bring the chicken soup back to a simmer, add the corn kernels and accumulated juices, and cook, uncovered, until the corn is tender, about 10 minutes.

**Serve:** Roughly chop the hard-boiled eggs and stir all but a handful into the soup.

Divide the soup among bowls, mound a few of the remaining diced eggs in the center of each, sprinkle the parsley on top if you'd like, and enjoy!

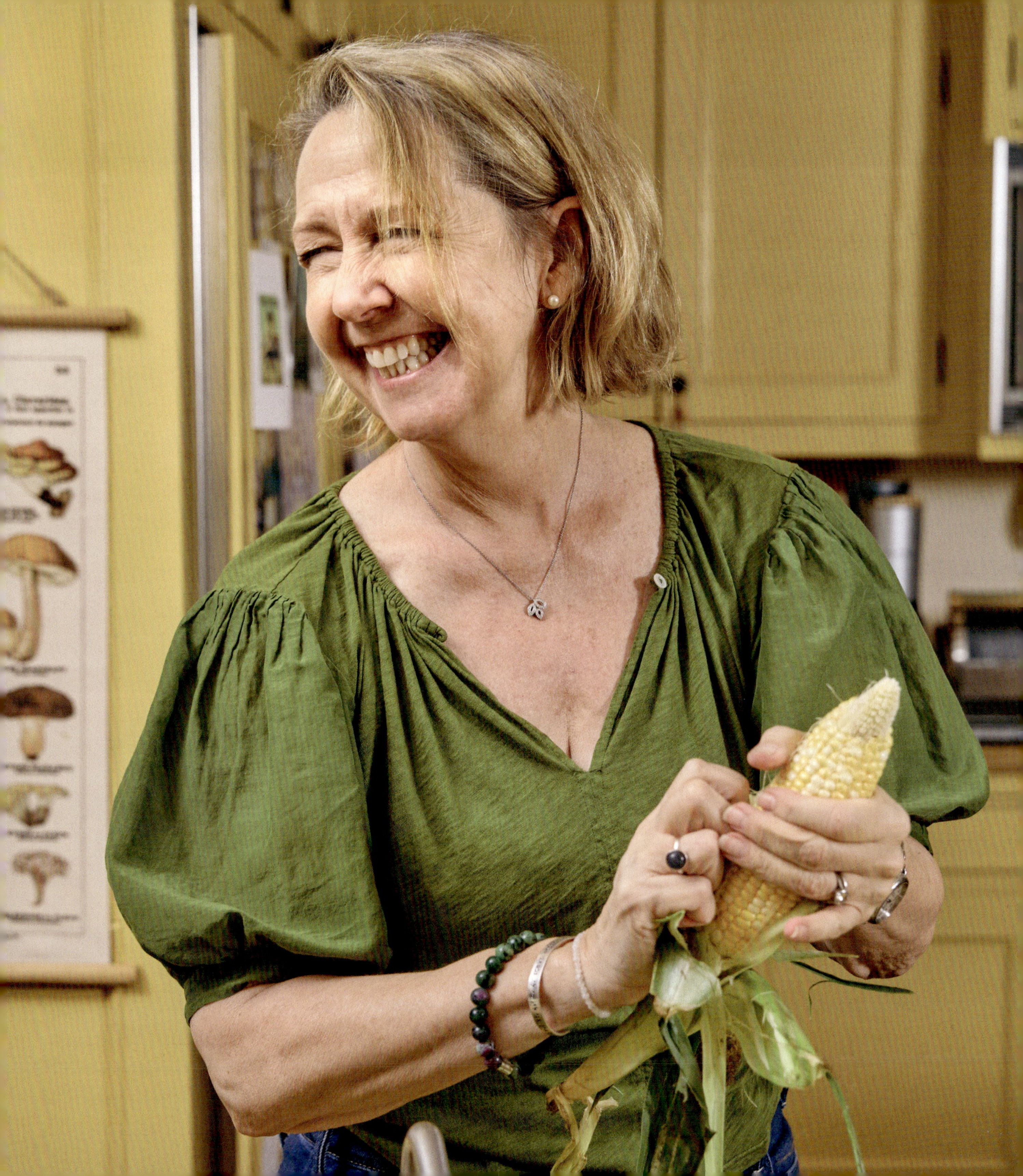

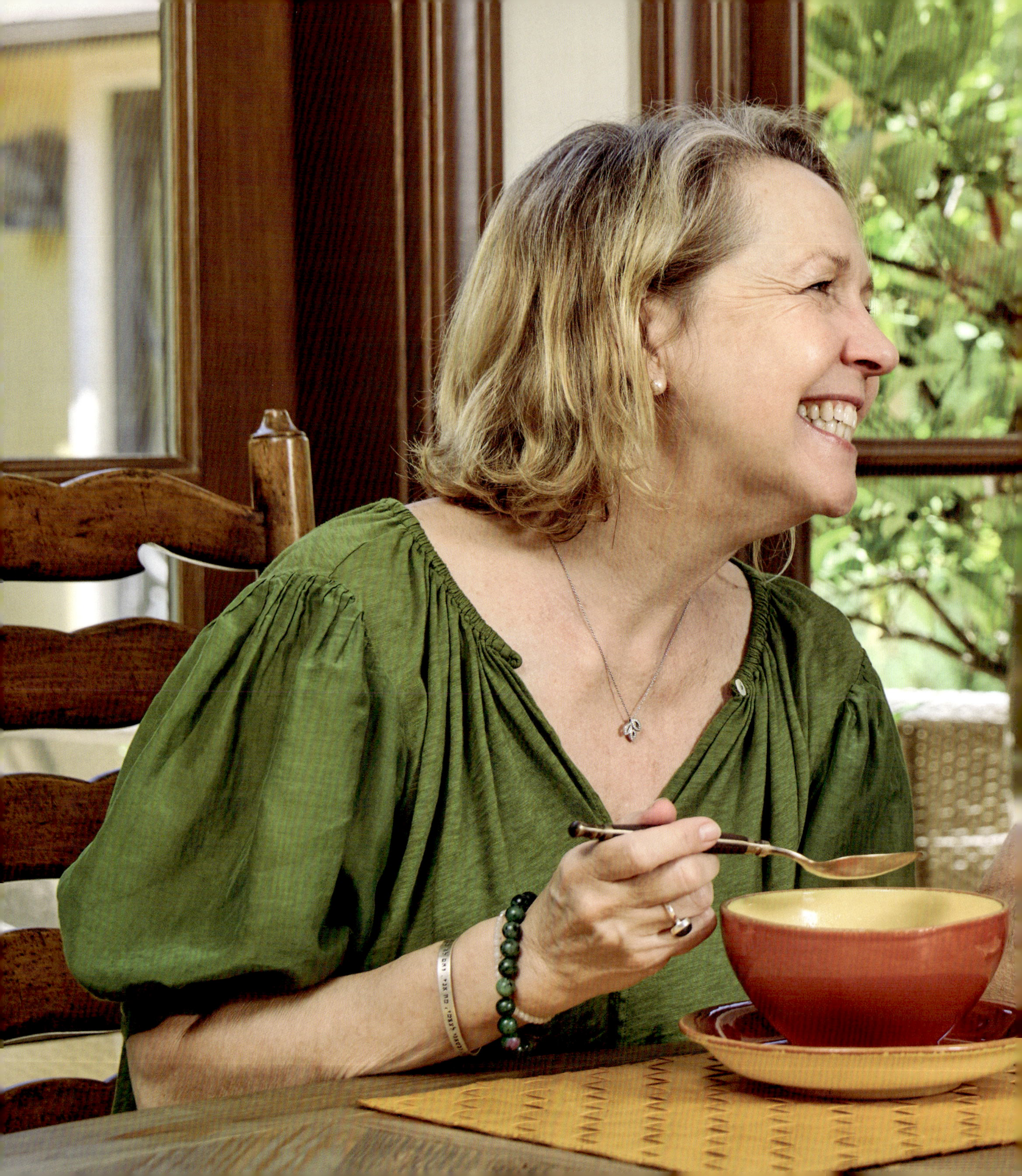

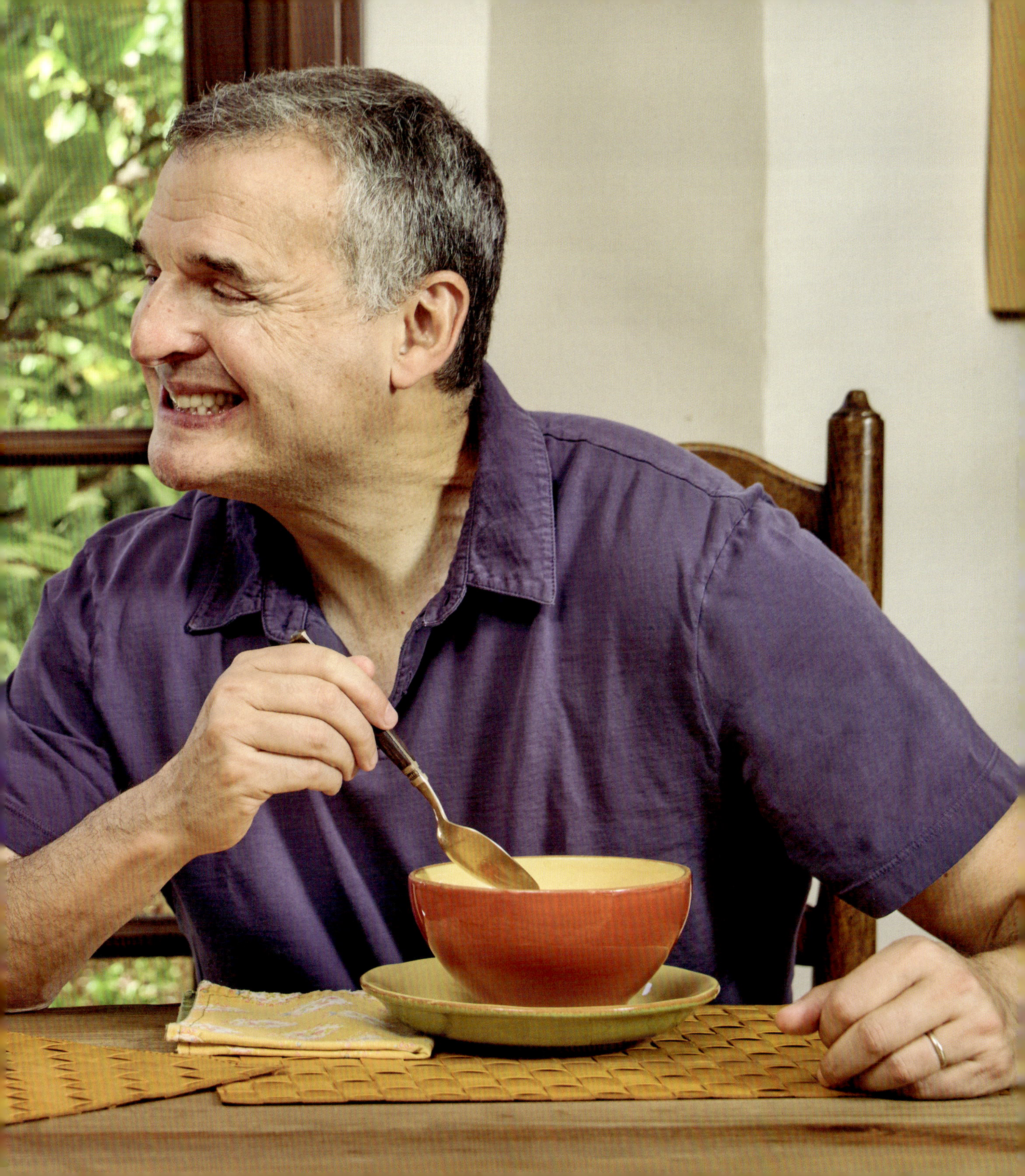

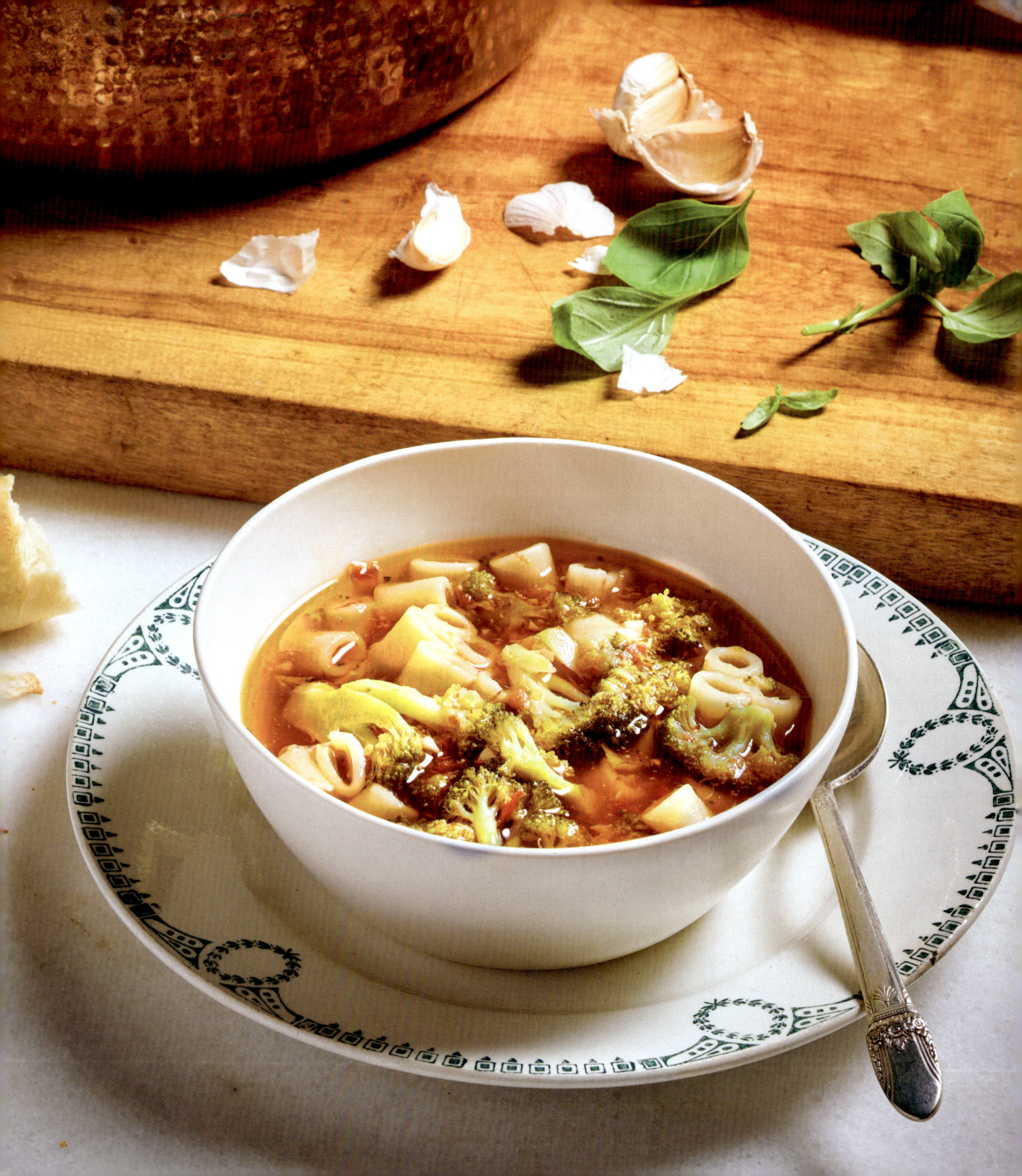

# The Only Way Ray Will Eat Broccoli

## (Anna Romano's Sicilian Broccoli-Pasta Soup)

When you make a television show with somebody, you spend a lot of time with them and get to know them very well. Monica and I are so lucky to call Anna and Ray Romano two of our closest friends. We've watched our kids grow up together, go to college, and get married, our families travel together every year at the holidays, and we get together whenever we can. Our families are one family.

In the introduction to *Somebody Feed Phil the Book*, I told you the story about how I got Ray to finally travel outside the United States for the first time when we were filming *Everybody Loves Raymond* in Italy, and how that one trip was transformative. Watching my friend experience the joys of travel for the first time is something I remember every time we film an episode of *Somebody Feed Phil*. It's why I do the show. One thing that has not changed about Ray is that he can be very particular about what he eats. I still can't get him to eat spicy food, even when he's in front of the camera like when we were filming the "Los Angeles" episode of *I'll Have What Phil's Having* and Ray and Anna met us at the Original Farmers Market to taste Jimmy Shaw's Huevos Rancheros (page 43).

The one person who can get Ray to eat something he thinks he doesn't like is Anna, who is a very good cook and makes this fantastic Sicilian-style broccoli soup that has been passed down through her family. She says it's the only way Ray will eat broccoli. Because this is my book and I do like spicy things, I put some spicy Calabrian chili peppers in my soup. If you don't already know about them, you're gonna want to get a jar for your pantry because the peppers happen to be in a couple of the recipes in this book (the aioli on page 302 that Nancy Silverton uses on her burger and Daniele Uditi's charred spaghetti on page 185). You decide.

> *This soup that my mom used to make is the only way to have Ray eat broccoli. It's easy to make and delicious on a cold day! I don't measure the water to cook the broccoli and pasta (it's meant to be very soupy), and I don't like the pasta al dente for this dish, so I cook it all the way through.* —ANNA

SOUPS, STEWS, AND CURRIES • 119

**FEEDS 5 TO 6**

1 medium head broccoli or 1½ bunches broccolini (about 1¼ pounds/570g)

Salt (any kind)

½ cup (120ml) extra-virgin olive oil

3 to 4 garlic cloves, minced

½ 15-ounce (425g) can crushed tomatoes (about 1 cup)

2 to 3 large basil leaves

Freshly ground black pepper

8 ounces (1⅓ cups/225g) ditalini or other small pasta (elbow macaroni, 1¾ cups)

2 to 3 teaspoons Calabrian chili pepper paste (Tutto Calabria crushed peppers or paste; optional)

**TO SERVE**

Plenty of crusty or garlic bread

**Prep:** Trim the stems off the broccoli and discard, then chop the crowns into bite-size pieces. For broccolini, chop both the crowns and tender top stems.

In a Dutch oven or large pot, combine 2 quarts (8 cups/2L) water and 3 to 4 generous pinches salt. Cover the pot and bring to a low boil.

**Make the tomato sauce:** While the water heats up, heat the olive oil in a medium saucepan or skillet over medium heat. Add the garlic and cook until fragrant but not brown, about 1 minute. Add the crushed tomatoes. Tear the basil leaves into 3 or 4 pieces and add them to the saucepan along with 2 to 3 pinches salt and several grinds of pepper. Simmer the tomatoes, stirring occasionally, until slightly thickened, about 5 minutes. Remove the saucepan from the heat.

**Boil the broccoli and pasta:** Add the pasta to the boiling water, stir, and cook for 5 minutes. Add the chopped broccoli or broccolini, return to a boil, and cook until the pasta is tender, 3 to 5 minutes, depending on the shape. Scrape the tomato sauce into the pot, stir, turn off the heat, and let the flavors meld for 5 minutes. If the pasta soaked up a bit too much of the cooking water (it depends on the shape, but it should have a nice amount of broth), add a little more water. Season the soup with salt and pepper and the Calabrian chili pepper paste, if you'd like.

**Serve:** Serve the soup in big bowls with crusty bread.

**TIP**

*Don't skimp on the quantity of olive oil; it's essential for both the flavor and texture of the soup, since there isn't any vegetable or other stock.*

# Saw Naing's Pe Hainn
## (Coconut Chickpea Curry with Greens)

*The Dutchess, Ojai*

If you've never been, Ojai is only about an hour-and-a-half drive north of LA and worth the trip. One place you have to go is The Dutchess, opened by pastry chef Zoe Nathan (her dad, my good friend Steve Nathan, taught me how to make the pancakes on page 47) and her two chef partners. During the day, pastry chef Kelsey Brito runs the bakery and café, then at night Saw Naing takes over and turns it into a Burmese Indian restaurant. Go at different times of day, and it's like you went to two completely different places in the same location.

> *I put this curry on the menu not long after we opened, and I can't take it off. I love eating chickpeas really, really soft. I don't use baking soda in the soaking or cooking water to soften them (it foams up the curry more); I just cook them longer. With black mustard seeds, it's important to wait until the seeds pop, but don't cook them too long or they will burn. We use local produce as much as we can—usually kale or Swiss chard with this curry—but get whatever is in season.*
> **—SAW**

### DAY 1

**Soak the beans:** In a large bowl or container, cover the garbanzo beans with at least 3 inches (7.5cm) cold water and let soak at room temperature for at least 12 hours. Strain.

### DAY 2

**Make the curry:** In a small dish, combine the garam masala, cumin seeds, turmeric, and sugar.

---

**FEEDS 6 TO 8**

16 ounces (about 500g, 2½ cups) dried garbanzo beans (chickpeas)

1 tablespoon plus 1 teaspoon garam masala

1 tablespoon cumin seeds

1 teaspoon ground turmeric

3 tablespoons granulated sugar

Neutral oil, for sautéing

1 teaspoon black mustard seeds

1 medium red onion, finely chopped

Kosher or coarse sea salt

1 tablespoon Everyday Garlic-Ginger Paste (page 314)

1 cup (240ml) full-fat coconut milk, well stirred

*(ingredients continue)*

SOUPS, STEWS, AND CURRIES • 121

**10 dried bay leaves, tied together with kitchen twine, if you'd like**

**1 lemongrass stalk, trimmed and outer leaves removed**

**2 medium bunches (1 to 1¼ pounds/500kg) leafy greens (Tuscan kale, Swiss chard, or similar), rinsed**

TO SERVE

**1 handful (about ¼ large bunch) cilantro, roughly chopped, or whole baby cilantro sprigs**

**Cooked basmati rice (optional)**

**Flatbread (naan, manakeesh, Greek pita, or Bombay Canteen Kulcha, page 324)**

---

TIP

*Black mustard seeds, which have a bright, spicy flavor vaguely reminiscent of wasabi, must be bloomed at high heat to release their oils. You can find them at Indian markets and at online retailers like thespiceway.com.*

---

In a large Dutch oven or soup pot, add enough vegetable oil to generously coat the bottom (3 to 4 tablespoons) and heat over medium-high heat until very hot, about 3 minutes. Add a few mustard seeds; they should sizzle and pop when they hit the oil. Add the remaining mustard seeds and stir constantly with a wooden spoon until fragrant, about 20 seconds.

Reduce the heat to medium-low, add the red onion and 1 tablespoon plus 1 teaspoon salt, and cook, stirring occasionally with a wooden spoon, until translucent but not brown, 6 to 8 minutes.

Add the garam masala mixture and Garlic-Ginger Paste and stir constantly until very fragrant, about 45 seconds, then add the coconut milk and stir to incorporate. Add the drained garbanzo beans, bay leaves, lemongrass, and 1½ quarts (1.4L) water and bring to a boil. (The cooking broth will foam up the first 10 to 15 minutes but will subside.) Reduce the heat to a simmer and cook (uncovered), stirring and scraping the sides of the pot occasionally, until the garbanzo beans are very tender and the broth is roughly at the level of the beans, about 1½ hours; the beans should taste almost creamy. Remove the bay leaves and lemongrass.

You can finish the curry now, set it aside for 2 to 3 hours, or let it cool completely, cover, and refrigerate for up to 3 days.

**Finish the curry:** Remove the thick inner rib from the kale, Swiss chard, or other greens and, if the leaves are very large, tear each into several pieces.

Reheat the curry over medium heat, if needed. Add the greens and stir a few times. Reduce the heat to low and gently cook the greens for 10 to 15 minutes, and season with salt.

**Serve:** Serve the curry family-style or divide it among bowls and garnish with the cilantro. Serve the curry with the rice, if you'd like, and flatbread.

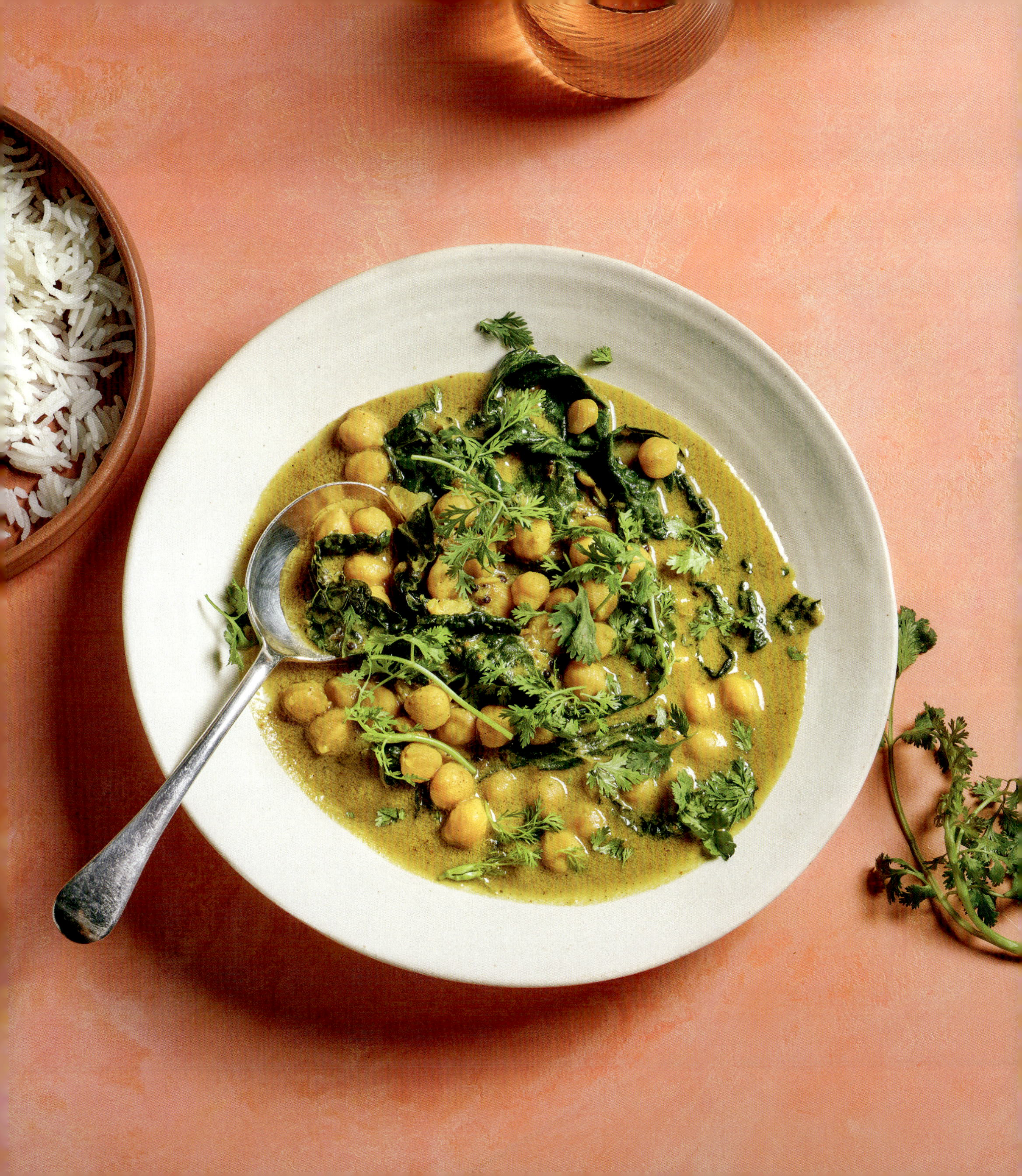

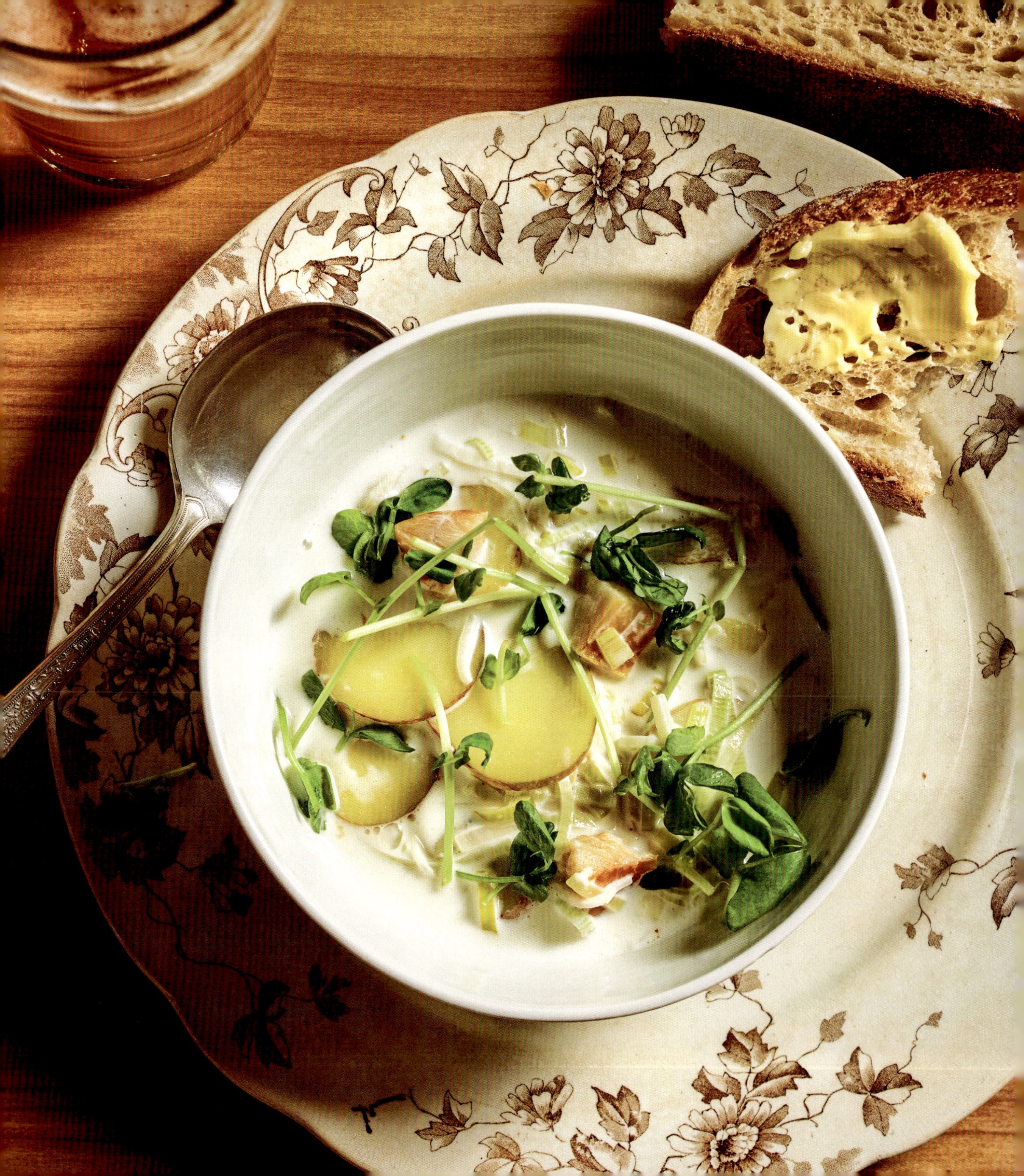

# Roseleaf's Cullen Skink
## (Scottish Smoked Fish Chowder)

*Roseleaf, Edinburgh*

In Leith, on Edinburgh's North Side, there's a pub we went to for a proper Scottish breakfast called Roseleaf. The owner, Jonny Kane, couldn't be more welcoming, and as soon as you walk in you feel like you know everybody who's there. Tony Singh, an amazing chef who grew up in the neighborhood and took me there, said, "Hospitality is about hospitality. That's why Roseleaf is amazing. You feel like part of a family here." You'll feel that way when you try their version of the local specialty, Cullen skink, a chowder with potatoes, leeks, and—this is the most important part—very good smoked fish. It's named after Cullen, an actual place, and skink, which is an old Scottish word for soup. It doesn't sound nice, but it's just what you want on a cold, rainy day, which means you can eat it pretty much every day in Scotland. I still think they should change the name.

> *Cullen skink has been on our menu since we opened, and the recipe has never changed. Ours is a lot more generous on the fish-to-tattie ratio than most, which is the way we like it. It's always best to use the naturally cold-smoked haddock, not those with fake yellow food coloring (people also regularly use Arbroath smokies, a hot-smoked haddock from Arbroath). Or you can substitute another smoked white-flesh fish. One rule: we never trim our tatties; all goes in the pot, no waste! And be sure to serve with chunks of crusty bread for mopping up.* —JONNY

**FEEDS 5 TO 6**

16 ounces (about 500g) finnan haddie (haddock) or Arbroath smokies fillets, smoked halibut, trout, or true cod (see Tips)

16 ounces (about 500g) baby red or yellow potatoes

16 ounces (about 500g; 2 medium) leeks, root ends and dark green tops trimmed

2 cups (480ml) whole milk, plus more as needed

2 cups (480ml) heavy cream, plus more as needed

Coarse sea salt and finely ground white pepper

**TO SERVE**

1 small handful pea shoots (whole) or parsley leaves (chopped)

Plenty of crusty bread

## TIPS

*Outside the UK, you can now order quality, freshly smoked finnan haddie from a handful of seafood markets in Maine, like Brown Trading Company (browntrading.com), that smoke and ship their own wild-caught local haddock. (Finnan haddie with a dark, almost golden yellow color, like most available at British and Scottish trinket shops in the US, are highly processed and the fake smoke flavor will overwhelm the soup.)*

*Arbroath smokies or your favorite non-oily smoked white-flesh fish (halibut, rainbow trout, or true cod) are good substitutes. The smoking process will affect the flavor intensity of the soup. Don't use smoked "whitefish" or black cod, also called sablefish (not true cod but an Alaskan fish); both are too oily for this soup.*

**Prep:** Peel the skin off the smoked fish and remove any pin bones; if the skin is difficult to peel, put the fish in the freezer for 30 to 45 minutes to firm up. Cut the fish into small bite-size pieces.

Scrub the potatoes (don't peel) and use a mandoline or sharp knife to slice them into thin medallions.

Slice the leeks in half lengthwise and rinse well under cold running water; flip through the sections like you are shuffling a deck of cards to remove every bit of dirt. Thinly slice the white bulb and the very lightest tender green stems.

**Make the soup:** In a large saucepan or medium stockpot, combine the milk, cream, and potatoes and bring to a low simmer over medium heat; watch the pot and reduce the heat as needed so the cream doesn't boil and overflow.

Reduce the heat to low and simmer the potatoes, stirring occasionally with a wooden spoon, until they can be easily pierced with a fork but are still somewhat firm, 8 to 10 minutes.

Add the leeks and smoked fish and gently simmer the soup until the leeks are crisp-tender, about 10 minutes; if using finnan haddie or another cold-smoked fish that isn't fully cooked, taste a piece to be sure the flesh is firm. The soup broth should be balanced and light; if too thick or your smoked fish is particularly strong, add a splash or two of milk or cream.

The smoked fish will have salted the soup, but add a pinch or two of salt if needed, and 3 to 4 pinches white pepper.

**Serve:** Divide the soup among five or six bowls, sprinkle the pea shoots over the soup, and serve with the crusty bread.

Cover and refrigerate any leftover soup for up to 3 days.

SOUPS, STEWS, AND CURRIES • 127

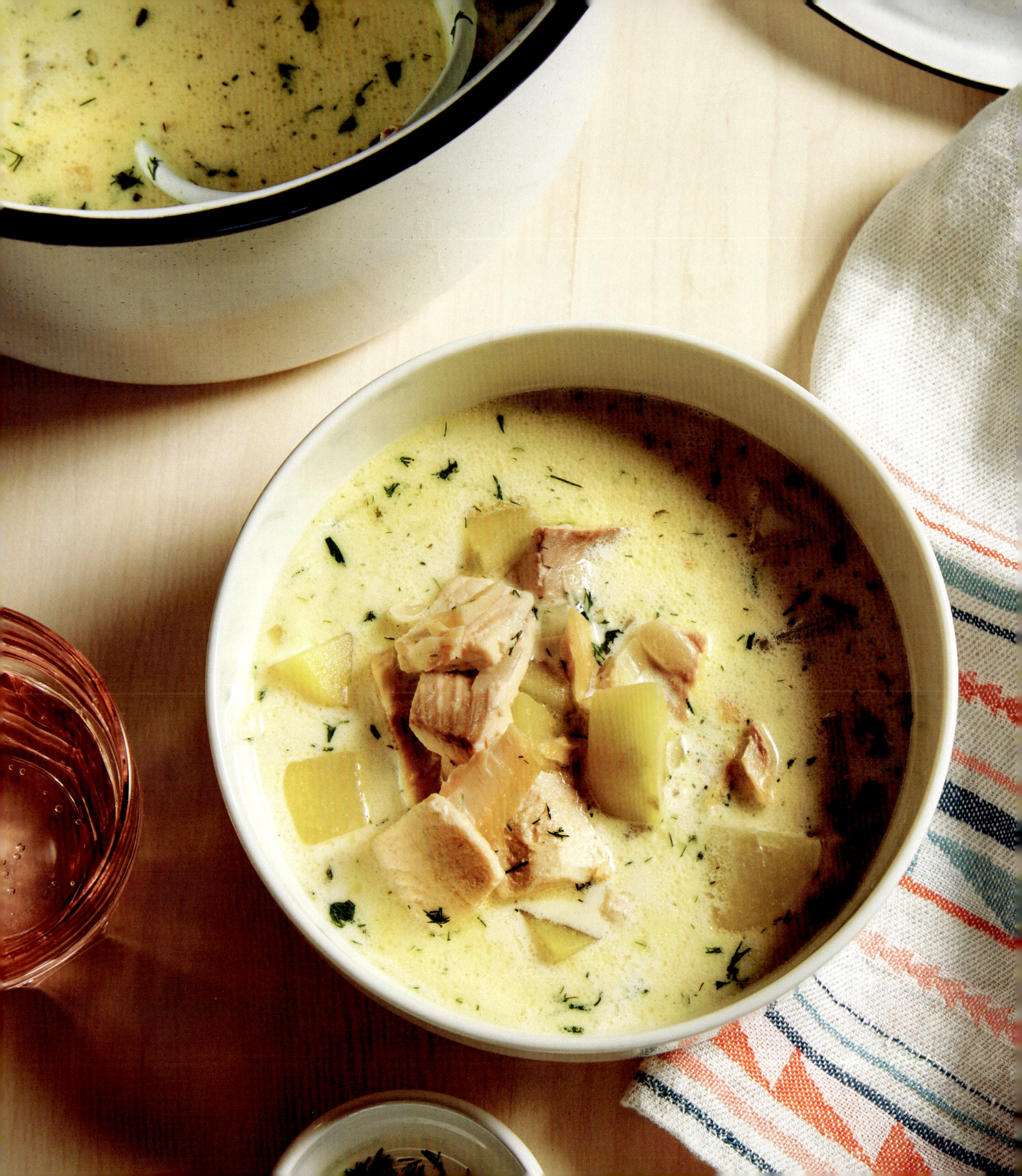

# Jasper Pääkkönen's Lohikeitto (Finnish Smoked Fish Soup)

*Löyly, Helsinki*

When you're in Edinburgh, go to Roseleaf, the local pub in Leith, and try Jonny's Cullen skink, the classic Scottish smoked fish chowder on page 125. Then, when you're in Helsinki (it's only a two-and-a-half-hour flight), go to Löyly, actor Jasper Pääkkönen's restaurant and sauna that overlooks the Baltic Sea, for an entirely different experience—and a completely different smoked fish and potato soup called lohikeitto. The view alone is a reason to visit, and if you need another, the architecture is incredible. It feels like you're walking into a contemporary museum dedicated to the art of the sauna, or "sowna."

Jasper's version uses smoked rainbow trout instead of the traditional smoked salmon because it's the more sustainable choice. And, it tastes phenomenal. When we were filming the episode, Jasper talked about how we should all work a little harder to find the most sustainable seafood when we're shopping, and one of the things I learned from him is that the fish farmed in open pens in the ocean is not good for everything else swimming in the sea. I happen to really like all those delicious things in the sea, so I'm going to work a little harder at keeping them happy.

> *Today, it's so important we all make the most educated fish choices. At Löyly, we never use endangered Atlantic salmon or oceanic farmed fish, whether salmon or rainbow trout (or the anadromous version, steelhead). Above all else, avoid seafood from open sea fish farms, one of the most environmentally damaging industries in the world. When done well, the alternative, land-based fish farming, is a much better choice, as most of the incredibly harmful aspects of oceanic farming are eliminated when you move the farms to closed containment systems on land (the salmon farm Sustainable Blue is a good example). That said, choose the best choice where you live, which in some regions might even be wild salmon like Alaskan wild caught.* —**JASPER**

**FEEDS 5 TO 6**

8 ounces (225g) fresh, sustainable rainbow trout or salmon

3 ounces (85g) cold-smoked, sustainable rainbow trout, salmon, or similar fish fillets

2 tablespoons (28g) unsalted butter

1 medium white or yellow onion, diced

16 ounces (about 500g) waxy potatoes, any size, peeled and cut into bite-size chunks

Generous pour (3 to 4 tablespoons) unoaked white wine

3½ cups (840ml) Fish Stock (recipe follows) or good-quality store-bought stock

1⅓ cups (320ml) heavy cream

Coarse sea salt and finely ground black or white pepper

**TO SERVE**

2 to 3 sprigs dill, finely chopped

**Prep:** Remove the skin from the fresh fish, pick out any bones, and cut the fish into generous bite-size pieces (1 inch/2.5cm). Thinly slice the smoked fish; it's fine if it falls apart.

**Make the soup:** In a soup pot, melt the butter over medium-high heat. Add the onion and potatoes and sauté, stirring occasionally with a wooden spoon, until the onion just begins to brown on the edges, 10 to 12 minutes. Add the wine and scrape up any brown bits on the bottom of the pot, then add the fish stock and bring to a low boil. Cook the potatoes until tender; once the stock begins to boil, prick 2 to 3 potatoes with a fork to test the texture; they may only need a minute or two longer.

Reduce the heat to low, add the fresh and smoked fish and heavy cream, and gently cook just until the flesh of the fresh fish is firm, 3 to 4 minutes. (Do not boil or the cream will curdle.) Season the soup with salt and pepper. You can set the soup aside for up to 1 hour.

**Serve:** Rewarm the soup, if needed, sprinkle the fresh dill on top, and serve family-style. Be sure to scoop up some of the onion and smoked fish on the bottom of the pot as you serve it.

Cover and refrigerate any leftover soup for up to 2 days.

**TIPS**

*Like Cullen Skink (page 125), this is a much lighter soup than many fish chowders and deserves really good smoked fish. If you break down a whole smoked fish, remove the bones.*

*Use whatever cleaned fish bones, heads, and tails you have to make the stock (collect them to freeze from whole fish, or ask your fishmonger for a few pounds). Be sure to remove the innards and gills, which will give the stock an off flavor.*

## FISH STOCK

In a stockpot, combine the fish parts, onion, celery, carrot, and 2 quarts (2L) water, and bring to a low boil. Skim off and discard the foam that rises to the surface for the first few minutes, then add the fennel stalk and fronds, thyme, and bay leaf. Simmer the stock for 20 minutes, strain, and season very lightly with salt (don't over season; the stock will be seasoned in the dish). Refrigerate the stock for up to 3 days or freeze in batches for up to 3 months.

**MAKES ABOUT 1¾ QUARTS (1.8L), ENOUGH FOR 2 BATCHES OF JASPER'S SOUP**

1½ to 2 pounds (680g) fish bones, heads, and/or tails, well cleaned

½ large yellow or white onion

1 celery stalk

1 carrot, peeled

Stalk and fronds from 1 fennel bulb, or 2 to 3 bushy dill sprigs

1 leafy sprig thyme

1 bay leaf

Coarse sea salt

SOUPS, STEWS, AND CURRIES • 131

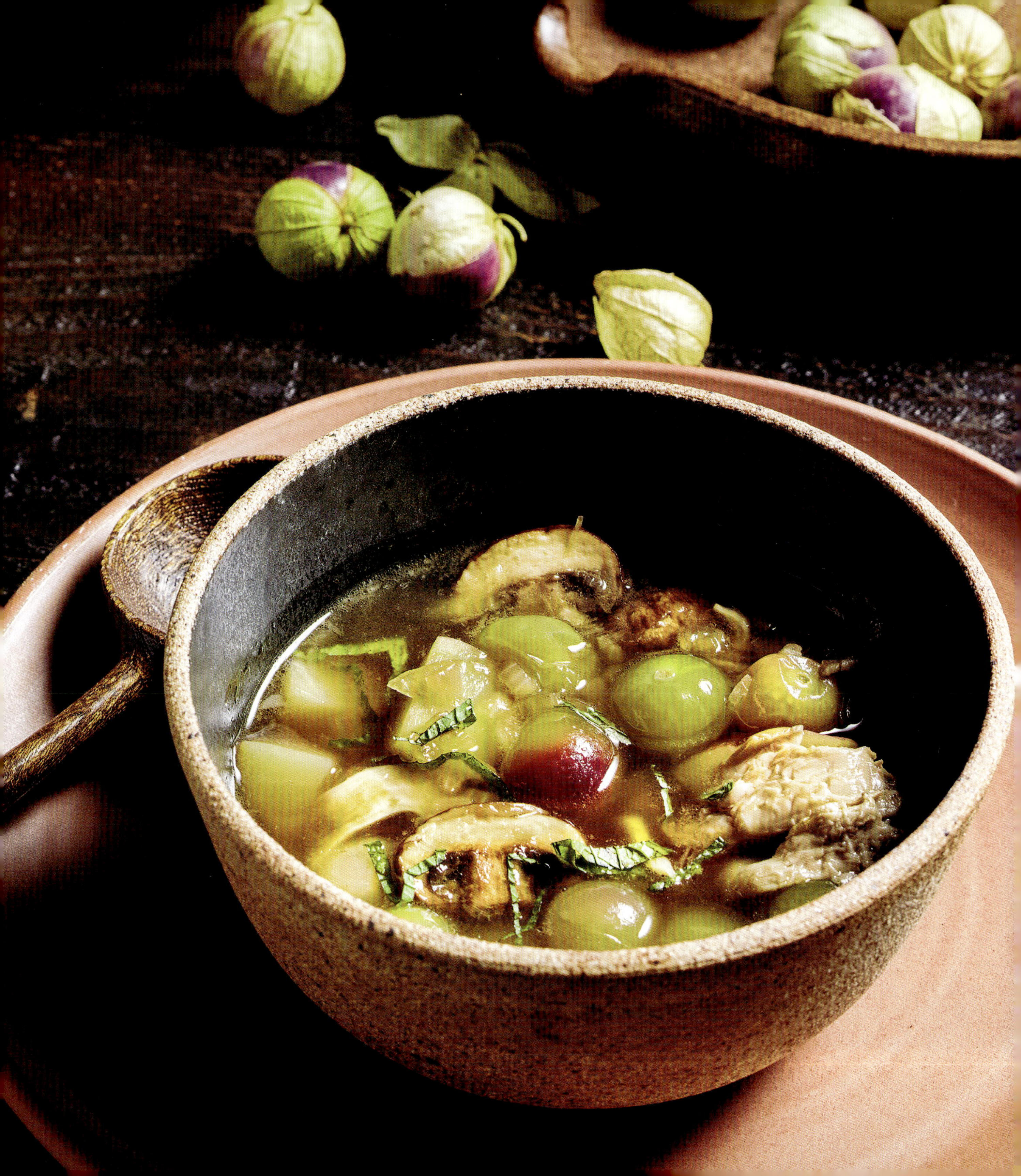

# Thalía Barrios García's Mushroom-Tomatillo Soup

📍 *La Cocina de Humo at Levadura de Olla, Oaxaca*

When we went to Mexico City for the very first season of *Somebody Feed Phil*, people kept telling me that if I really wanted to taste the origin of the cuisine, I had to go to Oaxaca in the southwestern part of the country. For season five, nearly four years later, I finally got the chance. As soon as I got there, I understood why Oaxaca is the cultural and culinary capital of Mexico. Everything is so colorful, from the way the buildings and pottery are painted and the way people dress to the beautiful rugs that I got to see being woven at the Vida Nueva Women's Weaving Cooperative. But mostly, it's the kind hearts of the wonderful people and the food they make from their hearts that's so bright, warm, and full of flavor. There's nobody who shows that more than Thalía Barrios García.

Thalía is the young, talented chef behind Levadura de Olla, one of the most talked about restaurants in Oaxaca. I went there with Ana Quintero, a cultural gastronomist, and we got to eat in a very special room called La Cocina de Humo (the Smoke Kitchen). It's where Thalía has replicated the experience of cooking and sharing a meal in a home kitchen in the small village where she grew up, San Mateo Yucutindoo, which is in the southern part of the state. She takes the traditional ingredients that locals grow and forage for and makes them into something unexpected and new, like this tomatillo soup. People traditionally make this soup when they're feeling a little under the weather, but with Thalía's version, you make it because you want to eat something delicious. It's very light and a little citrusy from the tomatillos, and it has poleo, a type of wild mint people find in the mountains. It's like you are tasting the history of the place.

*Soups are very comforting foods, but mine are very fresh, not overcooked. The poleo (wild mint) at the end gives that feeling of being awake and alive and full of life. We have many varieties of tomatillos in Mexico, all sizes and types. When I find the very small purplish-green ones, I drop those into the soup whole and let them do their magic on their own without chopping them. When you eat the soup, the tiny tomatillos explode in your mouth like blueberries, releasing all of their flavor and acidity. If you don't have small tomatillos, you can chop up the larger ones and get a similar effect. It's also important not to overcook the mushrooms.* —THALÍA

**FEEDS 4; 8 AS A STARTER**

4 large handfuls
(9 to 10 ounces/about 270g)
wild mushrooms,
or a mix of farmed
mushrooms like cremini
and oyster

1 pint very small (berry-size) or 8 medium fresh tomatillos (10 ounces/280g), preferably a mix of varieties

8 ounces (225g)
red or yellow potatoes
(5 small)

¼ small white
or yellow onion

1 large jalapeño

Generous pour
(2 to 3 tablespoons)
neutral oil

Kosher or coarse sea salt

10 to 12 fresh poleo
(wild brook mint) leaves,
or 3 to 4 large
mint leaves

**Prep:** Brush any grit off the mushrooms. Slice or break the mushrooms into bite-size pieces (it's easiest to slice the cremini and break apart the oyster mushrooms with your fingers).

Remove the papery husks from the tomatillos and rinse well to remove the sticky residue. Leave any berry-size tomatillos whole and cut any larger tomatillos into small bite-size pieces.

Slice off both ends of the potatoes, stand the potatoes upright, and trim all four sides to form a rectangle. Cut the potatoes into roughly ½-inch (12mm) cubes.

Finely chop the onion and score the jalapeño by making five to six small slits in the flesh.

**Make the soup:** In a medium soup pot or large saucepan, heat the vegetable oil over medium-high heat until hot, about 2 minutes. Add the onion and jalapeño and sauté, stirring occasionally with a wooden spoon, until the onion begins to brown on the edges, about 5 minutes. Add the potatoes and continue to cook until the onion is golden brown on the edges, 2 to 3 minutes, then add the tomatillos. Quickly sear the tomatillos, stirring constantly, for about 30 seconds (they shouldn't brown). Then add the mushrooms and sprinkle ¾ teaspoon salt over the vegetables. Add a splash of water (2 to 3 tablespoons), scrape any brown bits off the bottom of the pot, then add another 3 cups (720ml) water. Increase the heat to medium-high, bring the soup to a low boil, and cook the potatoes just until fork-tender. Once the broth is boiling, watch the potatoes closely; they should be ready within a few minutes. Turn off the heat and season the soup with salt.

**Serve:** Just before serving, tear the fresh poleo or mint leaves into small pieces, add the herbs to the pot, cover, and steep for about 5 minutes. Remove the jalapeño.

Divide the soup among large serving bowls or smaller appetizer cups and serve.

Cover and refrigerate any leftover soup for up to 2 days.

### TIPS

*Small tomatillo varieties like purple and milpero (look for them at farmers' markets during tomato season) make this simple vegan soup special, but even large green tomatillos are delicious.*

*Fresh poleo (wild brook mint) can be difficult to find outside of areas where it is foraged. Fresh mint (spearmint or similar) is a good substitute; don't use dried poleo.*

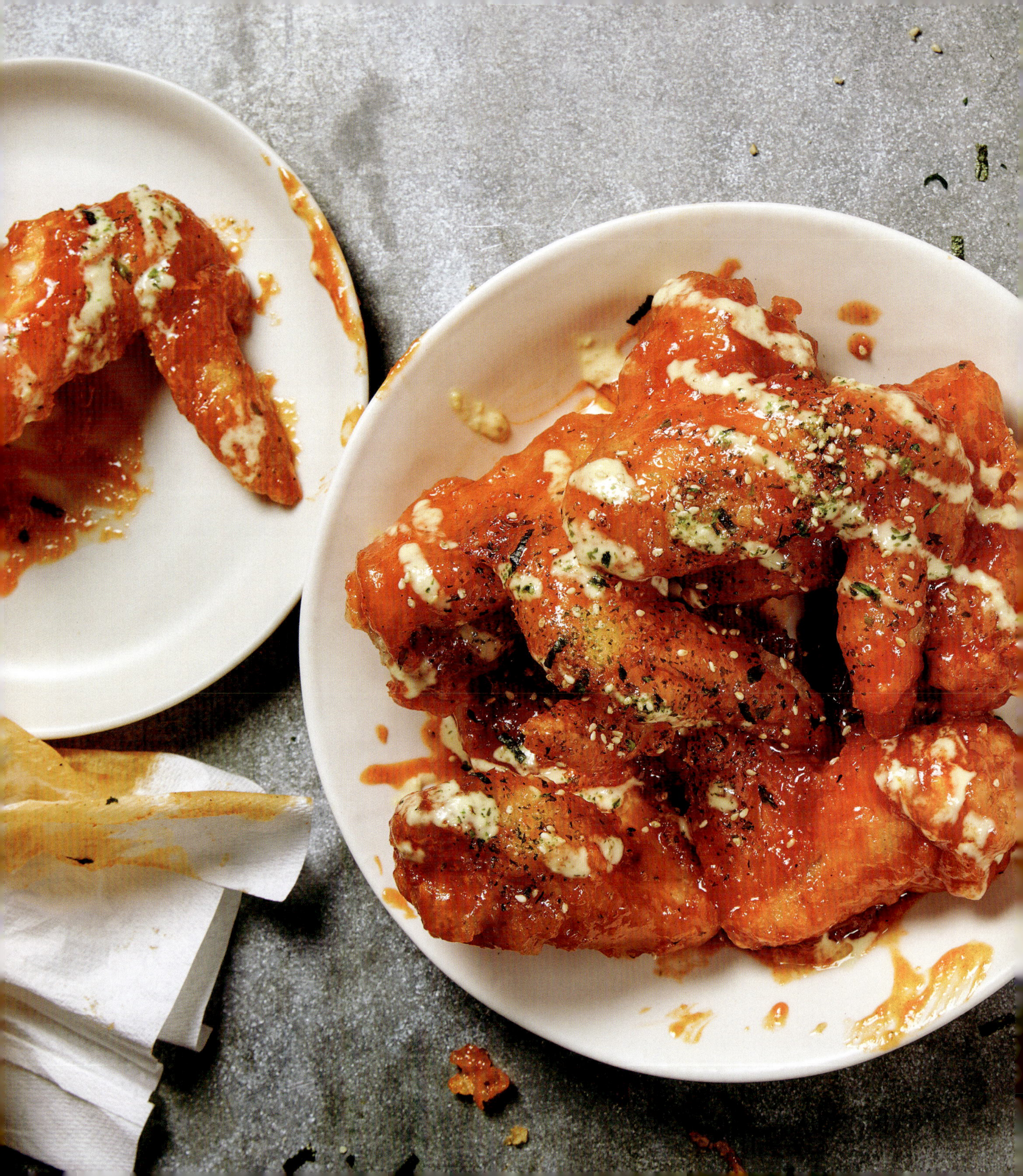

# THINGS TO SHARE

These dishes are for you people to share. I'm not sharing anything made for me in this chapter.

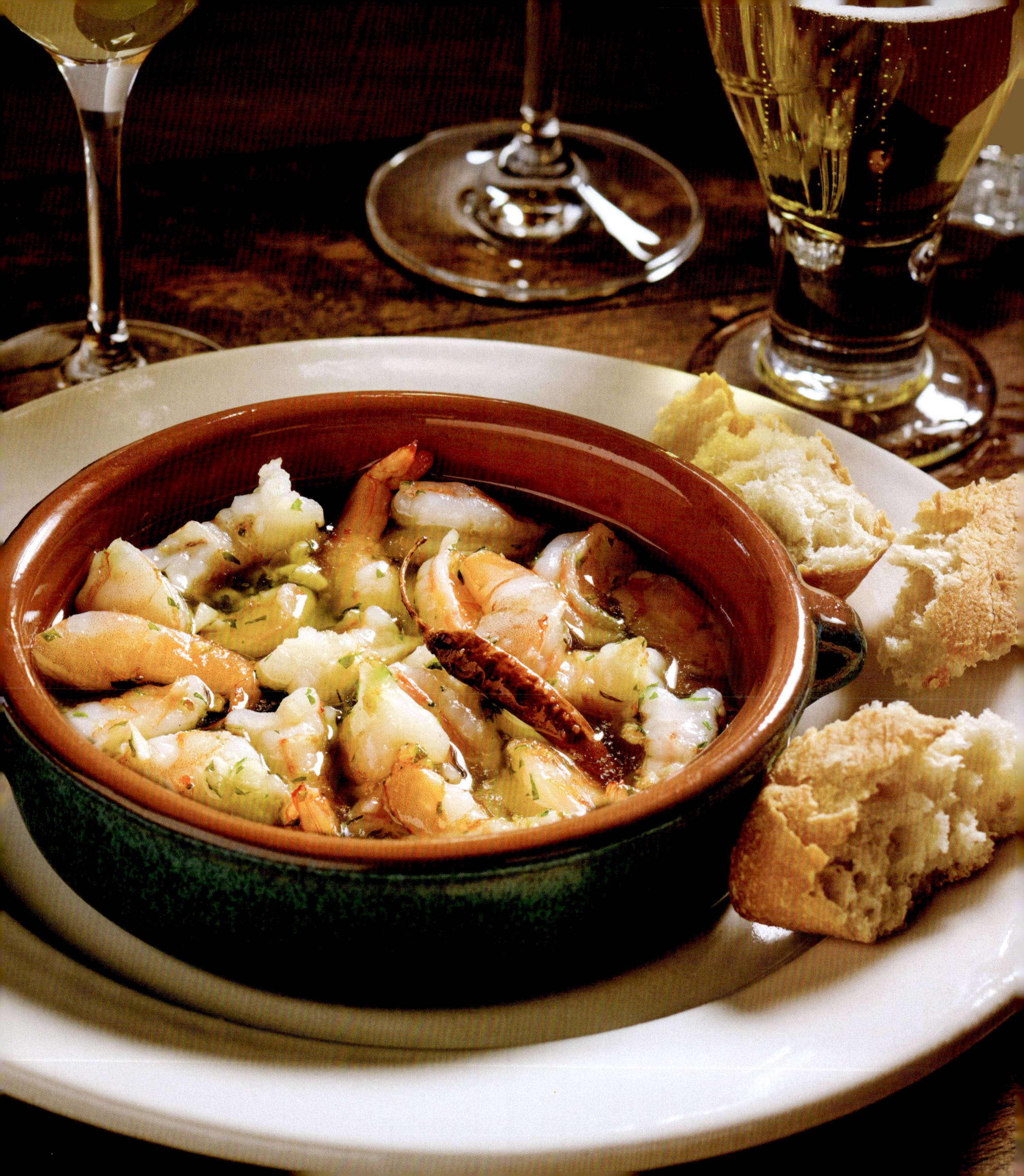

# La Casa del Abuelo's Gambas al Ajillo (Garlic Shrimp)

*Madrid*

When we're filming, usually there's a restaurant we'll eat at that's so good, the whole crew asks if we can go back off camera so we can hit it again. When we were in Madrid for season five, the opposite happened. We ate at the original La Casa del Abuelo (The House of My Grandfather) off camera for one of our crew meals, and it was so good that I had to go back and put it on camera. It was my duty to eat the very best garlic shrimp I've ever had in my life, again, as a public service for all of you kind people watching the show. (If you go, the one we went to is on Calle de la Victoria 12, the original restaurant that's been there since 1906; the family has several locations now.) You can get gambas al ajillo at tapas bars all over the city, but theirs is different from any garlic shrimp I've had anywhere. The shrimp are completely covered in the most delicious garlicky olive oil, which is the real reason why you order it. You don't even need the shrimp. By the way, I said in the show the shrimp was "so garlicky, so buttery" that I couldn't get over it. Daniel Waldburger, who runs the restaurant and is the great-grandson of the founder, gave me the recipe to share with you, and it turns out there's no butter at all, just the freshest local olive oil, which is a little sweet and probably why I thought it tasted like butter. You're gonna need some big, crusty Spanish rolls, the ones that are soft on the inside like they serve at La Casa del Abuelo. They're made for zobbling.

## TIPS

*It's worth getting a set of cazuelas, shallow terra-cotta cooking vessels, to make this fantastically simple dish (available at Spanish retailers like LaTienda.com). They induct high heat very slowly, so the shrimp and garlic truly poach in the olive oil. If you don't have a cazuela, you can mimic the cooking process by very slowly poaching the garlic in a skillet (it should not color), then adding the shrimp and cooking over very low heat.*

*Be sure to season a cazuela before you use it (follow the manufacturer's instructions); when new, they can break on the stove. It's best to use an inexpensive stovetop heat diffuser.*

*If you have a larger cazuela or similar clay pot, you can adjust the quantities of ingredients easily: there should be enough olive oil to come about one third up the sides of the dish, a single layer of the garlic-parsley mixture over the bottom of the cazuela, and later, another layer of shrimp.*

---

*This is one of Madrid's classic seafood dishes (even though we don't have a beach). We get our garlic from Chinchón, which is the best local garlic, and sweet white Mediterranean shrimp. Don't peel the garlic or shrimp until the day they are going to be eaten, and use good olive oil—a lot, you are in Spain tonight! It is also important to only cook the shrimp partway on the stove so they can finish cooking before your eyes at the table.* —DANIEL

**FEEDS 2 FOR TAPAS**

6 to 7 ounces (about 180g) medium or large shell-on shrimp, preferably Atlantic white

Coarse sea salt

4 to 5 medium very fresh garlic cloves

3 to 4 generous pinches (1 to 1½ teaspoons) finely chopped flat-leaf parsley, leaves only

About ⅔ cup (165ml) extra-virgin olive oil (Arbequina)

1 dried whole cayenne pepper or chile de árbol

Freshly ground black pepper

**TO SERVE**

3 to 4 panecillo tetiña (Spanish rolls), or ciabatta or rustic sandwich rolls

**TIPS**

*Use very fresh garlic (those with yellow cloves or that have sprouted often have a bitter flavor) and a bright, fruity extra-virgin olive oil like Arbequina, the primary olive variety grown for both Spanish and Californian olive oils.*

**Prep:** Put a small (roughly 6-inch/15cm) cazuela or similar terra-cotta cooking dish on the stove; if the cazuela is new, put a heat diffuser beneath it (see Tips). Have hot pads or kitchen towels near the stove.

Peel and devein the shrimp, and rinse under cold water. If large, cut the shrimp in half to make large bite-size pieces, and season lightly with salt.

Slice off the root end from the garlic cloves and peel them with your fingers without smashing the cloves.

Chop the cloves to roughly the size of whole black peppercorns. Mix about 2½ tablespoons chopped garlic with the parsley.

**Cook the shrimp:** Pour enough olive oil into the cazuela to come about one third up the sides of the dish. Add the whole cayenne pepper and heat the oil slowly over medium heat. When tiny bubbles begin to rise to the surface of the oil around the edges of the cazuela, about 5 minutes, add the garlic-parsley mixture (it should bubble vigorously). Use a metal spoon to spread it out in a single layer and poach the garlic in the oil until fragrant, 30 to 45 seconds; the garlic should not color. Stir the garlic, then add the shrimp and spread it out in a single layer. Cook the shrimp just until pink on the edges but the center is still translucent, about 1½ minutes. (The shrimp will continue to cook off the stove.) Lightly season the shrimp with salt and pepper.

**Serve:** Use hot pads to carefully transfer the cazuela (it will be very hot) to a heat-proof countertop or plate. Serve the shrimp right away with the bread.

# Angel Barreto's Korean Fried Chikin Wings

📍 *Anju, Washington, DC*

People don't think of Washington, DC, as a food town, but there's so much incredible food there today, we could have done two episodes. This Korean-style fried chicken at Anju, one of chef Danny Lee's restaurants that's run by chef Angel Barreto III, is the best I've ever had. It tastes like nothing I've had in Korea or anywhere else. The skin is so crispy and light, and the sauce is spicy with just enough sweetness. It's another good example of what happens when a young chef perfects a classic dish that they've always loved. (Angel grew up on an American military base in Korea.) Angel cuts up a whole chicken to fry at the restaurant, but he likes to do chicken wings at home (it's easier, and the flavor is exactly the same). You're going to need a lot of napkins. Good ABSORBENT napkins.

> *With Korean fried chicken, you want to both double coat it in potato flour and double fry it (fry, let the chicken rest, and fry again) so the coating gets extra crispy. You can do all the leg work, through the first frying, ahead. We break down and fry whole chickens; this recipe uses wings, which are easier to make at home because you don't have to regulate the different cook times of the chicken parts. The main thing is the potato starch needs to be cold before frying the chicken or the coating will start to blacken.* —ANGEL

---

**FEEDS 4 TO 6**

**BRINED CHICKEN WINGS**

2½ ounces (70g) kosher salt (a scant ⅓ cup Morton's or ½ cup Diamond Crystal)

4 medium garlic cloves, smashed

1 2-inch (5cm) piece ginger, peeled

About 3½ pounds (1.6kg) medium whole untrimmed chicken wings (14 to 16), or 3 pounds (1.4kg) drumettes and flats/wingettes

**FRIED WINGS**

Kosher or coarse sea salt and freshly ground black pepper

About 1¼ cups (235g) potato starch, divided

Plenty of vegetable or other neutral oil, for frying

Angel's Gochujang Wing Sauce (page 312)

**TO SERVE**

Angel's White Barbecue Sauce (page 313), at room temperature

Furikake seasoning

THINGS TO SHARE • 141

#### DAY 1

**Brine the wings:** In a large pot, bring 2 cups (480ml) water to a simmer. Add the salt and stir until dissolved. Remove the pot from the heat, add the garlic, ginger, and 1½ quarts (1.4L) tap water, and cool completely.

Put the wings in a large bowl, container, or food storage bag and add enough brine (along with the garlic and ginger) to fully submerge the wings. Cover or seal and refrigerate overnight or up to 24 hours.

#### DAY 2

**Flour the wings:** Line a large casserole or similar dish with parchment paper.

Strain the chicken wings (don't pat them dry) and rub ½ teaspoon salt and ½ teaspoon pepper all over the skin.

Put ¾ cup (140g) potato starch in a medium bowl and dredge the chicken wings in the potato starch, completely coating all sides. If the wings are wet in any spots, add a little more potato starch to the bowl. Stand the wings upright (as best you can) in the casserole dish, cover with plastic wrap, and refrigerate for 2 to 3 hours.

**Re-flour the wings:** Put the remaining ½ cup (95g) potato starch in a bowl and dredge the chicken wings again in the starch; they won't absorb as much starch this time but should be well covered. Rearrange the wings in the casserole dish, cover, and refrigerate at least 2 hours or up to 6 hours before frying.

**Fry the wings:** Lay a baking rack on top of a rimmed sheet pan, and have a splatter guard nearby.

Fill a deep fryer with the manufacturer's recommended amount of vegetable oil and heat as instructed. Or fill a large Dutch oven with enough oil to come 3 to 4 inches (7.5 to 10cm) up the sides.

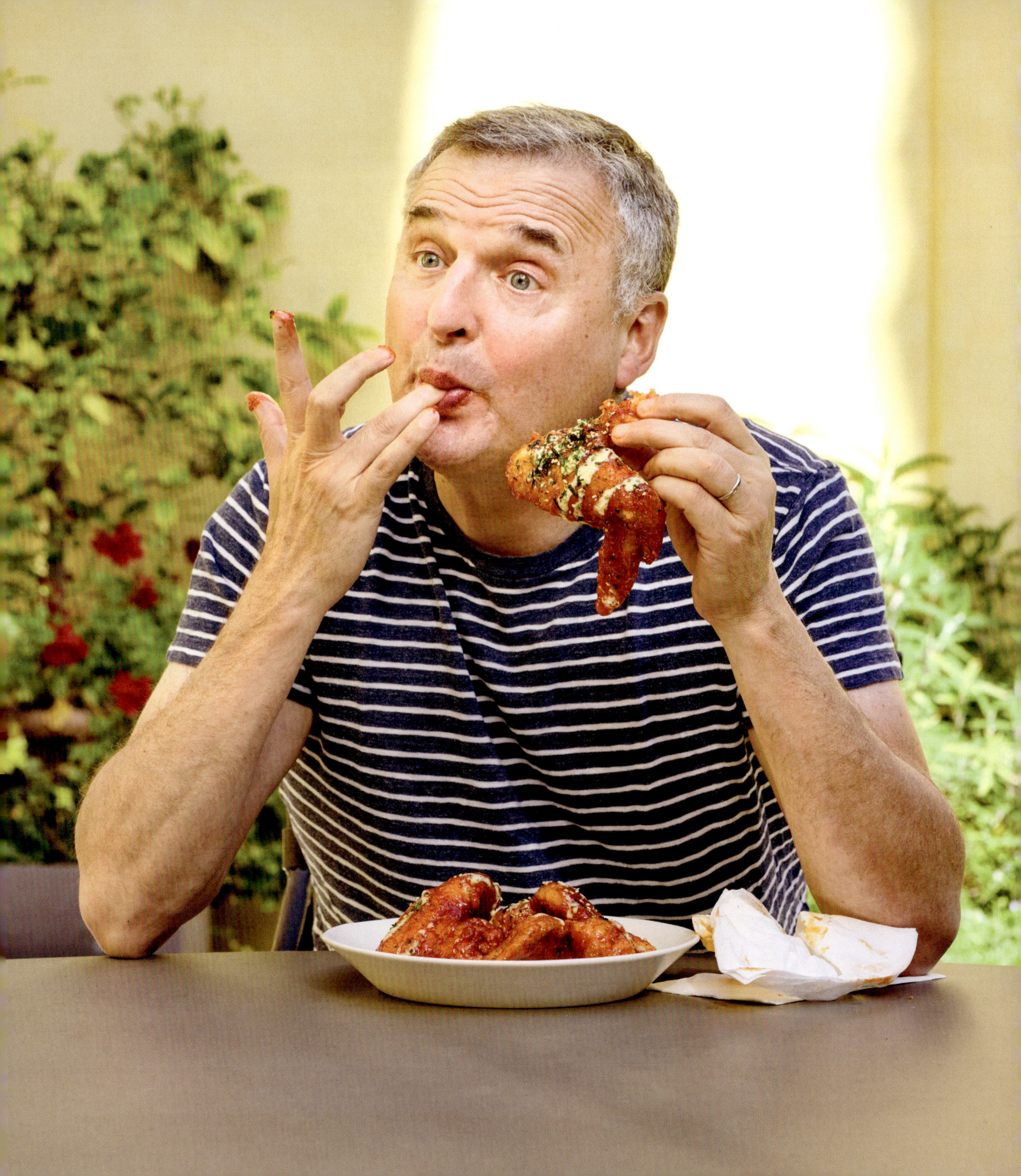

Heat the oil over medium-high until a digital thermometer reads 350 to 360°F (177 to 182°C), or test the heat by adding a sprinkle of flour; it should sizzle vigorously.

In batches, add the chilled wings to the hot oil (don't crowd the pan) and fry, flipping the wings a few times as they cook, until just beginning to lightly brown at the joints, 5 to 8 minutes (check a deep fryer on the earlier end, as the wings will take longer in a pot); the crust won't color much on the first fry. Transfer the wings to the baking rack, reheat the oil, and fry the remaining wings.

At this point, you can fry the wings a second time, or let them rest at room temperature for up to 1 hour before re-frying.

**Re-fry the wings:** Preheat the oven to 225°F (110°C) and line a rimmed baking sheet with parchment paper.

Rewarm the Gochujang Wing Sauce over low heat, just until no longer cold, and scrape about ¾ of the sauce into a large heat-proof bowl.

Reheat the deep fryer or oil in the pot (you will likely need to add more vegetable oil), this time to 360°F (182°C). Fry the wings, again in batches, until the crust is very crispy and begins to lightly brown, 3 to 5 minutes (check the deep fryer after 3 minutes). Transfer each batch of wings to the lined baking sheet and keep them warm in the oven while you fry the rest.

**Finish the wings and serve:** In batches, toss the hot wings in the gochujang sauce until completely covered. Arrange the wings on a large platter and drizzle about half (½ cup/120ml) of Angel's White Barbecue Sauce generously over the wings, then scatter the furikake lightly on top.

Serve the wings with the remaining white barbecue sauce on the side and any remaining gochujang sauce. And plenty of napkins.

## TIPS

*The double frying process is worth the effort, and relatively quick, as wings don't take long to fry. After brining the wings overnight, dredge them in the potato starch mixture early in the day so they have time to chill; then you're ready for the first fry an hour before serving them. All that's left is the second, and quick, five-minute fry.*

*These wings aren't suitable for air frying; the potato starch coating is completely dry and needs the hot oil to puff and crisp up.*

## Ibérico Ham

📍 *Barcelona, Spain*

In the "Barcelona" episode of *I'll Have What Phil's Having*, I went to Vila Viniteca, a gourmet food shop where you can have a snack while you shop. They specialize in one of my favorite things, the king of the pig world: Ibérico ham. You know it's really special when the guy who slices the ham trains for an entire year just to cut it the right way.

Here's my recipe.

Go to Spain and spend a lot of money on Ibérico ham.

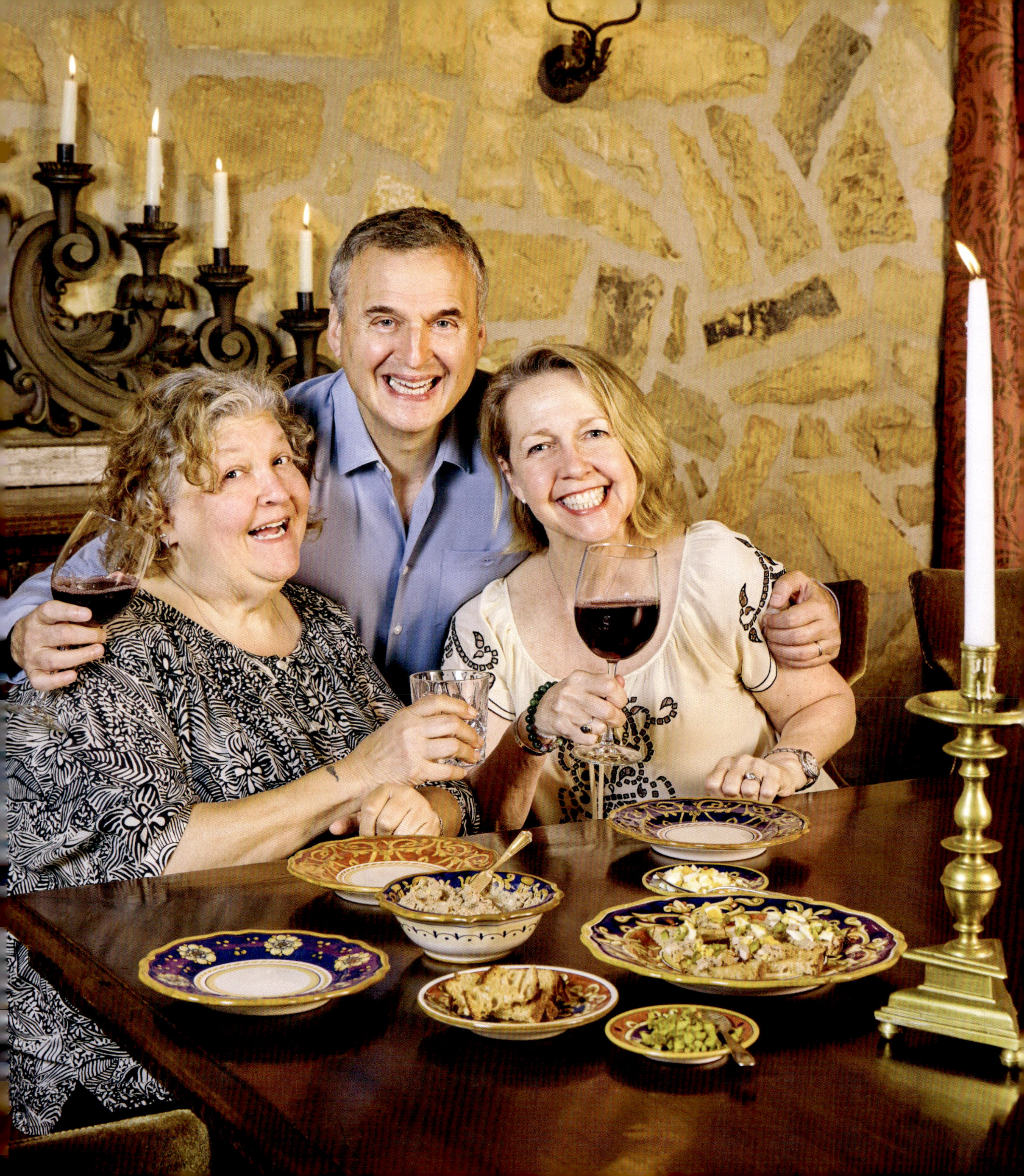

# Jennifer Heftler's Chopped Liver

One of my oldest friends, Jennifer Heftler, always brings her chopped liver to our house for holidays. I met Jen when we did theater together in New York in the 1980s. When we're both in town, we have breakfast every Saturday (she also loves to cook and has an Instagram page with all of her breakfast recipes: @squaremealdaily). I never miss it. She's family.

*I say this with zero modesty: You can put my chopped liver against your bubbe's or any Michelin-starred chef's fancy version. I know for those who love chopped liver, it looks like heaven. And for those who don't, it looks like, to put it bluntly, dog food. Wherever you stand on the liver continuum, I hope you'll still give this a try. Maybe this will convince you: chopped liver really isn't that different from foie gras mousse or pâté. It actually originated in what is now the French region of Alsace, where Ashkenazi Jews raised geese, so the first chopped liver was actually made from goose liver.*

*The recipe makes a lot, but I always hold some back when I bring it to Phil's. (And yes, you could cut the recipe in half.) You can make schmaltz by rendering chicken skin (the crunchy bits, called "gribenes" or chicken cracklings, that are left behind are a bonus, which some people sprinkle on top of their chopped liver), but I usually just buy my schmaltz frozen at the grocery store. If you don't have it, it's great with butter, or you could even use rendered duck fat (now you're even closer to foie gras). Just don't overcook the livers; you want them light pink in the middle but not dry. And no matter how short a time you keep the chopped liver in the fridge, the top of your mixture will oxidize and look darker (not a bad thing). Just stir the mixture before serving and it will all be fine. On Passover, I always serve this with matzoh, but for other holidays and events, challah or those little squares of "cocktail" Scandinavian dark rye or pumpernickel bread that are about the size of Post-it notes are great. You can also pre-top those small squares with the chopped liver and a little grated egg yolk for appetizers. For breakfast or lunch, try the chopped liver on rye bread or a bagel.* —JENNIFER

**FEEDS A BIG HOLIDAY CROWD (12 TO 16); MAKES ABOUT 4 CUPS (ABOUT 1KG)**

2 to 2¼ pounds (1kg) chicken livers

Kosher or coarse sea salt and freshly ground black pepper

4 tablespoons (½ stick/55g) unsalted butter, chilled

½ cup (120ml) schmaltz (rendered chicken fat) or duck fat, or ½ cup (1 stick/115g) unsalted butter, chilled and divided

2 cups (280g) finely chopped yellow onions (2 medium)

2 to 3 medium garlic cloves, minced

1 tablespoon granulated sugar

1 teaspoon balsamic vinegar

½ teaspoon dried thyme or 1 teaspoon thyme leaves

2 hard-boiled eggs, coarsely chopped

**Prep:** Use kitchen scissors to trim off any stringy connective tissue or membranes on the chicken livers and any greenish-colored sacs attached to the lobes. Rinse the chicken livers well, lightly dry them on a paper towel, and season both sides generously with salt and pepper.

**Cook the onions and liver:** If using poultry fat (chicken or duck), melt the 4 tablespoons (½ stick/55g) of butter and ¼ cup (60g) schmaltz in a large nonstick skillet over medium heat. If skipping the poultry fat, melt ½ cup (1 stick/115g) butter.

When the fat or butter is hot, add the onions, garlic, sugar, balsamic vinegar, thyme, and ½ teaspoon salt and cook, stirring occasionally with a wooden spoon, until the onions have completely softened and are beginning to brown, 12 to 15 minutes. Scrape the onions into a bowl.

Increase the heat to medium-high and add about half the chicken livers to the skillet (don't crowd the pan). Sear the livers, flipping occasionally with tongs to brown all sides, until the flesh feels firm to the touch and when you cut into a liver the interior is light pink and the juices run clear. Check the smallest pieces after 5 to 6 minutes; the larger, full lobes after 8 minutes. (The livers will continue to cook after you remove them from the skillet.) Scrape the livers into a bowl.

Wipe any burnt bits out of the pan and add a little of the oil from the bowl of onions to the pan. Sear the remaining livers.

**Finish the chopped liver:** Put the livers and onions in a food processor with the remaining ¼ cup (60ml) schmaltz. Or, cut the remaining 4 tablespoons (½ stick/55g) butter into small cubes and scatter it over the liver and onions.

Pulse the liver and onions 8 to 10 times, stirring to redistribute any larger pieces of liver; if using butter, you may need to break up any large clumps with your hands. Continue to pulse and stir the liver until coarsely ground; when only a few larger chunks remain, scrape the chopped liver into a bowl and break up the largest pieces with your fingers.

Gently fold the chopped eggs into the liver and season with salt and pepper. Press a piece of plastic wrap directly onto the surface of the chopped liver and refrigerate at least 4 hours or up to 3 days.

**Serve:** Stir the chopped liver to mix the oxidized, darker layer at the top back into the mixture. Transfer the chopped liver to a serving bowl and scatter the chopped hard-boiled eggs and cornichons on top or serve them on the side. Serve with the bread, matzoh, or crackers.

**TO SERVE**

**2 to 3 hard-boiled eggs, chopped**

**4 to 5 cornichons, chopped**

**Plenty of sliced bread (like dark rye, pumpernickel, challah, or sourdough), matzoh, or your favorite crackers**

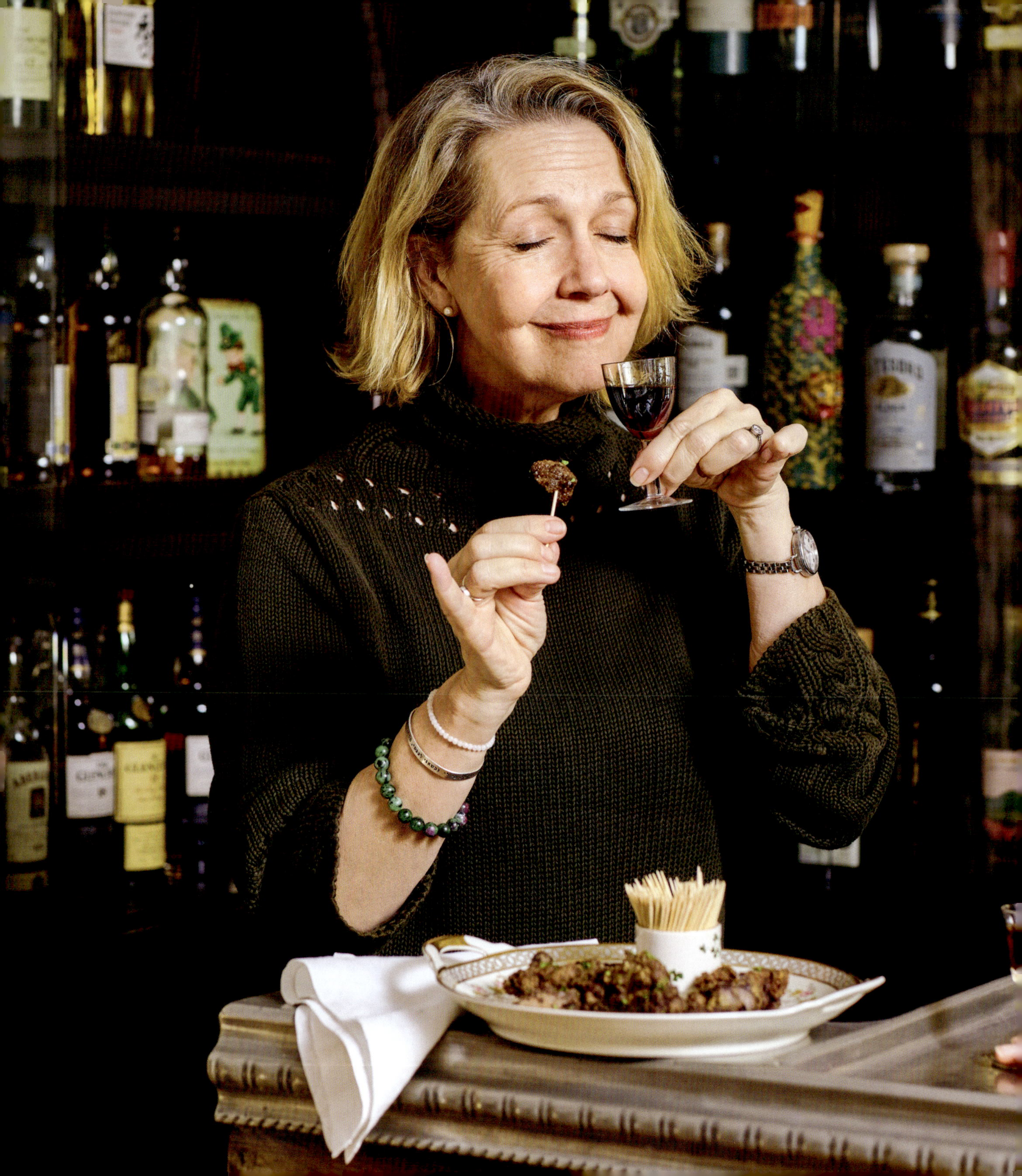

# Steve Horan's Fried Chicken Livers

Monica's brother, Steve Horan, is a great chef! He makes my other favorite chicken liver dish. His are deep-fried, so you get that crunchy crust and soft inside.

> *This was a favorite of my parents. It's very simple to make but delish. The only challenge in frying a chicken liver is that it's a bit of a mess and you need to be careful (they pop out hot oil when frying). Use an electric fryer with a lid, if you have one, or a deep pot. Mom would always serve them with toothpicks in each one . . . and a glass of sherry. L'chaim!*
> —STEVE

**Prep:** Pour yourself a glass of sherry to drink while cooking.

Line a plate with paper grocery bags or paper towels.

Use kitchen scissors to trim off any stringy connective tissue or membranes on the chicken livers and any greenish-colored sacs attached to the lobes. Rinse the chicken livers well, lightly dry them on a paper towel, and season both sides generously with salt and pepper.

In a medium bowl, combine the Bisquick, garlic powder, seasoned salt, onion powder, and 1 teaspoon pepper and mix well.

**Fry the livers:** Fill a deep fryer with the manufacturer's recommended amount of vegetable oil and heat as instructed. Or, add enough oil to a large Dutch oven to come about 2 inches (5cm) up the sides, and have a splatter guard, preferably, or the pot lid nearby. Heat the oil over medium-high until a digital thermometer

---

**FEEDS 4 TO 5 AS AN APPETIZER**

1 glass cream sherry, for the cook

About 1 pound (455g) chicken livers

Kosher or coarse sea salt and finely ground black pepper

1 cup (120g) Bisquick, or 1 cup all-purpose flour plus 1 teaspoon baking powder

1 tablespoon garlic powder

1 tablespoon seasoned salt (Lawry's or homemade; recipe follows)

1 teaspoon onion powder

**TO SERVE**

The rest of the bottle of cream sherry

3 to 4 flat-leaf parsley leaves, finely chopped

THINGS TO SHARE • 151

> **TIP**
>
> *Drinking a glass of cream sherry with the fried chicken livers isn't just a boozy gimmick (the word* cream *refers to sweetened, as opposed to various dry, sherry wines). The dried fruit flavors and sweetness balance the earthy richness of the livers. In Andalucía, the "sherry triangle" of Spain, chicken livers stewed in dry sherry is a classic tapas dish.*

reads 350 to 360°F (177 to 182°C), or test the heat by adding a sprinkle of flour; it should sizzle vigorously.

When the oil is hot, dredge the chicken livers in the flour mixture and toss well to completely coat all sides.

Carefully slide the livers into the hot oil (the oil will sizzle and pop) and quickly put the lid on the deep fryer or cover the Dutch oven with the splatter guard (or partly cover the pan with the lid).

In a deep fryer, cook the chicken livers until firm and barely pink in the middle, 5 to 6 minutes; cut a liver in half to check. In a Dutch oven, flip the chicken livers when the bottom begins to brown, about 2 minutes, re-cover the pot with the splatter guard or partially closed lid, and cook until the opposite side is golden brown and the livers are firm to the touch but slightly pink in the middle, 2 to 3 minutes.

Transfer the chicken livers to the paper-lined plate to drain and season lightly with salt.

**Serve:** Pour a glass of cream sherry for everybody ... and a second glass for the cook. Just before serving, sprinkle a few pinches of chopped parsley over the chicken livers, insert a toothpick into each, and serve.

## SEASONED SALT

In a small dish or jar, mix together 1½ tablespoons fine salt, 1 teaspoon granulated sugar, 1 teaspoon paprika, ¼ teaspoon ground turmeric, ¼ teaspoon garlic powder, and ¼ teaspoon onion powder. Store, covered, at room temperature for up to 1 month. Makes about 2½ tablespoons.

# The Bombay Canteen's Butter Garlic Crab Kulcha

*Mumbai*

If you saw the "New York" episode back in the second season of the show, then you met my friend Floyd Cardoz, a great chef and wonderful person. He took my friend Rupa Balasubramanian and me to an Indian temple in Queens, and we ate downstairs. Tragically, Floyd passed away due to COVID-19 in 2020, and we all miss him. When we were in Mumbai for season seven, I had to go to the Bombay Canteen, which Floyd cofounded with his partners Sameer Seth and Yash Bhanage. I had lunch with Sameer, Yash, and the head chef, Hussain Shahzad, and one of the things that I had was this flatbread with crab in a garlicky butter sauce. It's their tribute to the butter-garlic crab that I had at Trishna, where Vir Sanghvi, the top food critic in India, took me earlier in the episode. What I like about this version is it isn't supposed to be the "authentic" version of that crab at Trishna, which, as Vir was telling me, isn't an "authentic" Indian dish, either. And that's the whole point. It's what happens when creative people from all different backgrounds take something really great and make their own version that's as good or even better. You get a new "maximum" experience. When you go to Mumbai, go to Trishna and get their crab, then go to the Bombay Canteen and try this one. You can taste Floyd's influence, and it's worth every minute it takes to make.

> *We wouldn't be where we are without Floyd. He went from being a boss to a friend to a mentor to everything. He's left his thought process in each one of us, and we each interpret it in a different way on a different day, and that's the beauty of it.* —SAMEER

**FEEDS 6 TO 8**

6 to 8 small round flatbreads (Bombay Canteen Kulcha, page 324), naan, taboon, manakeesh, or Greek pita (roughly 6 inches/15cm each)

Hussain's Butter-Garlic Sauce (page 316)

8 ounces (225g) lump crab meat, picked over

2 green onions, finely chopped (white bulbs and tender top stems), divided

**TO SERVE**

6 to 8 poached eggs (or soft scrambled eggs; see Tips)

1 handful Pickled Red Onions (recipe follows), drained

Grated zest of ½ to 1 medium lemon

## TIPS

*For a party, you can make the kulcha components ahead and save poaching the eggs for the last minute. For a shared family dish, layer the ingredients onto a large, baked pizza dough round instead of multiple small flatbreads.*

*An egg poacher makes poaching multiple eggs at the same time easy; another option is to make silky soft scrambled eggs (whisk the raw eggs and sauté them gently in plenty of butter), as the Bombay Canteen also sometimes does.*

**MAKES ABOUT 2 CUPS (225G) ONIONS, PLUS PICKLING BRINE**

**1 medium red onion, sliced in half and shaved on a mandoline or very thinly sliced**

**2 to 3 teaspoons finely chopped spicy green chili (Jwala, serrano, or similar), deveined and seeds removed**

**½ cup (120ml) white vinegar**

**1 teaspoon granulated sugar**

**1 teaspoon coriander seeds**

**Kosher or coarse sea salt and freshly ground black pepper**

**Prep:** Heat a cast iron skillet or comal over medium-high heat. When the skillet is very hot, quickly sear the flatbreads, one at a time, on both sides to refresh the bread.

In a saucepan over low heat, very gently rewarm Hussain's Butter-Garlic Sauce, stirring constantly. (Don't simmer or the sauce may break.) Add the crab and about ¾ of the green onions. Stir a few times until the crab is no longer cold and remove the saucepan from the heat.

**Cook the eggs:** Poach the eggs on the stovetop, in an egg poacher, or in the microwave.

**Assemble and serve:** Dollop several generous spoonfuls (5 to 6 tablespoons) of Hussain's Butter-Garlic Sauce on each flatbread, spread the sauce out evenly, and scatter several pickled onion slices over the sauce. Lay 1 poached egg in the center of each flatbread. Sprinkle a little of the lemon zest over each kulcha, finish with the remaining green onions, and serve right away.

## PICKLED RED ONIONS

Pack the onions and chili snugly into a jar or glass measuring cup with at least 1 inch (2.5cm) room to spare at the top.

In a small saucepan, combine the vinegar, sugar, coriander seeds, 1 teaspoon salt, ¼ teaspoon pepper, and ½ cup (120ml) water. Bring to a simmer and stir to dissolve the sugar and salt.

Pour the hot brine over the onion slices and press down on the onions with a spoon to completely submerge them. Loosely cover the container and let cool completely.

Refrigerate the pickled onions for at least 24 hours before using, or up to 2 weeks; the flavor will intensify over time.

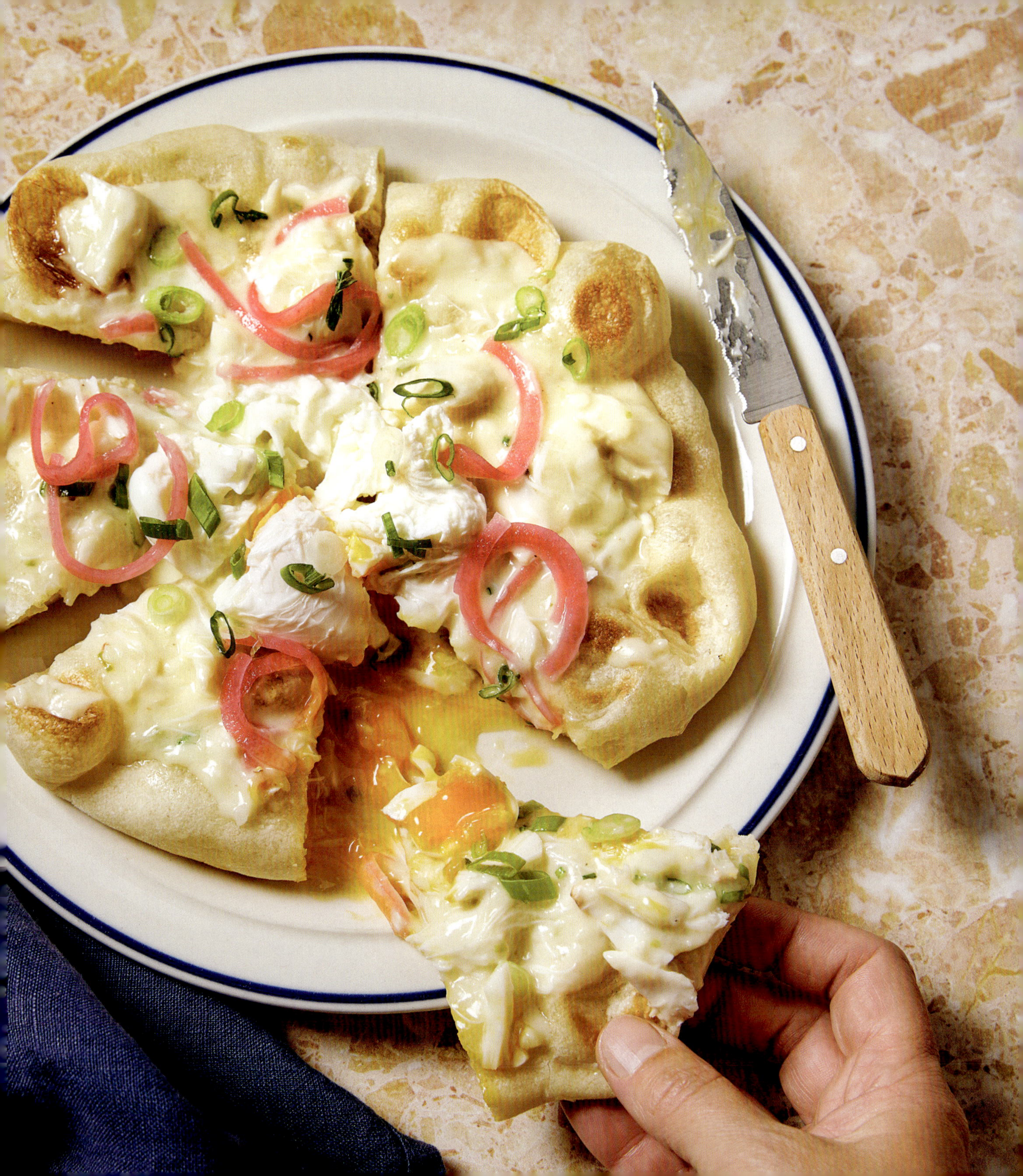

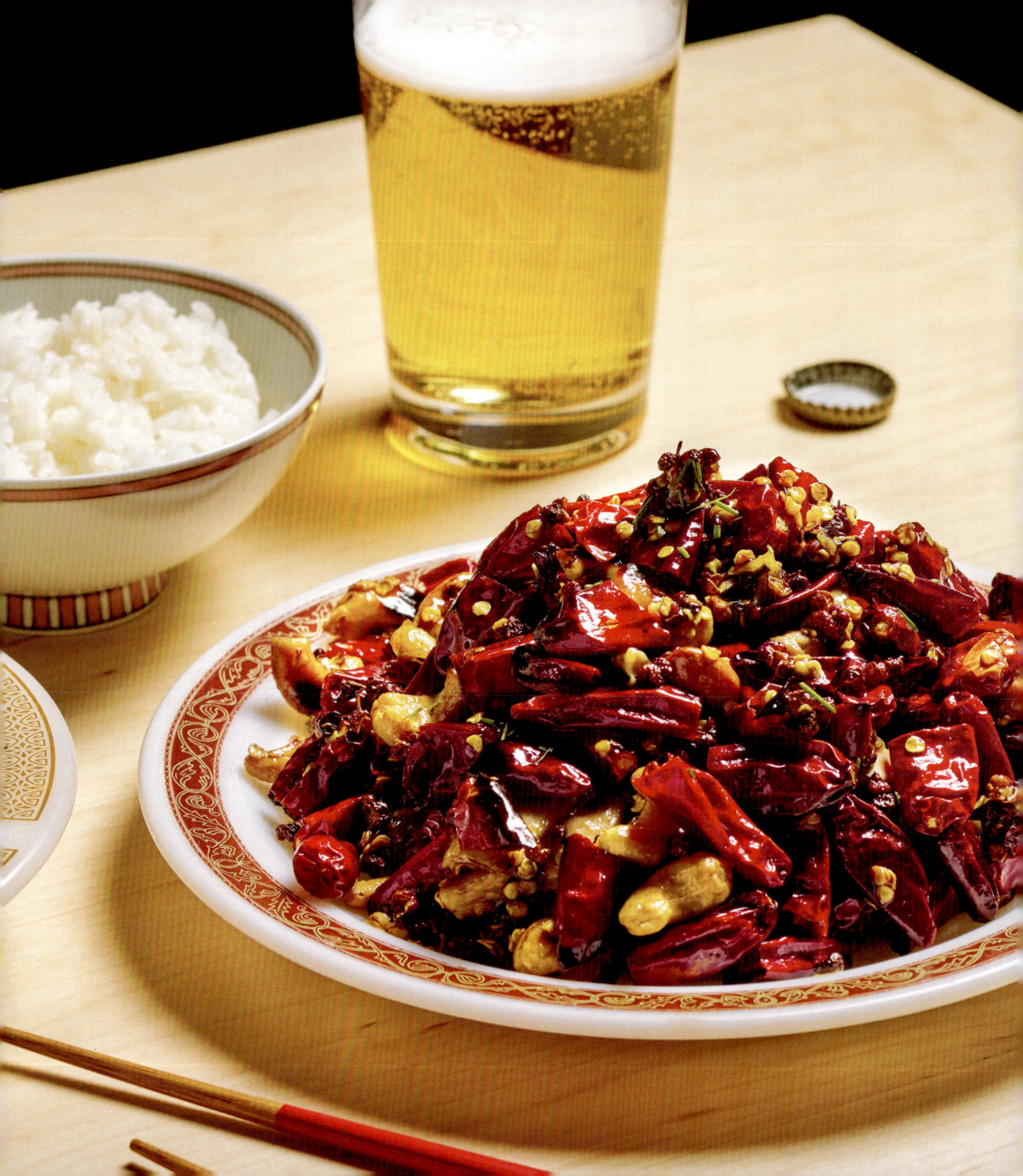

# San Xi Lou's Sichuan Spicy Chicken

*Hong Kong*

Here's what I love about San Xi Lou: they tread the edges. Their food is right on that razor's edge between great spicy, really good spicy, and too much. It took me years of building up to different levels of "spicy" to be able to say that. This crispy Sichuan chicken that I had back in 2015 when we were filming the "Hong Kong" episode of *I'll Have What Phil's Having* still ranks as one of the spiciest nights of my life.

Regional Chinese cuisine is all so different, but only Sichuan food uses both the uniquely addictive Sichuan chili pepper and peppercorn. The word they use to describe spiciness is *mala*. The first part, "ma," is the numbing feeling you get, and the "la" is the spicy part at the end. A lot of Sichuan dishes, like this one, are both "ma" and "la." I call it eating in 3D, because there's another effect literally in your mouth that you wouldn't get from just flavor and consistency. The chilis you need to get to make this are the dried red killer chili peppers (there's more on that at the end of this recipe), and you don't just need some but a huge pile, more than I've ever seen on a single plate in my life. This is very important: you don't eat the chili peppers; you just go in with your chopsticks and pick out the chicken and cashews.

By the way, since I was in Hong Kong, the "real" San Xi Lou moved to a new location in Causeway Bay: 17/f, Lee Theatre, 99 Percival Street. The restaurant business is constantly changing, so it's not uncommon that some place has a new chef, or a restaurant moves or even has closed since we did the show. When we asked for this recipe for the book, the owner, Stanley Chuk, said that when San Xi Lou moved, somebody else took over the original space, which is in the business district in central Hong Kong, and instead of opening a new restaurant, they kept everything the same, from the menu to how the waitstaff dress and the way the place is decorated. Even the restaurant's name is very similar. You'll think you are at the real San Xi Lou. But you're not.

*We don't use MSG in any of our dishes but instead a little of our secret flavoring ingredient that has a similar effect. (You can use your favorite MSG substitute.)* —STANLEY

**FEEDS 2 TO 3**

About 1 pound (455g) skin-on, boneless chicken thighs or 1⅓ pounds (500g) bone-in thighs

1 4-ounce bag (115g) whole dried Sichuan chili peppers (about 4½ cups; see Tip)

2 tablespoons Sichuan peppercorns

2 green onions, bulbs and stems thinly sliced, divided

¾ cup (110g) roasted, unsalted cashews

3 medium garlic cloves, minced

1 2-inch (5cm) piece ginger, peeled and finely chopped

1 teaspoon ground cumin

1 teaspoon powdered chicken bouillon (MSG free) or Better than Bouillon Roasted Chicken Base (see page 114)

1 teaspoon MSG substitute

**Prep:** Have a medium heat-proof plate or bowl, a large skimmer or spider (or large slotted spoon), and a ladle near the stove. Line a plate with paper towels or paper bags.

Use kitchen scissors to remove the bones from the chicken thighs, if needed; leave the skin intact. (Save the meaty bones for stock.) Cut the meat into bite-size pieces.

Over a medium bowl, use the scissors to cut the whole Sichuan chili peppers in half widthwise. (If using a knife, slice carefully, as the seeds scatter everywhere.) Lightly crush the Sichuan peppercorns in a mortar or with the bottom of a bowl and add to the chili peppers.

Put ¾ of the green onions in one dish or pile, the cashews in another, the garlic and ginger in another, and finally the cumin, powdered chicken bouillon, and MSG substitute together.

**Triple fry the chicken:** In a wok or Dutch oven, heat plenty of vegetable oil (about 3 inches/7.5cm) over high heat until very hot, 3 to 4 minutes; the surface should be shimmering. Test the heat with a piece of chicken; it should vigorously bubble.

Add the chicken to the hot oil and stir-fry, stirring occasionally with the ladle or spoon, for about 45 seconds. Scoop out the chicken with the skimmer or spider and transfer it to the plate. (If you're using a large skimmer or spider, just leave the chicken inside it.)

Let the oil heat back up to the frying temperature and fry the chicken again, stirring the pieces occasionally as they fry until the chicken begins to lightly brown, about 30 seconds. Scoop the chicken out of the oil, reheat the oil until very hot one more time, and fry the chicken until golden brown, 30 to 45 seconds, then transfer to the plate.

**Finish the stir-fry:** Pour off all but a thin layer of the frying oil. Reheat the oil in the wok, add the Sichuan chili peppers and peppercorns, and toss or stir a few times to coat the peppers in the oil. Add the cashews and fry, stirring, for about 10 seconds, then add the garlic and ginger and flip or stir a few more times. Add the cumin and chicken bouillon and keep tossing and stirring until aromatic, 10 to 15 seconds, then stir in the remaining green onions and sesame oil and turn off the heat.

**To serve:** Pile the stir-fry onto a large, shallow serving bowl and scatter the sesame seeds on top. Serve the stir-fry with the rice, if desired, and use chopsticks to pick out the chicken and cashews. (The whole chili peppers are not meant to be eaten.)

**Vegetable oil, for frying**

**Spoonful (about 1 tablespoon) toasted sesame oil**

TO SERVE

**Spoonful (about 1 tablespoon) untoasted sesame seeds**

**Cooked rice (optional)**

TIP

*You can find authentic xiao mi la peppers (a spicy dried chili pepper similar to Thai chilis) and Szechuan peppercorns (the lemony, "numbing" dried berries of the prickly ash tree) at Chinese markets and at specialty shops online like The Mala Market (themalamarket.com). The term "Sichuan chili peppers" refers to several varieties of peppers grown in the region, so if you get a bag of chili peppers from a general retailer that aren't very spicy, they likely are not xiao mi la peppers.*

THINGS TO SHARE • 159

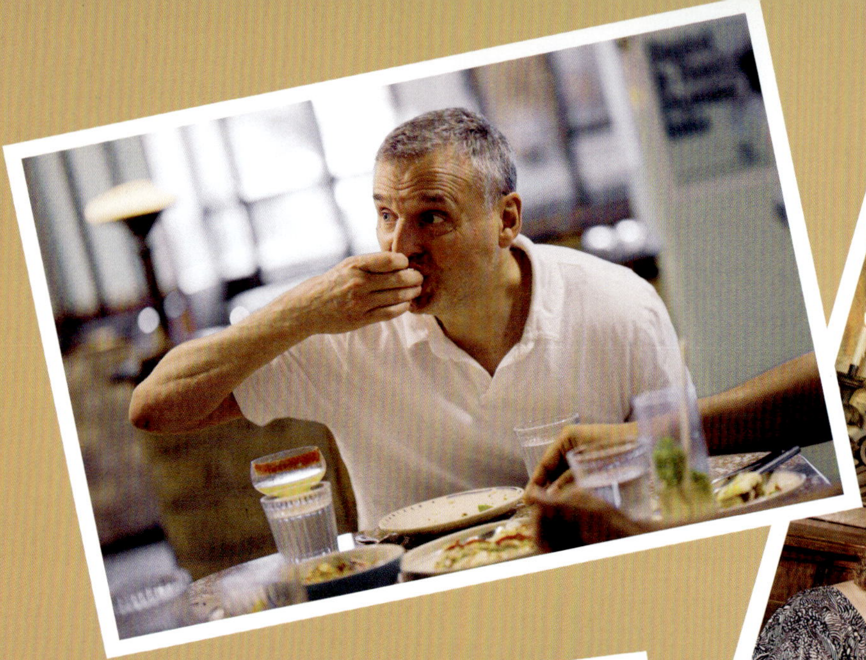
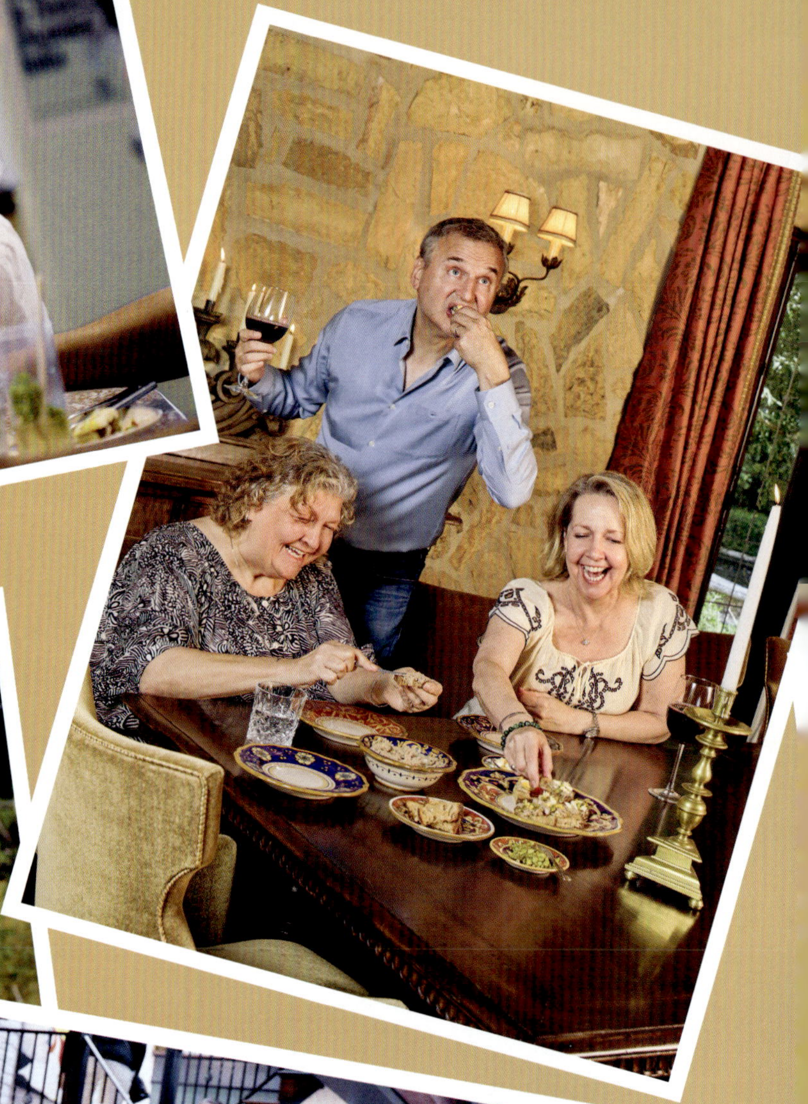
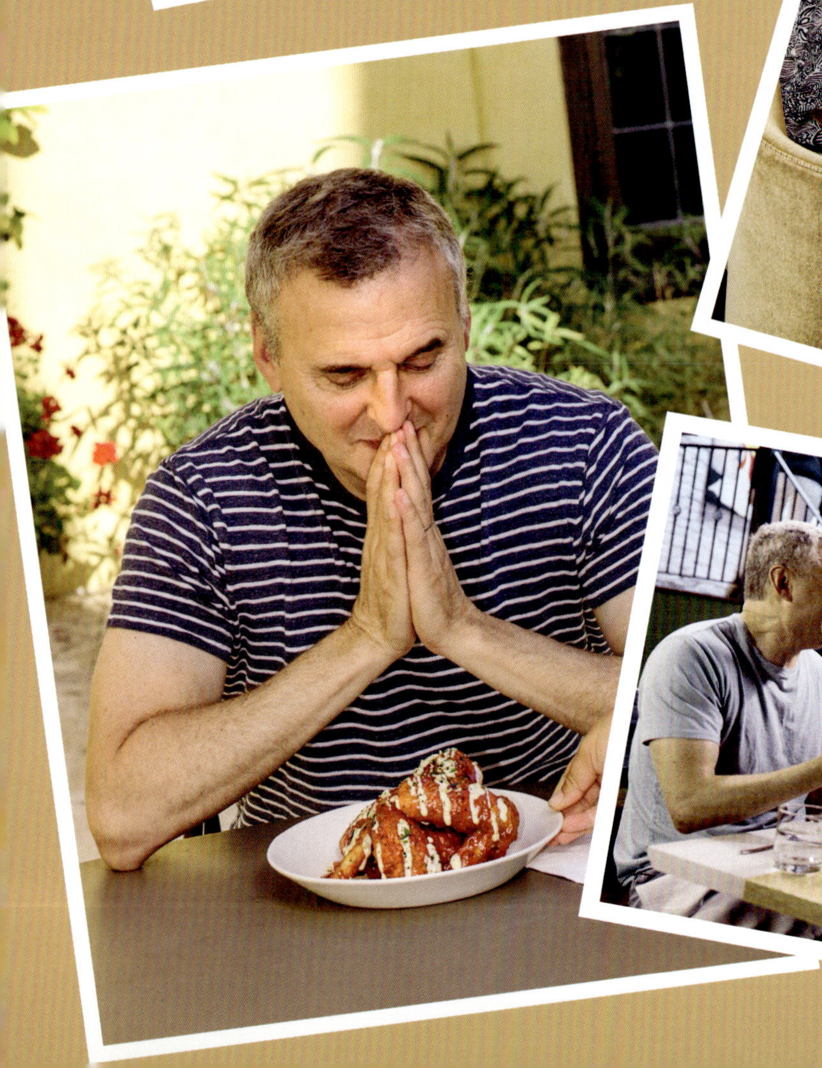
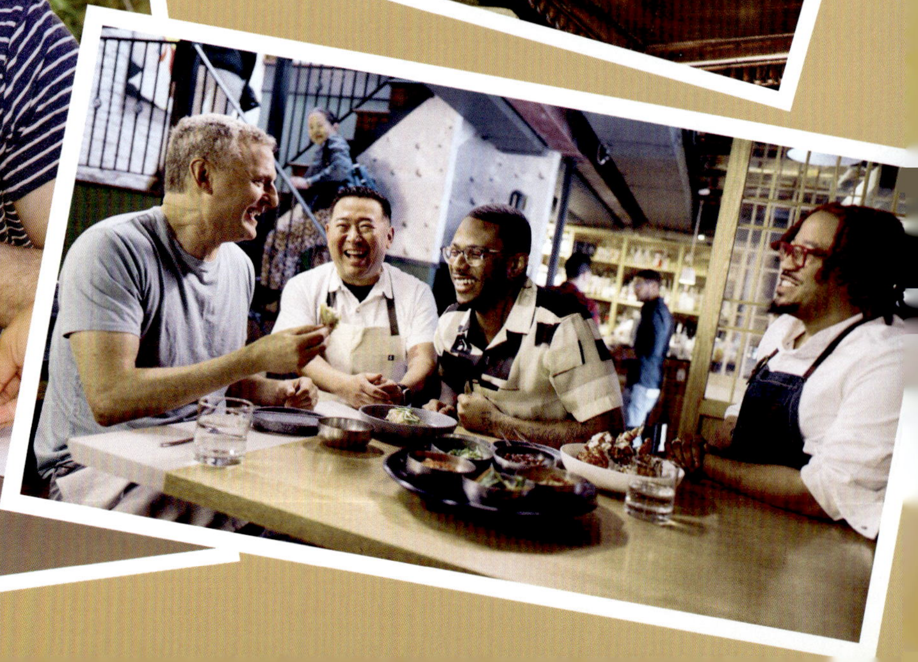

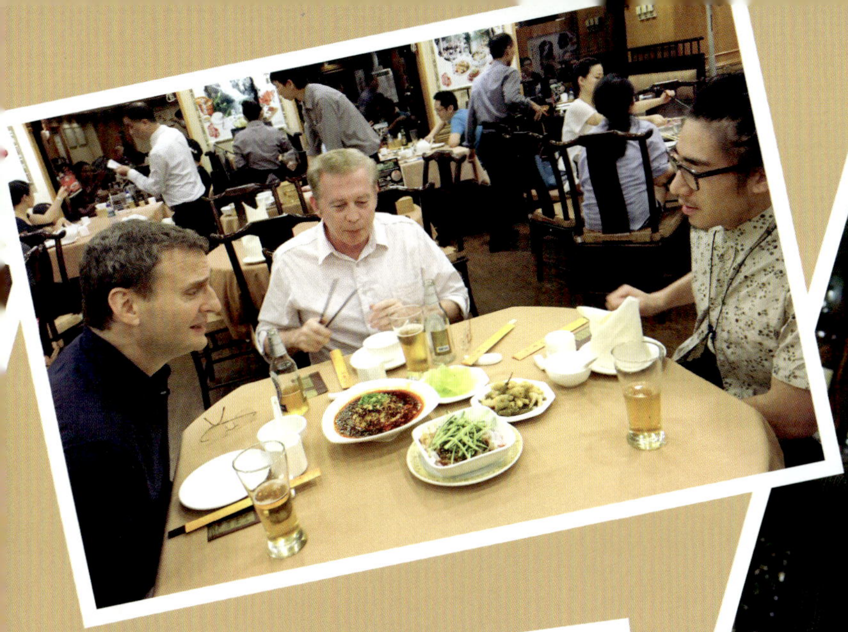
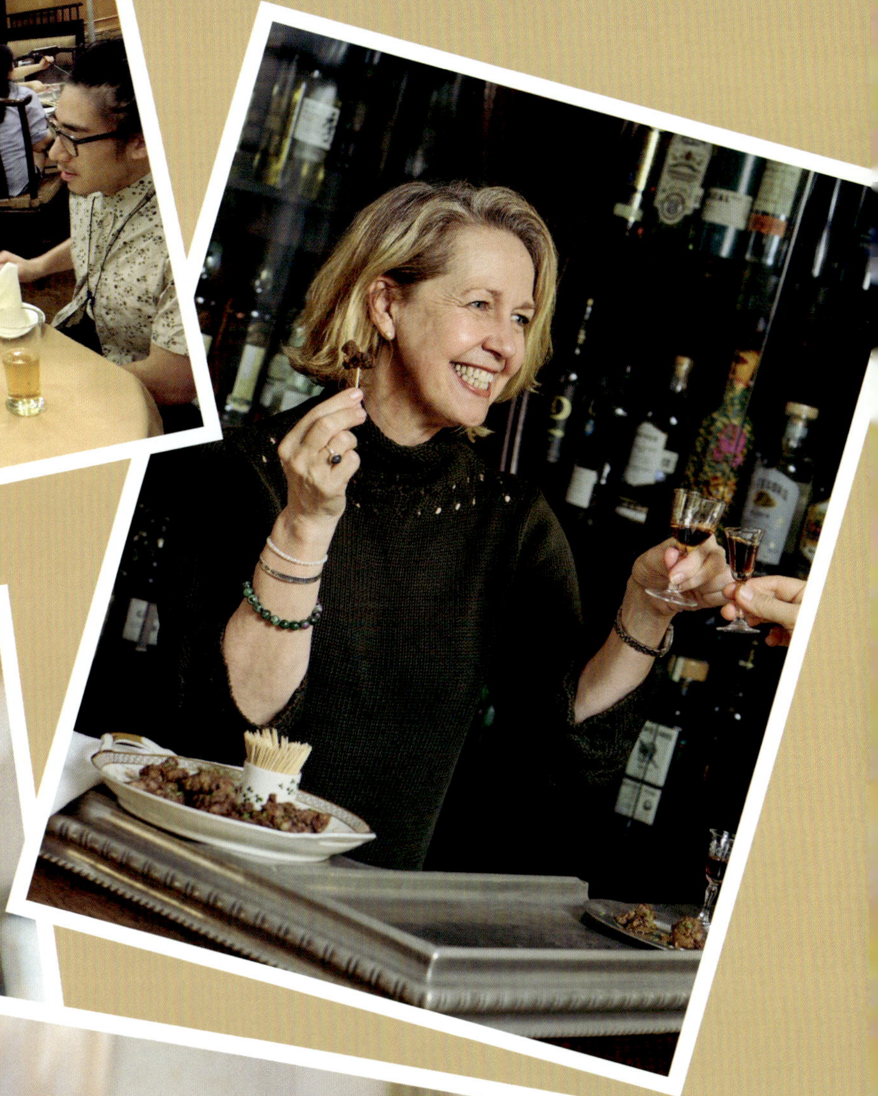
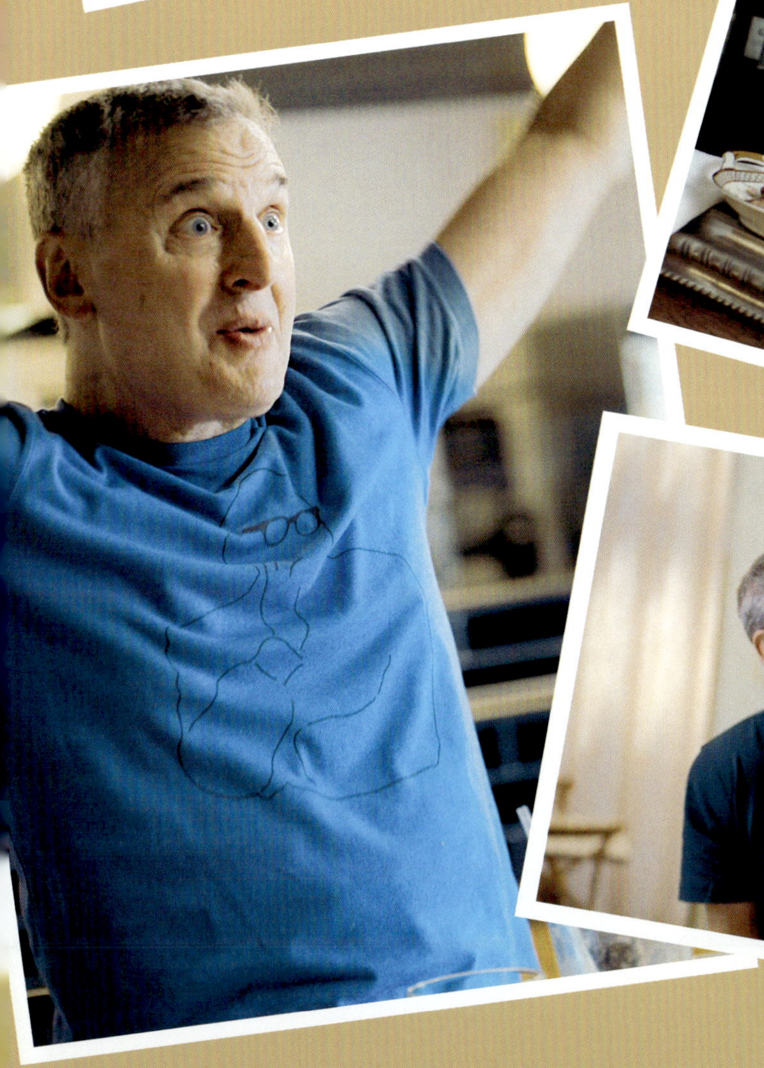
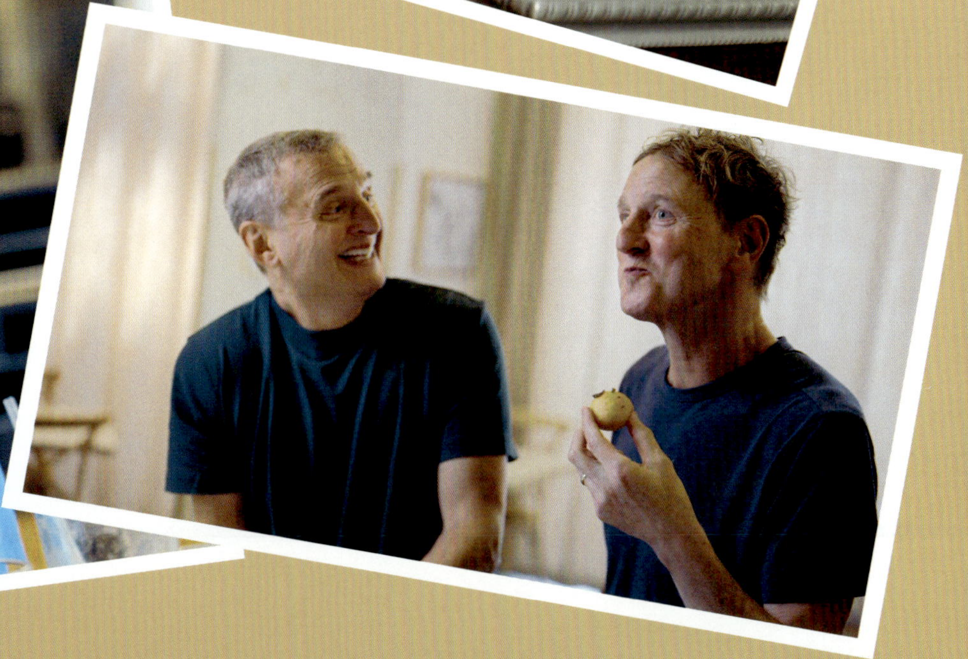

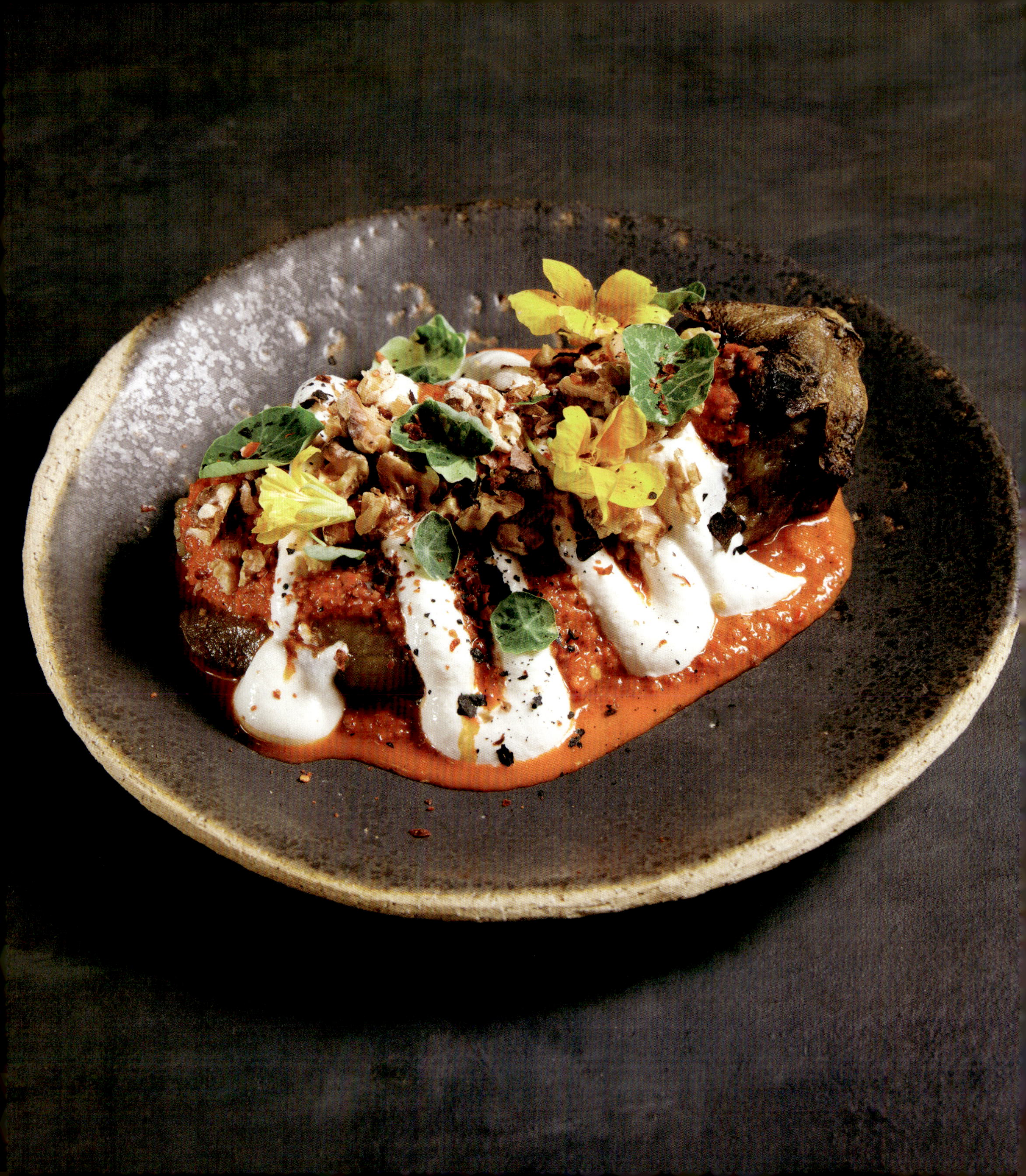

# Mohamad Orfali's Charred Eggplant Bayildi

*Orfali Bros, Dubai*

The first time I was in Dubai was when we were filming the "Cape Town" episode in the second season of the show. We had a long layover, it was over one hundred degrees, so what do you do? You go to the mall. I thought that was Dubai. It wasn't the first place I wanted to go back to for the show, but everybody told me I had to do it. We finally went in season seven, and I'm so glad we did. Dubai is probably the most dynamic city I've ever been to. It has a thriving immigrant population that makes up more than 85 percent of residents. Think about having that number of people from around the world in a single city with more than three million residents, and how it would change everything, especially the food. In Dubai, you can walk into a restaurant or café, go to a market, or walk up to a cart on the street, and you're transported to a whole other country—a country you might not ever be able to go to otherwise. I've never been anyplace like it.

Probably the best example of that food diversity in one spot is at Orfali Bros, where the head chef, Mohamad Orfali, and his brothers Wassim and Omar, the pastry chefs, take inspiration from Aleppo, Syria (where they grew up), and apply it to cuisines from all over the world. Every single thing I had there was fantastic, including this charred eggplant with a yogurt-tahini sauce (it's based on a traditional Syrian dish). I couldn't stop eating. When we're filming, I try to pace myself because we've usually got at least one other place, maybe two or three, to go to in a day. I had already hit that point when I was going to have to politely say I was stuffed, and then Mohamad says, "You know, I have a burger." (I recommend you stop reading this and go straight to page 95 for that recipe.) Then, after the burger, Mohamad brings out Wassim and Omar, and they start handing over plate after plate with the most incredible works of art on them. Their pastries were not only beautiful, they were better than some of the very best I've had in France, Italy, or anywhere else. That's the power of so much diversity in one city.

> *Dubai is a city of opportunities. Opening a restaurant here has given us the opportunity to create something new in our cuisine. There are no rules, but we respect traditions. Every dish has a story behind it that shows our roots, but we don't serve Syrian or even Emirati cuisine. We are modern chefs with our own modern thoughts. We call it Community Cuisine . . . food for everyone. This is my spin on imam bayildi, only with smoked eggplant (my personal favorite way to cook eggplant; it adds complexity).* —MOHAMAD

**FEEDS 4 AS A MAIN (GENEROUSLY); 8 OR MORE AS A SIDE DISH**

**Charred and Cured Eggplant and Red Peppers (recipe follows)**

**MAKDOUS MUHAMMARA**

1 medium garlic clove

7 tablespoons good-quality Syrian or Turkish chili pepper paste (see Tips)

2 tablespoons extra-virgin olive oil

1 tablespoon Turkish sour cherry vinegar, or 1 tablespoon white wine vinegar plus 1 teaspoon sour cherry or other tart jam

Coarse sea salt

Mohamad's Tarator (page 322)

¾ cup (100g) walnuts, lightly toasted

**TO SERVE**

About ½ teaspoon ground Aleppo pepper

A few pinches chili threads or cayenne pepper

Small handful nasturtiums (leaves and petals) or red vein sorrel leaves or watercress

---

**Prep:** Remove the Charred and Cured Eggplant and Red Peppers from the refrigerator a few hours before serving.

**Make the makdous muhammara:** Peel the charred red peppers and remove the seeds (don't rinse).

In a blender or food processor, combine the charred red peppers, garlic, Syrian chili pepper paste, extra-virgin olive oil, cherry vinegar, and ½ teaspoon salt and mix until smooth. Season with more salt, if needed, and set aside until ready to serve.

**Assemble the bayildi:** Spread a spoonful or two of the makdous muhammara down the center of four large plates, lay the eggplant on top of the sauce, and spread more makdous muhammara generously over the top of each. Dollop Mohamad's Tarator generously over each eggplant and spread it out with the back of a spoon; it should be very thick (for a more formal presentation, pipe the yogurt sauce in a tight zigzag pattern across the eggplant).

Break up the largest toasted walnuts with your hands and scatter them over the eggplant. For a shared plate or buffet, at this point you can cut each eggplant horizontally to make several smaller portions and reassemble each on a serving platter.

**Serve:** Just before serving, sprinkle several pinches of Aleppo pepper over each eggplant and a few chili threads or a pinch of cayenne pepper, then sprinkle a few pinches of the chopped, charred eggplant skin over each. Tuck a few baby nasturtiums, red vein sorrel, watercress, or baby arugula leaves on top of each eggplant, and serve.

## CHARRED AND CURED EGGPLANT AND RED PEPPERS

**Prep:** At least 1 day before you plan to make the bayildi, prepare a grill for direct cooking over high heat, heat a pizza oven until moderately hot (around 500°F [260°C]), or preheat the oven to 400°F (205°C).

Pierce the eggplant in several places with a small knife.

**Grill method:** Grill the eggplant and red peppers (if using a pizza oven, put them on a baking sheet or in a cast iron skillet), flipping each occasionally.

Grill the red peppers until softened and well charred on all sides. Transfer the whole peppers to a bowl, cover with plastic wrap, let cool, and refrigerate.

Grill the eggplant until the skin is completely blackened like a roasted marshmallow and the flesh is buttery soft throughout; it should be very squishy when gently squeezed with tongs. The time will vary depending on the thickness of the eggplant and heat source.

**Oven method:** Wrap each eggplant in foil and put them on a rimmed sheet pan. Put the red peppers (unwrapped) on another sheet pan.

Roast the eggplant until a knife easily pierces the flesh to the very center but the eggplant has not fully collapsed, 40 minutes to 1 hour; with very thick eggplants, the roasting time may be longer to truly soften the flesh.

Roast the peppers, flipping occasionally to char all sides, until fully softened and blackened in spots, 25 to 30 minutes. Transfer the hot peppers to a bowl, cover, and let cool completely.

4 medium Globe or Italian eggplants, all roughly the same size

1 pound (about 500g) red bell peppers (2 large or 3 medium)

## TIPS

*Yes, any dish from a great chef like Mohamad is going to take some time to make, but after charring and curing the eggplant and bell peppers, it's easy to assemble. You can skip the harder-to-find garnishes like nasturtiums and chili threads and use staple ingredients like arugula and a pinch of cayenne to make this a special weeknight vegetarian main course; the components also pack well for a picnic or potluck (add the final garnishes just before serving).*

*For the makdous muhammara, which can also be made ahead (and is excellent on top of hummus or a bowl of white beans), a good-quality Syrian (or Turkish) pepper paste (a thick, smoky paste made from Aleppo peppers) is worth seeking out; most commercial jarred pastes lack a fresh pepper flavor. The paste from Kōy (koypantry.com), an artisan importer, is a great stand-in for Mohamad's homemade paste.*

Remove the foil and move the sheet pan close to the broiler so the skins of the eggplant are very close to the flames. Broil the eggplant, flipping each occasionally to evenly char all sides, until the skin blackens and begins to split. Or, remove the grate of a gas stovetop burner, turn the flame to high, and hold 1 eggplant at a time directly in the flame like you're toasting a marshmallow until it chars and blackens on all sides. Be patient, as it takes longer than on a grill.

**Cure the eggplant:** Gently peel the eggplant with your fingers, leaving the stem of the eggplant attached and the flesh in one piece. Set aside 3 or 4 tablespoons of the most blackened bits of eggplant skin (for garnish) and lay them out on a paper towel or cutting board to thoroughly dry overnight, then loosely cover and store at room temperature.

Season the peeled eggplants generously on all sides with salt (about ½ teaspoon per eggplant), stack them in a strainer or colander set over a bowl to catch the juices, and loosely cover.

Refrigerate the eggplant and red peppers overnight.

The next day, remove the eggplant from the strainer (discard the liquid). You can use the eggplant and peppers now, or cover refrigerate them for 1 more day. (The charred flavor will start to dissipate the longer they are refrigerated.)

# Sieger Bayer's Golden Beets with Tofu Crema and Verjus

*Here's Looking At You, Los Angeles*

Here's Looking At You, which goes by HLAY, is an example of how the restaurant scene in LA has changed from excellent to be on the level of some of the very best restaurants in the world. Lien Ta, who is one of the most gracious people and will probably be there when you go, and Jonathan Whitener, the founding chef (he sadly passed away), opened it together back in 2016. Everything is fantastic, like these beets that Sieger Bayer, who was the head chef when we were working on this book, puts on the menu when they're in season.

> *When I was at the farmers' market one week, a farmer I know had all of these golden beets and just handed over pounds of them. We didn't have a lot of vegan options on the menu at the time, and this is what they became. For the marinade, you want to cook the caramel sauce until it's a little darker and smokier than a regular caramel, but not totally burnt out. When the beets go in the marinade, they can hang in for a while (even the leftovers), so if you're serving this for a party, you can even grill them ahead. With the pepita crumble, it's the more the merrier.* —SIEGER

**Grill or sear the beets (optional):** An hour or two before serving, preheat a grill over medium heat. Or heat a grill pan or cast iron skillet over medium heat until very hot.

Brush the peeled beets lightly with olive oil and grill both cut sides until charred but not softened, 1 to 2 minutes per side. Or sear the beets in batches in the hot pan until golden brown in spots (don't crowd the pan).

**FEEDS 6**

Roasted Golden Beets with Verjus Marinade (recipe follows)

Extra-virgin olive oil, for grilling

Sieger's Vegan Soya Crema (page 311), at cold room temperature

Freshly ground black pepper

1 lemon, quartered

**TO SERVE**

Generous spoonful (about 2 tablespoons) Toasted Pepita Crumble (recipe follows)

- 2 pounds (910g) golden beets (about 2 large bunches)
- 2 large, juicy oranges (Navel), quartered
- 4 medium garlic cloves, smashed
- 2 leafy sprigs fresh thyme
- ¼ cup (60ml) champagne or white wine vinegar
- ½ teaspoon coriander seeds, smashed, or 3 to 4 generous pinches ground coriander
- ½ teaspoon black peppercorns
- ¼ teaspoon red pepper flakes
- Kosher or coarse sea salt
- ½ cup (60ml) white sour grape juice (verjus or husroum; see Tips), or unoaked white wine plus 1½ tablespoons white wine vinegar
- ¼ cup (50g) granulated sugar
- ¼ cup (56g) packed light brown sugar
- 1 tablespoon tamari or good-quality soy sauce

**Marinate the beets:** Pour the Verjus Marinade over the beets, toss to combine, and let marinate for at least 1 hour or up to 4 hours.

**Assemble and serve:** Mound a generous spoonful (about 3 tablespoons) of Sieger's Vegan Soya Crema in the center of each serving plate. Scoop the beets out of the Verjus Marinade (reserve the marinade) and arrange them around the crema. Lightly drizzle the marinade (about ½ tablespoon) over the beets and season with pepper and a squeeze of lemon juice. Sprinkle the Toasted Pepita Crumble generously over the beets and crema and serve.

For a shared plate, arrange everything on a large serving platter, or simply serve the vegan crema in a bowl alongside the beets.

Cover and refrigerate any leftover beets in the marinade overnight (for a more intense flavor), or drain and reserve the marinade.

## ROASTED GOLDEN BEETS WITH VERJUS MARINADE

**Prep:** Preheat the oven to 350°F (175°C).

Trim off the beet tops and root ends and wash the bulbs well to remove any grit. Cut the beets into wedges roughly 2 inches (5cm) thick.

**Roast the beets:** Arrange the beets and oranges snugly in a single layer in a large casserole dish (9x13 inches/23x33cm or similar) and tuck the garlic cloves and thyme in between. (Don't use a large sheet pan, as too much of the liquid will evaporate.)

In a measuring cup, combine the champagne vinegar and ½ cup (120ml) water and pour the marinade over the beets. Scatter the coriander seeds, black peppercorns, red pepper flakes, and 1 teaspoon salt evenly over the beets. Cover the baking dish with aluminum foil and bake until the beets can be pierced easily with a fork but are still fairly firm, about 1¼ hours. (Taste a beet; they will continue to cook as they cool but shouldn't be too firm to eat at this point.) Set the beets aside to cool, covered, for at least 30 minutes.

Peel the beets (reserve the beet pan juices and oranges) and transfer to a bowl.

Squeeze the juice from the oranges into the beet pan juices and strain through a sieve.

**Make the marinade:** Have everything ready by the stove: a whisk or heatproof spatula, the sour grape juice, and reserved beet pan juices.

In a medium saucepan with tall sides (the hot sugar syrup will bubble up as you make the caramel sauce), spread out the granulated sugar and brown sugar in a single layer.

Cook the sugar mixture (don't stir) over medium-high heat until almost fully melted, 4 to 5 minutes. Stir and continue to cook, swirling the pan or stirring occasionally to redistribute the sugar caramelizing at the edges, until it's deep amber in color and smells toasty and is bubbling vigorously, 3 to 4 minutes.

Immediately remove the pan from the heat and, while stirring, slowly and carefully pour in the sour grape juice; the hot sugar will seize and bubble up at first. When the sugar has melted fully into the juice, whisk in the reserved beet pan juices, tamari, and ¼ teaspoon salt and boil for about 30 seconds to integrate the ingredients. Remove the pan from the heat and let the marinade cool completely.

Cover and refrigerate the roasted beets and marinade, separately, for at least 4 hours or up to 4 days.

## TIPS

*Instead of roasting the beets at high heat, these are almost poached in a spiced orange juice liquid as the oranges break down, so they take longer to cook than the typical roasted beets. Roast the beets and make the caramel marinade, crema, and pepita crumble ahead, and this is a quick and impressive vegan main course or salad for a party.*

*Verjus (French) or husroum (Arabic) is the juice of very sour, unfermented "green" (unripened) grapes. Most are made from a blend of grape varietals (single varietal verjus can get pricey, as it's often marketed as an alcohol-free wine). Husroum (often labeled "sour grape juice" at Middle Eastern markets) is usually the most affordable option. For a similar flavor, you can substitute an unoaked white wine like pinot grigio with a little white wine vinegar.*

THINGS TO SHARE • 169

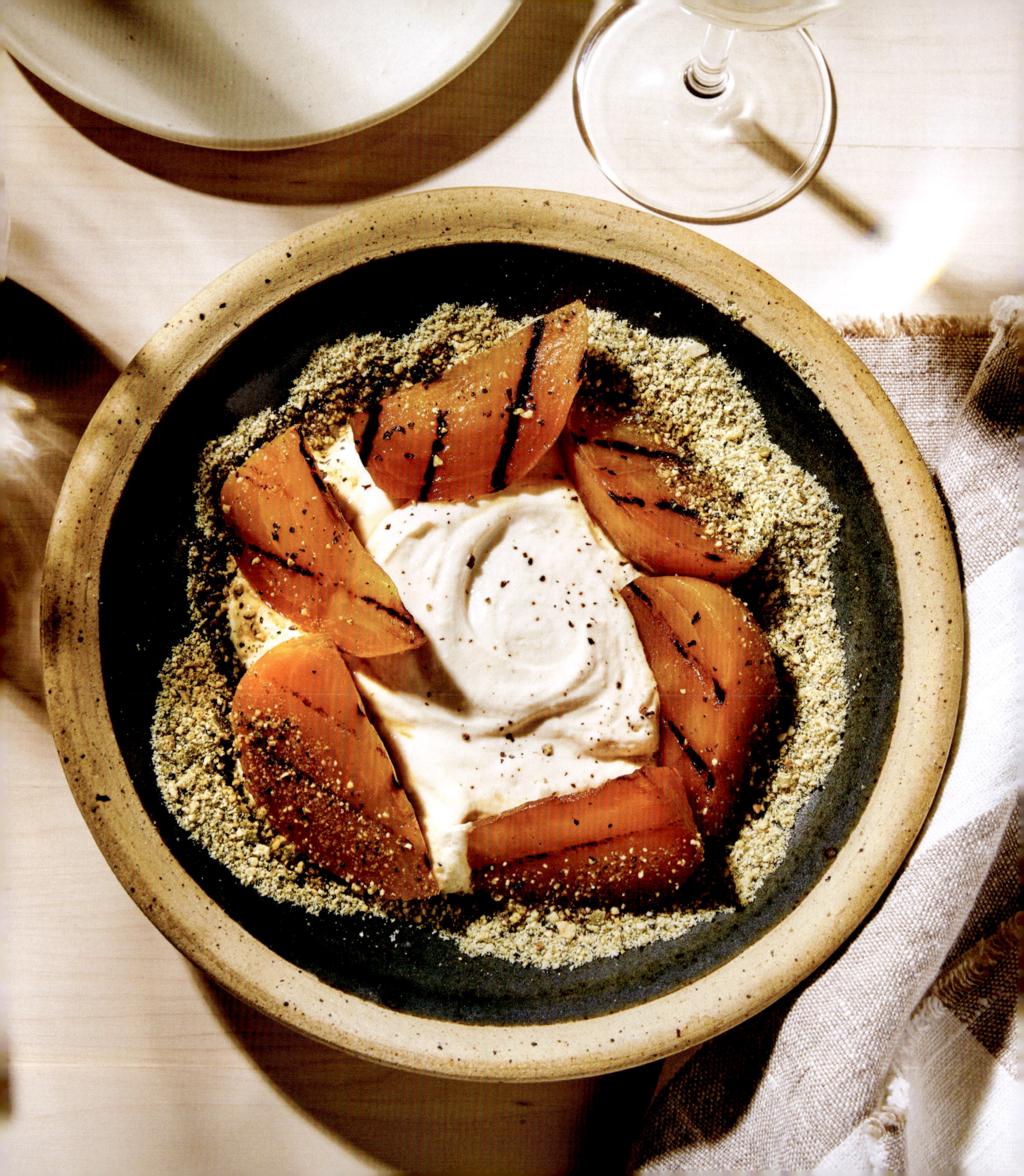

## TOASTED PEPITA CRUMBLE

Preheat the oven to 350°F (175°C).

On a rimmed sheet pan, mound the pepitas, sesame seeds, olive oil, and 1 teaspoon salt and mix well to evenly distribute the olive oil and salt.

Spread out the seed mix in an even layer and toast the seeds, stirring occasionally to redistribute them, until aromatic and the pepitas begin to brown along the edges, about 10 minutes. Transfer the seeds to a plate to cool.

In a blender, grind the seeds to a fine crumble, or grind them in batches in a molcajete or large mortar with a pestle. Season the seed crumble with salt; the mixture should be well salted, as it serves as a seasoning for the beets and crema.

Store in a dry, sealed container and store at room temperature for up to 1 week.

**MAKES A GENEROUS 1/2 CUP (ABOUT 90G)**

½ cup (60g) raw, unsalted pepitas

2 tablespoons sesame seeds

1 tablespoon extra-virgin olive oil

**Kosher or coarse sea salt**

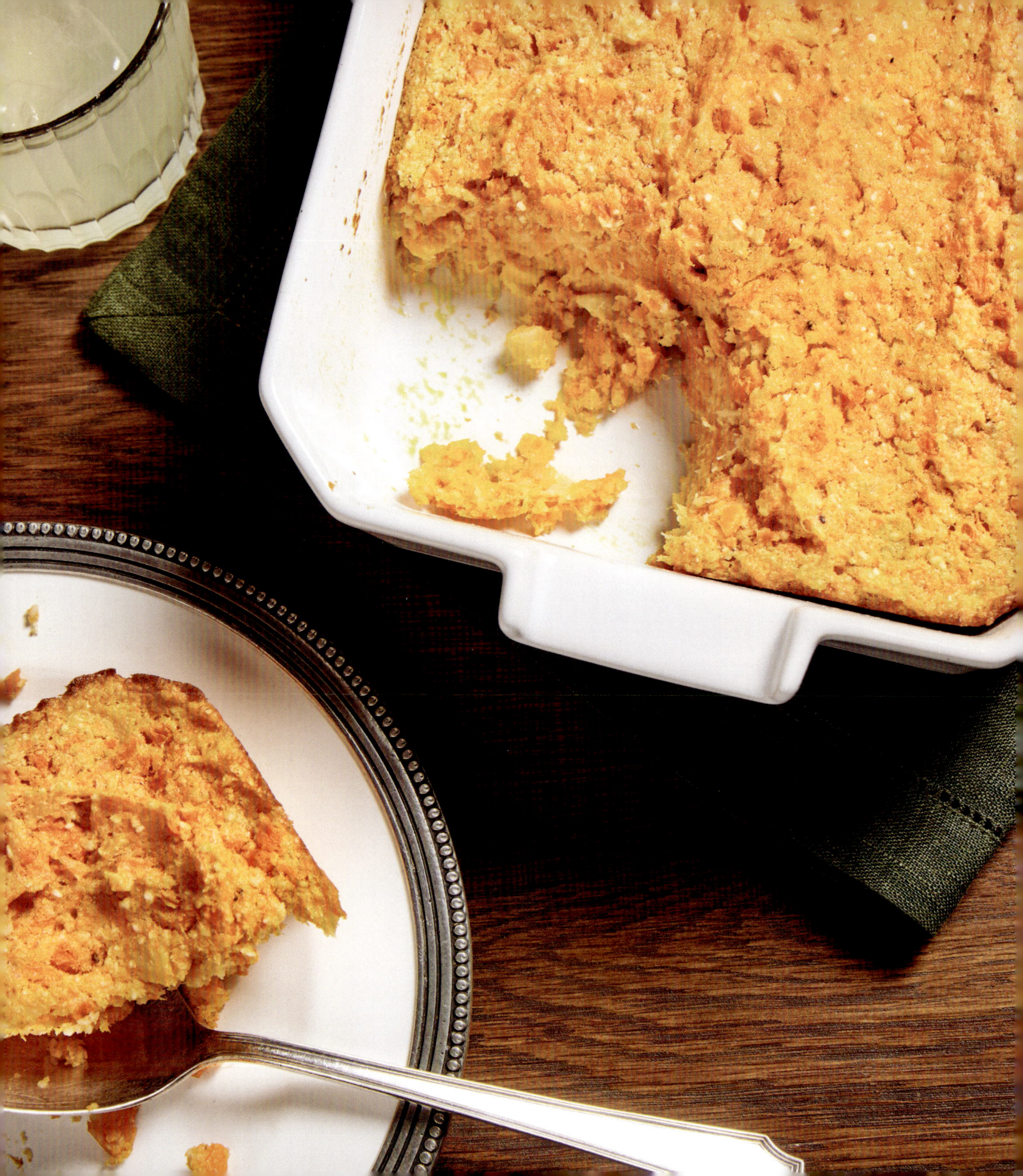

# Judy Gold's Carrot Kugel

📍 *New York*

The reason you see Judy Gold in so many episodes of the show is because she's one of the funniest people I know. Just shop with her at Zabar's sometime. We've been good friends for years; she would even go over to my parents' apartment to check in on them when they were getting older. She's the sister I never had.

> *Don't let the name fool you. This is not like chocolate or vanilla pudding; it's a kugel (Yiddish for a baked casserole). I grew up in a kosher home, and my mother would make carrot pudding for Passover because the recipe calls for matzoh meal. She would make it for Rosh Hashanah as well because it tastes so good with brisket or turkey. This kugel actually tastes great with everything, and it's vegetarian. The key to making it to perfection is beating the egg whites until they are very firm and then folding them in gently. Also, when you drain the juice from the can of crushed pineapple, put it in a glass, add some ice and vodka, and enjoy.*
>
> *Recently, I've taken to substituting bread crumbs for the matzoh meal for Thanksgiving, and it's been a huge hit! I love how the skeptics always question it: "Carrot pudding? I've never heard of that . . . okay, Judy, I'll try a little piece." That piece always turns into another and then another. And the best part: kids love it, too! I never weigh the carrots. I get one large bunch, nothing scrawny, plus two extra carrots. And I ALWAYS make a double batch because there are never any leftovers. (The baking time—exactly one hour—is the same.) My mouth is watering as I write this.* —JUDY

---

**FEEDS 8**

1¾ pounds (800g) carrots (about 1 dozen medium to large)

Kosher salt

1 8-ounce (225g) can crushed pineapple (about ⅔ cup/140g pulp)

3 large eggs, yolks and whites separated, at room temperature

½ cup (120ml) vegetable oil, plus more for the baking dish

1 cup (120g) matzoh meal

½ cup (100g) granulated sugar

THINGS TO SHARE • 173

**TO FEED 16
(JUDY'S DOUBLE BATCH)**

3½ pounds (1.6kg) carrots (2 dozen)

Kosher salt

2 8-ounce (225g) cans crushed pineapple (about 1⅓ cup/280g pulp)

6 large eggs, yolks and whites separated, at room temperature

1 cup (240ml) vegetable oil

2 cups (240g) matzoh meal

1 cup (200g) granulated sugar

**Boil the carrots:** Peel the carrots and cut them into thick medallions (1 inch/2.5cm).

Fill a large pot with enough water to generously cover the carrots, bring the water to a boil, and add 1 to 2 tablespoons of salt; it should taste like very well salted pasta water (this is the only salt in the kugel). Add the carrots, cover, and boil until easily pierced with a fork but not falling apart, about 15 minutes; test several of the largest carrots. Strain.

Return the carrots to the pot and, while still warm, mash with a potato masher until only small lumps remain, and transfer to a large bowl.

**Make the kugel:** Preheat the oven to 350°F (175°C). Lightly oil a 2-quart (2L) baking dish (roughly 8x8 inches/20cm), or to double the recipe, a 9x13-inch (23x33cm) casserole dish.

Strain the crushed pineapple over a small bowl and press down on the pulp to strain off most of the juice. Add the pulp to the bowl with the carrots. (Make a cocktail with the juice!)

Pour the egg whites into a stand mixer bowl fitted with a whisk attachment and put the yolks in the bowl with the (fully cooled!) carrots. To the carrots, add the vegetable oil, matzoh meal, and sugar, and mix until the matzoh is fully incorporated.

Beat the egg whites on medium-high speed until stiff peaks form, 2 to 3 minutes; they should hold their shape when the whisk is lifted. Use a rubber spatula to gently fold about a quarter of the egg whites into the carrot mixture, then gently fold in the remaining whites, scraping the bottom of the bowl to fully incorporate them; don't overmix. Scrape the batter into the prepared baking dish and roughly smooth out the top.

Bake, rotating the dish front to back halfway through, for 1 hour; the kugel will only brown at the very edges. (Follow Judy's method:

the baking time is the exact same for a single and double recipe.) Run a knife along the edges of the kugel and let cool for about 15 minutes, or cool completely.

**Serve:** Cut the kugel into squares and serve.

To rewarm the kugel, cover the baking dish tightly with foil and bake in a low oven (275°F/135°C) just until warm in the center, 20 to 25 minutes.

Cover and refrigerate any leftovers for up to 5 days.

### TIP

*If you're using unseasoned "plain" bread crumbs instead of matzoh meal (made from only flour and water), check the ingredients; many brands contain sodium and other ingredients (reduce the salt to about 1 tablespoon when boiling the carrots).*

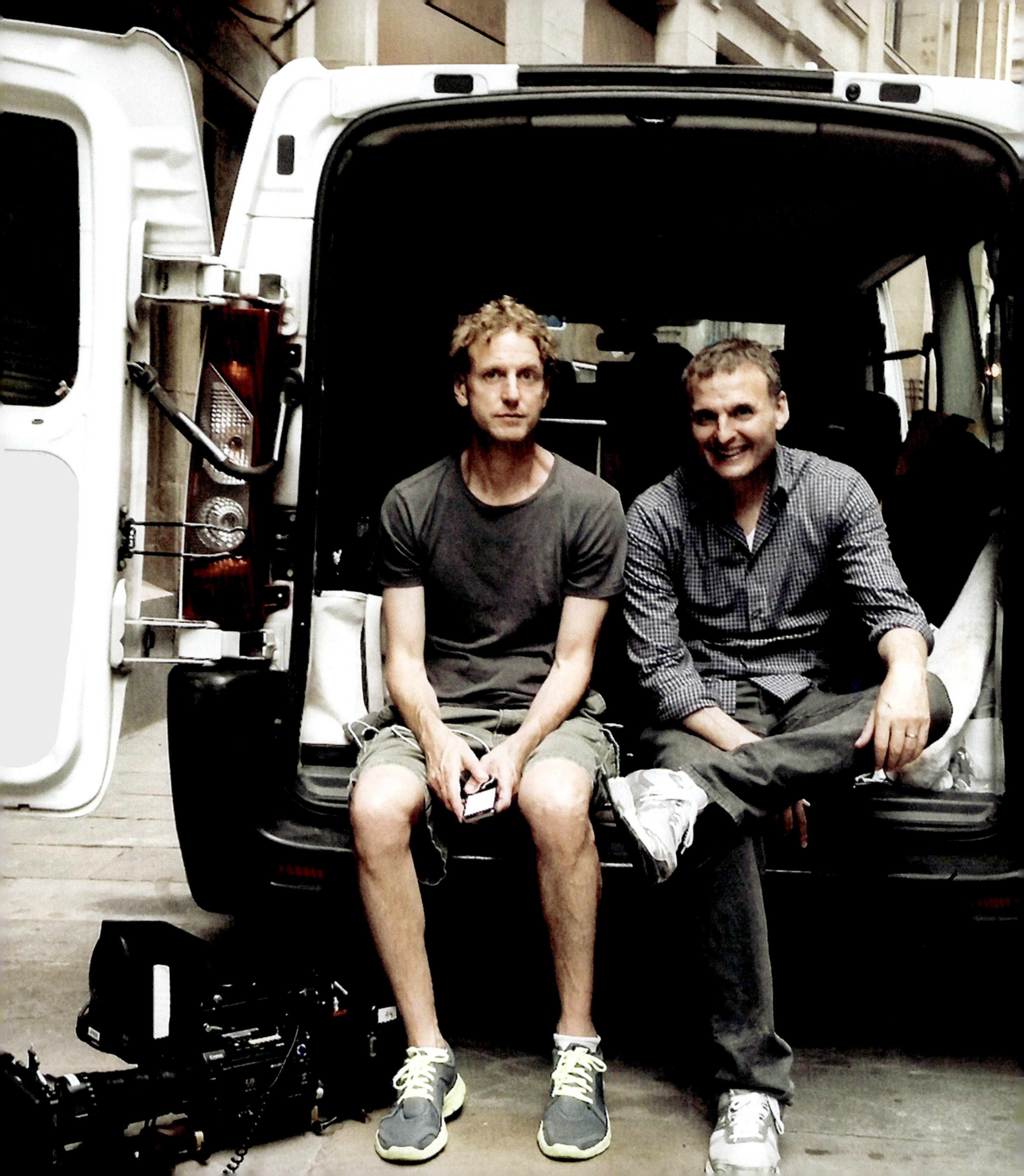

# AN ENTIRE CHAPTER FOR RICHARD

I make fun of Richard, because he deserves it. But the truth is he's the world's best brother, my best friend, and even my business partner. If you like the show at all, it's because of him.

I told him he could put anything he wanted in this book, and this is what he picked. Alcohol. He should be ashamed of himself.

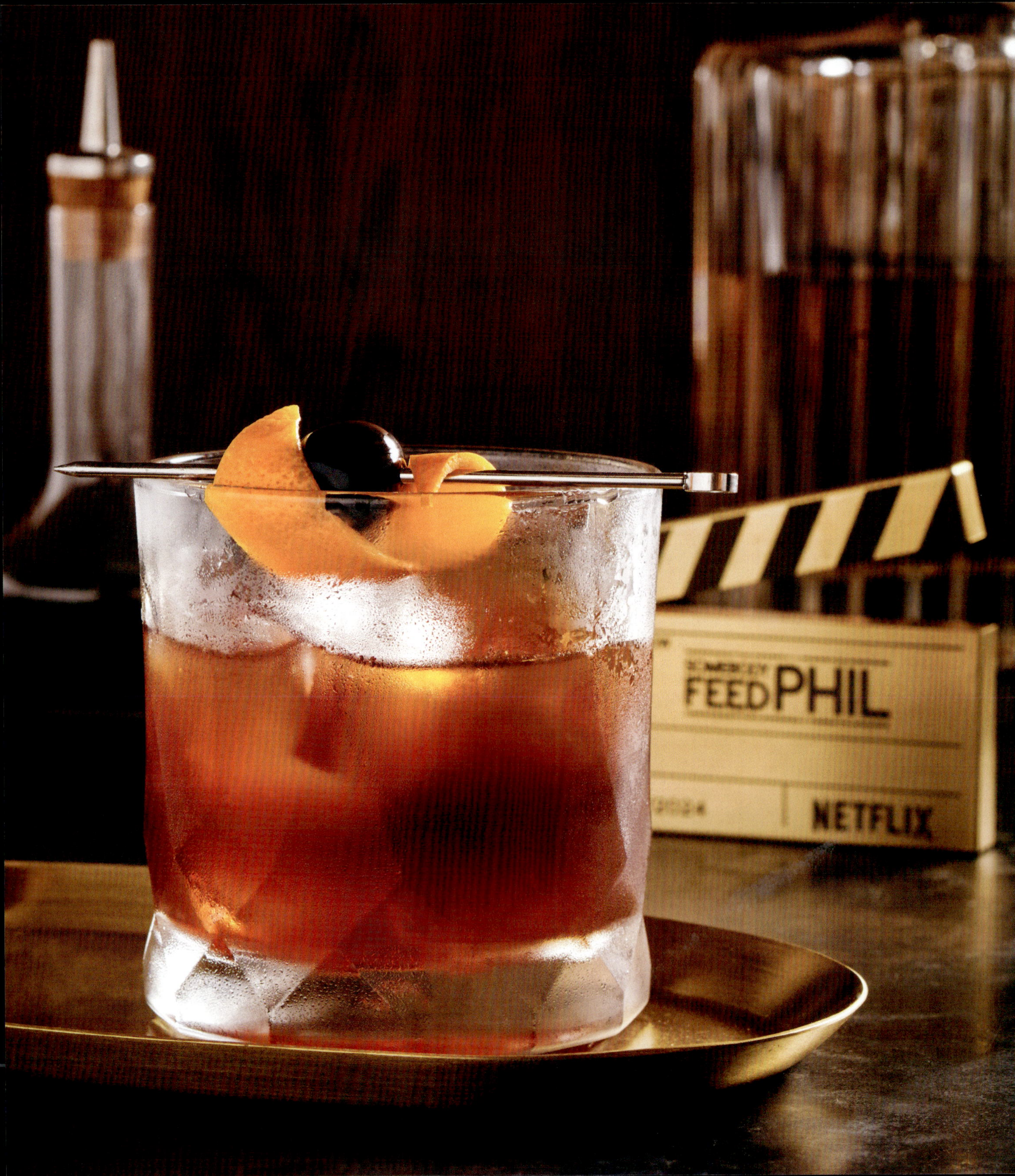
FEED PHIL
NETFLIX

# Richard's Staten Island

*I love old-fashioneds (rye or bourbon, sugar cube, bitters, twist of lemon peel) and Manhattans (rye, sweet vermouth, bitters, maraschino cherry), as well as Brooklyns (rye, dry vermouth, amaro, maraschino liqueur), so I made a bastardized version of all three one night for myself and my daughter, Tess. It's become our thing. She dubbed it the Staten Island. (No offense.)*

*Blood oranges are nice if you have them, but I use whatever citrus I've got in the house. I like this with rye; Tess prefers bourbon. I like a maraschino cherry (get a good brand like Luxardo); she leaves it out (doesn't like them). I don't measure anything out precisely. You can adjust the flavors once you make the cocktail. For a dryer cocktail, start with about half a shot of amaro.* —RICHARD

**MAKES 1 COCKTAIL**

¼ small blood orange, tangerine, mandarin, or orange, plus 1 strip of zest

1 shot (1½ ounces/45 ml) rye or bourbon

About ⅔ shot (1 ounce/30ml) dry vermouth

About ⅔ shot (1 ounce/30ml) amaro (Averna)

Dash of bitters (Angostura)

1 good-quality maraschino cherry (Luxardo), plus a splash of the syrup

In an old-fashioned glass, muddle the citrus well. Discard the orange if you'd like, or just leave it.

Fill the glass with ice, add the rye or bourbon, dry vermouth, amaro, bitters, and cherry syrup, and stir. Adjust the flavors if needed (more rye or bourbon for a less sweet cocktail; more amaro or cherry juice for sweetness).

Garnish with the orange twist and cherry and serve.

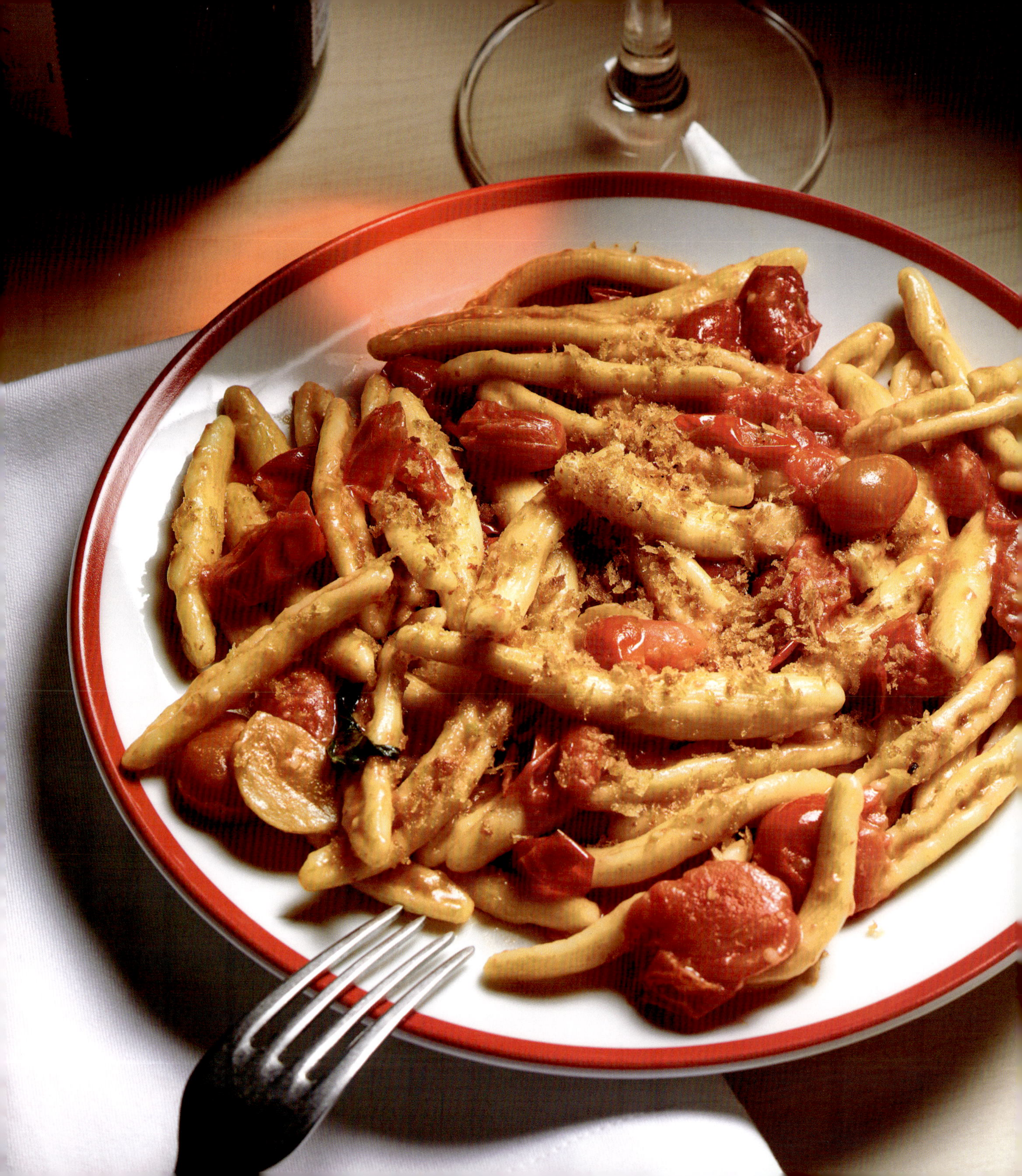

# THE REASON I PACE MYSELF

This chapter starts with two of my favorite pastas—because who doesn't like pasta—and ends with braciole and seafood risotto. I probably should have called this book *Everybody Loves Italian Food*.

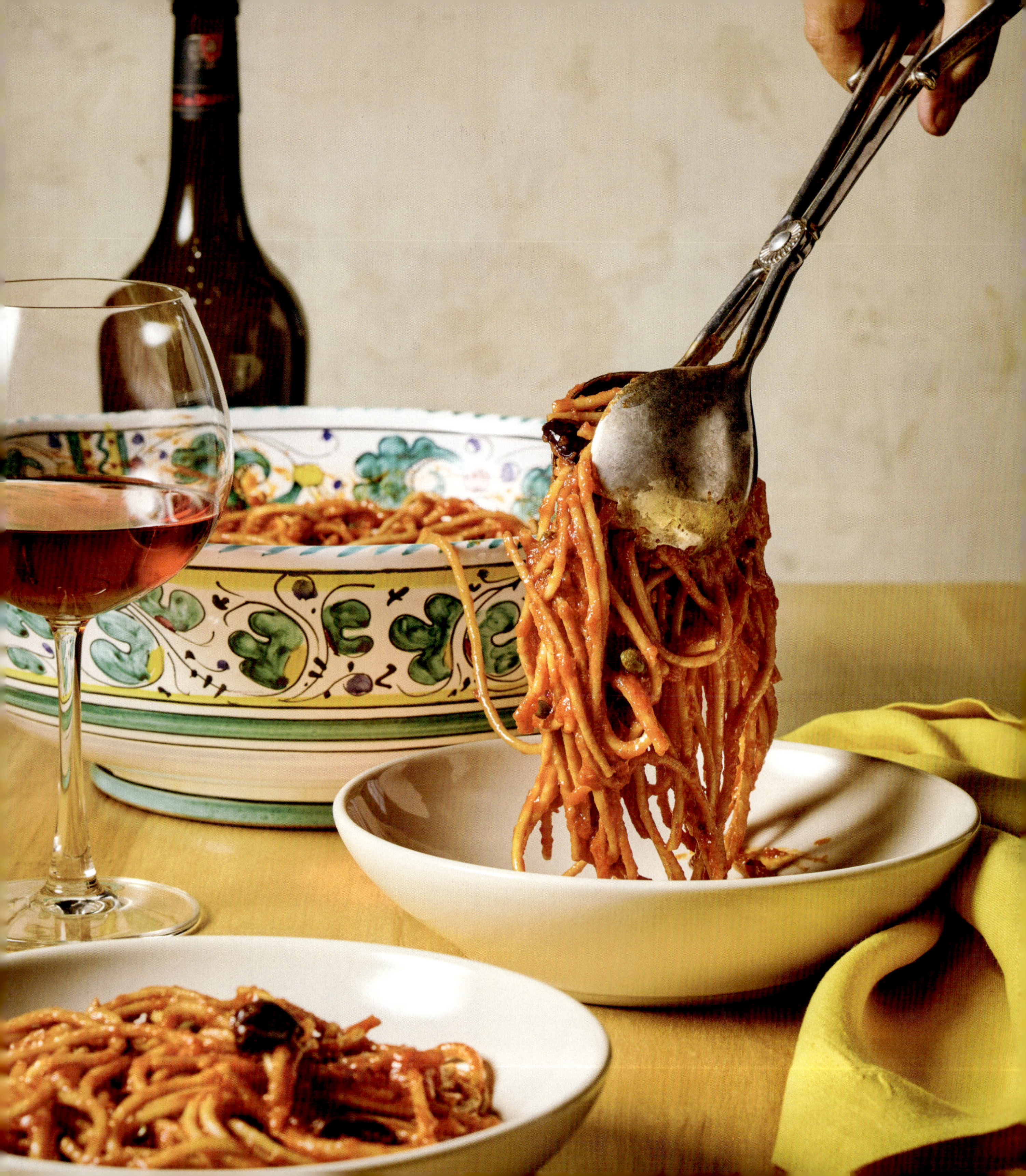

# Daniele Uditi's Spaghetti alla Puttanesca

*Pizzana, Los Angeles*

We have a tremendous pizza scene in LA. I would dare even say it's better here today than anywhere else. The reason I don't have a single pizza recipe in this book is pizza is something I always want to buy from somebody who makes it every single day. I have a wood-burning pizza oven in my kitchen; it was one thing I always dreamed of. We use it when a great chef like Daniele Uditi comes over; it's special for the whole family and anyone who comes to Movie Night. Daniele is from Naples and has been baking bread, making pizza, and cooking since he was a kid. (His aunt ran a bakery, his mother was a chef, and his grandfather was a pastry chef.) When he came to LA to consult on a couple of restaurants, like a lot of us here, he decided to stay. You can taste that family history and California influence in his food. If you're in LA, you need to go to Pizzana, his pizza and pasta place. (The original is in Brentwood; he's got a couple around town now.)

During COVID, Daniele would come over to our house and prepare these outdoor lunches for the family. It was one of the things we looked forward to the most. This pasta is my favorite, and he actually taught me how to make it. It's a classic spaghetti alla puttanesca with olives, anchovies, and capers, only Daniele toasts the dry spaghetti in his pizza oven to give it that incredible freshly baked bread flavor. And, unlike making a really good pizza crust, you can toast the spaghetti at home in the oven and get the same result—you just have to be careful not to burn the pasta. You do need to get good fresh Italian tomato sauce, the kind that comes in a jar like Mutti. It's different from the American ones in a can. Daniele never shows up at our house without a few jars.

---

**FEEDS 4 TO 5**

**TOMATO BROTH**

Extra-virgin olive oil

1 garlic clove, minced

1 24.5-ounce (700g) jar fresh tomato puree (passata or "strained tomatoes"; Mutti or Pomi)

Kosher or coarse sea salt

**PASTA**

16 ounces (about 500g) Charred Spaghetti (recipe follows)

½ cup (120ml) good-quality classic Italian marinara or tomato-basil sauce (Mutti)

2 to 3 teaspoons Calabrian chili pepper paste (Tutto Calabria crushed peppers or paste)

*(ingredients continue)*

10 good-quality oil packed anchovy fillets (Agostino Recca, chili pepper–spiced or regular)

⅓ cup (50g) drained and rinsed capers

⅓ cup (50g) drained, pitted kalamata olives, broken into 4 to 5 pieces with your fingers

Small handful (3 to 4 tablespoons) finely chopped flat-leaf parsley, divided

Extra-virgin finishing olive oil, for drizzling

**Make the tomato broth:** Drizzle enough olive oil in a medium, cold stockpot or Dutch oven to lightly coat the bottom (about 2 tablespoons). Add the garlic and turn the heat to medium. Gently sauté the garlic, stirring occasionally with a wooden spoon, until fragrant and barely beginning to brown on the edges, 3 to 4 minutes. Add the fresh tomato puree, 3 cups (720ml) of water, and 2½ to 3 teaspoons salt and bring to a simmer. Turn off the heat, taste, and season the tomato broth with more salt, if needed.

**Cook the pasta and make the sauce:** In an extra-large skillet or pan large enough to fit the Charred Spaghetti with a little extra room (see Tips), heat about ¼ cup (60ml) of olive oil over medium heat. Add the charred spaghetti, pushing it around the pan with a wooden spoon until the strands are evenly coated in olive oil, and gently cook for about 1 minute.

Add 1½ to 2 cups (480ml) of the hot tomato broth to the skillet, just to barely cover the pasta.

Increase the heat to medium-high, bring the broth to a boil, and gently shuffle the pasta back and forth across the bottom of the pan with the wooden spoon to keep it from sticking.

When the pasta soaks up the broth, keep adding more, about 1 cup (240ml) at a time, and push the pasta around in the pot until it's soft enough to stir. After about 10 minutes, most of the broth should have been absorbed by the pasta. Add the tomato sauce and 2 teaspoons Calabrian chili pepper paste and continue to cook the pasta, stirring, for about 2 minutes. Adjust the spiciness with more chili peppers, then gently stir in the anchovies, capers, olives, and two-thirds of the parsley.

**Serve:** Divide the pasta among four to five plates, drizzle a little finishing olive oil on top, and scatter a little parsley over each. Eat the pasta like an Italian: right now.

# CHARRED SPAGHETTI

> *I do this in a pizza oven, but here you use an oven. The spaghetti must be fully toasted for the flavor, but you need to watch the pan closely; if it gets too dark, it will taste bitter.*
> **—DANIELE**

**MAKES 16 OUNCES (ABOUT 500G)**

1 16-ounce (about 450g) package good-quality spaghetti (Mancini or De Cecco; see Tips)

**Prep:** Put a sheet pan or other rimmed metal pan that will fit the spaghetti without breaking it within 2 to 3 inches (5 to 7.5cm) of the broiler. Turn the broiler to high and let the pan heat for about 2 minutes.

**Toast the spaghetti:** Remove the hot pan from the oven.

If your broiler covers a larger surface area, arrange as much spaghetti on the pan as will fit beneath or within a few inches of the heat source. For example, if your broiler has a single flame running down the center of the oven, put about a third of the spaghetti in the middle of the hot pan and fan out the spaghetti so the pile is only 3 to 4 inches (7.5 to 10cm) wide. The strands don't need to be in a single layer but shouldn't be more than two to three layers deep.

Broil the spaghetti for about 30 seconds, take the pan out of the oven, and use tongs to gently redistribute the strands so they toast evenly. Continue to broil the spaghetti strands, checking and redistributing them every 15 to 20 seconds (remove any that are already well toasted), until most are light golden brown and the surface has blistered, 1½ to 3 minutes; the pasta should look like little toasted bread sticks. (The length of time to toast all the spaghetti will depend on your broiler's strength and proximity.) Remove the toasted spaghetti from the hot sheet pan.

Discard any strands of pasta that are dark brown or deeply burnt in

## TIPS

*Like when toasting nuts, the oven-toasted spaghetti quickly goes from barely colored to burnt. It's a good idea to get a backup package of spaghetti in case you burn the first.*

*An extra-large (14-inch/35.5cm) sauté pan, cast iron skillet, or round braising dish is large enough to cook the dry, toasted spaghetti strands (the spaghetti will lay flat in most 12-inch/30.5cm skillets, but it is difficult to move the pasta as it cooks without breaking it in half). A metal or cast iron rectangular roasting pan or dish (8x12-inch/20x30.5cm) can also be used. If you're doubling or tripling the recipe, you can even use a large turkey roasting pan.*

*Daniele's favorite anchovies, Agostino Recca, are larger and meatier than most; if you use another brand, use 12 to 14 anchovies. Fresh Italian-style tomato puree, also called passata or "strained tomatoes," is sold in jars or boxes and made from fresh, not cooked, tomatoes.*

spots (taste a small piece to make sure it's not bitter); if you've only discarded a dozen or so strands, you'll have plenty for the pasta, but otherwise toast a few more strands.

If not making the pasta right away, let the spaghetti cool completely, wrap in plastic wrap, and set aside for up to 6 hours.

*When you make the spaghetti a la puttanesca, the method of cooking dry spaghetti directly in the pan by slowly adding a tomato broth is called risottare (like when you make risotto). This version is easy to make at home, but you must remember one Italian rule: there is to be no broken spaghetti! Once you char the spaghetti in the oven, you need a pan large enough to fit the spaghetti so it lays flat. Also remember that the smoke point of olive oil is very low, so start with a cold pan to brown your garlic (medium heat, never higher!), then increase the heat when cooking the spaghetti. Use good Italian ingredients like Mutti tomatoes, big Angostino Recca anchovies (I like the ones with hot chili peppers), kalamata olives (pinched with your fingers, never sliced or chopped!), and the best spaghetti. I like Mancini, but even De Cecco will do.* —DANIELE

# Tracy Malachek's Cavatelli with Tomatoes, Anchovies, and Garlic Bread Crumbs

*Birdie's, Austin*

Austin is a place I always love to go. It's the most fun city with more music venues than even Nashville; the food is awesome; and best of all, the people are lovely. Two of those people are chef Tracy Malechek and her husband, Arjav Ezekiel, who I met when we were shooting the "Austin" episode for the sixth season of the show. My longtime friend Matthew Odam, the food critic for the *Austin American-Statesman*, said we had to go to their neighborhood restaurant, Birdie's, and he couldn't have been more right. Tracy and Arjav met in New York, where they both worked at Gramercy Tavern; she does the food, he does the wine. The whole place is about being together with people eating really good food. (Since we shot that episode, Birdie's was named *Food & Wine*'s Restaurant of the Year, and Tracy was nominated for the James Beard Award's "Best Chef: Texas.") There's no waitstaff—you get in line to place your order, go find a table and, if you're like me, maybe make a new friend at the table sitting next to you while you wait. The effect is the same as eating at the counter at a diner. The menu is constantly changing, and when we were there Tracy brought out this cavatelli. Make this and tell me it doesn't taste like you're in Italy.

### TIPS

*Tracy's home version of this pasta uses dried cavatelli (penne or rigatoni can be substituted); unlike Tracy's homemade cavatelli, most of the fresh cavatelli available in stores is made with ricotta, a flavor that doesn't work here.*

*Agostino Recca anchovies are very large and meaty; if you use another brand, use 5 or 6 anchovies.*

---

*Beyond really good ingredients, the most important technique in this otherwise simple recipe is controlling the sauce viscosity. You don't want a pasta that's too dry (add a little more pasta cooking water if so) or too soupy (cook the sauce a little bit longer). The sauce is really at its sweet spot when it "hugs" the pasta. (I tell my cooks at Birdie's this all the time!) For the finishing oil, the freshness, or the olive oil press date, really matters for the most vibrancy and flavor. It's the epitome of the saying "If you don't use it, you lose it."* —TRACY

**FEEDS 4 TO 5**

**Kosher or coarse sea salt**

**1½ pints (about 500g) very ripe, sweet cherry tomatoes**

**16 to 17 ounces (500g) good-quality dry cavatelli (Rustichella d'Abruzzo or Colacchio)**

**Extra-virgin olive oil, for sautéing**

**3 medium garlic cloves, thinly sliced**

**4 good-quality oil-packed anchovy fillets (Agostino Recca, chili pepper–spiced or regular), roughly chopped**

**½ teaspoon Italian pepperoncino or other crushed red pepper flakes**

**Generous pinch (about ¼ teaspoon) granulated sugar**

**8 large basil leaves**

**¼ cup (2 ounces/55g) unsalted butter, cut into cubes**

**¼ cup (20g) finely grated Pecorino Romano**

**Extra-virgin finishing olive oil, for drizzling**

**Prep:** Bring a large pot of well-salted water to a boil.

Cut the largest cherry tomatoes in half; leave the smallest whole.

**Cook the pasta and make the sauce:** When the water is boiling, cook the cavatelli according to the package directions just until al dente, 12 to 14 minutes; strain over a bowl and reserve about 1 cup (240ml) of the cooking water.

While the pasta cooks, drizzle enough olive oil in a large, cold saucepan to lightly coat the bottom (about 2 tablespoons). Add the garlic, and turn the heat to medium. Gently sauté the garlic, stirring occasionally with a wooden spoon, until fragrant and barely beginning to brown on the edges, 3 to 4 minutes. Add the anchovies and stir constantly until the fillets dissolve into the oil, about 30 seconds. Increase the heat to medium-high, add the cherry tomatoes, red pepper flakes, and sugar to the pan, and cook, stirring often, until the tomatoes have softened, about 5 minutes. Use the wooden spoon to lightly crush about half the tomatoes, starting with the largest; some should be smashed more than others to create a variety of textures.

**Finish the pasta:** When the pasta is ready, add about ¼ cup (60ml) of the reserved pasta cooking water to the sauce and stir vigorously until the smashed tomatoes cook down somewhat and the sauce reduces and thickens up slightly, about 1½ minutes. Add the hot cavatelli and continue to stir vigorously until the pasta has released its starch, about 1 minute; you will see the ingredients start to come together and form a more cohesive sauce. Tear the basil leaves in half and add them to the pan, then the butter, and stir constantly until the butter has melted. At this point, the cavatelli should be well coated in the sauce. If it seems dry, add another splash of the reserved pasta water; if it seems too loose, simmer the sauce 30 seconds to 1 minute longer to reduce the liquid. Turn off the heat.

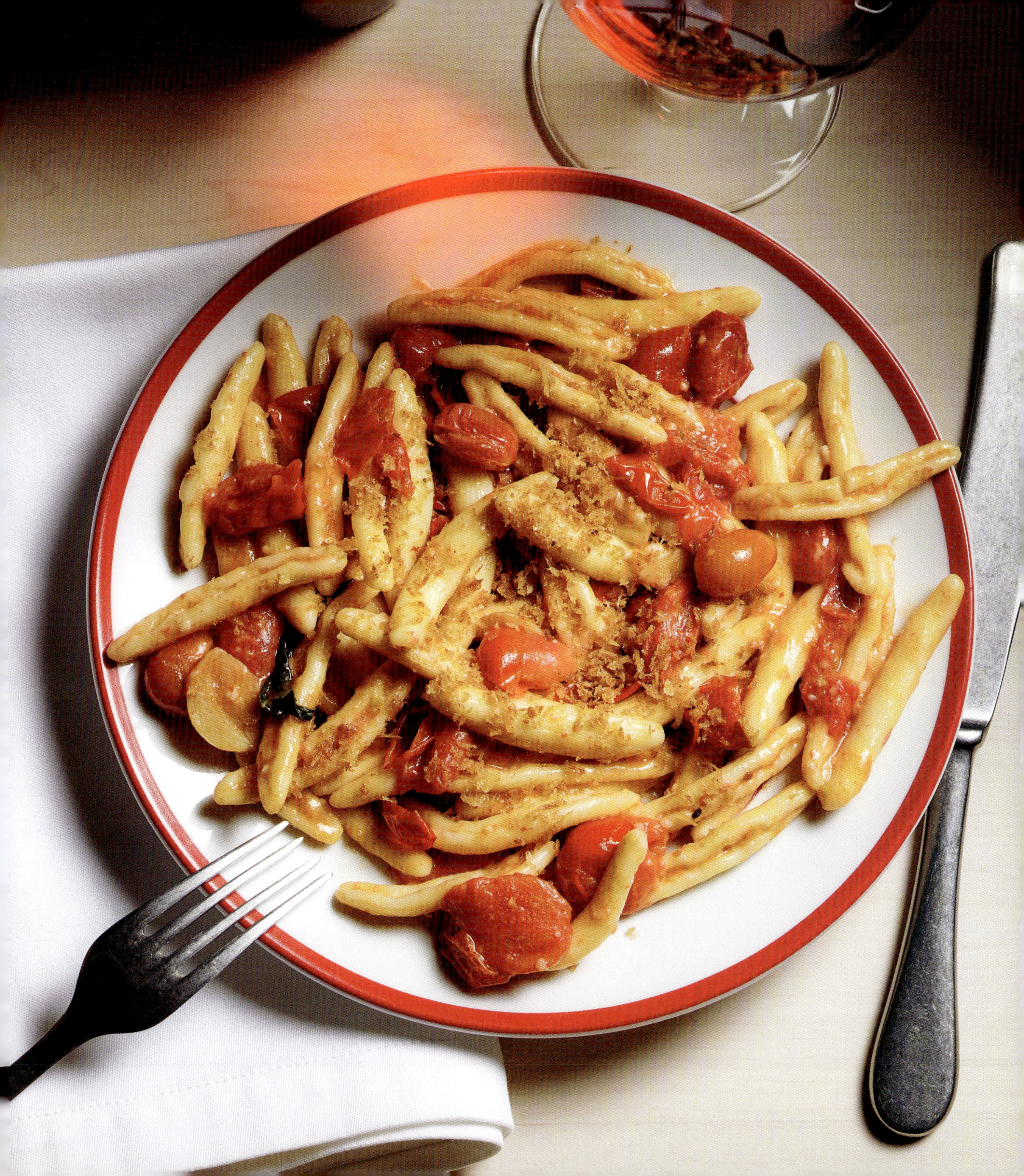

**TO SERVE**

3 to 4 tablespoons
Garlic Bread Crumbs
(recipe follows)

Sprinkle the Pecorino Romano over the pasta, then drizzle a little finishing olive oil (1 to 2 tablespoons) on top. Stir vigorously several times to further emulsify the ingredients together into a sauce.

**Serve:** Scrape the pasta and the very last bits of the sauce into four wide, shallow bowls. Sprinkle the bread crumbs evenly over the pasta and serve right away.

## GARLIC BREAD CRUMBS

**MAKES ABOUT ½ CUP (75G)**

2 tablespoons (28g)
unsalted butter,
cut into 3 or 4 chunks

2 to 3 medium
garlic cloves, smashed

3 leafy sprigs thyme

Kosher or coarse sea salt

1½ tablespoons
extra-virgin olive oil

½ cup (30g)
panko bread crumbs

*This makes more than you need for the pasta, but they keep for a few days and also make a great topping for roasted vegetables like broccoli rabe.* —TRACY

**Prep:** Line a small plate with paper towels.

**Toast the bread crumbs:** Put the butter in a large, cold sauté pan or nonstick skillet and turn the heat to medium. When the butter just begins to melt, add the garlic, thyme, and a generous pinch of salt. Swirl the pan occasionally until the butter has fully melted.

Add the olive oil, stir to incorporate, then scatter the panko evenly throughout the pan. Toast the panko, stirring often, until golden brown, about 3 minutes; watch the pan closely the last 30 seconds. Transfer the bread crumbs to the plate (discard the garlic and thyme) and season with salt.

If not using within a few hours, store the bread crumbs in an airtight container at room temperature for up to 3 days.

# Mason Royal's Lemony Chicken with Garlic-Anchovy Sauce

Lily's husband, Mason Royal, is not only a wonderful guy, he's a fantastic chef. I win again! He made this chicken one Sunday night at the house for everybody. It's got a ton of garlic, and two other things that I happen to really like: anchovies and olives. He knows what he's doing. And I know what I'm doing by having a daughter he could marry.

> *I like to make this with boneless, skin-on chicken thighs that cook up evenly and quickly. If you can't find them with the skins, get bone-in thighs. They're easy to debone yourself. It's the crispy skin you're after.* —MASON

**Prep:** For bone-in chicken thighs, use kitchen scissors to remove the bones; keep the whole thigh and skin intact. (Save the meaty bones for stock.) Trim any excess fat and skin from the edges of the thighs and pat the skin dry with paper towels. Season both sides generously with salt and pepper. Lay the chicken skin side up on a plate.

Juice 3 of the lemons; you should have about 6 tablespoons (90ml) of juice. Cut the remaining 2 lemons in half through the equator.

If the olives are whole, smash them lightly (the bottom of a bowl or mug works well) and remove the pits. Break up the flesh into large pieces with your fingers.

**Sear the chicken:** In a large cast iron skillet or heavy sauté pan, heat the olive oil over medium heat until hot but not smoking, about 1 minute. Sear the chicken thighs, skin side facing down and undisturbed, in batches (don't crowd the pan), until the fat begins

---

**FEEDS 4 TO 5**

6 medium skin-on chicken thighs, boneless (about 1½ pounds/680g) or bone-in (2 pounds/910g)

Kosher or coarse sea salt

Freshly ground black pepper

4 to 5 large lemons, divided

2 large handfuls (about ⅔ cup) drained Castelvetrano olives, whole or pitted

¼ cup (60ml) extra-virgin olive oil

1 medium shallot, diced

5 to 6 garlic cloves, minced

3 to 4 good-quality oil-packed anchovy fillets (Agostino Recca, chili pepper–spiced or regular), roughly chopped

*(ingredients continue)*

¼ cup (40g) capers, drained and 1 tablespoon of the juice reserved

4 tablespoons (½ stick/55g) unsalted butter, cubed

3 to 4 sprigs parsley, leaves only, roughly chopped

**TO SERVE**

Plenty of crusty bread

**TIPS**

*Beyond the buttery lemon-garlic sauce, the beauty of this one-skillet recipe is you make the sauce using the same pan that you sear the chicken thighs in (be sure to get the skin golden brown).*

*Agostina Recca anchovies are quite meaty; if you use another brand, increase the quantity to 5 or 6 anchovies.*

to render and the skin is nicely browned and crispy, 7 to 8 minutes. If any thighs aren't golden brown, move them to the hottest part of the pan for a minute or two. (Color is flavor in this dish; don't skimp on the browning process.) Use a large spatula to get fully underneath the skin and flip the chicken thighs onto a plate, skin side facing up; don't stack the thighs or they will lose their crispiness. Sear the remaining chicken thighs and turn off the heat.

**Make the lemon-garlic sauce:** Let the cooking oil in the pan cool for a minute or two. Turn the heat to low and add the shallot, garlic, and anchovies, stirring with a wooden spoon to break up the anchovies. Sauté, stirring regularly, until the shallot and garlic are deep golden brown, 3 to 4 minutes. Add the olives, capers and their juice, and the lemon juice to the pan, scraping up any brown bits in the bottom of the pan. Simmer the sauce until reduced by about half, 4 to 5 minutes.

At this point, you can finish cooking the chicken or take the pan off the heat for up to 30 minutes.

**Finish the chicken:** Pick out any visible seeds on the cut surface of the lemon halves and char the lemons, cut side facing down, directly over the flame of a gas stovetop until the flesh is well blackened in spots. Or, heat a small skillet and sear the lemon flesh for 2 to 3 minutes.

Reheat the pan you used to sear the chicken and add all the chicken thighs, this time skin side facing up. Cook the thighs until the juices run clear when pierced with a knife or a digital thermometer inserted in the thickest part of the thigh reads 165°F (74°C), 3 to 5 minutes. Transfer to a large serving platter.

Add the butter and parsley to the pan and stir or whisk until the butter has fully melted. Season the sauce with salt and pepper.

**Serve:** Pour the lemon-garlic sauce over the chicken thighs, tuck the charred lemon halves among the thighs, and serve with the crusty bread.

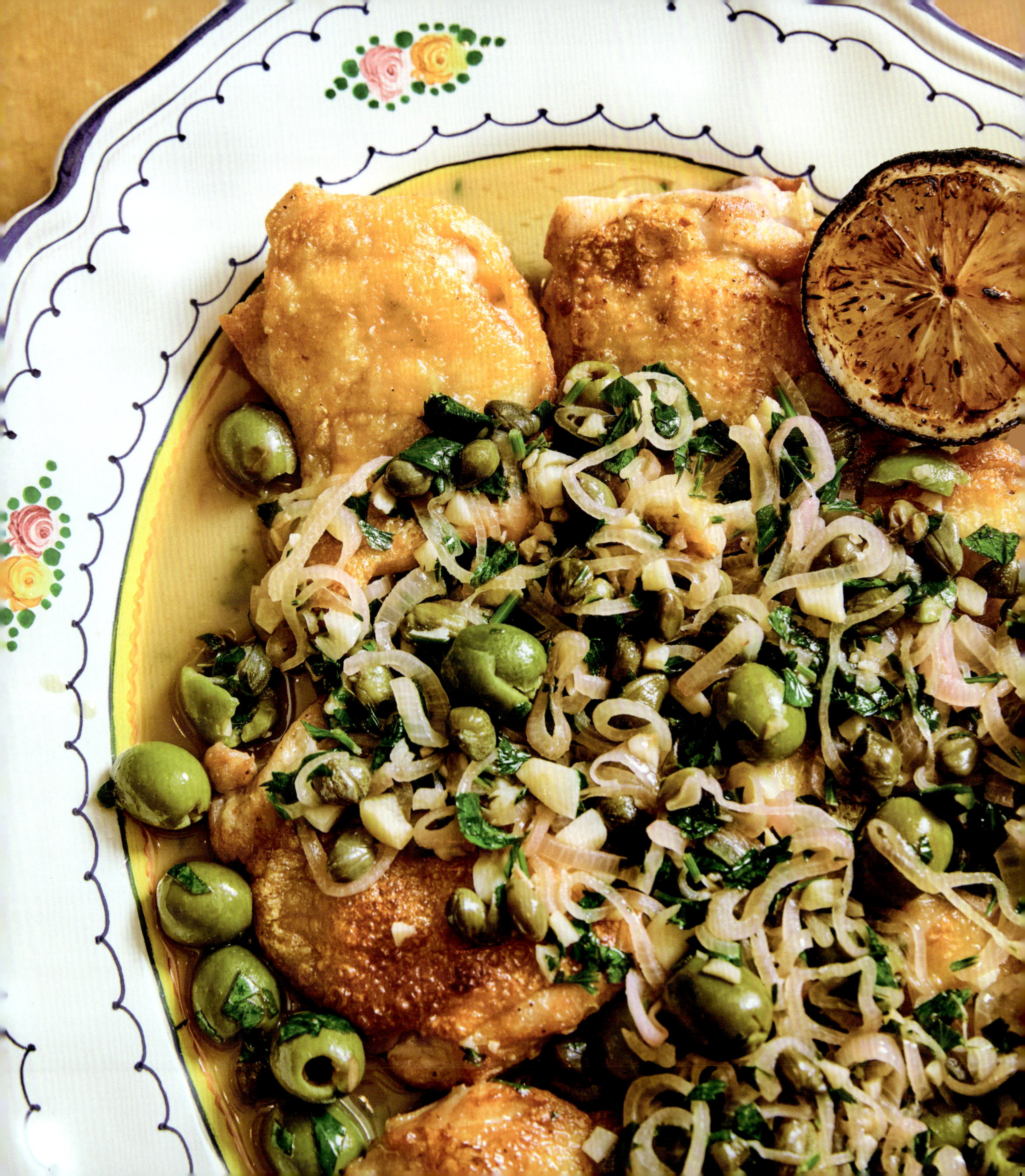

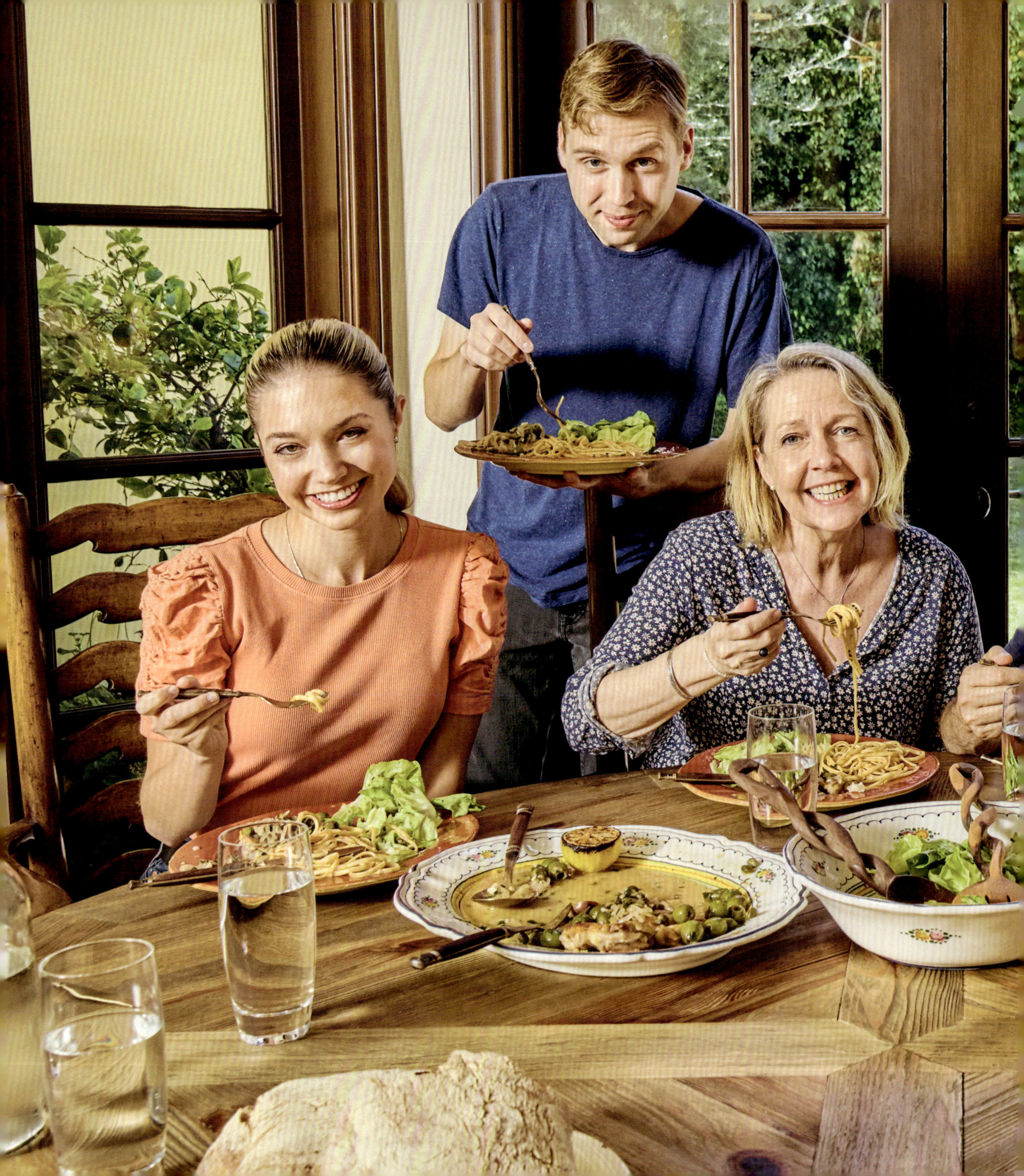

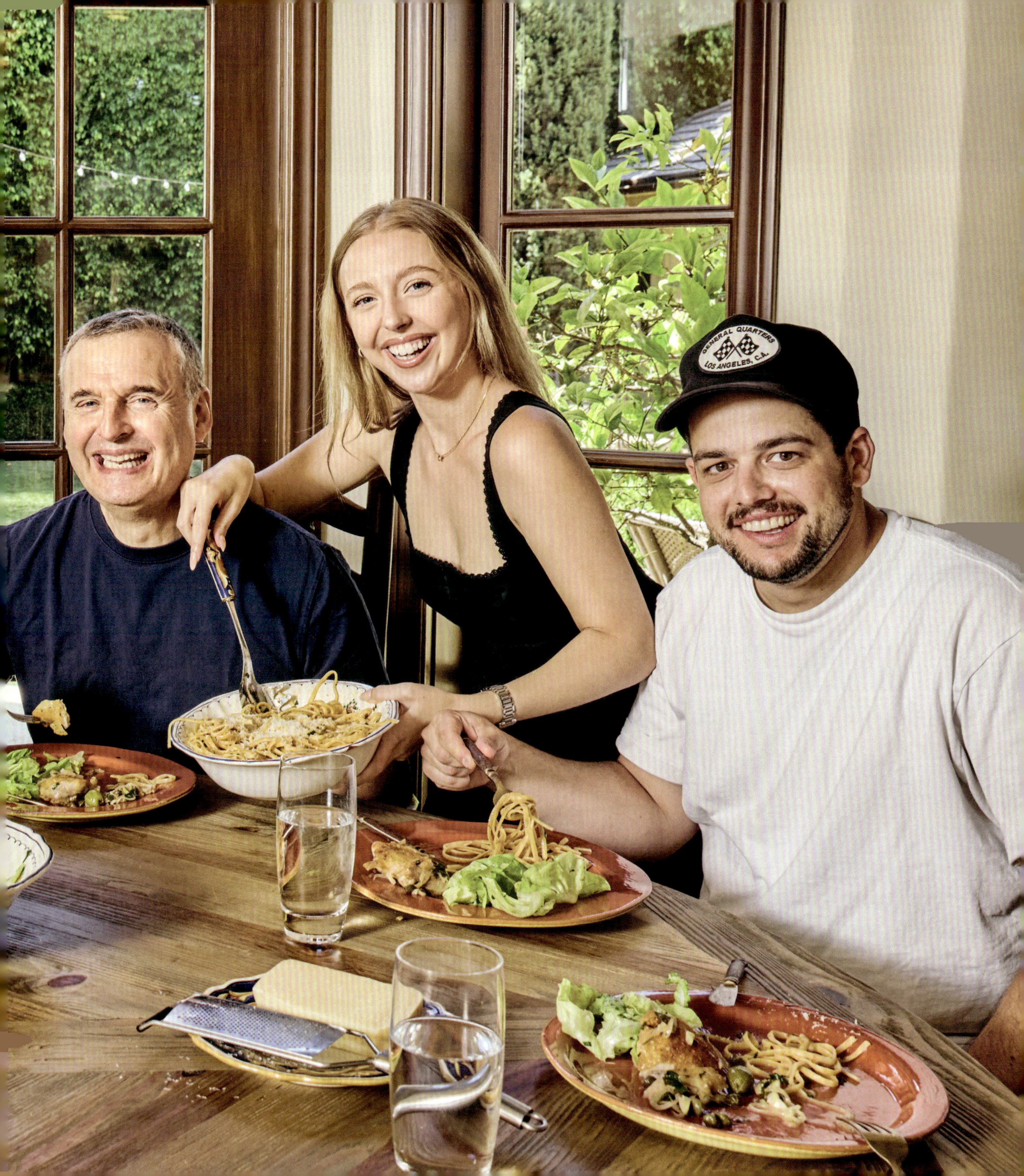
GENERAL QUARTERS
LOS ANGELES, C.A.

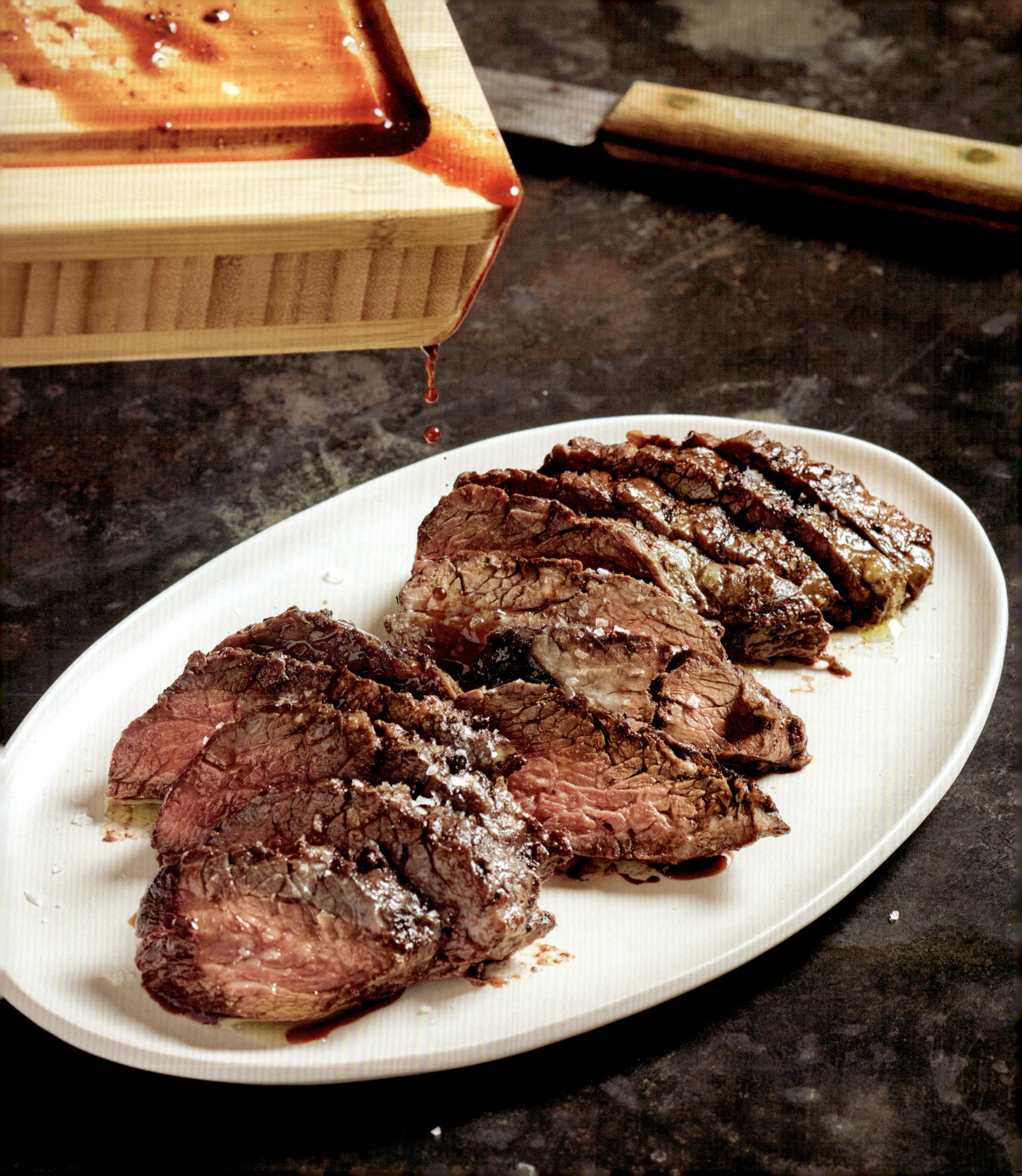

# Shola Olunloyo's Charred Steak with Olive Oil

📍 *Philadelphia*

It's always nice being invited to someone's home for a meal no matter what's on the menu, but when Shola Olunloyo, a great chef in Philadelphia, has you over, it's probably not gonna be burgers and hot dogs. When we have a full day of filming ahead, I normally try to pace myself, but everything Shola brought out that day was so delicious, I couldn't stop. I should point out that nothing he made was a complicated dish. It was simply prepared food done very well, the kind of food we all want to eat most days.

After he grilled some whole squid and made a quick shakshuka, he cooked this hanger steak for dessert. It's so easy, even I can do it. His secret is getting the grill very hot, to 700°F, so the steak sears really quickly. (You don't need the special grill he has to make this.) I recommend getting one of those cutting boards with channels around the edges like Shola used in the episode; it captures all the delicious steak juices. (It doesn't need to be expensive; he got his cutting board from IKEA.) Shola doesn't add anything except good olive oil and Maldon, but this steak would also be delicious with the seasoned sea salt my friend Dario Cecchini, the great Tuscan butcher, uses on his steaks (which I use on my tuna sandwich on page 77, so now you have another reason to get a jar). But the most important part of this recipe is to share. As Shola said, "Luxury without generosity is not luxury."

**FEEDS 2**

1 really good boneless hanger (butcher's) steak or New York strip, any size

Flaky sea salt (Maldon) or other good sea salt

Really good extra-virgin olive oil, for finishing

---

*A large cross-section hanger steak has incredible flavor. Cooked properly to medium rare, first over direct heat, then over indirect, the cut is as tender as a rib eye or New York strip. Dousing the meat heavily with olive oil when it comes off the grill, then a little flaky sea salt (no pepper), prevents the meat from losing all of its juices as it rests.* —SHOLA

### TIP

*You can cook the steak with this method on any grill (charcoal or gas), or even broil it. To try a really hot grill closer to what Shola uses (he has a professional-grade outdoor grill/oven), set a few bricks on top of the grill grate with the charcoal in between them, like for the kebab grill setup (see page 238). Lay a grate or baking rack on top of the bricks; you'll have a very close heat source for direct cooking. Close the lid for a few minutes to finish the steak.*

**Prep:** Heat a grill as hot as you can get it. Season the meat lightly with the salt.

**Cook the steak:** Char the meat over really hot direct heat for no more than a minute or two, then move the steak to indirect heat, close the lid, and cook until medium rare, or however you like your steak. Right when it comes off the grill, pour a lot of good olive oil over the steak, then sprinkle more salt on top. Let the steak sit for a few minutes, transfer it to a plate, then pour all of the good juices on the cutting board over the steak. Slice the steak and find somebody to share it with.

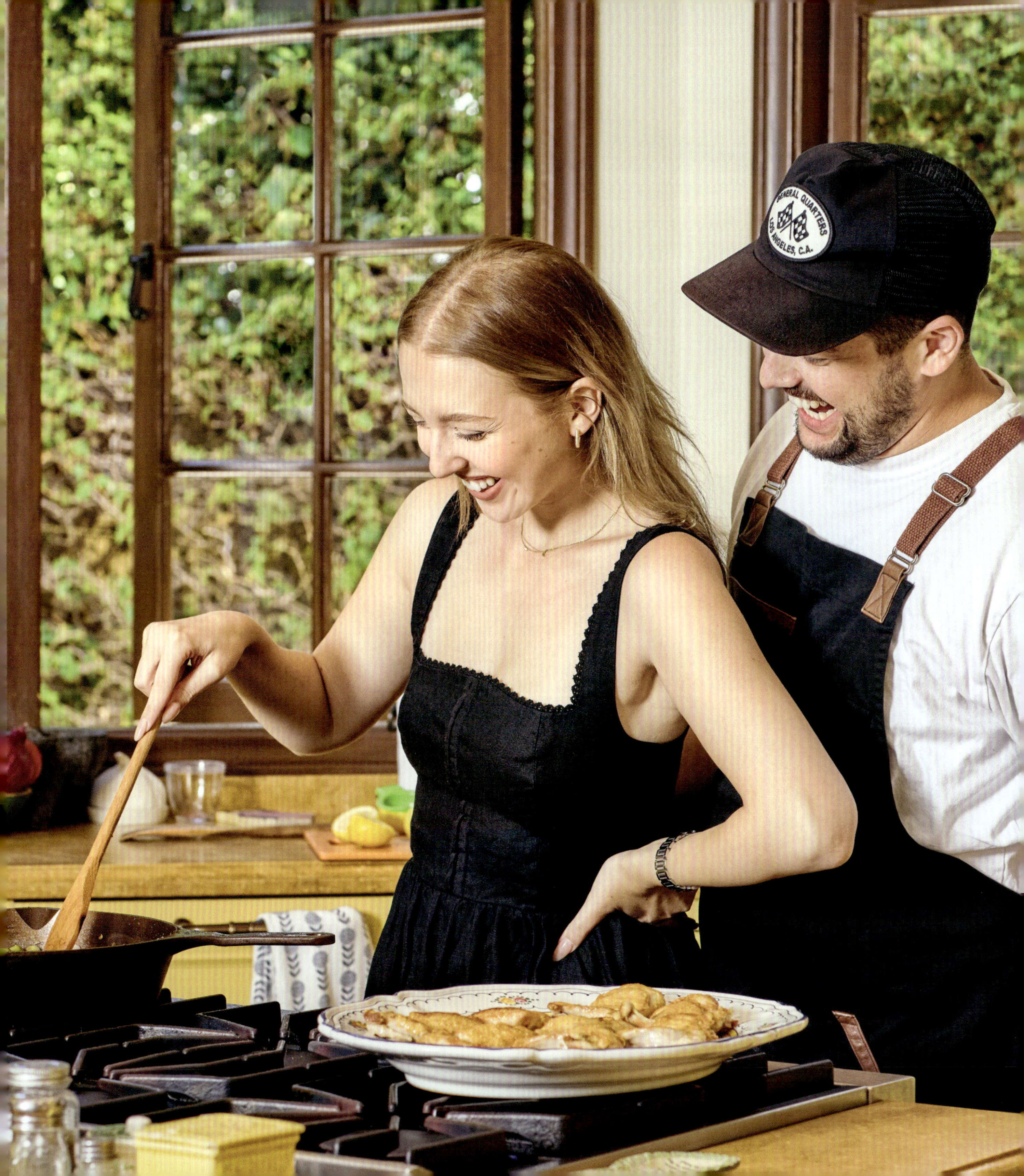
GENERAL QUARTERS
LOS ANGELES, C.A.

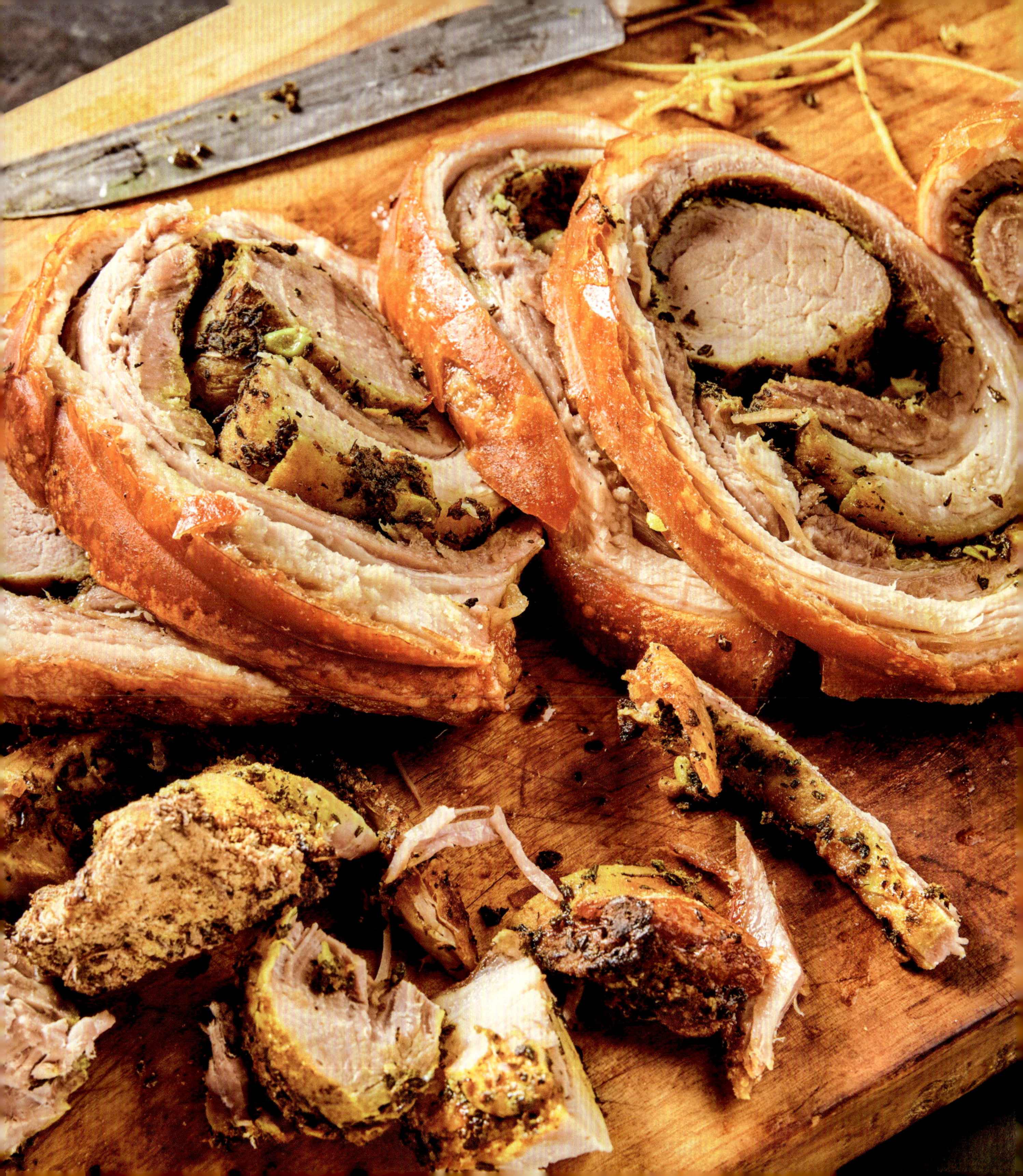

# Yamuel Bigio's Puerto Rican Porchetta

📍 *Crocante, Orlando*

The first place we went in the "Orlando" episode was Crocante, which means "crispy and crunchy." Yamuel Bigio is the genius who has perfected those two words. You've probably noticed that I get excited when somebody brings out a big chunk of meat, but this porchetta was the most beautiful piece of meat I think we've ever shot in the series. Porchetta is traditionally Italian, but Yamuel gives his version a Latin-Caribbean twist by filling it with Dominican oregano (which is stronger than Mediterranean oregano), cumin, turmeric, and lemon and lime juice. Yamuel could stuff his porchetta with a shoe and I'd eat it. The whole point of this is the crispy skin. You can actually hear the crack when you cut through it. Pork for everybody!

> *This is a smaller cut of pork than we roast on our rotisseries, so it's easy to do at home in the oven. Make sure you get a true pork "middle," which includes some of the leaner loin meat with the fattier belly; you can also use plenty of lemon juice on the meat before you add the spices. (You don't want juice or spices on the skin.) The lemon juice gives the pork a great flavor and also helps the rub stick better. You need to use thick twine and really apply force to roll and tie up the belly into a nice, tight roll. And, most importantly, when you cook the porchetta, have patience. This is something that is best cooked low and slow.* —YAMUEL

## TIPS

*Like a brined turkey, making a porchetta requires some advance planning, but the process is relatively simple and the leftovers make great fillings for tacos, tamales, and sandwiches.*

*Dominican oregano, also called Jamaican or Cuban oregano, has a very intense and distinct flavor; you can find it at Puerto Rican markets and some spice shops (nyspiceshop.com). The closest substitute is dried Mexican oregano, but you can also use more common Italian oregano.*

*At higher-end markets and butchers, the pork belly is often smaller (often less than 5 pounds/2.3kg), fattier cuts that have been trimmed of most of the meat. Ask your butcher for a boneless, skin-on belly that still has some of the loin meat attached at one end. (Filipino and Chinese markets with a large pork selection can be a good place to find deals on a large, whole center-cut belly; ask at the butcher counter.) If you can't find one, cut a 2- to 3-inch (5 to 7.5cm) strip from a pork loin and lay it across one end of the belly before rolling up the porchetta for extra meatiness (brine the loin with the pork belly).*

**FEEDS A LARGE CROWD (10 TO 12)**

**BRINED PORK BELLY**

12 ounces (340g) kosher salt (about 1½ cups Morton's or 2¼ cups Diamond Crystal), divided

1 10-to 12-pound (4.5 to 5.5kg) skin-on pork belly with loin meat (if not available, a trimmed pork belly plus a small boneless pork loin; see Tips)

**PORK RUB**

6 ounces (170g) kosher salt (¾ cup Morton's or 1 generous cup Diamond Crystal)

2 tablespoons coarsely ground black pepper

4 tablespoons dried Dominican or Mexican oregano (see Tips), or 5 tablespoons dried Italian oregano

1 tablespoon ground cumin

1 tablespoon turmeric

2 to 3 large lemons

8 to 10 garlic cloves, thinly sliced

**DAY 1 (UP TO 2 DAYS BEFORE ROASTING THE PORCHETTA)**

**Brine the pork:** In a large stockpot, bring 2 quarts (2L) water to a simmer, add the 12 ounces (340g) salt, and stir until dissolved. Remove the pot from the heat, add 2 quarts (2L) cold tap water, and let cool completely.

Put the pork belly in a large, deep roasting pan or heavy-duty brining bag. Add equal amounts of cold tap water and the cooled salt water to the pan or bag, 2 quarts (2L) at a time. Keep adding a 50/50 ratio of tap to salted water to the pan or bag until the pork belly is completely submerged; the amount you'll need depends on the size of the pan or bag. Cover the pan with plastic wrap or press the air out of the bag and seal, and refrigerate overnight (12 to 16 hours; don't leave the pork in the marinade longer or it can get too salty).

**DAY 2**

**Season the pork:** Lay a thick kitchen towel on a large rimmed sheet pan.

Remove the pork belly from the brine (discard the brine) and lay it, flesh side facing down, on the kitchen towel to dry the flesh. Pat the edges dry, then flip the belly so the skin side is facing down.

Mix together the 6 ounces (170g) of salt (if your pork belly is not the full 10 to 12 pounds, reduce the amount of salt accordingly), pepper, oregano, cumin, and turmeric.

Squeeze the juice of the lemons directly over the pork flesh and rub the juice over the meat evenly; there should be small pools of juice. Pick off any lemon seeds, scatter the spice mixture evenly over the pork, and rub it into the meat and all over the sides of the belly (avoid the skin), then scatter the sliced garlic on top.

**Roll the porchetta:** Lay the pork belly vertically on your work surface with the thicker, meaty end facing you (or if you are adding a pork loin, place it closest to you). Slide four to five pieces of butcher's twine, each several inches longer than the width of the belly, width-wise underneath the pork belly at intervals.

Snugly roll up the pork belly like a cigar and tie it tightly closed with one piece of twine. It takes some muscle to really pull the belly into a tight roll; have someone hold the roll closed as you tie it, or use your forearms like a clamp on one end and tie that spot first. (This isn't a time when a butcher's knot is an advantage; a firm, straight tie works best.) Flip the belly so the seam is near the bottom and keep tightly tying the other pieces of twine at roughly 2-inch (5cm) intervals. If needed, snip off the first knot you tied if it's loosened up and re-tie that spot tighter. Slide the towel out from underneath the belly and wipe any excess seasoning mix off the pork belly skin.

You can roast the porchetta now, or to roast it the following day, overlap several large pieces of plastic wrap, lay the pork on top, and roll the pork up snugly. Line a rimmed sheet pan or roasting pan with a clean, dry kitchen towel to catch the drippings, lay the porchetta on top, seam side facing up, and refrigerate overnight or up to 16 hours; longer and it will start to lose moisture from the salt.

**Roast the porchetta:** If refrigerated, let the porchetta sit at room temperature for about 1 hour.

Put an oven rack in the lower third of the oven, preheat the oven to 325°F (165°C), and lay a grill or sturdy baking rack on top of a large, rimmed sheet pan.

Wipe the skin of the porchetta with kitchen or paper towels so it is very dry and put the pork on the rack-covered sheet pan; if using the oven, make sure the entire pork roll is directly over the sheet pan to catch the fat drippings.

**TO SERVE**

**1 large bunch fresh cilantro, leaves and tender top stems roughly chopped**

**6 to 8 limes, cut into wedges**

Roast the porchetta for 2 hours, occasionally basting the skin with some of the accumulated fat in the sheet pan. Rotate the sheet pan front to back, and if the skin is already very brown at this point, reduce the oven temperature to 300°F (150°C).

Continue to roast the porchetta, checking every hour and basting the skin, until a digital thermometer inserted in the middle reads 180°F (82°C) and the skin is crispy, 2 to 2½ more hours, depending on the size, for a total of 4½ to 5 hours.

Remove the porchetta from the oven and set aside to rest for about 30 minutes.

**Serve:** Transfer the porchetta to a clean rimmed sheet pan to catch the drippings (there is too much jus even for most channeled cutting boards). Slice the meat into thick pieces and arrange on a serving platter.

Serve the porchetta with the cilantro and lime wedges.

Cover and refrigerate any leftovers for up to 5 days, or freeze for up to 3 months.

# Seng Luangrath's Moak Paa (Steamed Fish in Sticky Rice Marinade)

*Thip Khao, Washington, DC*

What's great about the food scene in DC right now is that some of the most interesting cuisines you're going to find in the capital hail from cultures outside our borders. Food from Laos, which they call Lao food, is one of them. When we were filming season seven, I went to Thip Khao, one of three restaurants in the city run by Seng Luangrath and her son, Boby Pradachith. It's a true family business: both Seng and Boby are chefs, and everything is fantastic. This fish steamed in banana leaves was my favorite thing we had there; Richard's, too. With Lao food, you use the bowl of sticky rice that comes on the side like a utensil to scoop up the fish and sauce. It's a very satisfying way to eat.

> *Moak Paa is one of the staple dishes in our local cuisine. Laos is known particularly for the technique of steaming marinated fish in banana leaves. We like to say that banana leaves are "nature's parchment paper," as their sturdy structure retains flavors within the parcel wrap. And, it's a nice presentation for guests who get to unwrap the leaves and the finished product is revealed, all while the perfuming aromas escape. The banana leaves also impart their own slightly coconutty and floral rice flavors to the fish. We steam the parcels, but there is a variation where it is grilled to impart smokier flavors. I recommend using skinless fish unless, like me, you enjoy fish skin. We also make a version with tofu that I've included here.* —BOBY

**FEEDS 6**

6 8-ounce (225g) skinless black sea bass (not Chilean), salmon, flounder, or catfish fillets

**Sticky Rice Marinade (recipe follows)**

3 to 4 large banana leaf sheets, or 8 pre-cut square or 12 round banana leaf sections (about ½ 16-ounce/455g package), thawed and trimmed (technique follows)

2 medium shallots, very thinly sliced

2 3.5-ounce (100g) packages hon shimeji (brown beech/clamshell) mushrooms, ends trimmed

1 medium bunch dill, ends trimmed, stems and fronds roughly chopped

Steamed Thai sticky (khao niew) or Japanese sushi rice, for the table

## TIPS

*With the sticky rice marinade made ahead, you simply need to make your fish (or tofu) packets and steam them for an impressive entertaining dish.*

*Padaek (labeled "ground preserved fish") is a very thick, Lao-style unfiltered fish sauce made from fermented freshwater fish, and is very different from other fish sauces. Look for brands like Pantai at Lao and some Thai markets and online (shopsoutheats.com).*

**TOFU MOAK PAA:**

*Substitute 2 14-ounce (400g) blocks medium or firm tofu for the fish, pat dry very well, and cut into cubes. Increase the amount of mushrooms to 3 packages (all hon shimeju or mix with wood ear mushrooms). Fill, wrap, and steam the tofu (with the other ingredients) as instructed for 12 to 15 minutes.*

**Prep:** Put the fish fillets in a wide, medium bowl. Stir the Sticky Rice Marinade and pour it over the fish; each fillet should be completely submerged. Cover the bowl and refrigerate the fish for 15 to 20 minutes.

Fill a deep pot with a steamer basket with 3 to 4 inches (7.5 to 10cm) water. Or, to make a steamer, put a large colander in a soup pot; if needed, raise the height of the colander by an inch or two so there is plenty of room to add water by laying it on round metal biscuit cutters or balls of wadded-up aluminum foil.

**Wrap the fish packets:** Rinse the banana leaves well, shake off the excess water, and lay them on a damp kitchen towel.

If you have pre-cut circular or smaller rectangular banana leaves, leave them whole. For large sheets, use kitchen scissors to cut out any tough brown ribs, then cut the leaves into large, roughly 8x8-inch (20cm) rectangles. (Save the scraps.) Turn on a gas burner and run the banana leaves, one by one, back and forth over the flame a few times until they soften up. Or, cover the stack of leaves in the damp kitchen towel and microwave until they soften up, about 30 seconds.

Choose the most pliable banana leaves without any tears. On a rimmed sheet pan, arrange 1 large rectangular banana leaf vertically or 2 smaller banana leaves, overlapping the smaller leaves in the center to create a larger surface area; keep the rest of the leaves covered in the damp towel as you work. Put 1 marinated fish fillet in the center of the leaf or leaves; if the fish fillet is long and thin like flounder or catfish, you may need more banana leaves so you can wrap the package and fully enclose the fish.

Stir the Sticky Rice Marinade well and drizzle about 3 tablespoons over the fish (you can use the marinade used to soak the fish or any remaining marinade); the fillets should be evenly covered in sauce. Scatter the shallots evenly on top, then separate the mushrooms and tuck them all around the fish and divide the dill among the fillets.

To enclose the fish, fold down the top and fold up the bottom of the leaves, then fold in both sides to make a package. Flip the fish package over and set it aside while you make the rest. A little marinade will leak out of the packages; if most comes out, the banana leaf likely has a large tear and should be rewrapped. Gently set the packet aside and wrap the remaining fish; it's fine if there is a little marinade on your work surface, but if there was a spill, wipe it up first.

**Steam the fish:** Line the bottom of the steamer basket with banana leaf scraps and bring the water to a boil.

Arrange the fish packages, seam side facing down, in the steamer basket or colander; they can be stacked on top of one another but lay each as flat as possible to help keep the sauce from spilling. Cover the pot with the lid, or if you're using a colander and the pot lid doesn't close, cover snugly with aluminum foil.

Steam the fish until the flesh is firm and the rice is cooked, about 20 minutes for long, thin fillets (flounder, catfish) or 25 minutes for thicker center-cut fillets (black sea bass, salmon). Open one banana leaf package to check the rice.

**Serve:** Remove the steamer basket or colander from the pot and slide a spatula underneath each fish package to carefully remove it from the steamer basket or colander; hold on to the top of the packages as you remove each so they don't open. Flip the packages upside down onto serving plates, seam side facing up so they can easily be unwrapped at the table. Serve the moak paa with the steamed Thai sticky rice.

## TIPS

*Thai (or Filipino) khao niew, a long-grain sticky rice, is available at most Thai and Filipino markets; common brands include Cock, Sanpatong, Three Rings, and Malagkit. A short-grain sticky rice like Japanese sushi rice also works.*

*Banana leaf preparation: The size and shape of both the banana leaves (large pieces or pre-cut) and the fish (a long and lean fillet or a chunky center-section cut from a larger fish) will determine how many banana leaves you need to fully enclose each fish package. For full leaves, use scissors to cut out the main rib in the center of each leaf and leave smaller circular or rectangular banana leaves whole; cut full sheets into large, roughly 12x6-inch (30x40cm) rectangles (cut more than one per fish packet, as some will likely tear). Searing the leaves on the stove (or putting them briefly in the microwave to steam) before wrapping the fish helps prevent the leaves from tearing.*

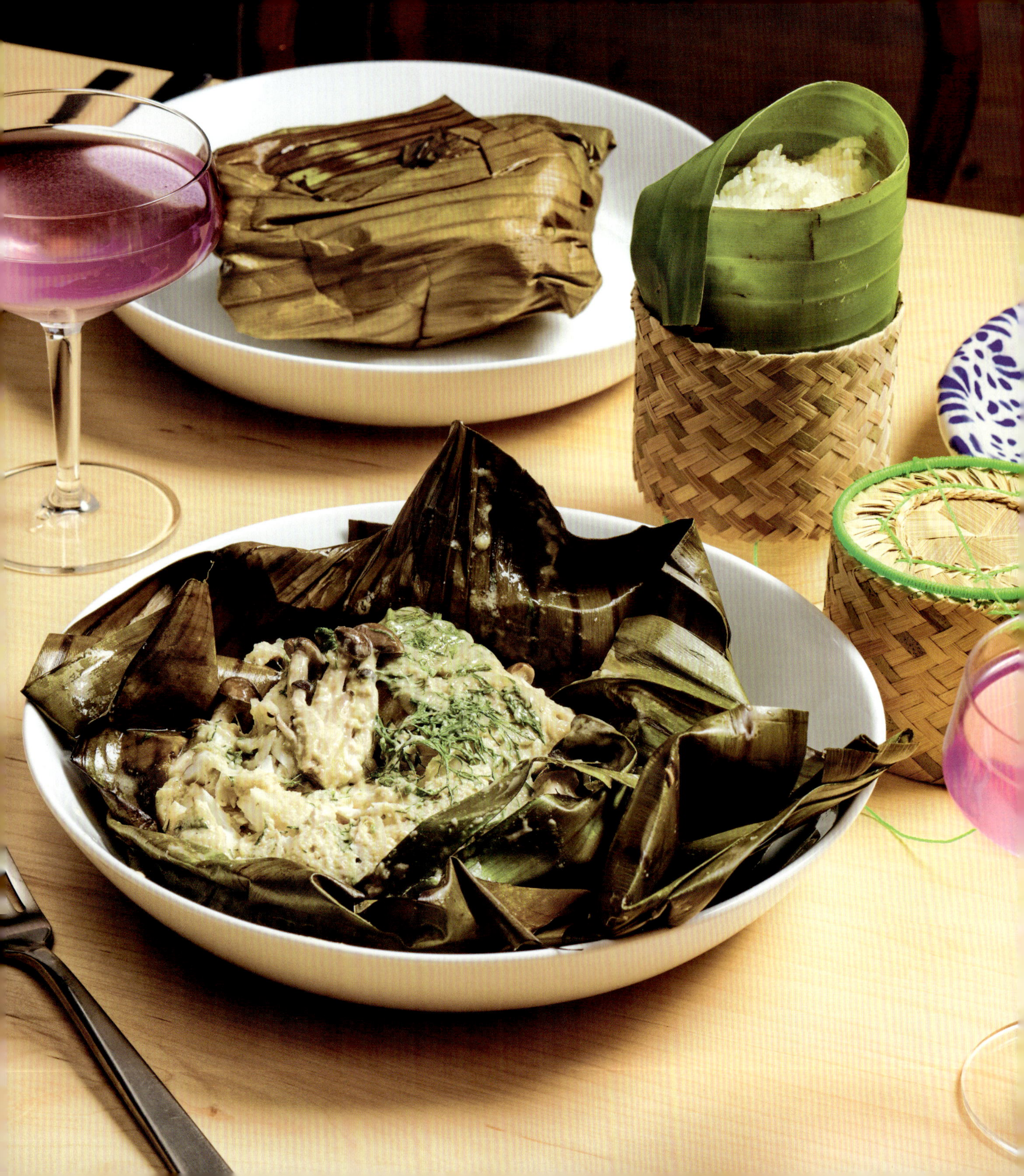

# STICKY RICE MARINADE

**MAKES ABOUT 2 CUPS (480ML), ENOUGH FOR 6 FISH FILLET OR TOFU PACKAGES**

> *If you're not used to cooking with lemongrass, you first want to cut a good amount off the root end, then cut off the green tops where the leaves start to turn yellow in the center of the stalk. Peel off one or two layers (they're woody) and save all of your trimmings for stocks!* —BOBY

⅓ cup (70g) Thai sticky rice (khao niew) or Japanese sushi rice (see Tips)

4 lemongrass stalks, root ends trimmed and outer leaves removed; tender inner core cut in thirds

3 to 4 garlic cloves, smashed

3 tablespoons Thai green curry paste

3 tablespoons Vietnamese fish sauce

2 tablespoons Thai ground preserved fish sauce (Pantai; see Tips), well shaken, or more Vietnamese fish sauce

1 tablespoon oyster sauce

3 tablespoons vegetable or other neutral oil

1 fresh kaffir lime leaf or 1 teaspoon freshly grated lime zest

Kosher or coarse sea salt

1 scant cup (220ml) full-fat coconut milk, well stirred or briefly warmed if solidified

**Soak and pound the rice:** Put the rice in a sieve or small colander, lay the sieve in a small bowl, and fill the bowl with enough cold water to generously cover the rice. Stir with your fingers until the water is cloudy, dump out the water, and repeat the soaking process three or four times until the water runs clear. Cover the rice with cold water one more time and set aside to soak for 2 to 3 hours. Strain the rice and shake off the excess water.

In a mortar with a pestle, grind the rice to a medium-fine grind, like freshly ground black pepper. Or, on a flat work surface, use a meat mallet to gently smash the rice, pressing down to really crush the pieces.

**Make the marinade:** In a blender, combine the lemongrass, garlic, Thai green curry paste, Vietnamese fish sauce, Thai ground preserved fish sauce, oyster sauce, vegetable oil, kaffir leaf, and 2 pinches kosher salt and blend on medium speed until smooth, about 20 seconds. Add the coconut milk and pounded rice and pulse on low speed 2 or 3 times, just until combined.

Cover and refrigerate the marinade for at least 1 hour or up to 6 hours.

Filled Cabbage

Have water boil in a big pot then put the "Cabbage head" in. Leave the cabbage in for 20/30 minutes. Then try to seperate the leaves. The leaves should not be too hard not too soft so that one can fill them with the prepared chopped meat. Chopped meat (for 5/6 persons. Prepare the chopped meat w/ one egg. Spices: ginger, broth, salt, (matza crumbs))

# Oma's Stuffed Cabbage Rolls

I'm so grateful that Richard likes to cook. If he didn't, recipes like our grandmother's stuffed cabbage rolls might have gotten lost instead of being passed down to the next generation in our family. Here's to all our grandmas, and especially this one: Martha Adler.

> *For Passover, our grandmother would put these out on the table as an appetizer. I've still got her handwritten recipe and sometimes make it for dinner. This is one recipe that doesn't benefit from "chef-ing up"—meaning stick to dried spices, basic canned tomato sauce and chicken broth, and margarine (never butter; that would significantly change the overall flavor). For the sauce, you need ketchup for that classic flavor, but not too much or it will be too sweet. I start with a little and taste the sauce as it cooks down to see if it needs more. My grandmother would cook everything in one of those really thin aluminum pasta pots that everyone had back then, but it's easier to brown the cabbage rolls in a Dutch oven or other sturdy pot so they don't stick. She would sprinkle the matzoh on top at the same time she cooked the cabbage rolls, but if you brown the rolls on their own in the margarine first, then add the matzoh to the pot like you would when making a roux with flour, the matzoh toasts up. When you add the broth and tomato sauce, it cooks down into more of a brown gravy—what you're after, not so much a really tomato-y sauce.* —RICHARD

**Boil the cabbage (or freeze it; see Tips):** Use a small knife to make an angled cut around the core of the cabbage so you can pop it out.

Fill a stockpot about halfway with water, bring to a boil, and gently slide the cabbage into the pot, core side facing down, with two

---

**FEEDS A SMALL CROWD (6 TO 8), MORE AS PART OF A HOLIDAY SPREAD (MAKES 16 CABBAGE ROLLS)**

**CABBAGE ROLLS**

1 very large, heavy green cabbage (3½ to 4 pounds/1.6 to 1.8kg)

3 tablespoons matzoh meal or unseasoned fine bread crumbs

1 teaspoon dried parsley

½ teaspoon ground ginger

½ teaspoon onion powder

½ teaspoon garlic powder

Salt (any kind)

Finely ground black pepper

1½ pounds (680g) ground beef

1 large egg

1 tablespoon meerrettich (prepared horseradish), drained (optional)

About 6 pats (5 to 6 tablespoons/85g) margarine

*(ingredients continue)*

### SAUCE

**2 pats
(about 2 tablespoons/28g) margarine**

**3 tablespoons
matzoh meal or unseasoned fine bread crumbs**

**1 8-ounce (225g)
can tomato sauce**

**2½ to 3 cups
(600 to 720ml) canned or boxed chicken broth (not low-sodium)**

**2 to 3 tablespoons
ketchup**

### TO SERVE

**Meerrettich (prepared horseradish), drained**

large spoons (don't just drop the cabbage in the pot, as the boiling water will splash). Cover the pot, boil for 20 minutes, flip the cabbage so the top side is now submerged, and boil, covered, for another 5 to 10 minutes; the outermost leaves should be almost translucent. Strain, transfer the cabbage to a bowl, and let cool for at least 30 minutes.

Lay the cabbage on several kitchen towels (it will release a lot of moisture) and peel off and discard the outermost leaves. Gently peel back the remaining leaves; some will tear, but try to keep them whole. Stop when you get to the small, firm leaves closest to the core.

**Make the cabbage rolls:** In a large bowl, mix together the matzoh meal, dried parsley, ginger, onion powder, garlic powder, ½ teaspoon finely ground salt or 1 teaspoon kosher salt, and 1 teaspoon pepper. Add the ground beef, egg, and meerrettich, if you'd like. Knead the beef with your hands until the seasonings are well incorporated. Divide the mixture into 16 to 18 large meatballs, about 1½ ounces (45g) each if you want to be precise, but the size doesn't matter.

Lay out the cabbage leaves on a large work surface. Cut off the very bottom of any large leaves with very thick stems. If a leaf still isn't easy to bend, use a knife to make a few horizontal slashes on the thickest part of the stem so it rolls up easily. Put a meatball at the base of each leaf and roll it up snugly like a burrito, folding in the sides to enclose the filling as you go. Secure the seam of each cabbage roll with toothpicks, if you'd like, or you can forgo the toothpicks (see Tips) and simply set each aside, seam side facing down. When you get down to smaller leaves, piece together several scraps to make one larger wrap, or divide the meatballs into smaller pieces so they fit in the leaves.

If you'd like to fry up the extra cabbage leaves (including those near the core) to serve with the cabbage rolls, tear them into large chunks and set them aside with the cabbage rolls.

**Fry the cabbage rolls:** In a large Dutch oven, melt 2 pats (about 2 tablespoons/28g) of margarine over medium-high heat. Sear the cabbage rolls in batches (don't crowd the pan) until golden brown in spots, 3 to 4 minutes. Flip the cabbage rolls and sear the opposite side. If the pot becomes watery, let some of the water evaporate before adding another pat or two of margarine and frying more cabbage rolls. If you'd like, fry any reserved cabbage leaves until just beginning to brown.

**Make the sauce:** Reduce the heat to medium-low, add 2 more pats (about 2 tablespoons) of margarine, and when melted, add the 3 tablespoons of matzoh meal. Toast the matzoh, stirring regularly with a wooden spoon, until golden brown, 3 to 4 minutes. Add the tomato sauce, scrape any brown bits off the bottom of the pot, then stir in about 2½ cups (600ml) of chicken broth and 2 tablespoons ketchup. Bring the sauce to a boil, reduce to a simmer, and snugly pack cabbage rolls in the pot. Scatter the fried cabbage scraps in between and on top of the rolls, if using, partly cover the pot, and cook the cabbage rolls for 30 minutes.

Season the sauce with salt, pepper, and another small squeeze of ketchup, if you'd like (the sauce shouldn't be too sweet). Simmer the cabbage rolls, this time uncovered, until the sauce is has reduced somewhat and has darkened in color, 45 minutes to 1 hour. If the sauce ever appears dry, add another splash of chicken broth.

You can serve the cabbage rolls now, or remove them from the heat, cover the pot, and set aside for 2 to 3 hours.

**Serve:** Rewarm the stuffed cabbage rolls over low heat, if needed.

Transfer the cabbage rolls and leaves to a large, deep serving platter and remove the toothpicks. Pour the sauce over the cabbage rolls and serve with the horseradish on the side.

## TIPS

*Especially if serving kids, be sure to remove the toothpicks, as they can be difficult to see.*

*Instead of boiling the cabbage, you can freeze the cabbage until fully frozen (at least 24 hours), then completely thaw it in a bowl in the refrigerator (another 24 hours, sometimes longer, or partly thaw it on the countertop). When completely thawed, the leaves will be soft and pliable.*

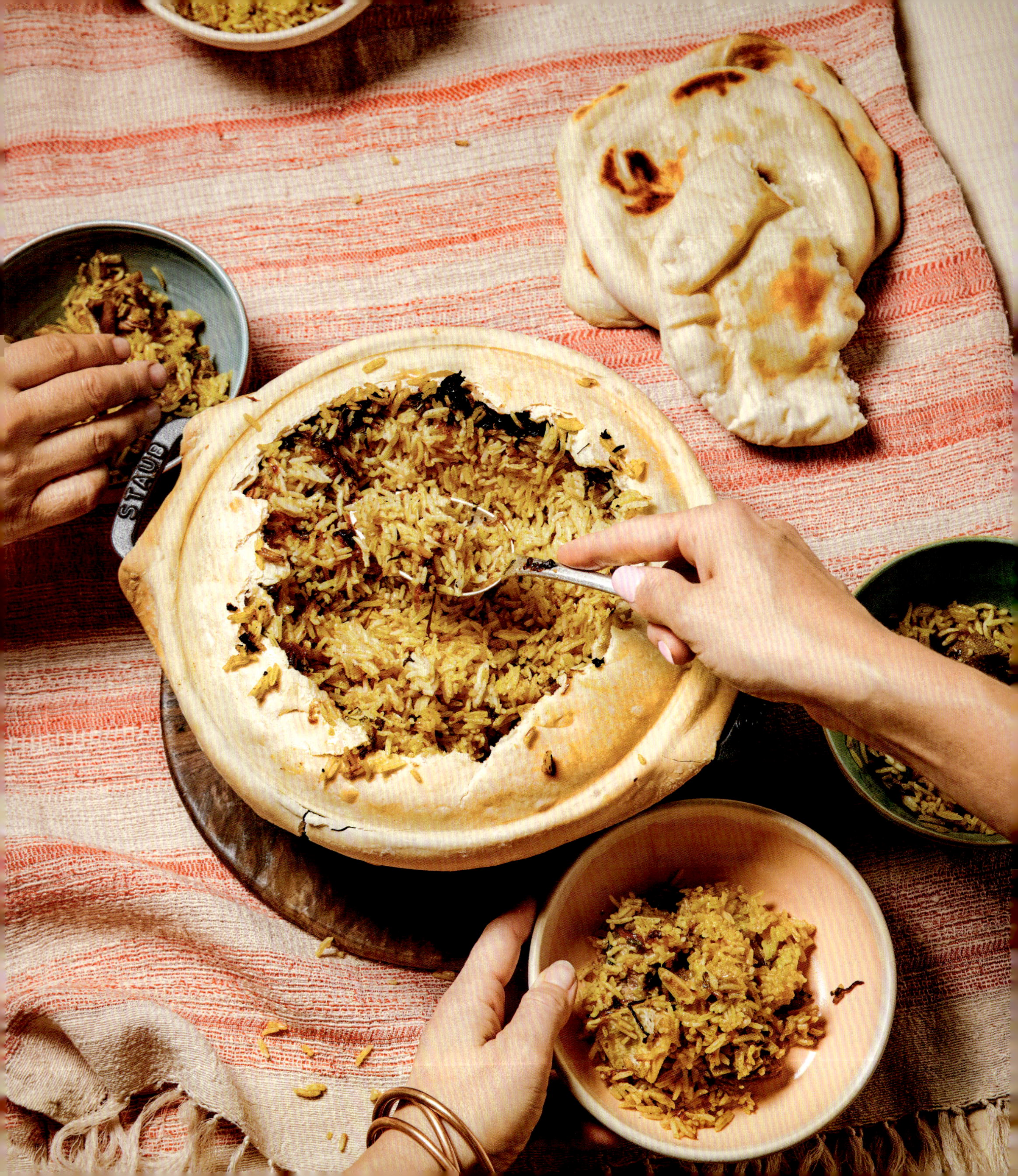
STAUB

# Chintan Pandya's Lucknow Dum Biryani

*Adda, Queens*

Indian food is one of my favorite cuisines. I go out for Indian or order it at home at least once a week, and when I'm in New York, I never miss the opportunity to go to one of my friend Chintan Pandya's restaurants, Dhamaka, Semma, Rowdy Rooster, or Adda. I've had some of the best meals ever, regardless of the type of cuisine, at his restaurants. Chintan grew up in Mumbai, and he happened to be there when we were filming the episode. He took me to one of his favorite restaurants, Soam, where they serve the comforting and delicious things people make at home. Like so many other places I went to in Mumbai, it tastes like you're eating at someone's house.

Chintan is a master at taking home-cooked dishes like this biryani and making them the best versions of what they can be. If you've never had one, a biryani is a spicy curry layered with seasoned rice, fried onions, spices, and other ingredients, and because this one is based on the style of biryanis people make in Lucknow in northern India, you cover the top of the pot with dough before you bake it to seal the pot. This one is with goat meat, something I love. By the way, if you missed it, you need to go to the "Austin" episode and watch the scene when we were at Suerte. Fermín Núñez brings out his goat barbacoa, and I said, on camera, that goat was "the most popular [and] the most consumed meat in the world." You will understand why Richard is no longer allowed to speak when the cameras are rolling.

**FEEDS 6**

**BASMATI RICE**

2½ cups (16 ounces/about 500g) white basmati or other long-grain rice (jasmine)

**WHOLE GARAM MASALA SPICE MIX**

2-inch (5cm) piece ginger, peeled

1½ teaspoons cumin seeds, or 1 teaspoon ground cumin

1½ teaspoons whole coriander, or 1 teaspoon ground coriander

4 green cardamom pods

1 black cardamom pod (optional; see Tips)

6 black peppercorns

1 cinnamon stick

1 mace blade, or 2 pinches ground mace or nutmeg

1 bay leaf

Kosher or coarse sea salt

## TIPS

*Kewra water, the distilled extract of the flowers of the pandanus tree, is used more for its rose water–like aroma (and fine to leave out of the stew).*

*Many Halal butchers stock bone-in goat stew meat or will order it, as do some online ranches and meat purveyors (wildforkfoods.com). The lean meat benefits from a long, slow cooking process and, because the stew meat is cut from the entire animal rather than one meaty section, the bone-to-meat ratio will vary in each batch.*

**SAFFRON-CARDAMOM CREAM**

⅓ cup (80ml) heavy cream

1 teaspoon saffron threads (about ⅓ of a 1-gram tin)

4 tablespoons (55g) ghee or unsalted butter (½ stick/55g)

1½ teaspoons ground cardamom, or seeds from 12 green cardamom pods, ground in a mortar

Few drops kewra water (optional)

> *I grew up in a vegetarian household, and my mother would cook biryani on special days with whatever vegetables were at their best. We make it with goat at Adda, and I think mine is very tasty. (I would never dare say that to my mother; otherwise I would be kicked out of my house.) It is simple food transformed into perfection. You layer up curry and rice in a ceramic pot, seal it with dough, and bake it all together (the bread is for cooking, not eating). When you serve biryani, you reach all the way to the bottom of the bowl to get each of the ingredients.* —CHINTAN

**Cook the rice:** Soak rice in cold water for 30 to 45 minutes and strain.

In a sachet or cheesecloth tied with a string, combine the ginger, cumin seeds, whole coriander, green and black cardamom pods, black peppercorns, cinnamon stick, mace blade, and bay leaf.

In a medium pot, combine 1½ quarts (6 cups) water, the sachet with the garam masala mix, and 2 to 3 pinches salt and bring to a vigorous boil. Add the strained rice and stir, then reduce the heat to low, cover the pot, and simmer for 3 minutes. Taste the rice; it should be soft on the outside but firm in the middle; it will finish cooking in the oven. Immediately strain and fluff the rice several times with a fork to release the steam. Remove the sachet and leave the rice in the strainer to cool.

**Bloom the saffron and make the cream:** In a small saucepan, warm the heavy cream over low heat just until hot but not boiling. Crumble the saffron over the cream, transfer to a dish, and let bloom for 5 minutes.

Add the ghee and cardamom to the saucepan and melt the ghee over low heat, swirling the pan, then scrape the ghee into the saffron cream. When cool, add a few drops of kewra water to the saffron cream, if you'd like.

**Assemble the biryani:** If the curry is chilled, gently rewarm it over low heat just until no longer cold.

Toss together the cilantro, mint, ginger, and peppers and set aside.

Scrape the saffron-cardamom cream into a large Dutch oven or clay pot with a lid and swirl to coat the bottom of the pot. Spread half of the spiced basmati rice evenly over the cream, then pick the stew meat out of the curry and arrange it on top of the rice (reserve the curry sauce). Scatter half of the cilantro-mint mixture over the meat, spread out half the fried onions in an even layer, then top the onions with the remaining rice. Dollop all the curry sauce over the rice, spreading out the sauce as much as possible so it goes all the way to the edges of the rice. Finish the layers with the remaining cilantro-mint mixture and fried onions.

**Bake the biryani:** Put both racks in the lower third of the oven and preheat the oven to 300°F (150°C).

Roll out the biryani dough out and seal the pot (technique follows) or cover the pot very snugly with aluminum foil. Either way, close the pot with the lid and bake the biryani for 1 hour. Remove the pot from the oven and let it rest for about 15 minutes.

**Serve:** Put the yogurt in a large, shallow serving bowl and scatter the pomegranate seeds on top.

Transfer the Dutch oven or pot to the serving area. Crack the dough and peel it off the top of the pot (discard the dough) or remove the foil.

Serve the biryani with the yogurt and a large spoon so everyone can scoop all the way to the bottom of the pot to get to each layer.

**BIRYANI ASSEMBLY**

Chintan's Goat (or Lamb) Curry with Fried Onions (recipe follows)

2 handfuls chopped cilantro, leaves and tender top stems (about 1 cup)

2 handfuls chopped mint leaves (about 1 cup)

1 3-inch (7.5cm) piece ginger, peeled and finely chopped

2 to 3 jwala or 1 to 2 medium serrano peppers, seeds removed and finely chopped

Saffron-Cardamom Cream

Garam masala–spiced basmati rice

Biryani Dough to seal the pot (technique follows; optional)

**TO SERVE**

About 2 cups (480g) full-fat plain yogurt

Generous handful pomegranate seeds

# CHINTAN'S GOAT (OR LAMB) CURRY WITH FRIED ONIONS

**FEEDS 5 TO 6 (SERVED WITH RICE); MAKES ENOUGH FOR THE BIRYANI**

**FRIED ONIONS**

3 medium yellow onions, divided

Neutral oil, for frying

**GOAT OR LAMB CURRY**

2½ to 3 pounds (1.2 to 1.4kg) bone-in goat stew meat or 2 to 2¼ pounds (1kg) bone-in lamb stew meat or shoulder, cut into 1- to 2-inch (2.5 to 5cm) chunks

Kosher or coarse sea salt

5 green cardamom pods

3 black cardamom pods (optional; see Tips)

3 cloves

3 mace blades or ¼ teaspoon ground mace or nutmeg

2 dried bay leaves

2 teaspoons ground turmeric

3 to 3½ teaspoons Kashmiri or other mild red chili powder

3 tablespoons Everyday Garlic-Ginger Paste (page 314)

Line a sheet pan or large plate with paper towels.

**Fry the onions:** Quarter 2 onions and slice them into very thin rings (save the ends and scraps).

Roughly chop the onion scraps and the remaining onion and set the chopped onions aside for the curry.

Add enough vegetable oil to a Dutch oven or other large pot to come about ½ inch (12mm) up the sides. Heat the oil over medium heat, add the sliced onions, and slowly fry, stirring occasionally with a wooden spoon, until caramelized and a deep, dark golden brown, 30 to 35 minutes. You can leave the onions largely unattended the first 15 minutes or so, but once they start to brown, watch and stir them more often; pick out any clumps of onions that darken quickly so they don't burn. Strain the onions over a heatproof bowl (reserve the frying oil). Transfer the onions to the sheet pan and separate the slices.

**Make the curry:** Remove any small shards of bone that are loosely attached to the goat stew meat. Season the meat generously with salt (about 2 teaspoons) and toss to coat all sides.

In a small dish, combine the green and black cardamom pods, cloves, mace blades, bay leaves, turmeric, and chili powder.

Wipe out the Dutch oven and add enough of the reserved frying oil to coat the bottom (about 3 tablespoons). Heat the oil over medium heat, add the chopped onions, and sauté, stirring occasionally, until beginning to brown, about 10 minutes. Add the Garlic-Ginger Paste and spice mixture and stir constantly until aromatic, about 1 minute. Add 5 cups (1.2L) water and scrape the spices off the bottom of the pot. Add the goat stew meat and bring to a boil.

Reduce the heat to a simmer and cook, uncovered and stirring occasionally, until the stew meat is tender, 2 to 2½ hours. The goat will be firmer than most stew meats but should be easy to nibble. If the curry broth reduces beyond roughly the level of the meat, add a little water (about ½ cup/120ml). Season the curry with salt.

Pick out the chunks of meat and transfer them to a bowl or food storage container; you can leave the meat on the bone (check the goat meat and remove any small bits of bone that are falling off the meat) or debone the meat completely. Strain the curry sauce over the bowl and pick out the green and black cardamom pods, cloves, bay leaves, and any small bone shards in the sauce (look carefully; with goat the pieces can be quite small).

At this point, you can assemble the biryani or let the curry cool completely, cover, and refrigerate overnight. (Refrigerate the fried onions separately.)

## BIRYANI DOUGH (OPTIONAL)

A dum biryani is topped with simple flour and water dough to tightly seal the pot and steam the rice without letting any air escape ("dum" means to cook slowly, traditionally over a low fire). The dough needs to be sturdy enough to cover the top of a large pot without falling in, so it should be on the drier side.

Mound the flour on a work surface or in a bowl. Drizzle about ⅓ cup (80ml) water over the flour and knead until the flour starts to come together. Keep adding water (or more flour) until you have a smooth dough; it shouldn't be sticky. Let the dough rest for about 15 minutes.

On a lightly floured surface, roll out the dough into a circle about 1 inch (2.5cm) larger than the baking pot. Lay the dough over the pot, stretching it out slightly so it doesn't sag too much in the middle. Tightly seal the dough to the edges of the pot, then cover the pot with the lid. Break open the dough and discard it after baking.

**TIPS**

*You'll need to set aside time to make the curry (which is also delicious served on its own, with flatbread), but the cooking process is mainly hands off—great for a weekend project, and the flavors deepen after an overnight rest.*

*Like many home cooks throughout India, Chintan uses whole spices to make a garam masala spice mix. You can play around with the type and ratio of spices (or substitute ground spices), but one worth seeking out is black cardamom, the much larger, fully matured pods of the cardamom plant that have a unique flavor from being smoked and dried. Beyond Indian markets, you can find black cardamom at online purveyors that specialize in South Asian spices (thespiceway.com).*

**MAKES ENOUGH TO COVER 1 LARGE DUTCH OVEN OR POT**

1½ cups (180g) all-purpose flour, plus more as needed

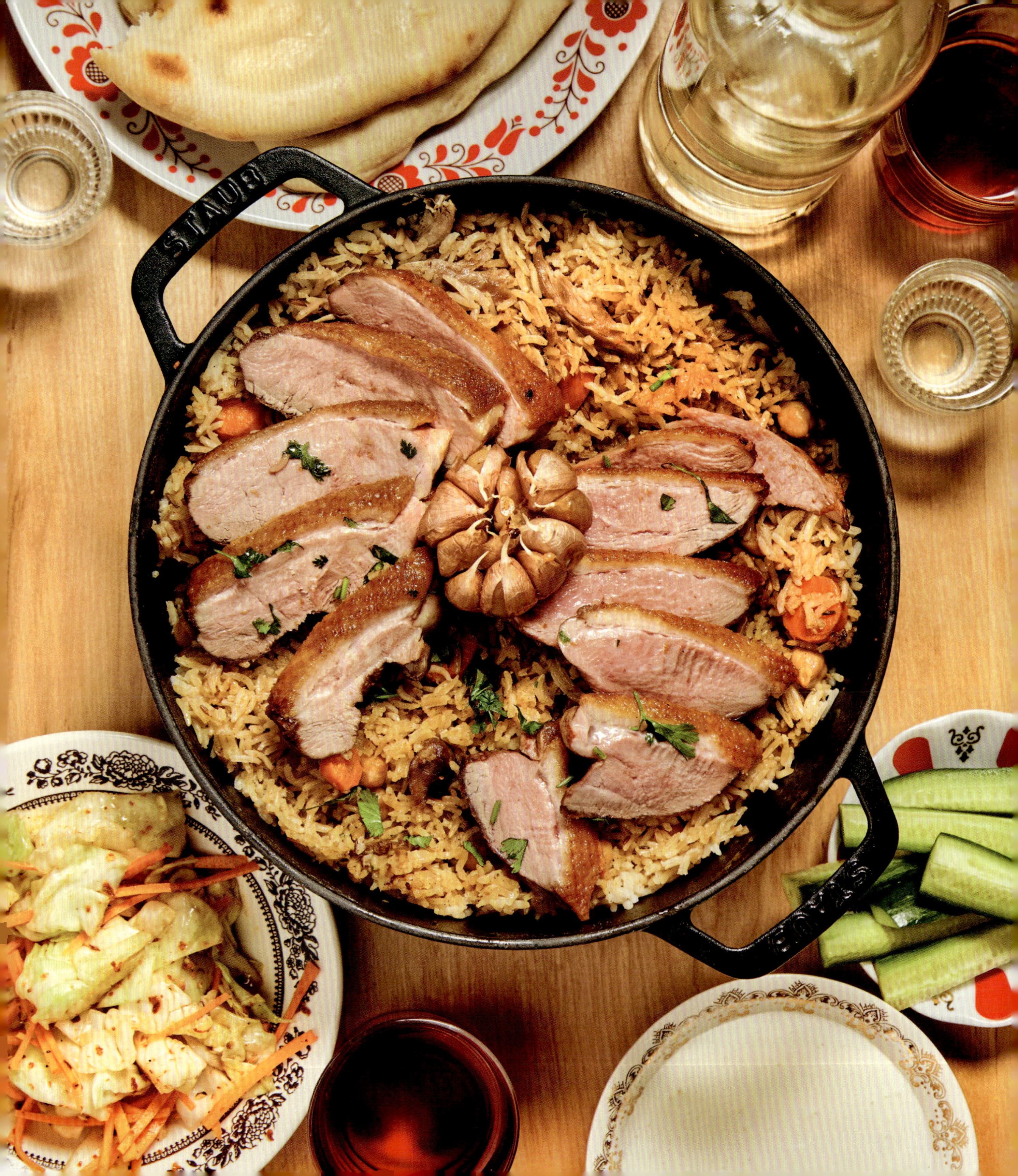
STAUB

# Bonnie Morales's Duck Plov

*Kachka, Portland (Oregon)*

When we went to Portland in season five, I heard that one of the best places to go in the city was Kachka, where the food is influenced by Russia and other former Soviet Republics. It's run by Bonnie Morales and her husband, Israel. Everything you get there sounds simple, things like homemade dumplings and horseradish vodka, but it all has an unexpected explosion of flavor. It's the very best comfort food can be.

During that scene, Bonnie told a beautiful story about why they named the restaurant Kachka. During World War II, when Germans were advancing into Belarus, her grandmother Rakhil was telling her family that they had to get out and leave the ghetto at that moment. They couldn't wait any longer. The family felt if they left together, they would be caught, so Rakhil left with her baby and started heading toward Russia. Along the way, Rakhil was stopped by German soldiers and asked if she was Jewish. She said, "No, no, I'm Ukrainian, I'm going to my in-laws." The soldiers asked her to prove it by telling them how you say "duck" in Ukrainian. She spoke Yiddish, Russian, and a little Belarusian, but not Ukrainian. She guessed and said, "kachka," the word for duck in several languages. The soldiers let her go. That one word saved her life. As Bonnie said, "Everyone has their version of kachka." It's the thinnest line of luck we all live on.

This Uzbek-style duck plov that they make at Kachka for special occasions is a tribute to Bonnie's grandmother. It's a garlicky rice pilaf with duck confit and seared duck breast. Bonnie serves it with her cabbage slaw, suzma (which is the Uzbek version of sour cream), and, to drink, pomegranate juice. You're also going to need a bottle of vodka so you can make the same toast Bonnie made when I was there: "For everything that joins us."

---

*Every couple of years, we take our management team on a discovery trip to a former Soviet bloc country. In 2021, as we traversed Uzbekistan, we collectively ate our weight in plov. Plov happens to be the national dish, a celebratory rice affair studded with dried fruits, decadent lamb, and heady spices. We even managed to cram a massive, thirty-liter cast iron kazan, the traditional cooking vessel for plov, in a suitcase that our chef de cuisine, Francisco, dragged back to Portland so we could create our own iteration of this magical dish. In ours, we substitute duck in place of the more traditional lamb, both in honor of our name and because, well, duck is pretty darn delicious.* —BONNIE

**FEEDS 6**

Duck Stock and Confit (recipe follows), plus the 2 reserved duck breasts

Kosher or coarse sea salt

1½ teaspoons cumin seeds, or 1 teaspoon ground cumin

¾ teaspoon whole caraway seeds, or ½ teaspoon ground caraway

1 teaspoon ground coriander

¾ teaspoon onion powder

¾ teaspoon garlic powder

¾ teaspoon sweet paprika

½ teaspoon freshly ground black pepper

¼ teaspoon ground mustard

¼ teaspoon ground fenugreek

⅓ cup (80ml) neutral oil

¼ cup (60ml) duck fat, chilled or at room temperature, reserved from making the confit

1 15.5-ounce (430g) can garbanzo beans (chickpeas), drained (about 1½ cups)

---

*At the restaurant, we use short-grain Uzbek lazer rice; it can be difficult to find, so this recipe uses basmati. All of the plov components and sides—the duck stock, confit, cabbage salad, and suzma—are made a day ahead and everything is served family-style, so it's a good party dish.* —BONNIE

**Make the rice pilaf:** Take the duck breasts out of the refrigerator about 45 minutes before you plan to serve the plov and season generously with salt.

Put the cumin and caraway seeds in a small dish by the stove. In another small dish, combine the coriander, onion powder, garlic powder, paprika, black pepper, ground mustard, and fenugreek.

Heat a large Dutch oven, kazan, or cast iron wok with a lid over medium-high heat. Add the cumin and caraway seeds and toast, stirring occasionally with a wooden spoon, for about 20 seconds. Add the rest of the spices and stir constantly until fragrant, 15 to 20 seconds. (Be careful not to burn the spices.) Quickly add the oil, stir a few times, then add the duck fat, 3½ cups (840ml) duck stock, the chickpeas, raisins, barberries, and 1 teaspoon salt. Bring the stock to a boil, reduce to a simmer, and simmer for a few minutes to allow the spices infuse the stock.

Stir in the rice and add the confit duck and vegetables (the duck meat, offal, carrots, garlic cloves, and whole garlic head). Cover the pot, reduce the heat to low, and cook for 20 minutes. Scrape any brown bits off the bottom of the pot and check the liquid; if the rice has absorbed all the stock, add a generous splash of duck stock or water (about ⅓ cup/120ml). Cover the pot, cook until the rice is tender, about 15 minutes, and turn off the heat.

Fish out the whole head of garlic and nestle it on top of the pilaf in the very center of the pot.

Cover the pot and let the rice steam while you cook the duck breasts.

**Sear the duck breasts:** While the rice steams, pat the duck breasts dry with paper towels.

Heat a large, dry cast iron skillet or comal over medium-high heat until very hot, about 2 minutes. Add the duck breasts, skin side facing down, to the skillet, reduce the heat to medium, and sear, undisturbed, until the skin is nicely browned and crispy, about 6 minutes. Use a large spatula to get fully underneath the skin, flip the duck breasts, and cook until medium rare or a digital thermometer inserted in the thickest part of the breast reads 130°F (55°C), 3 to 5 minutes.

Transfer the duck breasts to a cutting board and let rest, uncovered, for about 5 minutes. Slice each crosswise into roughly ½-inch (12mm) thick slices.

**Serve:** Fan out the duck breast slices on the plov to make a circle around the head of garlic. Tuck the quartered eggs around the duck breast and scatter the cilantro leaves over the plov.

Serve the plov family-style with the cabbage salad, suzma, sliced radishes, and bread along with the pomegranate juice and vodka for the table.

¼ cup (40g) raisins, roughly chopped

1 tablespoon dried barberries or goji berries or finely chopped unsweetened cranberries

2 cups (13 ounces/370g) white basmati or other long-grain rice

**TO SERVE**

2 hard-boiled eggs, peeled and quartered

Leaves from 5 to 6 sprigs of fresh cilantro

Bonnie's Korean-Style Cabbage and Carrot Salad (recipe follows)

2 cups (465g) suzma (store-bought) or Homemade Suzma (technique follows)

Sliced green radishes or peeled daikon

Plenty of lepyoshka or other flatbread

**TO DRINK**

Fresh pomegranate juice and vodka

# DUCK STOCK AND CONFIT

**MAKES ABOUT 4 CUPS (960ML) STOCK AND ENOUGH CONFIT DUCK AND VEGETABLES FOR THE PLOV**

1 large (5- to 5½-pound/ 2.3 to 2.5kg) whole duck

Kosher or coarse sea salt

**DUCK STOCK**

2 whole heads garlic

3 tablespoons whole black peppercorns

1 medium yellow or white onion, peeled and cut in half through the root ends

Reserved duck bones (skeleton and wings)

**DUCK CONFIT**

Reserved seasoned duck legs

16 ounces (about 500g/6 large) carrots, peeled and cut into ½-inch (12mm) medallions

3 whole heads garlic

About 3 cups (720ml) melted rendered duck fat (2 11-ounce/310g jars)

> *If you aren't comfortable breaking down a whole duck, ask your butcher to cut it up into two boneless breasts and two bone-in legs, and keep the offal and frame along with the trimmings. We save the skin from the trimmings and also remove the skin from the legs (before they're confited) to fry up to make crispy gribenes that we serve on top of the plov. Here, the skin is left on the legs, but take it off if you want to make them (it's easy to do if you have the time). For the best flavor, we use every part of the duck, including the offal, in the plov (and it's more economical), but if you're short on time you could make this with two large boneless duck breasts and two bone-in thighs, and use good-quality chicken stock (make sure it's not very salty) in the rice.* **—BONNIE**

### DAY 1

**Break down the duck:** Use a sharp knife or kitchen scissors to cut the duck into 2 breasts, 2 legs (with the thigh), 2 wings, the duck frame, and offal (heart, liver, gizzards). Start by cutting out the neckbone, then cut off the thighs and wings, then the breasts. Trim away any bits of offal from the cavity of the duck and discard, then remove the bones from the breast (save the bones). Trim off any excess skin around the duck cavity, legs, and breasts and save it to fry up to make gribenes as a crispy snack or plov topping, if you'd like.

Rinse all the duck parts well and pat dry with paper towels.

Generously season the duck legs with salt (about 1 teaspoon) and put in a bowl with the reserved offal. Cover and refrigerate for at least 3 hours, or preferably overnight for the best flavor before making the confit.

You can use the meaty duck bones to make the duck stock now, or refrigerate them as well to make the stock later.

In a separate bowl or in plastic wrap, cover the unseasoned breasts; they will be cooked on the day you plan to serve the plov.

### DAY 2

**Make the duck stock:** Cut 1 garlic bulb in half through the equator.

Heat a large Dutch oven or stockpot over medium-high heat until hot, add the black peppercorns, and toast until fragrant, about 30 seconds. Add 1½ quarts (1.4L) of water, the halved and whole heads of garlic, onion, and duck bones and wings. Bring the water to a boil, reduce the heat, and simmer until the stock has reduced by almost half, about 3 hours.

Let the stock cool completely and strain through a fine-mesh sieve (discard the solids). If not using within an hour or two, cover and refrigerate the stock for up to 3 days.

**Confit the duck legs and offal:** Meanwhile, put a rack in the middle of the oven. Preheat the oven to 250°F (120°C).

Arrange the duck legs in a single layer in the bottom of a medium Dutch oven or other oven-safe wide pot that will snugly fit the duck legs and carrots in a single layer. Be sure the pot has high enough sides to keep the duck fat from overflowing as the duck cooks and more fat is rendered. Tuck the firm offal (the heart and gizzards) between the duck legs.

Peel the outmost layer of papery skin off 1 garlic bulb and tuck it in the middle of the duck legs. Remove the cloves from the remaining 2 garlic bulbs, slice off the hard root ends, and peel the cloves with your fingers (don't smash them). Scatter the garlic cloves over the duck and carrots and add enough melted duck fat to fully submerge the legs. (Refrigerate the empty duck fat jars to refill with

### TIPS

*This recipe looks daunting, but most of the components are made ahead so the dish can be finished relatively quickly. You need to plan at least two days ahead to allow time to season the duck legs overnight, then confit the legs and offal and make the duck stock the following day; you can make the plov that same day or refrigerate everything another day or two. The lightly pickled cabbage salad also needs an overnight rest to cure.*

*Use the leftover strained duck fat to roast potatoes and other vegetables, fry meats and vegetables, or to make another plov; it will keep in the refrigerator for up to 2 months.*

*Barberries, available at Middle Eastern markets, are small berries with a uniquely tangy flavor. Dried goji berries or finely chopped unsweetened cranberries can be substituted.*

fat after you make the confit.) Gently tuck the duck liver in the fat wherever there is room.

Slowly roast the duck, uncovered, until the meat has pulled away from the end of the bone and is easy to remove when pricked with a fork, about 3 hours.

Let the duck confit cool for about 1 hour.

**Finish the plov base:** Fish out the liver and break it apart with your fingers over a medium bowl.

Pick the meat off the duck legs, shred or chop the meat, and add it to the bowl. (Discard the bones and any coarse bits of cartilage.) Chop the firm offal (heart and gizzards) and add them to the bowl.

**Strain off the duck fat and prepare the vegetables:** Set a fine-mesh strainer over a 1 quart (1L) or larger measuring cup and strain off the duck fat; stop when you get to the garlic, vegetables, and sediment at the bottom of the pot. Let the duck fat cool before pouring it into the reserved jars.

Over the bowl with the duck meat, squeeze out the cloves from 1 head of garlic and gently toss everything together well. Add the carrots and the remaining garlic cloves and whole head of garlic. Don't stir at this point; the garlic cloves and remaining head of garlic fall apart easily.

If you're not making the plov within an hour, cover and refrigerate the duck and vegetables overnight or up to 3 days.

You'll need a portion of the duck fat to make the plov; cover and refrigerate any leftover fat, well sealed, for up to 2 months.

# KOREAN-STYLE CABBAGE AND CARROT SALAD

*This coriander-spiced salad with both cabbage and carrots is a nice contrast to the plov. It's inspired by the carrot salads that are the ubiquitous dish on every Uzbek table. The influence of Korean cooking on Uzbek cuisine goes back to the 1930s, when Stalin ordered the deportation of nearly two hundred thousand Koreans living in the easternmost regions of Russia (closest to Korea and Japan) to areas of the former Soviet Union thousands of miles to the west, including what is today Uzbekistan. The Koryo-Saram ("Korea-people," as they refer to themselves) have significantly influenced Uzbek culture, including the food and drink.* —BONNIE

**FEEDS 6**

1 small, heavy green cabbage, cored (2 to 2¼ pounds/1kg)

Kosher or coarse sea salt

2 medium carrots, peeled and cut into thin matchsticks

⅓ cup (80ml) distilled white vinegar

3 to 4 teaspoons gochugaru (Korean red chili flakes)

2 teaspoons granulated sugar

2 teaspoons whole black peppercorns

1 tablespoon plus 1 teaspoon coriander seeds

1½ tablespoons grapeseed, linseed, cold-pressed sunflower, or vegetable oil

2 garlic cloves, minced

**Wilt the cabbage:** Roughly chop the cabbage into large chunks (roughly 1½ inches/4cm) and put in a large bowl.

Sprinkle 1 tablespoon plus 1 teaspoon salt over the cabbage and use your hands to firmly massage the salt into the cabbage until the leaves start to soften and are moist, about 2 minutes. Set the cabbage aside for 45 minutes to 1 hour.

**Finish the salad:** Add the carrots, vinegar, gochugaru, and sugar to the wilted cabbage and toss to combine.

In a mortar with a pestle or with the bottom of a bowl or mug, lightly crush the black peppercorns until they just begin to break apart; add the coriander seeds, and smash to the texture of freshly ground pepper. (Or, lightly crush the spices in a spice grinder.)

In a small saucepan, heat the oil over medium-high heat until very hot but not smoking, about 1 minute. Take the pan off the heat, add the peppercorns, coriander, and garlic, and stir vigorously until the spices are fragrant, 10 to 15 seconds. Scrape the seasoned oil into the cabbage mixture and toss to combine.

Cover the surface of the salad with plastic wrap and set a wide bowl filled with several heavy cans of food on top. Let the salad cure at room temperature for 2½ to 3 hours. Remove the weights and refrigerate the salad overnight or up to 3 days.

## HOMEMADE SUZMA

**MAKES ABOUT 2 CUPS (465G)**

8 ounces (225g) soft sheep's milk or goat cheese, room temperature

½ cup (120ml) labneh or full-fat yogurt (goat, Greek, or Icelandic)

½ cup (120ml) smetana or crème fraiche

2 tablespoons finely grated Pecorino Romano cheese

Kosher or coarse sea salt

If you've got a Russian or Eastern European market nearby, get some Uzbek-style suzma, a thick, cultured dairy product somewhat like crème fraîche, to serve with the plov. Otherwise, this homemade version is a good stand-in. Keep it in the fridge to serve with other dishes or use in drinks, as locals do.

In a blender or food processor, combine the sheep's milk cheese, labneh, smetana, Pecorino Romano, and ½ teaspoon salt and blend until smooth. Cover and refrigerate the suzma for up to 5 days.

# Salam Dakkak's Fatet Muskhan

*Bait Maryam, Dubai*

In Dubai, you need to go to Bait Maryam ("House of Maryam"). It's a very special restaurant where Salam Dakkak cooks the Palestinian-Jordanian food she grew up eating at home. (Maryam was Salam's mother.) It's not often in the restaurant world that you find a place run by a great chef that feels like you're eating in someone's home. Everything about it, the food and the way it looks (even the curtains that were from Salam's mother's house), is so genuine. And for anybody who thinks it's too late to change the direction of their life, Salam didn't open the restaurant until she was in her fifties. When we were there for season seven of the show, she had just been named the Middle East & North Africa's female chef of the year.

I had lunch with Nada, Salam's daughter who runs the restaurant, and her mom prepared a special dish for me to try called kibbeh nayyeh. It's a specialty of the village where Salam grew up, which is known for the quality of their meats, especially lamb. (In the show, I told you the story that I had actually had another very special mother's version of kibbeh from my mom. She used to make snacks for Richard and me that were raw ground beef rolled up in a little ball with some salt, because that's what you did in Germany.) Salam mixed the ground lamb with spices like cinnamon, cloves, marjoram, and some others I can't remember. The important part is how you eat the kibbeh: on a very thin flatbread topped with some bulgur and a little onion. I don't know what happened, but when I bit into this dish, I was transported to another time and place or human being. I still can't explain it. It's like I saw a UFO. It was so crazy, I felt so emotional. I don't know if it was because Salam and Nada had shared their story with me, but I was feeling an emotion *in* the food. It was magic. Certain dishes are delicious and that's good enough; that's always the bottom line. But some dishes have another dimension.

The only way you can experience kibbeh nayyeh is to go to Bait Maryam and have Salam make it for you. The ground lamb is prepared in a certain way so it's safe to eat raw (it must be from a specific part of the leg, and it must be very, very fresh). This chicken with sumac and red onions is also from Salam's mother, and how you eat it is just as important as the kibbeh. You take a little piece of taboon, the local flatbread that Salam fries up so it's crispy like a pita chip, and you scoop up the chicken and some of the garlicky yogurt sauce. Salam told me that her mom put all of her heart, all of her love in her food. When you try this, you'll understand.

**FEEDS 5 TO 6, MORE AS PART OF A TASTING MENU**

About 4 pounds (1.6kg) red onions, peeled (8 large)

1 4-ounce (115g) bag ground sumac, divided (1 scant cup)

1 teaspoon Baharat (Seven Spice Blend), store-bought or homemade (recipe follows)

1 teaspoon ground cinnamon

Coarse sea salt and freshly ground black pepper

¾ cup (180ml) extra-virgin olive oil, plus more for frying

1 small carrot, peeled

1 slice (wheel) dried lemon or ¼ whole lemon, seeds removed

1 cinnamon stick

1 bay leaf

1 to 1¼ pounds (500g) boneless chicken breast, cut into large chunks, or chicken tenders (tenderloins), cut in half if large

---

*This dish is extremely close to my heart, as in this form it is not very well-known, and we believe Maryam herself may have created it. My mom had a big family that she needed to feed, so she would always use any leftovers in different ways to make it seem like she cooked a new dish the next day. Whenever she would make muskhan (also spelled musakhan), a popular Palestinian dish composed of chicken with onions, sumac, and fried pine nuts served over taboon bread, she would shred the leftover chicken the next day and stir it into a big new batch of red onions that she cooked down with a lot of sumac. She topped it with her lemony, garlicky yogurt sauce, crunchy fried bread (day-old bread works well), parsley, and fried pine nuts and almonds (in our culture we believe that the more nuts you add, the more generous you are), and called it fatet muskhan. (Fatet is also a classic dish that relies on leftover fried bread and yogurt sauce.) I hope you enjoy it as much as my family has over the years.* —**SALAM**

**Sweat the onions:** Trim the tops off the onions and cut each in half lengthwise through the root end. Thinly slice each onion in half crosswise, and put them in a large, dry Dutch oven.

Cook the onions over medium-high heat, uncovered, stirring occasionally with a wooden spoon and scraping the bottom of the pot, until they have released most of their water and have reduced by more than half, 35 to 40 minutes. Turn off the heat.

Set aside 1 small spoonful (about 1 teaspoon) of the ground sumac for serving. Add the remainder of the sumac, the Baharat, ground cinnamon, 1 teaspoon each salt and pepper, and the olive oil to the pot, and stir until the spices are fully incorporated.

**Boil the chicken:** While the onions cook, fill a medium saucepot about halfway with water. Add the carrot, dried lemon slice, cinnamon stick, and bay leaf and bring to a low boil. Add the chicken to the pot and cook until the flesh is firm and no longer pink in the center (cut the thickest piece in half), 8 to 12 minutes, depending on the size of the pieces. Drain the chicken and, when cool enough to handle, shred it into bite-size pieces. Add the meat to the spiced onions, stir to completely coat the chicken in the onions and spices, and season with salt and pepper.

Cover the pot and let the flavors meld for at least 30 minutes. Or, if not serving right way, let the muskhan cool completely, cover, and refrigerate overnight or up to 3 days.

**Fry the flatbread and almonds:** Line a sheet pan with paper towels or bags.

Pour enough olive or other frying oil into a large sauté pan to generously coat the bottom and heat over medium-high heat. Tear any large pieces of bread in half to fit in the pan, and fry the bread in batches (don't crowd the pan) until golden brown and crispy, 30 to 45 seconds per side. Transfer the bread to the sheet pan. Between batches, reheat (and add more of) the oil in the pan as needed.

Pour off all but a thin layer of the oil from the pan, then add the almonds and toast, stirring constantly, until just beginning to brown, about 30 seconds. Scrape the almonds onto the pan with the fried bread.

If not serving the muskhan right away, you can set aside the flatbreads and almonds at room temperature, uncovered, for several hours.

**To serve:** Rewarm the onion and chicken muskhan over medium-low heat, stirring often.

Break the fried flatbread into large bite-size pieces.

Divide the chicken-onion muskhan among six shallow bowls (or

### FLATBREAD

Olive oil or vegetable oil

Plenty of flatbreads: Bombay Canteen Kulcha (page 324), naan, taboon, manakeesh, or Greek pita

2 handfuls (about ½ cup/45g) slivered or sliced almonds

### TO SERVE

Salam's Fatet (Fatteh) Sauce (page 323)

3 to 4 sprigs parsley, finely chopped

### TIPS

*You can enjoy the muskhan the day it is made, but the flavors meld after an overnight rest in the refrigerator. A great family dish, it also works well for a buffet (increase the amount of flatbread so there's plenty to go around).*

*Most muskhan recipes call for only a few tablespoons of sumac, but here there's no holding back on the citrusy, earthy berry flavor. Get a fresh bag from a good vendor like The Spice Way (thespiceway.com).*

pile it on one large plate) and mound Salam's Fatet Sauce (about ⅓ cup/80ml) in the center of each. Use the back of a spoon to spread the yogurt sauce into a large, wide circle, sprinkle the reserved teaspoon of sumac over the yogurt sauce, and scatter the almonds and parsley on top. Mound about half of the fried flatbreads in the center of the yogurt sauce and serve the remaining flatbreads on the side.

To serve the chicken-onion muskhan in a Dutch oven for a family-style dinner, mound the yogurt sauce in a bowl, sprinkle the sumac, almonds, and parsley on top, and serve with the fried flatbreads.

## BAHARAT (SEVEN SPICE BLEND)

Mix together all of the spices.

**MAKES ABOUT 2½ TABLESPOONS**

1½ teaspoons sweet paprika

1½ teaspoons ground cumin

1½ teaspoons finely ground black pepper

¾ teaspoon ground coriander

¾ teaspoon ground cloves

¼ teaspoon ground cinnamon

¼ teaspoon ground nutmeg

⅛ teaspoon ground cardamom

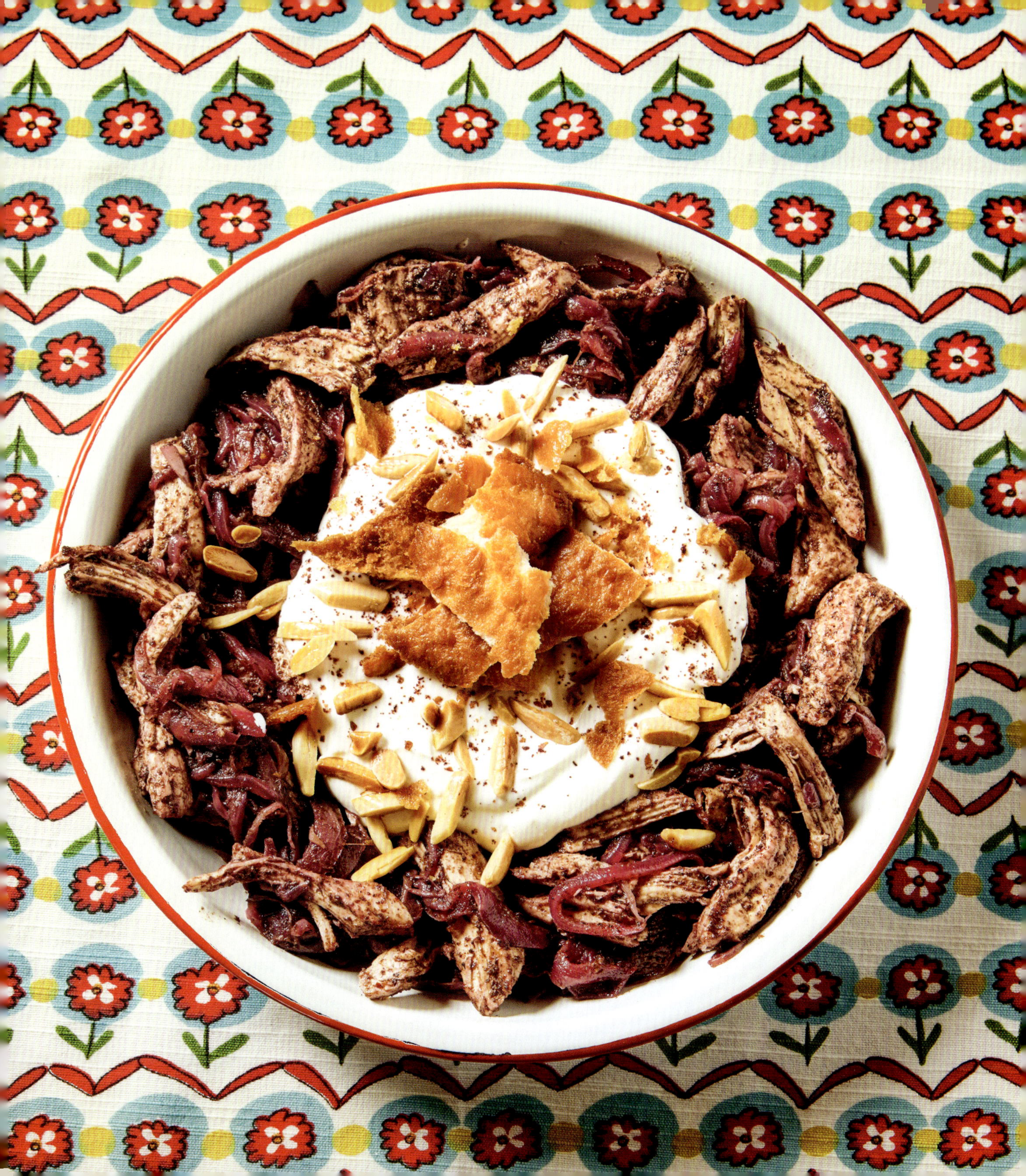

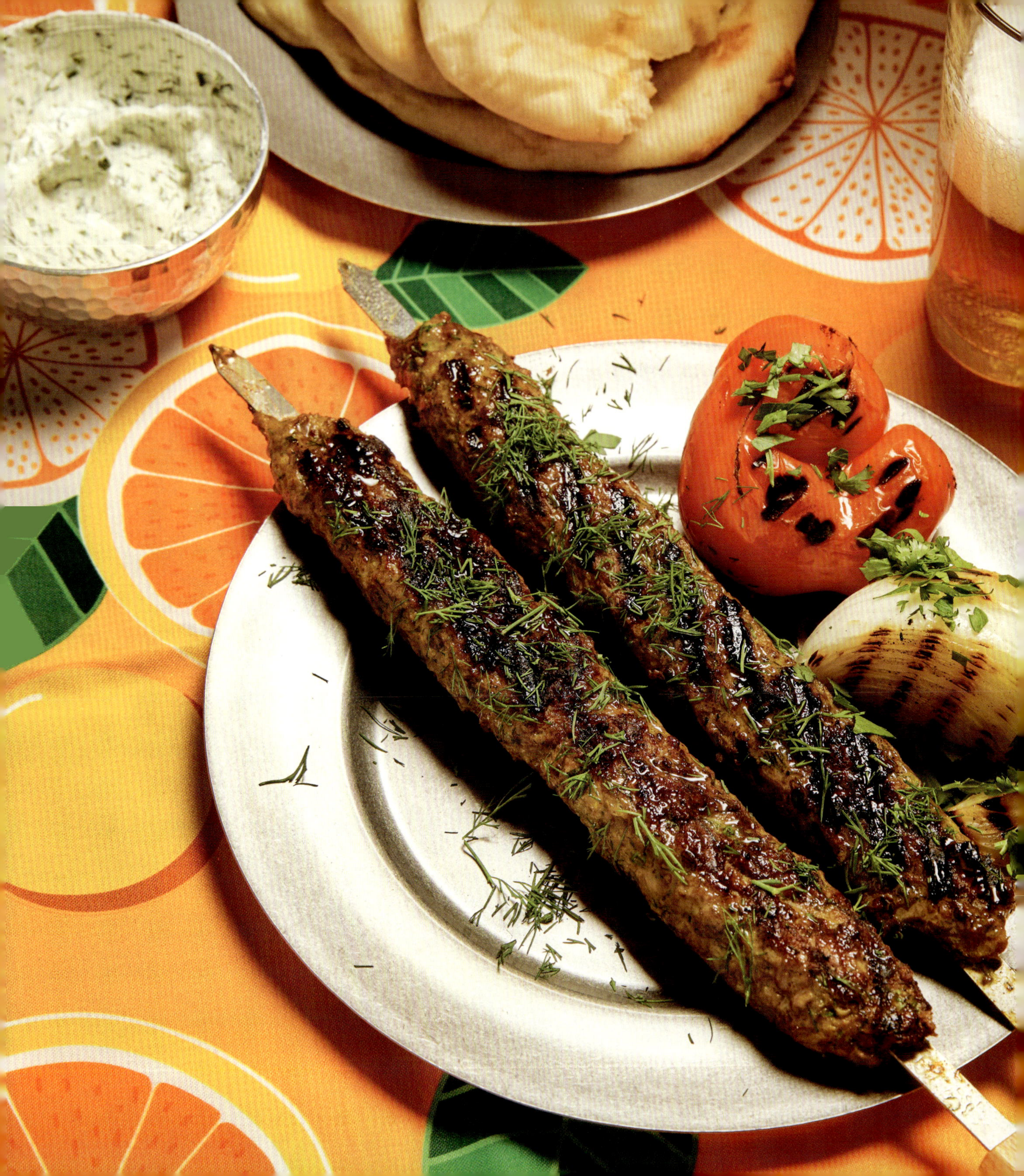

# Mike Solomonov and Andrew Henshaw's Lamb and Beef Koobideh

*Laser Wolf, Philadelphia*

I've known Mike Solomonov for years. He was one of my guides in the "Tel Aviv" episode of the very first season of *Somebody Feed Phil*, and beyond being a great friend, he's one of the most influential Jewish chefs in the country. He and two other younger chefs—Alon Shaya in New Orleans (there's a recipe from him in my first book) and Ori Menashe in LA—have put Israeli cuisine on the map in the US. We had a recipe for Ori's incredible hummus in this book, but we ran out of room and couldn't include it. If you're in LA, go to Bavel (I never miss ordering a plate of his hummus with duck 'nduja for the table) or Saffy's, his more casual place, where you can get his hummus with ful, which are fava beans.

When we shot the "Philadelphia" episode for season six, I finally got to take you to not just one but two of Mike's restaurants: Laser Wolf, his more casual place where Andrew Henshaw is the head chef, and Zahav, Mike's flagship restaurant where we had our final group dinner. You can't go wrong at either place. At Laser Wolf, one of the things Andrew brought out was this lamb and beef koobideh. A koobideh is a Middle Eastern kebab, only instead of big chunks of meat and vegetables like you get on American kebabs, it's like a giant hamburger patty with a lot of spices that has been molded onto a skewer.

*This is a winning-like-Phil's-smile kebab that is easy to prepare and wildly flavorful—what's not to love?* —**MIKE**

*At Laser Wolf, our grills are very shallow like what you see all over Israel, so everything cooks very close to the smoldering charcoal. It's almost like the meat and vegetables are grilled and smoked at the same time. We put bricks in our grills so we have a ledge to lay the koobideh skewers on (regular thin metal or bamboo skewers won't hold the meat), which you can also do at home on a standard grill. Get beef and lamb with a higher fat content, coarsely ground; ask your butcher. The bigger chunks of fat melt more slowly so the meat stays tender and juicy. Don't skip the step of refrigerating the kebabs; it helps keep the fat from melting too quickly and falling off the skewers or drying out. Once you get the hang of shaping and cooking them, it's a lot of fun.* —**ANDREW**

**FEEDS 6**

**KEBABS**

1 large white or yellow onion

1 large or 2 small bunches dill, finely chopped

1½ pounds (680g) 20% or 30% coarsely ground beef (not lean; see Tips)

1 pound (455g) coarsely ground lamb

2 tablespoons seltzer water or club soda

2 teaspoons turmeric

2 teaspoons ground sumac

1 teaspoon dill seed

1 teaspoon granulated sugar

½ teaspoon baking soda

Kosher or coarse sea salt and freshly ground black pepper

**Prep:** To grill the kebabs, you'll need six wide, flat metal koobideh skewers (see Tips; standard thin metal skewers work in an oven).

**Make the beef kebab base:** Slice the top off the onion, peel, and, holding the root end, coarsely grate the onion over a large bowl. Pour off and discard about half the onion juice, add 2 large handfuls (about 1 cup/32g) of chopped dill, the ground beef, ground lamb, and seltzer water. (Save the remaining dill for garnish.)

In a small dish, mix together the turmeric, sumac, dill seed, sugar, baking soda, 2 to 3 teaspoons salt, and 2 teaspoons pepper. Add the spices to the onion-meat mixture and knead the meat with the palm of your hand, like you're making a bread dough, until it becomes sticky and paste-like, 3 to 4 minutes. Divide the mixture into 16 large meatballs, about 3¼ ounces (90g) each.

**Shape the kebabs:** Wash the meat off your hands and shake off the excess water; moist hands help keep the meat from sticking.

Thread 1 meatball onto a skewer and slide it toward the middle. Wrap the palm of your hand around the meatball and open and close your hand, working down the length of the meatball, to gently flatten out the meat into a roughly 3-inch (7.5cm) torpedo shape.

Thread another meatball onto the skewer and shape the same way, working the meatballs toward one another until they touch and form a unified piece of meat roughly 9 inches (23cm) long. (If the meat sticks to your hands, run them under cold water.) Make a few shallow indentations at four or five intervals down the meat (this helps the meat stick to the skewer) by squeezing the meat gently, then pinch both ends closed so they hug the skewer. Lay the finished skewer over the edges of a large casserole dish so the meat is suspended in the middle. Loosely cover the kebabs with plastic wrap and refrigerate for at least 1 hour or up to 8 hours.

**Set up the grill or oven:** Set up a grill for direct cooking, or, if you'd like, you can set it up like a kebab grill (see Tips). To bake the kebabs, put a rack in the middle of the oven, lay a rimmed sheet pan on the rack, and preheat the oven to 425°F (220°C).

**Grill or roast the vegetables:** Put the tomatoes, cut side up, and the onions, cut side down, on the grill rack, or spread them out on the sheet pan in the oven.

Grill the tomatoes until softened, about 5 minutes (don't disturb them as they grill), or 10 minutes in the oven, and transfer to a plate. Flip the onions on the grill or sheet pan and cook just until beginning to soften but still firm, 4 to 5 minutes on the grill and 8 to 10 minutes in the oven.

Roughly chop the tomatoes and onions into large pieces, season with salt, and transfer to a serving bowl. Generously drizzle olive oil (about 3 tablespoons) over the vegetables and toss to combine.

**Cook the kebabs:** Grill the kebabs until the meat is charred on the bottom, 3 to 4 minutes, flip, and grill the opposite side until firm to the touch, 4 to 5 minutes on a very hot grill. Be careful not to overcook the meat or it can dry out.

To bake the kebabs, reheat the sheet pan you used to roast the vegetables for about 5 minutes. Slide the kebabs off the skewers and onto the hot sheet pan, roast for 5 minutes, flip the kebabs (use two spatulas so they don't break), and roast until the meat is firm, 6 to 8 minutes.

Transfer the koobideh to a serving platter.

**Serve:** Sprinkle a few pinches of the reserved chopped dill over the koobideh. Scatter the parsley and cilantro on top of the grilled tomatoes and onions, toss to combine, and serve the grilled vegetables with the koobideh and flatbread.

---

**GRILLED TOMATOES AND ONIONS**

4 to 5 large heirloom tomatoes (about 2½ pounds/1.2kg), cut in half

1 large white or yellow onion, quartered through the root end

Kosher or coarse sea salt

Extra-virgin olive oil, for drizzling

**TO SERVE**

Reserved finely chopped dill fronds

⅓ small bunch parsley, leaves only, chopped

⅓ small bunch cilantro, leaves only, chopped

Plenty of flatbread (any kind)

## TIPS

*To grill these kebabs, you will need the flat, wide metal skewers traditionally used to make koobideh and other Middle Eastern–style kebabs. (The meatballs are too heavy for thin metal or bamboo skewers on a grill, but in an oven, either can be used.)*

*Kebab grill setup (optional): You can grill the koobideh on a standard grill directly on the grill grate with great results. Or with just a few bricks, it's easy to mimic the shallow, rectangular grills used in the Middle East that char skewered meat and vegetables within 2 to 3 inches (5 to 7.5cm) of the heat source, which chars the meat while indirectly cooking it at the same time. (The setup is also a great high-heat steak grilling technique, like for Shola Olunloyo's Charred Steak with Olive Oil on page 197.)*

*Put the grill grate on the grill without any charcoal underneath. (You can also do this on a gas grill.) On top of the grate, lay two unglazed bricks upright (on their sides) and end-to-end off to one side of the grill to build a brick "wall." Build another brick wall on the opposite side of the grill, leaving enough room to fit the koobideh meat in between. You will have two "ledges" to suspend the koobideh skewers (pull out a skewer to make sure there is enough room to fit the meat between the bricks). Now stack two to three layers of briquettes or lump charcoal between the bricks, light the charcoal as usual (or preheat your gas grill), and when you have a smoldering pile, suspend the skewers between the bricks and grill your kebabs.*

*To grill the tomatoes and onions, lay another grate or rack across the bricks and lay the vegetables on top of the rack. (If you're grilling steak, fish, or anything else with this technique, you will need to lay them on the top rack.)*

# Ben and Jeremy's Seafood Boil

Ben and his cousin Jeremy Shartar (who also lives in LA with his wife, Kaye, and their baby, Jordan) have gotten into cooking together, which has been great because Monica and I get to be their guinea pigs. One of the things they make when the whole family gets together at our house is this seafood boil. You can make a lot like they do for our family and friends, or enough for five or six people.

*When I was a kid, we lived in Malibu for a couple months during the summer every year. For a special get-together, Dad would hire a great chef, Joshua Rosenstein, to do a big Cajun-style boil. It's such a fun way to eat, everyone together around the table with a big pile of seafood in the middle. Josh would dump it on the table, and everyone would just go at it.*

*When I got older, I started to cook more with my cousin Jeremy, and one of our favorite things to make together is our version of Joshua's spicy Cajun boil. One summer when my grandpa Max came to LA to visit, Jeremy and I had the idea to try a boil that would be easier on his palate (without the Cajun spices and beer and with fresh herbs and white wine instead). It turned out great, and Max loved it so much that he ate two entire lobsters.*

*Jeremy and I usually cook the lobsters first so we can break them down and no one needs tools at the table, but you can serve them whole or even get lobster tails (especially when lobsters aren't in season). We have one of those really giant seafood boil pots that you set up on a stand over a propane burner, but you can make a smaller amount in a turkey fryer or, for just a few people, in a pot on the stove like in this recipe. You need to salt the boil stock really well; it's what flavors everything.* —BEN

3 tablespoons fish sauce
3 loosely packed cups chicken meat (12 ounces, pulled from store-bought rotisserie chicken or roast chicken)
2 cups thinly sliced red or green cabbage
1 small English cucumber, thinly sliced (about 1½ cups)
1 medium bell pepper (any color), thinly sliced
1½ cups peppery leafy greens, such as watercress with tender stems, arugula or mizuna
1 loosely packed cup Thai or
On Reddit, menswear enthusiasts spar over the relative appeal (and loathsomeness) of pleats in denim.

9 A.M. | CAFFEINATE IN OLD TOWN
Marinette reminds you you're really in Europe, thanks to tables that spill out into a bright but narrow Nice alleyway in the middle of Old Town. Inside, charmingly mismatched lamps swing from the ceiling. The
The draw at Bocca, a popular lunch spot, is its nearly 2,700-square-foot rooftop terrace offering a shady view of the colorful square Cours Saleya. The menu of shared plates features flavors from all over the Mediterranean, such as a heaped platter of black-ink paella with fresh squid cooked in parsley and butter (€24 per person), or a delicate fried artichoke with raita, za'atar, basil and mint (€14). Enjoy them alongside a pitcher of fruity sangria de Cava (€45 for 1.5 liters).
HIT THE PROM
WHERE TO STAY
IT'S REASONABLE to keep a mask in your pocke
around you starts coughing, says infectious-disease

## FAMILY BOIL: FEEDS 5 TO 6

### BOIL STOCK

Vegetable oil

1 medium yellow or white onion, peeled and quartered

2 medium carrots, peeled and cut into thick medallions

1 celery stalk, quartered

1 head garlic, cut in half through the equator

4 to 5 leafy sprigs thyme

1 5- to 6-inch (14cm) sprig rosemary

2 lemons, preferably unwaxed, cut in half

1½ cups (360ml) unoaked white wine (pinot grigio or similar)

Kosher or coarse sea salt

### TIP

*Ben and Jeremy like to serve this fresh herb Mediterranean-style seafood boil with clarified butter. Joshua Rosenstein, the chef the recipe was inspired by, served it with good olive oil. Put out both and let everybody decide.*

**Prep:** Cover the table or wherever you plan to serve the seafood boil with butcher paper, newspaper, or brown paper grocery bags. You can also lay or tape the paper on top of large, rimmed sheet pans, which work well to catch the drippings.

Put a large colander in the sink.

**Make the boil stock:** Pour enough vegetable oil to lightly cover the bottom of an extra-large 12- to 16-quart (12 to 15L) stockpot and heat the oil over medium-high heat until very hot. Slide the onion, carrots, and celery into the pot, add the garlic, and sear the aromatics until golden brown on one side, about 5 minutes. Be patient; well-browned vegetables are key to flavoring the stock. Flip the vegetables and sear until the opposite sides begin to brown, 3 to 4 minutes. Add the thyme and rosemary, and toast the herbs until they smell very fragrant, about 30 seconds.

Flick off any visible seeds on the cut surface of the lemon halves, squeeze the juice over the vegetables, and toss the rinds into the pot. Add the white wine, using a wooden spoon to scrape up any brown bits on the bottom of the pot, and bring to a boil. Boil until the wine has reduced by about a third.

Fill the pot about ⅔ full of water, cover, bring to a boil, remove the lid, and boil the stock until reduced by about 1 inch (2.5cm); the time will vary depending on the size of the pot.

Add 4 tablespoons salt and taste the broth; it should taste like ocean water (the amount of salt you need depends on the amount of water in the pot). Turn off the heat and set the stock aside until you're ready to finish the boil.

**Prep the seafood and vegetables:** Keep each ingredient in separate piles. Rinse the whole lobsters or tails under cold water and set aside. Devein the shrimp (leave the shell on). Scrub and debeard the clams.

Cut the sausages into 2- to 3-inch (5 to 7.5cm) pieces.

242 • PHIL'S FAVORITES

Halve any potatoes, if needed, so all are roughly the same size. Break or cut each ear of corn into 2 to 3 pieces.

**Boil the whole lobsters:** (If using lobster tails, skip this step; they will be cooked later.) Fill a large bowl or pot about halfway with ice water to submerge the cooked lobsters.

Bring the boil stock to a rolling boil; add a little more water to the pot, if needed, so the lobsters will be completely covered. When the water is boiling, add 2 lobsters, headfirst, to the pot (wait to add more lobsters until the water is back at a boil). Boil the lobsters for about 10 minutes; the shells should be deep red. Use tongs to remove the lobsters and cut the tail off 1 lobster; if the flesh is still translucent in the center, return the lobsters to the pot for 1 to 2 minutes longer. Put the lobsters in the ice water bath and let cool for a few minutes.

Break the lobster tails and claws down with a nutcracker or clean pliers. Transfer the meat to a strainer or colander small enough to fit inside your stockpot (this will keep the delicate meat intact when it is rewarmed with the other seafood boil ingredients) and set aside.

**Finish the boil:** Have everything ready for serving before boiling the rest of the ingredients: the quartered lemons, chopped parsley leaves, Clarified Butter (rewarmed on the stovetop), and the extra-virgin olive oil.

Return the boil stock to a low boil, add the potatoes, cover the pot, and boil for 5 minutes. Add the corn, cover the pot again, and cook until the potatoes can easily be pierced with a fork but are not falling apart, 3 to 4 minutes. Add the sausage and the lobster tails, if using, to the pot and cook, now uncovered, for about 1 minute, then add the clams. Boil just until the first clams open, 2 to 3 minutes. Add the shrimp to the pot and cook until they begin to curl, about 1 minute. Turn off the heat.

**SEAFOOD BOIL**

2 small live lobsters (1½ pounds/680g each) or 2 medium raw lobster tails (about 4 ounces/115g each), thawed if frozen

1½ pounds (680kg) large, shell-on shrimp

1½ pounds (680kg) littleneck, steamer, or other small clams

1 pound (about 500kg) smoked chicken andouille sausage links

1½ pounds (680kg) small red or yellow potatoes

3 large ears corn, shucked

**TO SERVE**

2 to 3 lemons, cut into wedges

8 sprigs parsley (leaves only), chopped (optional)

Clarified Butter (recipe follows), warmed on the stovetop

Good-quality extra-virgin finishing olive oil

Plenty of crusty bread

### TIPS

*Save the jumbo shrimp, clams, and lobster for another dish. The larger the shellfish you buy, the fewer individual pieces you'll have to go around, and they're almost always more expensive by the pound than their smaller counterparts.*

*If you're short on time, lobster tails cook quickly without the work of breaking down whole lobsters. You can get raw, frozen tails at many grocery stores and seafood markets and thaw them out a few hours before boiling.*

If you boiled whole lobsters, submerge the strainer or colander with the lobster meat in the hot boil stock for about 30 seconds to rewarm it, then set the lobster meat aside.

Immediately strain the boil into the colander in the sink.

**Serve:** Gently dump out the seafood and vegetables onto the prepared serving area; be careful not to break the clam shells. (Discard any that did not open.) Pick out and discard the aromatics (the onions, carrots, celery, garlic, and herbs).

Cut the lobster tails in half or thirds, or scatter the meat from the whole lobsters throughout the boil.

Tuck the quartered lemons throughout the seafood, sprinkle the parsley over the boil, and serve with the warm Clarified Butter, finishing olive oil, and bread.

## CLARIFIED BUTTER

**MAKES ABOUT 4 CUPS (960ML) OR ¾ CUP (180ML)**

**1 cup (2 sticks/225g) unsalted butter**

In a saucepan, melt the butter over medium-low heat; don't stir. When the butter stops sizzling and foaming, remove the pan from the heat. (Don't let the butter brown.) Skim the foam off the top of the melted butter and pour the clarified butter into a bowl; stop when you get to mainly white milk solids in the bottom of the saucepan. (Discard the solids.)

Let the clarified butter cool completely, transfer to a glass jar or other container, cover, and refrigerate for up to 1 month.

To serve, gently rewarm the butter over low heat until fully melted.

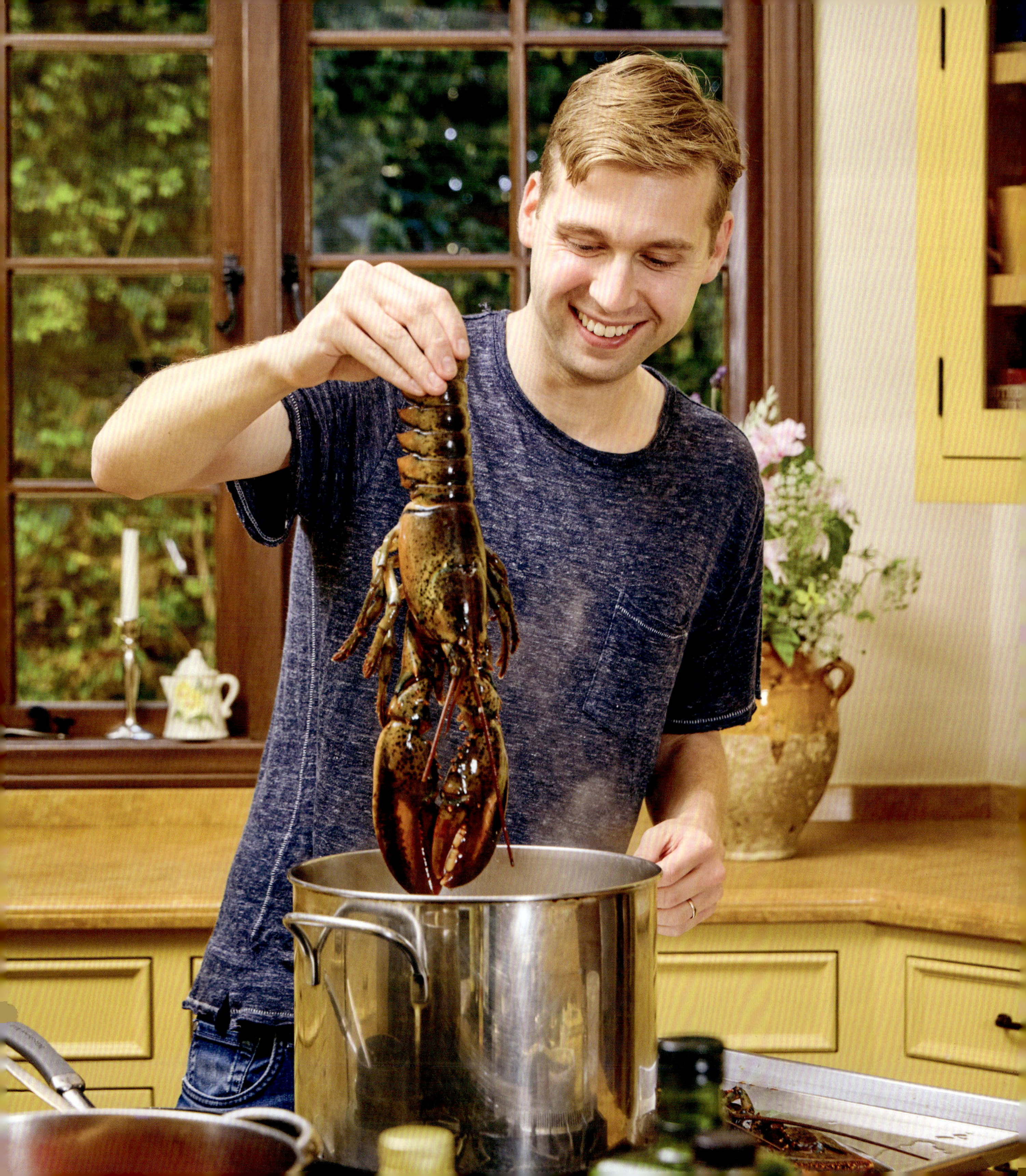

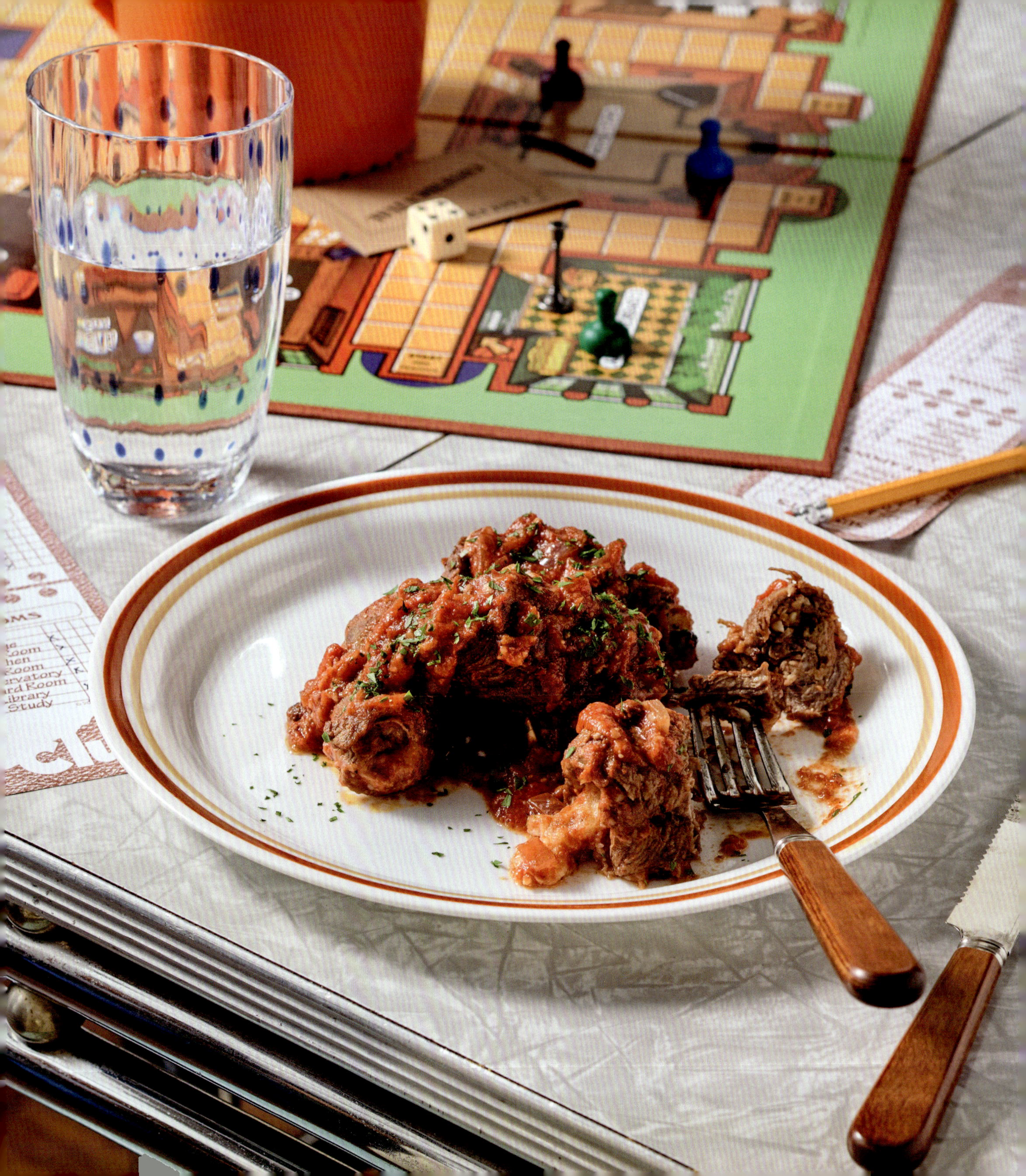

# Debra Barone's Braciole

📍 *"Debra Makes Something Good," season 4, episode 18 of* Everybody Loves Raymond

We featured food a lot on *Raymond*. I'd go so far as to say that the most powerful person in the family was Marie, because of her fantastic cooking abilities. And she ruled with that power. One day we thought, "What if Debra made something good?" The whole balance of power might be shifted. It couldn't be too easy a dish, it had to surprise the family that Debra could pull something like this off. And so, this is the braciole that Debra made in the episode "Debra Makes Something Good" from the fourth season of *Everybody Loves Raymond*. In the opening scene, Ray has just gotten back from a trip, and Debra hands him a plate of braciole she's made. He doesn't even want to try it, but it turns out to be so great, he takes it next door, and Frank and Robert love it. They swoon. Frank turns to Marie and says, "You should get the recipe from Debra." Marie gives him a look. She then scoffs and takes a bite. A moment. She throws her fork on the table and storms out of the room.

For the episode, Rhonda Schneider, the prop master for the show, made a version inspired by the braciole in *Savoring Italy*, a 1999 Williams-Sonoma cookbook by food writer Michele Scicolone. Debra replaced the raisins in the filling with black currants, and her version is more Italian American, with canned instead of fresh tomatoes, dried oregano, and, because everybody loves garlic, a lot of garlic. This is the actual, infamous recipe, which caused Frank to bring Debra flowers.

## TIPS

*These beef rolls aren't meant to look perfect. You can toss any beef rolls that fall apart back into the sauce; the little bits of beef and filling make the sauce even more delicious. The leftovers are great on pasta, even if you're down to mainly a beef-infused ragu.*

*Pounding the meat very thin is more important than the cut of beef you use (top or bottom round, sirloin, or thinly sliced flank and even breakfast steaks all work), and if you have very thick pieces of beef, it takes some patience. Chilling the beef rolls before securing them with toothpicks firms up the meat so they seal more securely and makes weaving a toothpick through the meat lengthwise down the roll easier (instead of crosswise), which both holds them together better and allows you to brown all sides of the rolls.*

*Dried black currants, also called Zante currants, are not true currants (a berry that is usually eaten fresh) but small dried Black Corinth grapes. Look for them at specialty markets and nut retailers; you can also use any chopped conventional raisins.*

**FEEDS 5 TO 6**

**BEEF ROLLS**

1½ pounds (680g) top or bottom round, breakfast, or flank steaks (8 to 10 thinly sliced ¼-inch/6mm filets, or 1 to 2 thick 1-inch/2.5cm filets)

Kosher or coarse sea salt and freshly ground black pepper

8 slices prosciutto (2½ ounces/70g)

8 slices provolone cheese (3 ounces/85g)

3 tablespoons (40g) unsalted butter

¼ cup (28g) fine bread crumbs (unseasoned) or matzoh meal

3 tablespoons pine nuts, lightly crushed in a mortar or with the bottom of a bowl

1 garlic clove, minced

3 tablespoons finely grated Pecorino Romano or parmesan cheese, packed

3 tablespoons dried black currants (or your favorite raisins), chopped

**Pound the filets:** If the steaks are thick, butterfly them by slicing them in half horizontally, then in half again to make several filets no more than ¼-inch (6mm) thick. (If difficult to slice, put them in the freezer for about 15 minutes to firm up.)

Pound each filet with the flat side of a meat mallet until very thin; they shouldn't be more than ⅛-inch (3mm thick), the thinner the better. Chop and reserve any meat scraps.

**Make the beef rolls:** Arrange the filets on a large work surface or sheet pan and season both sides lightly with salt and pepper. Lay a piece of prosciutto, then a slice of provolone cheese over each filet; tear the meat and cheese into smaller pieces so they are about the same size as each pounded steak.

Heat a large Dutch oven over medium heat, add the butter and, when melted, stir in the bread crumbs and pine nuts. Toast, stirring regularly with a wooden spoon, until both just begin to lightly brown, about 5 minutes. Add the minced garlic clove and sauté until fragrant, about 30 seconds. Scrape the mixture into a small bowl, add the Pecorino Romano and black currants, and toss to combine. Scatter the filling evenly over the beef filets.

Starting at the widest end, roll up each filet snugly like a cigar and arrange the beef rolls, seam side facing down, in a baking dish or on a plate. Scoop up any filling that spills out as you roll up the rolls and set it aside in a small dish.

Freeze the beef rolls for about 30 minutes or refrigerate for at least 1 hour or up to 4 hours, loosely covered; also refrigerate any beef scraps and extra filling.

Close the seam of each chilled beef roll by threading two toothpicks lengthwise (not crosswise) through the meat. As you close them, tuck in and secure any excess flaps of meat on the sides of the roll if needed.

**Fry the beef rolls:** Wipe out any excess bread crumb mixture from the Dutch oven. Add enough olive oil to generously coat the bottom (about 3 tablespoons) and heat the oil over medium heat until hot, about 2 minutes. Fry the beef rolls in batches (don't crowd the pan), seam side facing down, until deep golden brown, 3 to 4 minutes.

Use tongs to flip the rolls and fry the top side of each until golden brown, then lightly brown both sides as much as possible (the toothpicks can make it tricky). Transfer the beef rolls to a plate. Between batches, pick out any stray pine nuts or raisins so they don't burn and set them aside with the fried beef rolls.

Roughly chop and fry any leftover scraps of meat, if you have any, and set aside with the beef rolls.

**Make the sauce:** If the pot looks dry, add a little more olive oil and when hot, add the onion and sauté, stirring occasionally with a wooden spoon, until softened, 2 to 3 minutes. Add the chopped garlic cloves and any extra pine nut–bread crumb filling and stir until the garlic is fragrant, about 1 minute. Add the wine, bring to a boil, and cook until reduced by half, 2 to 3 minutes. Crush the tomatoes as you add them to the pot with their juices. Add the oregano, bay leaf, 1 teaspoon salt, and ½ teaspoon pepper and stir to combine.

Gently submerge the beef rolls in the sauce, bring the sauce to a simmer, reduce the heat to low, and braise, partially covered, for about 1 hour. Remove the lid, gently stir and scrape the bottom of the pot, and continue to simmer the sauce, stirring and scraping the bottom of the pot occasionally, until the sauce is reduced by about half, 1 to 1½ hours. Taste the pan juices and season with salt and pepper.

Turn off the heat and cover the pot until ready to serve.

### TOMATO SAUCE

Extra-virgin olive oil, for frying

1 large white or yellow onion, roughly chopped

3 garlic cloves, roughly chopped

1 cup (240ml) dry red wine (chianti or pinot noir)

2 28-ounce (800g) cans whole tomatoes

1½ teaspoons dried oregano

1 bay leaf

Kosher or coarse sea salt and freshly ground black pepper

### TO SERVE

Leaves from 2 sprigs parsley, finely chopped

Crusty bread

**Serve:** Gently rewarm the braciole over low heat, if needed. Remove the beef rolls from the pot and remove the toothpicks; if they are wedged in tightly, it helps to hold on to the toothpicks with a dry paper towel.

Slice the beef rolls into large bite-size pieces and roughly chop any meat that falls apart as you slice them. Put everything back into the pot, if serving the braciola family-style. Or, spoon a generous amount of sauce on the bottom of large, shallow bowls and arrange the sliced beef rolls on top. Scatter the parsley over the braciole and serve with the bread.

Cover and refrigerate any leftover braciole for up to 5 days.

# Gverović-Orsan's Black Risotto

*Dubrovnik*

Our last day in Croatia we went to Gverović-Orsan, which is just outside Dubrovnik. Not only is the scenery straight from heaven, I'd say it's one of the best seafood restaurants in the world. It's a family restaurant run by Igor Gverović; his wife and the chef, Eta; and their daughter, Nea. (Igor's parents opened it more than fifty years ago.) Their black risotto is the best I've ever had. The size of the langoustines alone is a reason to go there.

This recipe isn't worth making if you can't get really, really good seafood. It needs to be as fresh as the seawater that Nea scooped up straight from the ocean to wash our oysters in that final scene of the episode. Every recipe in this book is as close as possible to the original, and they've been tested and worked on with each chef many times to make them the best they can be at home, but there are some things that aren't going to ever be the way a certain dish tastes when you travel. The experience—and that includes the scenery, the sounds and smells, the people you're sharing that moment with—are all part of the flavor. (At home, even using squid instead of cuttlefish wasn't the same, and they use fresh ink, not the jarred kind you can buy.) I'm still giving you the recipe, only exactly as Nea sent it to me, so you can decide whether to make this or look for hotels in Croatia and go to Gverović-Orsan. You know what I'm gonna do.

Get some fresh cuttlefish (about 1 pound/500g) with the ink sac and the same amount of langoustines (or extra-large whole prawns) and mussels. Clean the cuttlefish and cut it into large pieces. Save the fresh ink. Clean the langoustines and mussels.

Heat up some homemade fish stock (6 to 7 cups/about 1.5L).

Put a lot of good olive oil in a pan and cook 3 or 4 chopped garlic cloves with 2 large spoonfuls of tomato concentrate (paste), 3 large spoonfuls chopped fresh parsley, and a few pinches of freshly ground black pepper. Add 2¼ cups (400g) arborio rice, stir a few times, and add enough cuttlefish ink to make the rice dark gray, almost black. Now add the langoustines, then the fish stock a few spoonfuls at a time, always stirring, until the fish stock is absorbed. Keep adding fish stock and stirring until the rice is almost al dente (taste), approximately 17 minutes. It should be very creamy, not dry (add a little more fish stock if needed). Add the mussels and stir until the mussels open. Now add a small glass (about ½ cup/120ml) Croatian Pošip (dry white wine) and keep stirring until the rice is al dente, 2 to 3 minutes. Season the risotto with sea salt. Pile everything onto a big platter and enjoy with a glass of white wine.

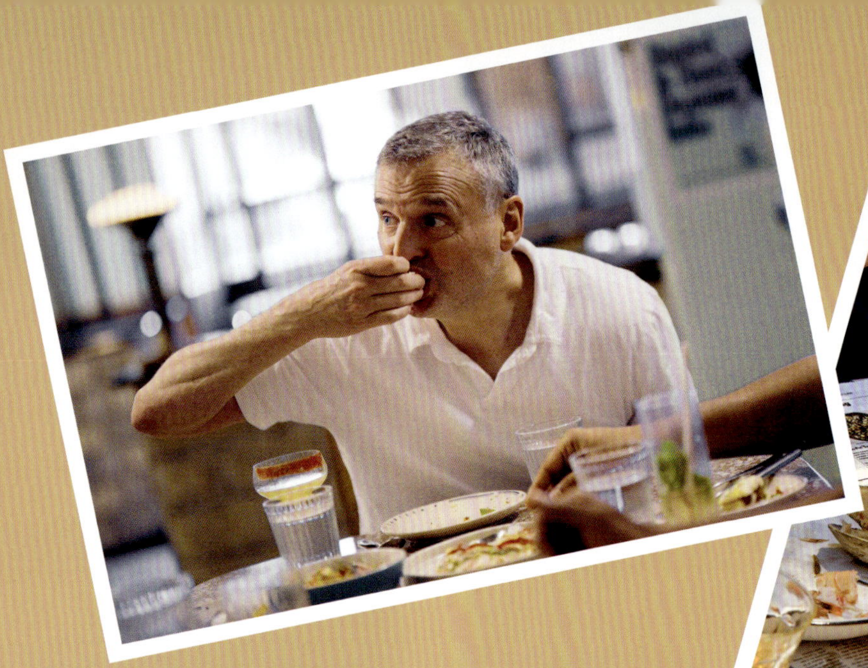

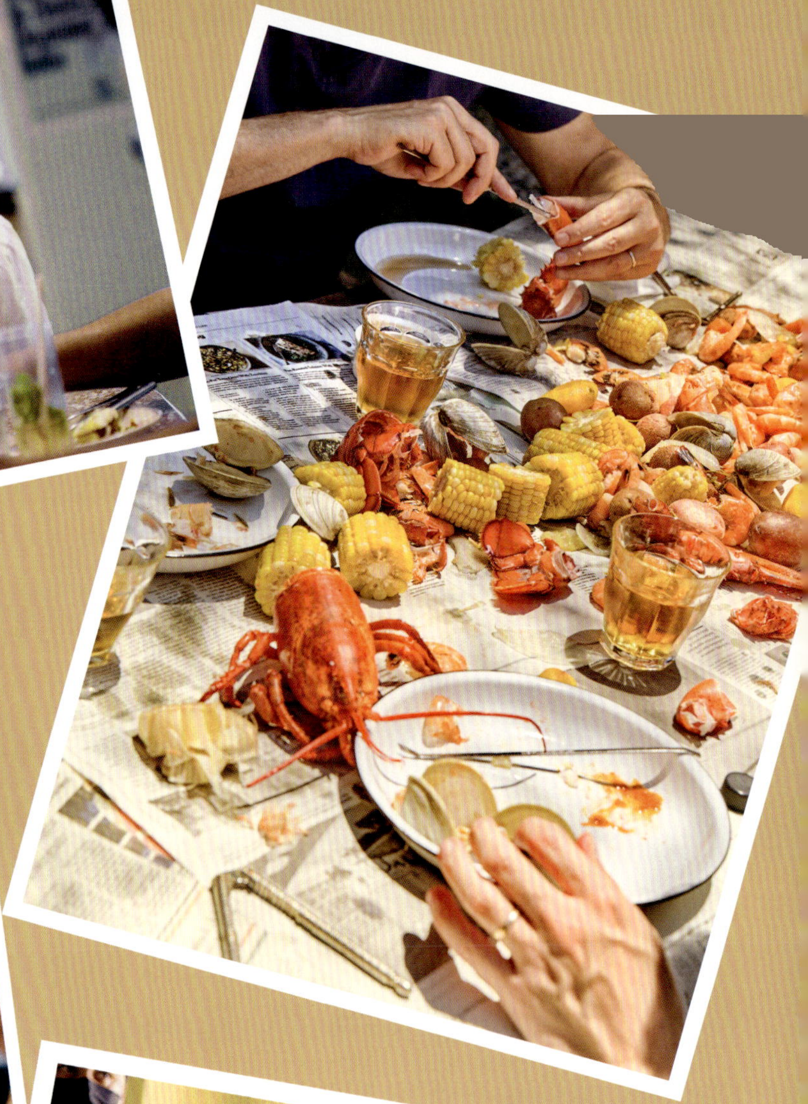

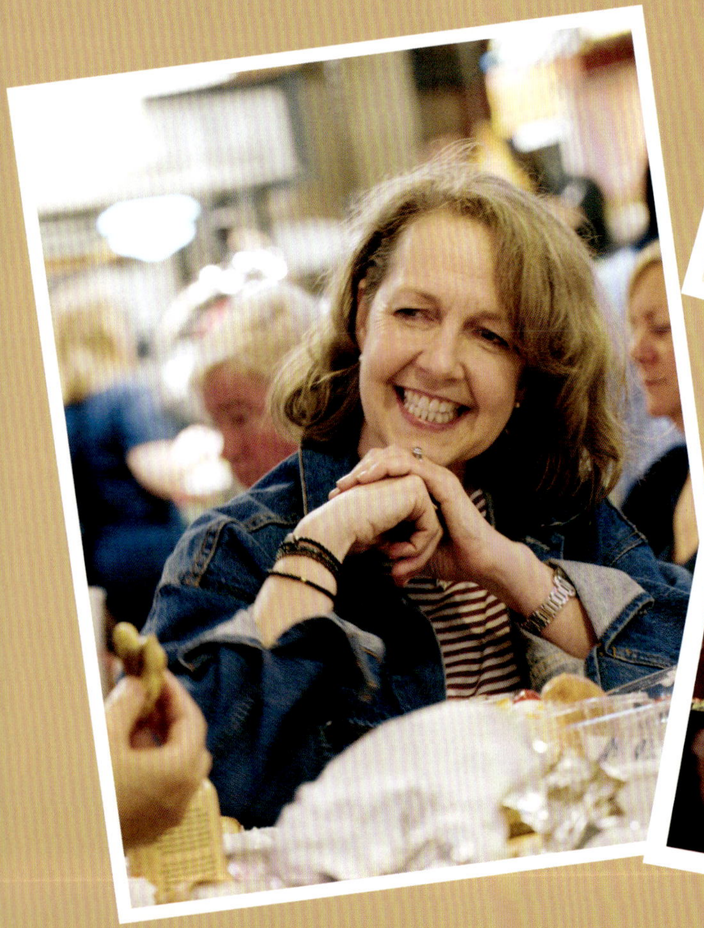

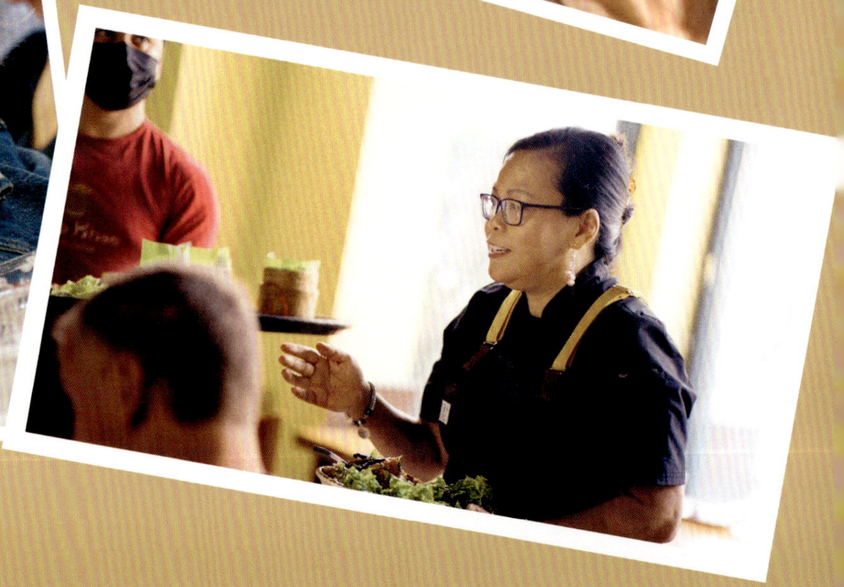

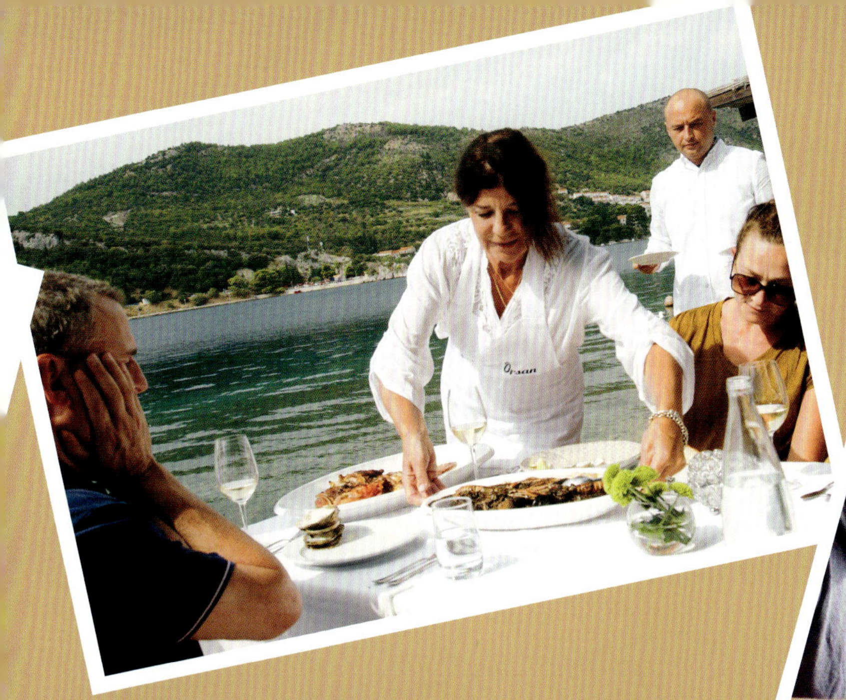

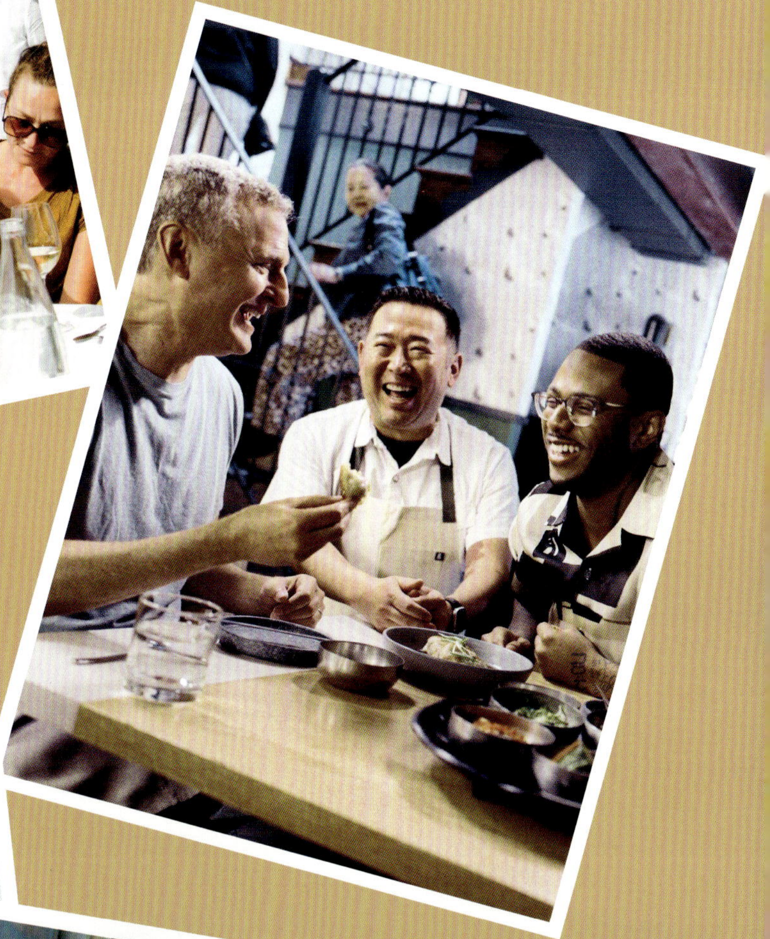

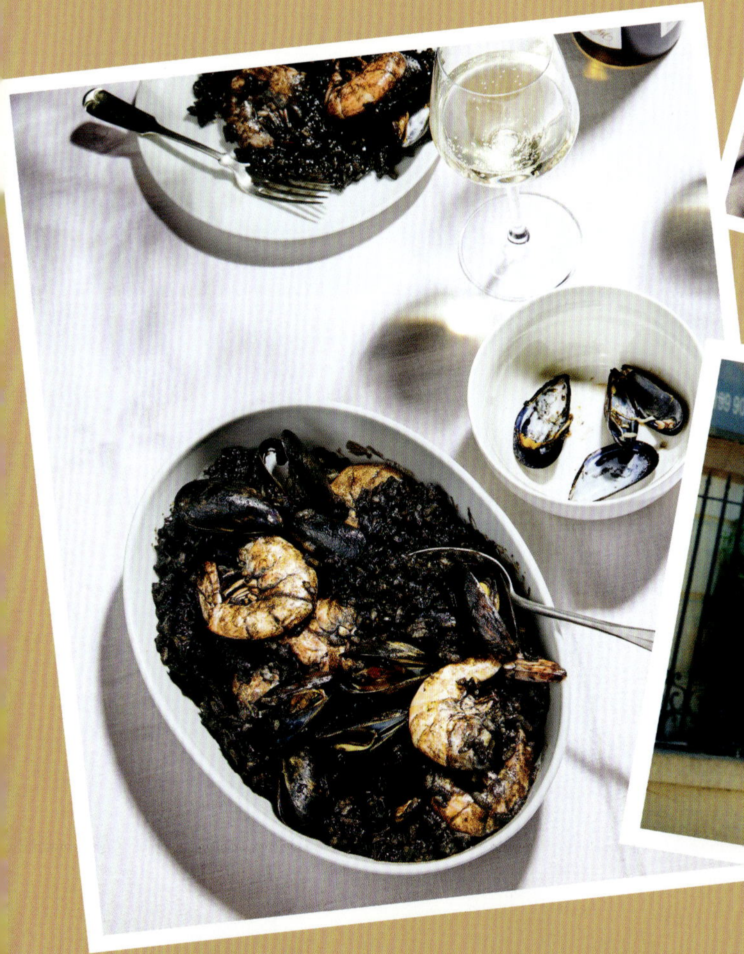

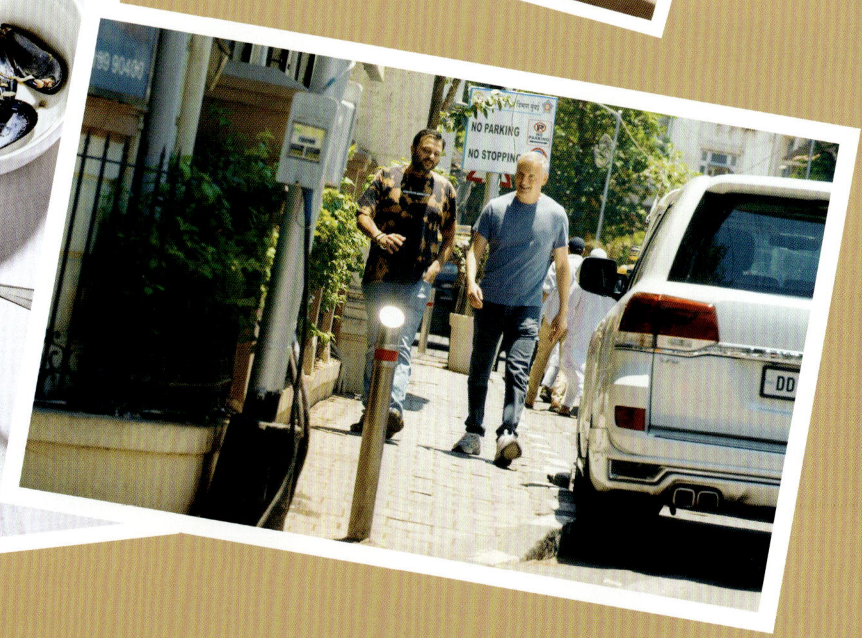
NO PARKING

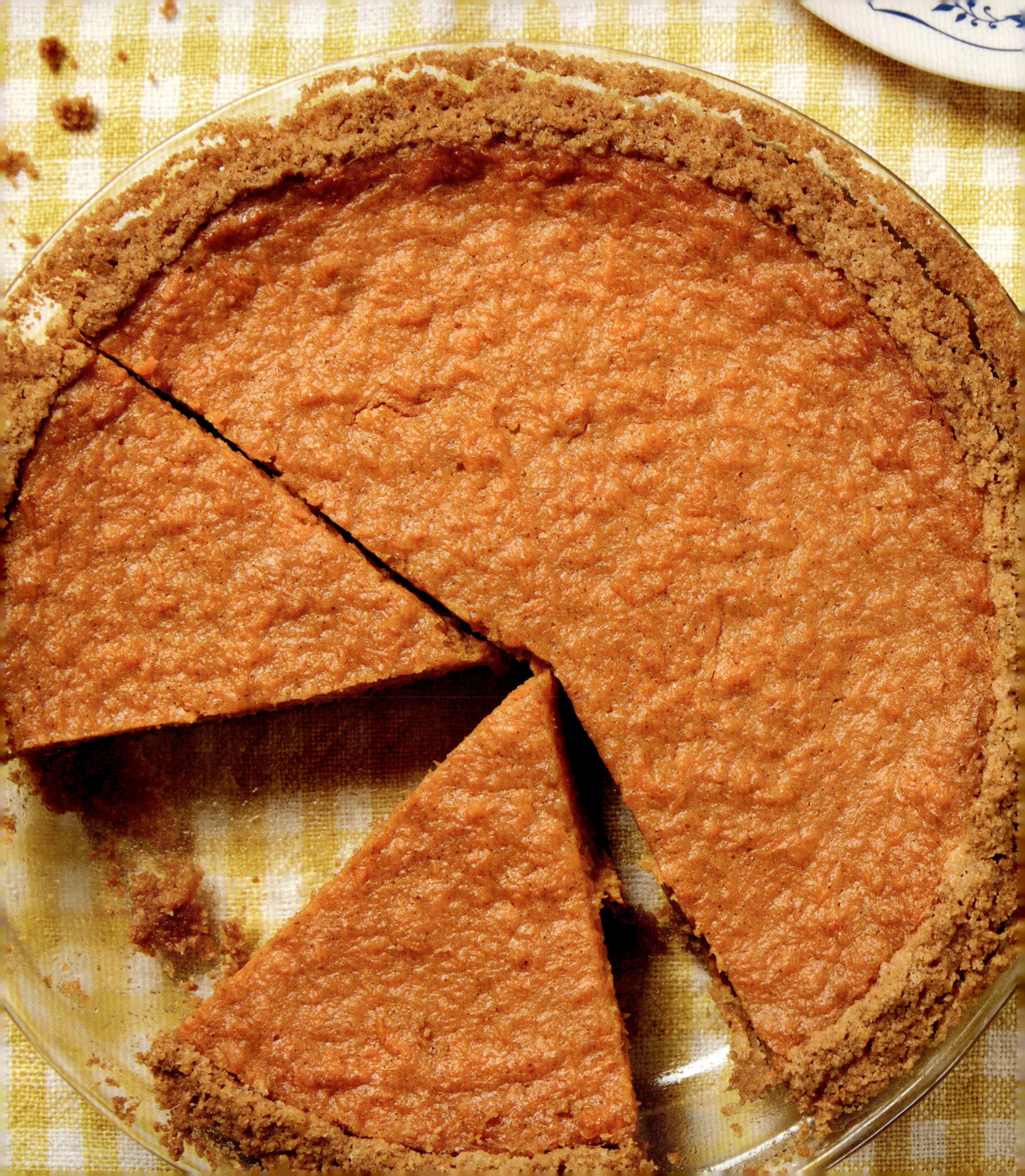

# THE BEST PART OF THE DAY

You've probably noticed in the show that I don't usually turn down dessert. This was probably the hardest chapter in the book to narrow down to less than ten recipes. Two of my favorite things in life are ice cream and dark chocolate. No matter how full I am, there's always room. In fact, I believe dessert has a separate room. When you're traveling abroad, another very good place to find flavors you've never tried is at candy shops or the local convenience store. One of my favorite candies is a Japanese yuzu gummy that I had in Kyoto and always keep in my pantry.

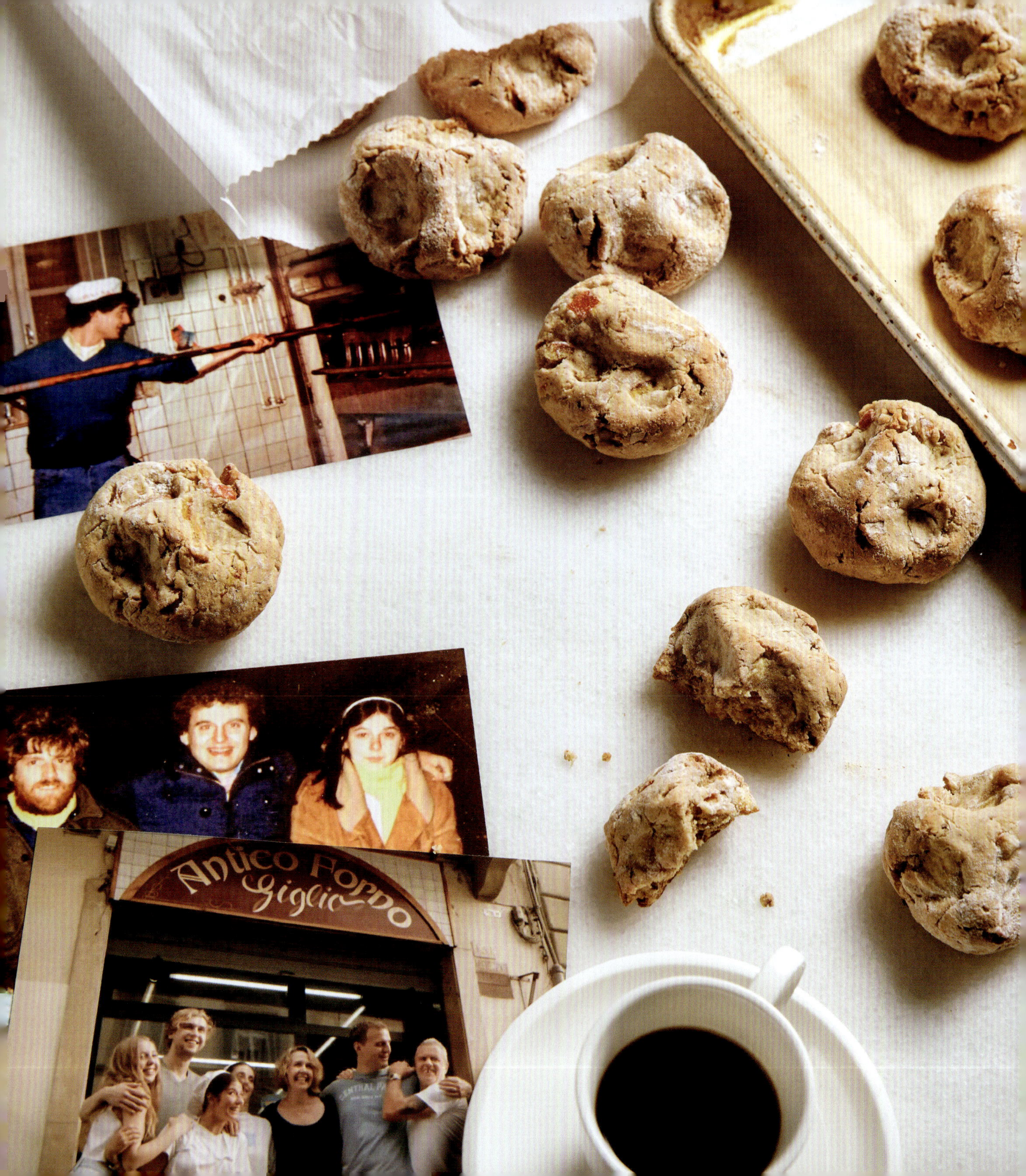
Antico Forno

# Dario Landi and Dania Nuti's Cavallucci Cookies

*Antico Forno Giglio, Florence*

The first place I fell in love with abroad was Florence. More than that, I fell in love with the people. I met Dania Nuti and Dario Landi on my very first trip abroad as a DHL cargo courier. The whole story is in the introduction to *Somebody Feed Phil the Book*: meeting Dania and Dario on the train from Paris to Florence, where they lived, and becoming instant friends, even though we didn't speak the same language. Then going to the bakery in Florence, Antico Forno Giglio, that Dario's father ran; a few years later taking my new girlfriend, Monica, to Italy to meet them; and then Dania and Dario coming to visit us in New York with their first baby, Ginevra.

As life happens, you get busy, and Monica and I moved to LA and lost touch with our good friends on the other side of the Atlantic. In 2015, when we were in Italy filming the second episode of *I'll Have What Phil's Having*, we finally got to reconnect with them at Antico Forno Giglio, now their bakery, for the first time in twenty-seven years. It was like we'd never been apart. Ben and Lily, who Dania and Dario got to meet, were grown, and so were their kids, Ginevra, Rebecca, and Bernardo. It will always be a special memory for Monica and me. It shows how much the people you meet when you travel change you, and will forever be in your life, even if you don't get to see them very often.

(A special thank-you to Lorenzo Nuti, Dania's nephew, who made extra batches of the cookies at the bakery to make sure we got this recipe just right for you.)

---

*In 1983, we met Phil on a train from Paris to Florence, and from then on we bonded a beautiful friendship. Years later, we got to know Monica, a wonderful person, and our families started to know each other. Every time they come to Florence, we don't waste any time to see them and have a nice time together. These cookies are a classic Tuscan recipe made at Christmas. If the cookies are dry, that means the sugar syrup boiled too long, or there is too much flour (it is always best to weigh your ingredients). We hope you enjoy them!* —DARIO AND DANIA

**MAKES 16 COOKIES**

**6 ounces (170g) drained Candied Orange Peels (about 1 cup, loosely packed; recipe follows)**

**¾ cup plus 1 tablespoon (162g) granulated sugar**

**3 tablespoons (45ml) honey**

**1½ cups (160g) walnut halves or pieces**

**1 teaspoon baking powder**

**2 tablespoons anise seeds**

**¾ teaspoon ground cinnamon**

**¾ teaspoon ground coriander**

**¾ teaspoon ground ginger**

**¾ teaspoon ground cloves**

**¾ teaspoon ground star anise**

**¾ teaspoon ground mace or nutmeg**

**Fine salt**

**2½ cups (300g) 0, 00, or all-purpose flour, divided, plus more for the work surface**

**Prep:** Put a baking rack in the top and bottom thirds of the oven and preheat to 375°F (190°C).

Line two baking sheets with baking mats or, if using parchment paper, put a few small dabs of the syrup from the Candied Orange Peels in the corners of the baking sheets first to keep the parchment paper from moving.

Lay out the Candied Orange Peels on several paper towels to soak up some of the excess sugar syrup (don't blot them dry, they should still be very juicy), then roughly chop the peels into small pieces.

**Make the honey syrup:** In a medium saucepan with tall sides (the sugar syrup will bubble up), combine the sugar, honey, and ¼ cup (60ml) water. Bring to a low boil over medium-high heat (do not stir) and boil, occasionally swirling the pot, until the bubbles and foam begin to subside and the temperature just reaches the thread stage, 228 to 230°F (110°C) on a digital thermometer; start checking the temperature when the bubbles start to deflate at about 2 minutes. The syrup shouldn't darken beyond a light honey color. Immediately remove the saucepan from the heat and set aside to cool for at least 10 minutes while you make the dough. The syrup will thicken as it cools but should not harden; if it does, discard and start over.

**Toast the nuts:** Put the walnuts on a baking sheet and lightly toast, stirring to redistribute the nuts halfway in between, until fragrant and just beginning to brown, 5 to 7 minutes. When cool enough to handle, use your fingers to break the walnut halves into small pieces. (If you chop the walnuts, discard the powdery nut residue.)

**Make the dough:** In a large bowl, mix together the baking powder, anise seeds, cinnamon, coriander, ginger, cloves, star anise, mace, and a pinch or two of fine salt. Add 1⅔ cups (200g) flour, stir to evenly distribute the spices, and add the toasted walnuts and chopped Candied Orange Peels. Toss the orange peels into the dry ingredients with your fingers until well combined.

Scrape the cooled honey syrup into the dry ingredients and mix with your hands or spoon until just combined; the dough will be very floury. Gradually work in the remaining 1 cup less 2 tablespoons (100g) of flour, about a quarter at a time, kneading the dough with your hands after each addition until the flour is fully incorporated.

Generously flour a work surface, turn out the dough, and knead ten to twelve times with your palms until smooth, like you are making a bread dough. Form the dough into 16 balls (a scant ¼ cup/50g each). Re-flour the work surface, if needed, and pack each ball between your palms like you're making a meatball. Lightly flour your hands and roll the balls around on the counter until smooth; the dough rounds should be lightly covered in flour.

Arrange the balls about 2 inches (5cm) apart on the baking sheets. Hold your thumb, index, and middle finger in a triangle shape while you gently press down to make three indentations in each cookie. Gently press down on the cookies to slightly flatten the balls; they should still be very thick.

**Bake the cookies:** Put the baking sheets in the oven and bake the cookies, rotating the pans back to front and top to bottom halfway through, until golden brown on the bottom (lift up one cookie to check) and just beginning to brown on top, 13 to 14 minutes. Watch the cookies closely the last 2 minutes to avoid overbaking. Let the cookies cool completely on the baking sheets.

Store the cookies, tightly covered, at room temperature for up to 2 weeks; they will be crunchy and firm the first few days, then soften as they age.

## TIPS

*These citrusy, heavily spiced cavallucci ("horsemen") are a cross between a cookie and a lightly sweetened bread. There's no butter or eggs, making them sturdier than most cookies (as the story goes, they were traditionally baked for travelers or workers on horseback). The texture evolves as they age. For a firmer cookie, eat them within a few days; for a softer cookie, wait several days or even a week.*

*Italian-style candied orange peels (often called "glazed" orange peels) add essential moisture to the cookie dough. It's worth the time to candy your own orange peels. The more common granulated sugar-covered peels are too dry for these cookies.*

# CANDIED ORANGE PEELS

**MAKES ABOUT 12 OUNCES (2 CUPS/340G) CANDIED ORANGE PEELS, ENOUGH FOR 2 BATCHES CAVALLUCCI COOKIES**

5 to 6 medium organic Navel oranges (2 to 2¼ pounds/1kg)

2 cups (400g) granulated sugar

2 tablespoons honey

Candying orange peels takes some time, but it's largely unattended stovetop time. Be sure to use Navel oranges (or a similar pithy variety), which have enough bitter pith to balance the sweetness; with easy-to-peel, thin-skinned citrus like mandarins and tangerines, you end up with more syrup than candied peels. The leftover syrup is delicious in cocktails and as a sweetener in citrusy marinades and salad dressings in place of honey or other sweeteners.

Slice off the very ends of the oranges, score the skin lengthwise into wide sections, and peel away the skin. Peel enough oranges to equal 4 cups (250g) of peels (save the flesh for another use).

Put the orange peels in a medium saucepot, cover completely with water, bring to a rapid boil, and blanch, stirring occasionally to redistribute the peels floating on top, for 10 minutes. Drain the peels and repeat the blanching process.

In the saucepot, combine the sugar and 1 cup (240ml) water, bring to a simmer, and stir to dissolve the sugar. Add the peels, return to a gentle simmer, and poach, stirring to redistribute the peels occasionally, for 30 minutes. Remove the pot from the heat, stir in the honey, and let cool completely.

Pack the orange peels into a container or jars, cover completely with the syrup, and press down on the peels so all are completely submerged. Let the peels cure at cool room temperature for 24 hours, then refrigerate for up to 2 months.

# DeLaney Harter Rosenthal's One-Bowl Black Brownies

DeLaney is the newest Rosenthal. She and Ben got married in June of 2024 after dating for six years. She's a terrific actress, an amazing violinist and composer, she's funny and sweet and fits right in with our crazy family. We love DeLaney; she's our second daughter. And, she makes a helluva brownie.

*These were inspired by a recipe for black cocoa brownies on the baking blog* Salt and Baker. *I love Oreo-flavored anything (and coffee), so when I saw the recipe, I had to try them. In my version, I do half regular cocoa and half black cocoa powder and make them a little less sweet so I can top them with a bunch of powdered sugar. I also scatter chocolate chips over the batter on one half of the pan because Ben likes them. (I don't.) They're not too thick, more like a cookie, and get a little gooey in the center . . . perfect with a cup of mint tea or coffee.* —DELANEY

**Prep:** Preheat oven to 350°F (175°C). Lightly coat the sides of an 8-inch (20cm) square baking pan with butter or cooking spray. Cut a piece of parchment paper to fit inside the bottom of the pan with several inches of overhang on both ends. Lay the paper in the pan and crease the edges to make "handles" to lift the brownies out of the pan.

**Make the batter:** In a medium bowl, combine the cooled butter, vegetable oil, granulated sugar, brown sugar, eggs, and vanilla and whisk vigorously until smooth and slightly thickened, about 1 minute.

### MAKES 16 BROWNIES

½ cup (1 stick/115g) unsalted butter, melted and cooled, plus more for the baking pan

1 tablespoon neutral oil

¾ cup plus 2 tablespoons (175g) granulated sugar

⅓ cup (78g) light or dark brown sugar, packed

2 large eggs

1½ teaspoons vanilla extract

½ cup (60g) all-purpose flour

¼ cup (22g) black cocoa powder

¼ cup (22g) cocoa powder (regular, not Dutch process)

Fine salt

Handful (about ½ cup/100g) dark or semisweet chocolate chips (optional)

### TO SERVE

2 to 3 spoonfuls powdered (confectioner's) sugar

## TIPS

*Black cocoa, also known as "ultra" Dutch processed, is rinsed in more of the alkaline solution that neutralizes the chocolate's acidity than Dutch-processed cocoa, so it has a very dark color and a smoother, more neutral chocolate flavor (think Oreos). It's available from specialty baking suppliers like King Arthur Flour. When used in combination with regular cocoa powder, it gives you a chewy, ultra-thin brownie that satisfies both ends of the chocolate spectrum.*

*Be sure to sift the dry ingredients so the batter is smooth (cocoa powder is often clumpy), and let the brownies set up for about 20 minutes after they come out of the oven before slicing.*

Over the bowl, sift together the flour, black cocoa, and regular cocoa powder. Add ¼ teaspoon fine salt and use a rubber spatula to fold the dry ingredients into the butter mixture, scraping the bottom and sides of the bowl, until well combined.

Scrape the batter into the prepared pan and use an offset spatula or the back of a spoon to spread out the batter in an even layer and smooth out the top; the batter will not come very far up the sides of the pan. Scatter the chocolate chips evenly over half the pan, if you'd like; you don't need to press them into the batter.

**Bake the brownies:** Bake, rotating the pan front to back halfway through, until the edges of the brownies are well set but the center is still slightly jiggly, 20 to 22 minutes; a toothpick inserted in the middle should have some moist bits but not be completely coated in wet batter.

Transfer the brownies to a baking rack or oven grate and let cool for at least 20 minutes; they will continue to set up as they cool.

Run a knife along the sides of the baking pan without the parchment paper and lift the brownies out of the pan. Cut the brownies into squares, wiping off any bits of brownie that stick to the knife; if you'd like cleaner-looking cuts, freeze the brownies for about 1 hour or refrigerate for several hours before slicing.

**Serve:** Just before serving, dust the brownies with as much sifted powdered sugar as you'd like. Store the brownies, tightly sealed, in a food storage container or zip-top bag at room temperature or refrigerate for up to 5 days.

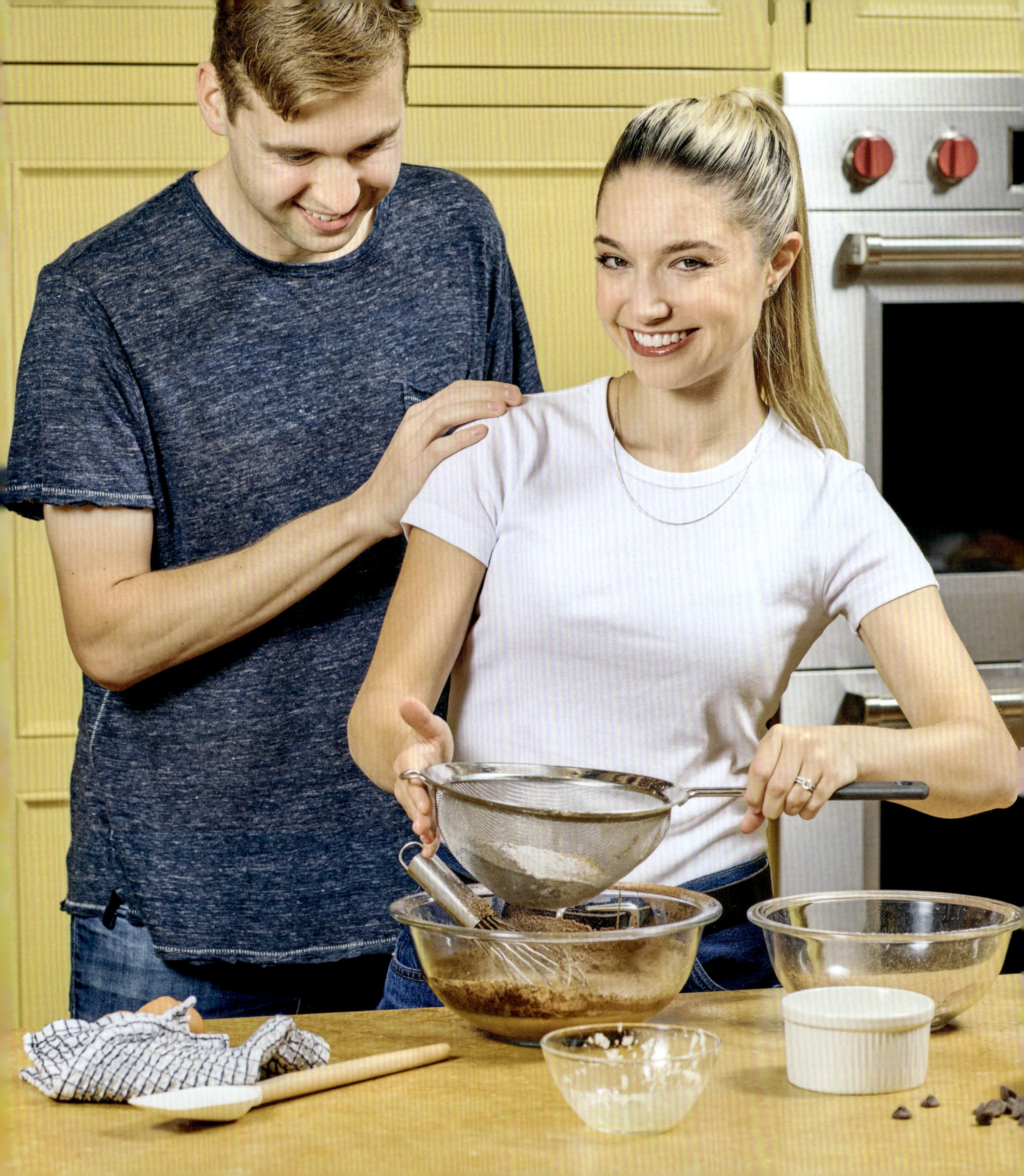

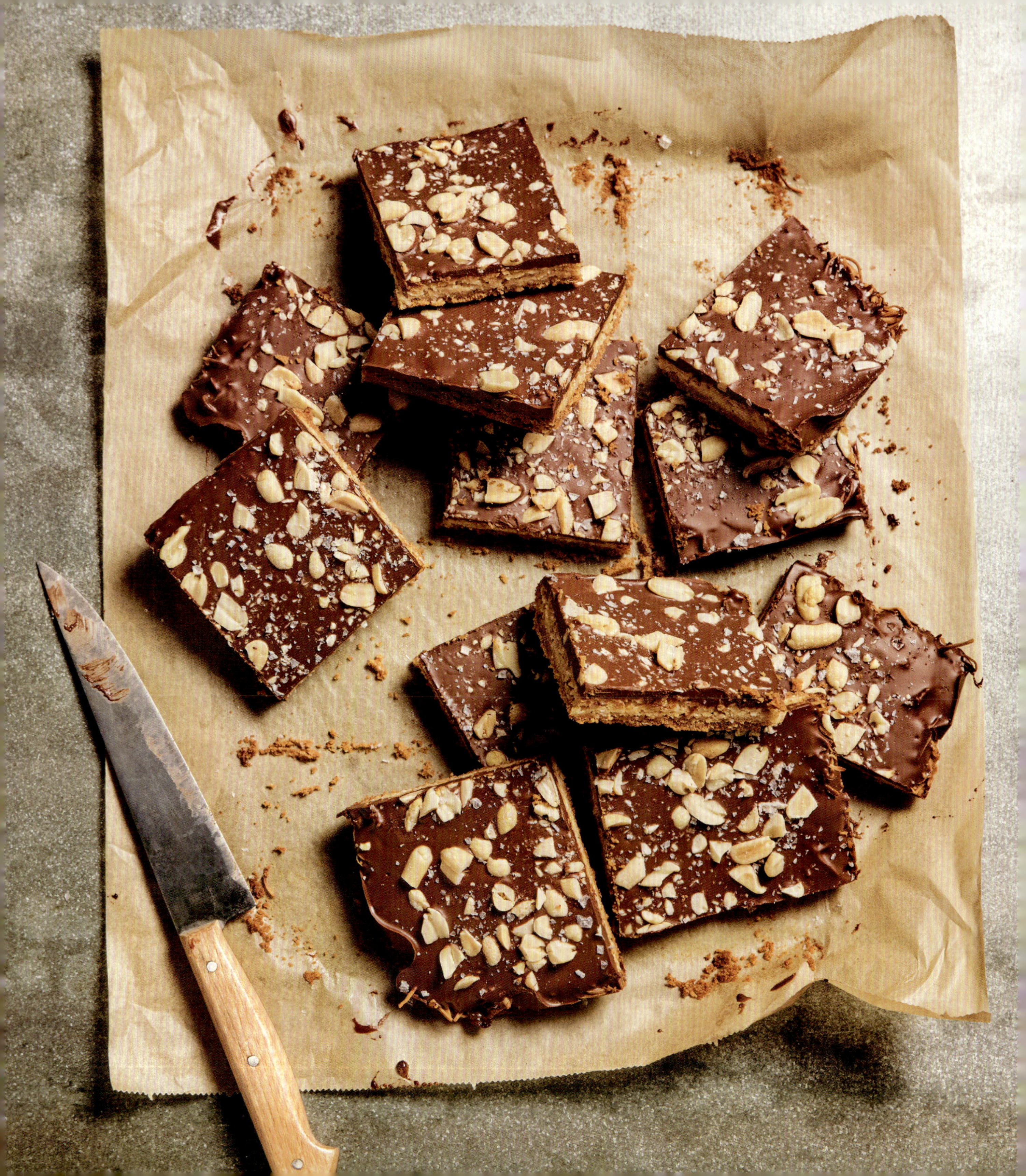

# Bob Champion's Chocolate Peanut Butter Triple Layer Bars

📍 *Los Angeles*

Erin Champion has been my phenomenal personal assistant since 1997. And, she is also family. On holidays, she bakes things for us (I win again!), and this one is my favorite. My one piece of advice is that you need Virginia-style peanuts, not the regular salted ones. Virginia peanuts are a specific variety that are bigger and crunchier, and they're never too salty.

> *My dad and hero, Bob Champion, is known for his cookies, especially those he would make at Christmas. Now I carry on his tradition by lovingly baking his bars and sharing them with friends and family, including the Rosenthals. This recipe is inspired by the classic three-layer bars with coconut, sweetened condensed milk, and a fudge-like chocolate–peanut butter spread that my dad always made. These are even more chocolatey, with brown butter and salted peanuts on top. (All Phil favorites!) Evenly dispersing the condensed milk is the only trick. Dad would sometimes tip the pan gently or use a spatula to nudge it. (Never spread! It will displace the coconut.) I just go slow and save a little in the can to try and fill in a few holes after the condensed milk settles, but mostly just let the oven handle things. The condensed milk will spread out as the bars bake.* —ERIN

**MAKES 40 BARS**

½ cup (1 stick/115g) unsalted butter, cut into 4 to 5 pieces, plus more for the pan

6 ounces (170g) graham crackers (11 full-size rectangular sheets; more if smaller squares)

2 cups (170g) finely shredded unsweetened coconut

1 14-ounce (400g) can sweetened condensed milk

½ cup (130g) creamy peanut butter (not natural peanut butter)

1 cup (6 ounces/170g) dark or bittersweet chocolate chips or 65% or higher dark chocolate bars, broken into pieces

Coarse sea salt (Maldon; optional)

½ cup (70g) roasted, salted Virginia-style peanuts, roughly chopped

THE BEST PART OF THE DAY

> **TIP**
>
> *If you're not using the standard large rectangular graham cracker sheets, check the package, as the smaller square cookies vary in size and weight.*

**Prep:** Preheat the oven to 350°F (175°C) and put a rack in the middle of the oven.

Lightly coat the sides of an 8-inch (20cm) square baking pan with butter. Cut a piece of parchment paper to fit inside the bottom of the pan with several inches of overhang on both ends. Lay the paper in the pan and crease the edges to make "handles" to lift the bars out of the pan.

Break up the graham crackers into smaller pieces and put them in a zip-top food storage bag or food processor. Gently crush the graham crackers in the food storage bag with a meat mallet or a can of food until very finely ground, or grind them in the food processor.

**Make and bake the base:** In a medium saucepan, melt the butter over medium heat and cook, swirling the pan occasionally, until the butter smells nutty and there are dark toasted bits on the bottom of the pan, 5 to 6 minutes; the butter will foam and pop as it cooks (watch closely toward the end so it doesn't burn). Turn off the heat, stir in the graham cracker crumbs, and press them into the bottom of the baking pan.

Scatter the coconut over the crust and drizzle the sweetened condensed milk evenly over the coconut. Use a rubber spatula to scrape out the last bits of condensed milk and pour it in the barest spots. It's fine if the condensed milk doesn't cover every single spot; it will redistribute in the oven.

Bake the bars until golden brown on the edges and lightly brown on top, rotating the pan front to back halfway through, 27 to 29 minutes. Transfer the bars to a wire rack or stovetop burner grate to cool for at least 30 minutes.

**Finish the bars:** Wipe out the saucepan you used to toast the butter, add the peanut butter, and melt over low heat just until it begins to soften. Add the chocolate chips and keep stirring regularly until the chocolate has melted and is well incorporated, about 45 seconds.

Pour the chocolate–peanut butter mixture over the crust and use the back of a spoon or rubber spatula to spread it out evenly. If you'd like, lightly sprinkle sea salt over the bars; crush the sea salt between your fingers as you sprinkle it. Scatter the chopped peanuts over the warm bars (discard any fine crumbs).

Transfer the bars to the refrigerator or freezer to chill until the chocolate has firmed up to the texture of fudge, about 45 minutes in the refrigerator or 25 minutes in the freezer.

**Serve:** Lift the bars out of the pan using the parchment paper and cut them into eight rows lengthwise and five rows across to make forty bars.

Store the bars in a single layer in zip-top food storage bags and refrigerate for up to 2 weeks or freeze for up to 3 months. You can also store the bars at room temperature for 4 to 5 days.

THE BEST PART OF THE DAY • 267

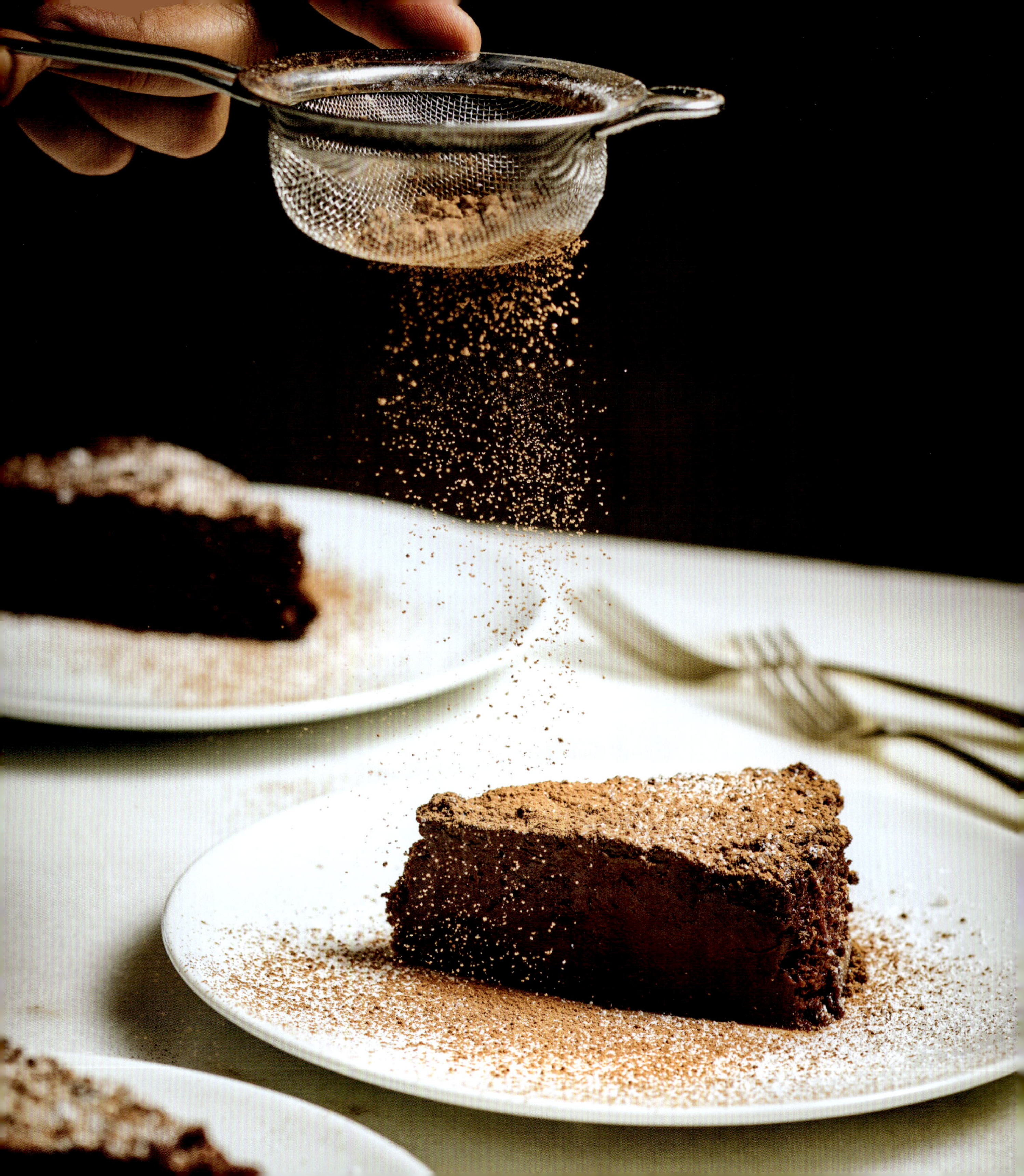

# Scott Linder's Flourless Chocolate Cake

*Matū, Beverly Hills*

Matū is probably the most unique and best steakhouse in Los Angeles. That's because all they serve is Wagyu beef, and not just any Wagyu but grass-fed Wagyu from New Zealand. (If you go to the restaurant's website, matusteak.com, you can read about how somebody you might know was the reason the owner, my friend Jerry Greenberg, got into grass-fed beef and, later, Wagyu.) Everything else there is also a home run, from the best French fries in the city to the salad. And then dessert comes, and you certainly don't expect anything as fantastic as everything else you just ate, and this chocolate cake comes out. Scott Linder, who is the chef and cofounder, makes one of the best chocolate cakes I've had in my life.

> *Like everything we do at Matū, this cake is incredibly simple, meaning using very few but only the very best ingredients, so good-quality chocolate is essential (Valrhona Guanaja 70% discs or other higher-quality bittersweet bar chocolate like Guittard). You also need to really pay attention to the technique. Make sure the eggs are room temperature when you whip them, and keep going for the full amount of time so they whip fully. After you pour the batter into the pan, you need to really bang the pan on the counter to get out the largest air bubbles for a light, smooth texture. (Don't use the fan or convection setting when you bake the cake.) After it's fully chilled overnight, you need to take the cake out of the fridge four to five hours before serving so it's truly room temperature.* —SCOTT

**MAKES 1 CAKE; FEEDS A LARGE CROWD (12 OR MORE)**

7 large eggs, at room temperature

1 cup (2 sticks/225g) unsalted butter, cut into cubes, plus more for the cake pan

Cocoa powder, for dusting

10 ounces (280g) bittersweet chocolate (65 to 70% discs or baking bars)

1¼ cups (250g) granulated sugar, divided

Powdered (confectioner's) sugar, for dusting

Flaky sea salt (Maldon)

## TIPS

*Don't let the exacting process deter you from making this flourless chocolate cake that's packed with bittersweet chocolate but far lighter in texture than most; after you make it the first time, you'll understand the process. Slicing the cake when well chilled is essential (and even still, you'll have plenty of cake stuck to the knife to enjoy yourself). You can freeze any leftover portions for up to 3 months (put them in a deep food storage container or on a plate that fits in a zip-top bag, but don't stack the slices, as they will collapse).*

*It's essential to use a 9-inch (23cm) cake pan with extra-tall 2½- or 3-inch (6 to 7.5cm) sides (like FatDaddio's anodized aluminum 9x3-inch pan, available fairly inexpensively online). The batter can spill over the edges of a standard cake pan with 2-inch (5cm) sides, particularly if not enough of the air bubbles are banged out of the batter.*

## DAY 1

**Prep:** Take the eggs out of the refrigerator 2 to 3 hours before making the cake.

Generously butter the bottom and sides of a deep-dish 9-inch (23cm) cake pan with 2½- or 3-inch (6 to 7.5cm) tall sides; it's important to use a deep cake pan (see Tips). Lightly sift cocoa powder all over the bottom and sides of the cake pan, then line the bottom with parchment paper.

For the water bath, find a deep-dish pizza pan, roasting pan, or similar dish large and deep enough to fit the cake pan with at least 1 inch (2.5cm) to spare on all sides. Arrange a kitchen towel flat on the bottom of the pan (the towel shouldn't be too thick). Fill a large saucepan with water, or if you're using a large roasting pan, fill a stockpot with water. Bring the water in the saucepan or stockpot to a boil, turn off the heat, and cover the pan to keep the water warm.

Put a rack in the middle of the oven and preheat the oven to 275°F (135°C).

**Make the chocolate base:** Set up a bain-marie by putting a medium metal bowl on top of a saucepan filled partway with water. Bring the water to a simmer over low heat, add the butter and chocolate discs to the bowl (or if using a chocolate bar, break it into small pieces), and stir constantly with a rubber spatula until the chocolate has melted and fully incorporated into the butter. (Hold on to the bowl with a kitchen towel; it will get very hot.) Set the chocolate aside and discard the water in the saucepan. Add ¼ cup (50g) of the granulated sugar and ⅓ cup (80ml) fresh water to the saucepan, heat until the water is almost simmering, and stir to dissolve the sugar. Stir the sugar syrup into the chocolate mixture and set aside for at least 15 minutes to cool.

**Finish the cake:** In a stand mixer fitted with the whisk attachment, combine the eggs and the remaining 1 cup (200g) granulated sugar and whip on high speed until more than quadrupled in volume and the color is off-white, 7 to 8 minutes (if using hand beaters, a total of 10 to 12 minutes). Don't skimp on the whipping time or the cake will deflate as it bakes.

Remove the bowl from the stand mixer and use a large rubber spatula to scrape the cooled chocolate into the stand mixer bowl. Firmly swipe the bottom and sides of the bowl about fifteen times, just until the chocolate is lightly incorporated. The batter will still be light in color and very streaky, and the eggs should not lose more than about a quarter of their volume.

Pour about half the batter into a large, clean bowl and stir a few times to fully incorporate the chocolate, but don't overmix or the batter will deflate. Now stir the batter in the stand mixer bowl several times to incorporate most of the chocolate at the bottom and sides of the bowl, then mix the two batters gently together until just combined. Pour the batter into the prepared cake pan.

To get out the largest air bubbles, firmly bang the cake pan on the counter ten times. (If you're not startling anyone else in the house, you're not banging hard enough.) The last few times, mainly only small air bubbles should rise to the surface; if there are still large air bubbles, bang the cake a few more times (not too many times or the cake will deflate as it bakes).

**Bake the cake:** Set the chocolate cake on the kitchen towel in the prepared pan and add hot water to come about halfway up the sides; stop when the cake pan just begins to float. Carefully slide the pan into the oven and bake for 2 hours. Touch the top crust and very gently move it back and forth; it should move only a small amount. If the crust moves easily, bake the cake for another 15 minutes.

Carefully remove the water bath pan from the oven and transfer the cake to a baking rack or stovetop burner to cool completely, about 3 hours.

Cover the cake with plastic wrap and refrigerate overnight.

**DAY 2**

**Slice the cake:** Take the cake out of the refrigerator 4 to 5 hours before it will be served so it can come to true room temperature. While the cake is cold, heat about a half inch (12mm) of water in a saucepan wide enough to fit the cake pan just until tiny bubbles form on the bottom of the pan. Remove from the heat.

Submerge the cake pan in the hot water for about 15 seconds and immediately remove the cake pan from the hot water (reserve the hot water). Lay a perfectly flat plate or baking sheet upside down on top of the cake pan and hold on to the plate or baking sheet while flipping the chocolate cake upside down. If the cake doesn't immediately release, return the cake pan to the warm water bath for about 10 seconds.

Dip part of a clean kitchen towel in the warm water, squeeze out the excess, and run a large, sharp knife (not serrated) through the moist towel. Run the knife around the edges of the cake to loosen it from the pan, stopping to wipe off the chocolate as you go, then carefully cut the cake into quarters with straight, vertical slices. Each time you make a cut, scrape the excess chocolate off the knife on the rim of the cake pan, then wipe the knife clean with the damp towel. As needed, dip the towel in the hot water.

Cut each cake quarter into three slices to make a total of twelve generous or more slightly smaller slices, depending on how many people you're serving. (If you're only serving a portion of the cake now, leave the remaining quarters whole to slice later.)

**Serve:** Slide a large, flat spatula underneath each slice of cake and carefully transfer to a serving plate. Use a fine-mesh sieve to dust an even layer of cocoa powder on the top of the cake and over each plate (pressing down on the cocoa powder in the sieve helps distribute it evenly). Bang the sieve to remove the cocoa powder, then very lightly dust each slice with powdered sugar. Sprinkle a few flakes of Maldon salt over each slice of chocolate cake and serve.

To store, return any leftover chocolate cake to the cake pan (or a plate), cover the top of the pan and any exposed sides of the cake with plastic wrap, and refrigerate for up to 5 days.

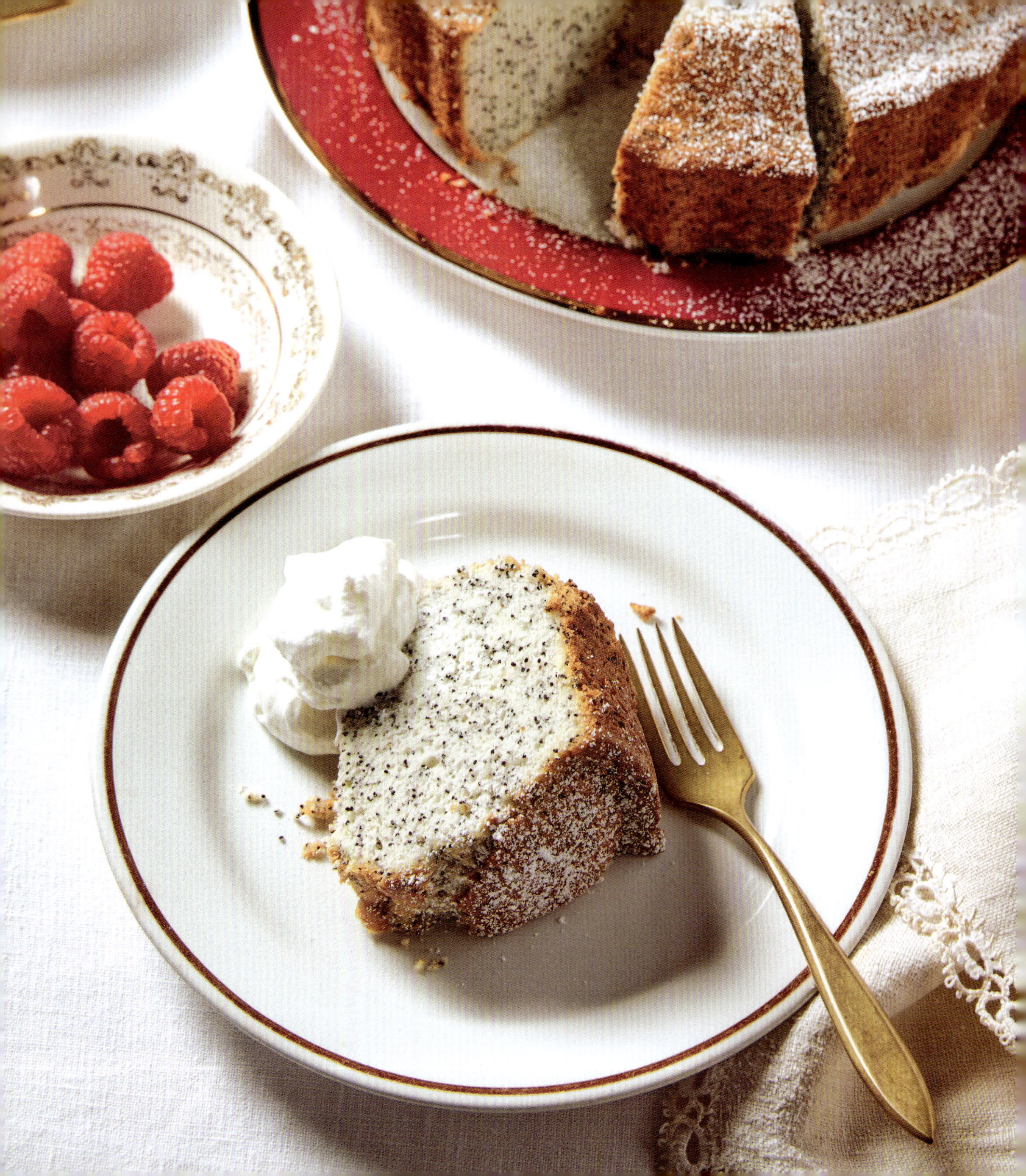

# Rob Weiner's Poppy Seed Cake

Rob Weiner is one of my oldest and closest friends. We met in college, and were roommates in New York. We've always loved to eat together, and he happens to be a great cook.

> *This is my aunt Marlene's recipe, and my most requested from a beloved relative. There's no lemon juice, only poppy seeds. She baked the cake in a tube pan, but I often use a Bundt pan. It needs to be a classic pan, not one with a lot of designs, and for the best release, be generous with the cooking spray! Powdered sugar is the traditional topping, but the cake doesn't need it.* —ROB

**Prep:** Put a rack in the top and bottom thirds of the oven. Preheat the oven to 350°F (175°C).

Coat a 9-inch (23cm) nonstick, rounded-edge Bundt pan (not one with intricate designs or sharp, angled edges) with cooking spray or vegetable oil; coat any grooves well to keep the cake from sticking (see Tips). Lightly dust the pan with sifted cake flour.

**Make the cake:** Over a medium bowl, sift together the cake flour, baking powder, and 1 teaspoon salt. (If you don't have a sifter, shake the dry ingredients through a mesh colander.) Scatter the poppy seeds over the dry ingredients and stir to incorporate.

Put the softened butter in a large bowl and gradually add 1¼ cups (250g) of the sugar in increments, about a quarter at a time; use the back of a spoon to mix the sugar completely into the butter before adding more. Add ¼ cup (60ml) of the milk and the vanilla and mix well. If the milk is very cold, the butter may firm up; smash the butter up a bit with the spoon so there are no large clumps.

---

**MAKES 1 CAKE; FEEDS 8 OR MORE**

Nonstick cooking spray or neutral vegetable oil, for the pan

2 cups (260g) cake flour, preferably, or pastry flour, plus more for the pan

2 teaspoons baking powder

Finely ground salt

½ cup (75g) black poppy seeds

½ cup (1 stick/115g) unsalted butter, at room temperature

1½ cups (300g) granulated sugar, divided

1 cup (240ml) whole milk, divided

1 teaspoon vanilla extract

4 large egg whites

**TO SERVE**

Powdered (confectioner's) sugar (optional)

Raspberries and fresh whipped cream (optional)

## TIPS

*The beauty of this cake, a hybrid of a poppy seed pound cake (made with butter and whole eggs) and angel food cake (lightened with beaten egg whites only), is that the cake is very light yet dense with poppy seeds. You can really taste their subtle, nutty flavor, as there's no citrus or other competing flavors. The slices can be served on their own or dusted with powdered sugar; either way, it's a true snacking cake.*

*A traditional 9-inch (23cm) nonstick Bundt pan with rounded sides and only 3-inch (7.5cm) tall sides is ideal for this cake. A much deeper, oversize Bundt pan like so many are today will also work as long as it has rounded sides; don't use any with intricate designs or sharp, angled edges, as the cake won't release well.*

*Get fresh poppy seeds from a bulk retailer (the poppy seeds sold in small jars in grocery store spice aisles are often stale and bitter) and store them in the freezer.*

Add about a third of the dry ingredients to the butter mixture and stir until roughly combined, then mix in about half of the remaining ¾ cup (180ml) of milk. Stir another third of the dry ingredients into the batter, then the rest of the milk, and end with the remaining dry ingredients.

In a stand mixer fitted with a whisk attachment (or use a large bowl with a hand mixer), beat the egg whites on high speed until soft peaks form, about 90 seconds. Add the remaining ¼ cup (50g) sugar and beat to stiff peaks, about 30 seconds; the whites should be glossy and hold their shape when the whisk is lifted.

Add a large spoonful of egg whites to the batter and use a rubber spatula to fold in the whites until almost combined. Gently fold the remaining egg whites into the batter, scraping the bottom and sides of the bowl, just until combined; don't overmix.

Scrape the batter evenly into the prepared cake pan and smooth out the top with the back of a spoon; it does not need to be perfectly smooth. Bake the cake, rotating the pan front to back halfway through, until light golden brown on top and a cake tester comes out with only a few crumbs, 45 to 48 minutes.

Let the cake cool completely on a baking rack or stovetop grate.

**Serve:** Insert a dull knife along the edges of the Bundt pan to push the cake forward slightly, working all the way around the cake to loosen the edges. Do the same within the interior ring of the pan. Lay a large, flat plate over the top of the cake and flip it upside down; bang on the pan a few times if needed until the cake releases.

Just before serving, lightly sift powdered sugar over the top of the cake, if you'd like. Slice and serve the cake on its own or with raspberries and whipped cream.

Tightly cover any leftover cake in plastic wrap or a cake storage bin and store at room temperature for up to 3 days or freeze for up to 3 months.

# The Pie Guy's Marionberry Pie

♦ *North Plains*

About twenty miles outside Portland, Oregon, there's a place you must visit called The Pie Guy. It's a pie shop from another era that's run by Bart VanDomelen; he's the pie guy, only it's not a shop but a refrigerator on the porch of Bart's house. Other than the delicious pies, this is what I love most: it's entirely run on the honor system. Bart puts whatever mini pies he bakes up that day in the refrigerator, you open it up, pick your pies, and leave your money. There's a spot outside where you can go eat and share the pies with anybody who's there.

In the "Portland" episode, instead of a reunion with everybody you saw in the episode like we usually do, we took the crew and our local fixers there for the final scene. I can't say enough great things about everyone who works on the show. Off camera, we all go out for meals together, and whenever we can, we'll often have crew meals at the place we just filmed so they can eat something amazing, too. But more often than I'd like, we have to move on to the next spot. Being able to sit outside someone's home and share pie together was something I'll always remember. This marionberry pie was everybody's favorite.

*Using frozen berries that have thawed so they have released much of their juices means I can be in control of the consistency of the pie by adding as much berry juice back into the filling as I want. (Be sure to measure the quantity of berries while frozen; they lose much of their volume when thawed.) By adjusting the sugar and lemon juice after the initial dry ingredients have been incorporated, I can also monitor the sweet-tart balance of the filling. As important, the filling can't be too runny from too much marionberry juice or lemon juice or the crumble will start to melt too much into the filling as it bakes. (It will sink somewhat into the filling.) I judge this consistency each time I make the pies, but it takes some practice, so this recipe has been adjusted with more specific quantities of filling ingredients to help you. I'm sure you'll get the hang of it. And everyone says it, but ovens vary so much in baking temperature, so pay close attention to the pie as it bakes and adjust the temperature if needed. I have two ovens; in one the pies bake at 345°F, and in my other oven I bake the pies at 375°F for exactly the same amount of time—and get the same result.* —BART

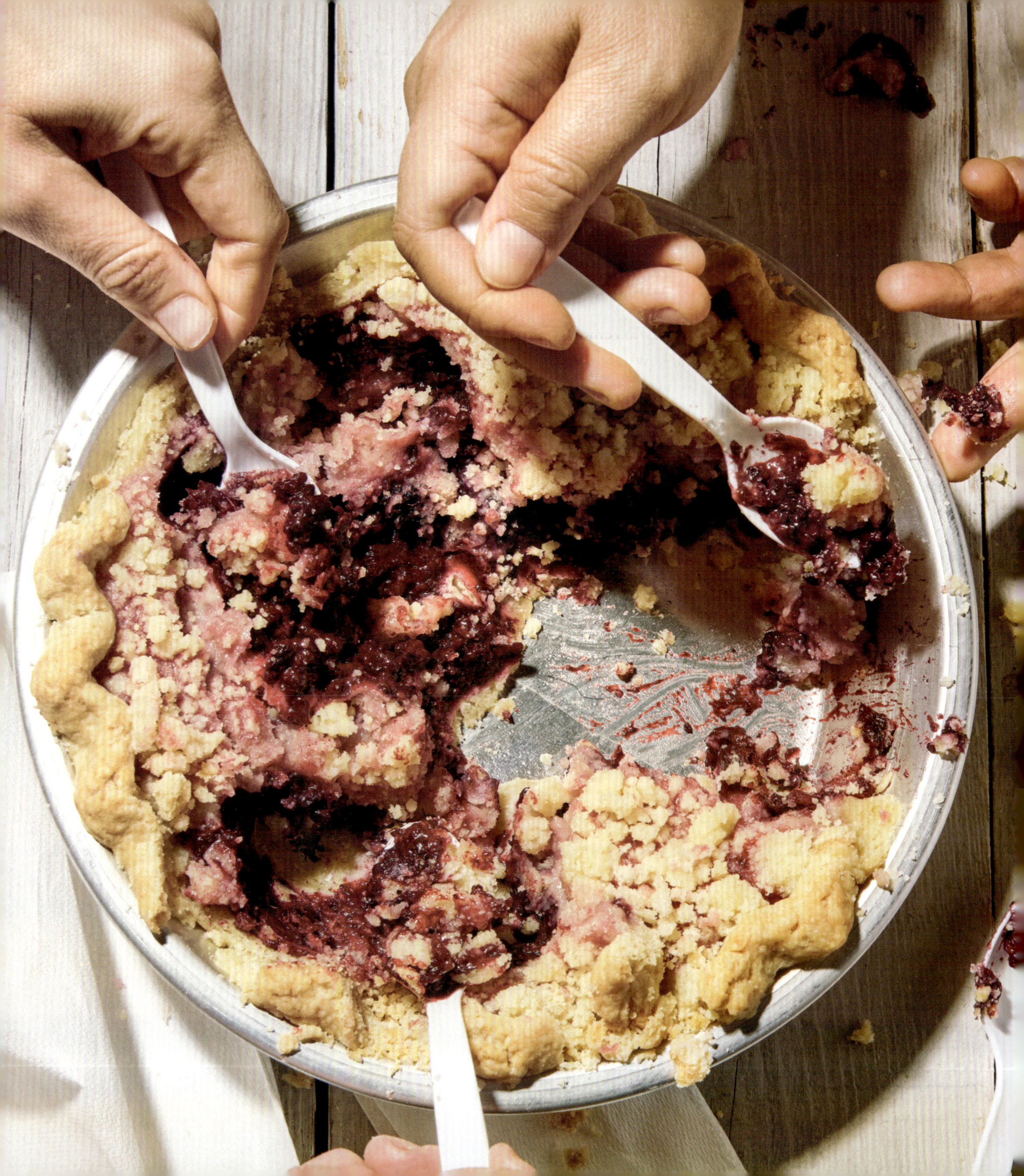

**Prep:** Put a baking rack in the middle of the oven and preheat the oven to 375°F (190°C).

**Make the berry filling:** Make sure the marionberries are completely thawed and very soft or it will affect the consistency of the filling. (If not completely thawed, you can microwave the berries in short bursts or warm them on the stovetop; it's fine if they fall apart.)

Over a medium bowl, strain the berries in a large colander and shake the colander a few times to remove the excess juice. Return the berries to their original bowl. You should have about 3 cups (600g) thawed berries; after about 5 minutes, there will be a little residual juice from the strained berries (leave the juice in the bowl).

Sprinkle 6 tablespoons of the flour, the sugar, and 2 pinches salt over the marionberries and gently toss the berries and dry ingredients together with your fingers or a large spoon. (Some of the berries will break apart as you mix.) The flour should have absorbed most of the residual marionberry juice in the bowl; if not, add another ½ tablespoon of flour. Add the lemon juice and 1½ tablespoons reserved marionberry juice and toss again. The filling should look like a juicy jam. Don't add the filling to the pie crust at this point. (Save the remaining marionberry juice for another use.)

**Make the butter crumble:** In a medium bowl, use your hands to mix together the flour, granulated sugar, and a generous pinch salt (2 to 3 pinches if using unsalted butter). Break up the butter into chunks and rub the butter into the dry ingredients until no clumps remain. Switch to your fist and firmly smash the butter against the bottom of the bowl to get the "sandy" bits at the bottom fully integrated; part of the mixture will look like sand, while the rest will be loose crumbles. Grab a clump of crumble, squeeze it firmly, then break up the chunk in your hand to create larger crumbles. Do this a few times until you have a mix of larger crumbles and smaller, finer grains.

---

**MAKES 1 LARGE PIE; FEEDS 8**

**MARIONBERRY FILLING**

7½ to 8 cups frozen marionberries
(3 10-ounce/280g bags), thawed (see Tips)

6 to 7 tablespoons all-purpose flour, divided

3 tablespoons granulated sugar

Kosher or coarse sea salt

2 tablespoons freshly squeezed lemon juice

**BUTTER CRUMBLE**

1½ cups (180g) all-purpose flour

1½ cups plus 1 tablespoon (312g) granulated sugar

Kosher or coarse sea salt

½ cup (1 stick) plus 3 tablespoons (155g) salted or unsalted butter, at warm room temperature

The Pie Guy's Pie Crust (page 336), rolled out into a 9-inch (23cm) deep-dish pie pan

**Fill and bake the pie:** Just before baking, recheck the moisture of the filling (the berries release more liquid the longer they sit at room temperature). If there is a lot of juice around the edges of the bowl, scatter the remaining ½ tablespoon of flour over the berries and toss to combine.

Pour the filling into the prepared pie crust and disperse the berries evenly throughout. Grab clumps of the crumble topping and squeeze it in your fist. Break up the large chunks of crumble and scatter them over the pie along with the finer, sand-like crumbs to create a mix of crumb sizes. Scatter the crumble all the way to the edges of the pie and slightly mound it up in the center.

Put the pie on a rimmed sheet pan and bake for 8 minutes; the crust and crumble should not have colored much. Reduce the heat to 350°F (175°C) and rotate the sheet pan front to back. Bake the pie, again rotating the pie front to back halfway through, until the crumble has some speckled light brown spots, 28 to 32 minutes in a metal pan, 30 to 36 minutes in a glass or ceramic pan.

Remove the pie from the sheet pan and transfer to a baking rack or stovetop grate. Let the pie cool completely before slicing, at least 4 hours; if not completely cool, the filling will not set up.

Cover the pie tightly with plastic wrap and store at room temperature for up to 5 days.

## TIPS

*With a tender, shortbread-like crust, tangy marionberry filling, and a mountain of delicate crumble, this pie is a contrast of big flavors and textures. The first time you make the pie, it feels "incorrect" in every way: the filling is very "thin" compared to most berry pie fillings, the crumble is extremely fine, and the crust is more the texture of cookie dough than a standard pie dough. (Don't use a standard pie crust here; it won't bake fully.) The biggest challenge is to create a filling that's sturdy enough to hold up the weighty pile of crumble yet still very moist by adjusting the "juiciness" with enough flour. As the pie bakes, the crumble is meant to sink into the berry filling, which creates a variety of textures. Take heed of Bart's note that this pie will need different lengths of time to bake in various ovens; the crumble will only be light golden brown in spots, much less brown than classic crumble pies.*

*Marionberries: Known as the "cabernet" of blackberries, tangy marionberries are what make this pie special. They're rarely available fresh beyond local Oregon markets during the growing season, but this pie filling was crafted to bake up better with frozen berries. Larger Oregon growers (Stahlbush Island Farms, Willamette Valley Fruit) sell the frozen berries at select grocery stores. You'll need three 10-ounce or one larger 32-ounce bag per pie; the exact quantity of berries doesn't matter (successfully making this pie relies on judging the moisture of the filling). Smaller farms like NorthWest Wild foods (nwwildfoods.com) ship their frozen marionberries. When thawed, the berries release most of their juices, so be sure to measure them when frozen. Freeze the leftover marionberry juice in ice cube trays for smoothies or to cook down for ice cream or meat sauces.*

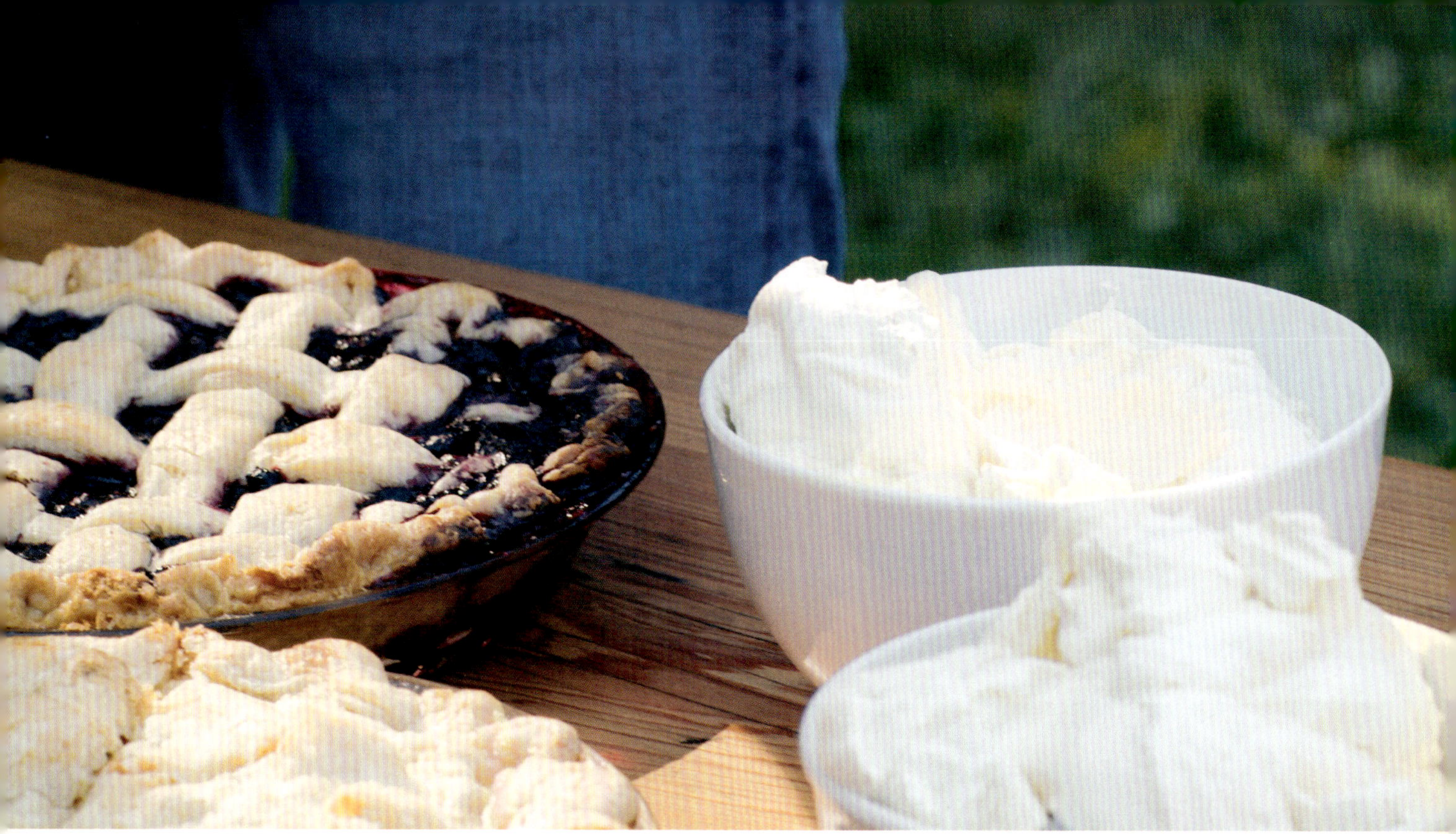

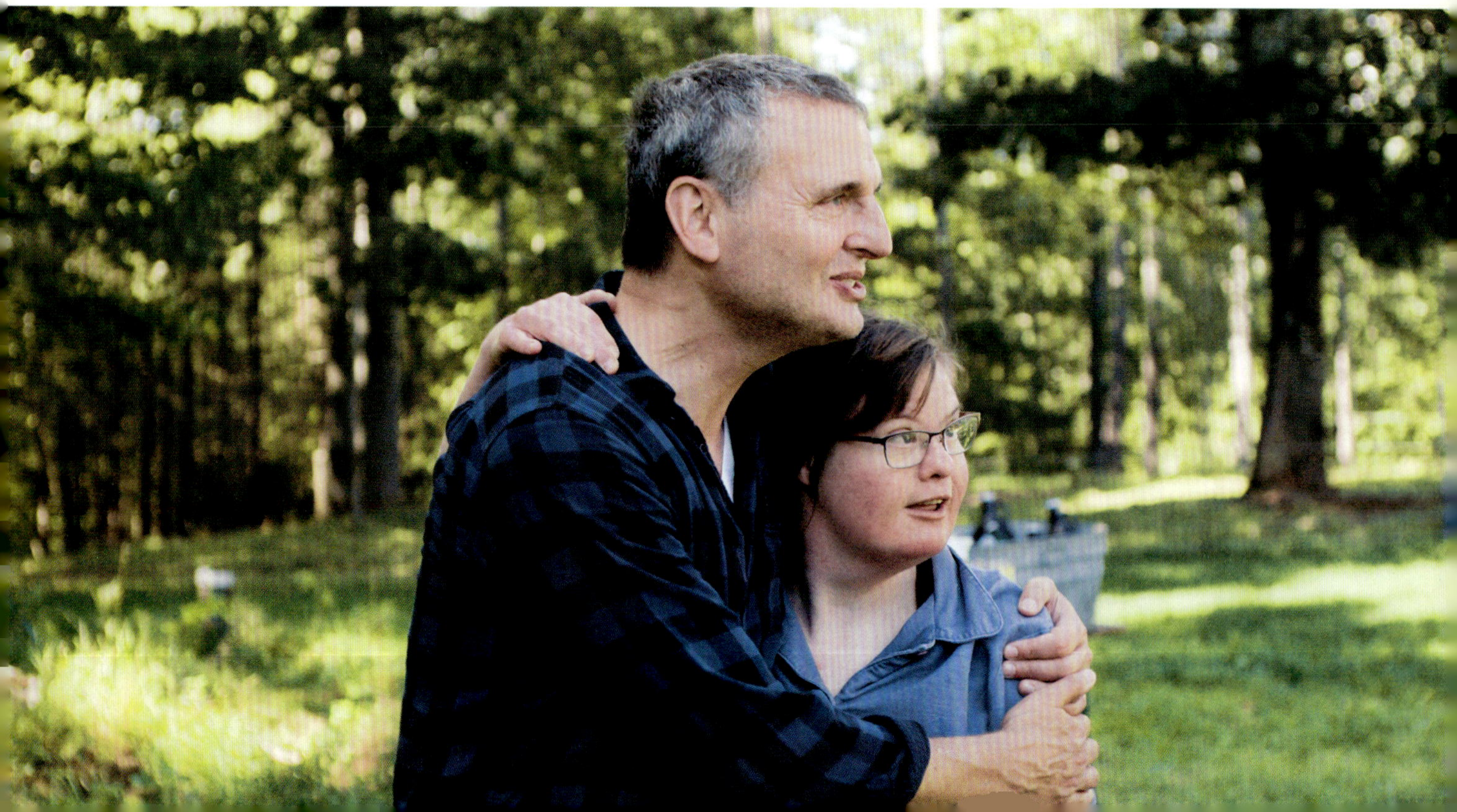

# Buckwheat Blossom Farm's Wild Blueberry Pie

*Wiscasset*

In the "Maine" episode in season five, we drove about an hour up the coast from Portland to Brunswick, where you got to meet my favorite cousin, Anna McDougal, and some of her friends at Spindleworks, the local nonprofit that empowers talented people like Anna to express themselves through their art. (You can buy artwork by Anna and her friends at spindleworks.independenceassociation.org. Monica and I have some in our house.) In the last scene, we went to Wiscasset for a family picnic at Buckwheat Blossom Farm, a totally organic and horse-powered farm where Anna lives with her sister, Amy; her husband, Jeff Burchstead; and their three wonderful kids, Ruth, Leah, and Asa. It's always special to be at their farm with the whole family, sharing good food together. (*Special* isn't the word I would use to describe how I felt in the scene where Jeff teaches me how to corral and shear sheep.) My favorite thing I ate that day were the wild blueberry pies that Ruth and Leah made for everybody. I wanted to get you their pie recipe, but you have to use the best wild blueberries from a small farm or it won't work. (The frozen wild Maine blueberries you can get at the grocery store don't taste as good and also mess up the filling, so you end up with pie soup.) Instead, I'm giving you my version.

By the way, the best way to get a slice of wild Maine blueberry pie is to go to Maine. It's the official state pie, and everybody loves the berries, so you're going to find the pie on the menu at a diner or restaurant somewhere. Wild Maine blueberries are so much better than the ones you get most places, and the blueberries really do grow wild there, so the farmers are just taking care of something that's already around. They're an example of what I love most about Maine, beyond the spirit and friendliness of the people. It's the way everybody is in harmony with nature. It reminds me that maybe we're at our best as a country, and maybe as a people in general around the world, when we work and live in harmony with what's around us, meaning, the gifts that we have from nature.

Go to Maine in the late summer. Get some wild blueberries from a local farm and ask the farmer for the best recipe. Eat a bunch of blueberries, then make a pie while Richard shears some sheep.

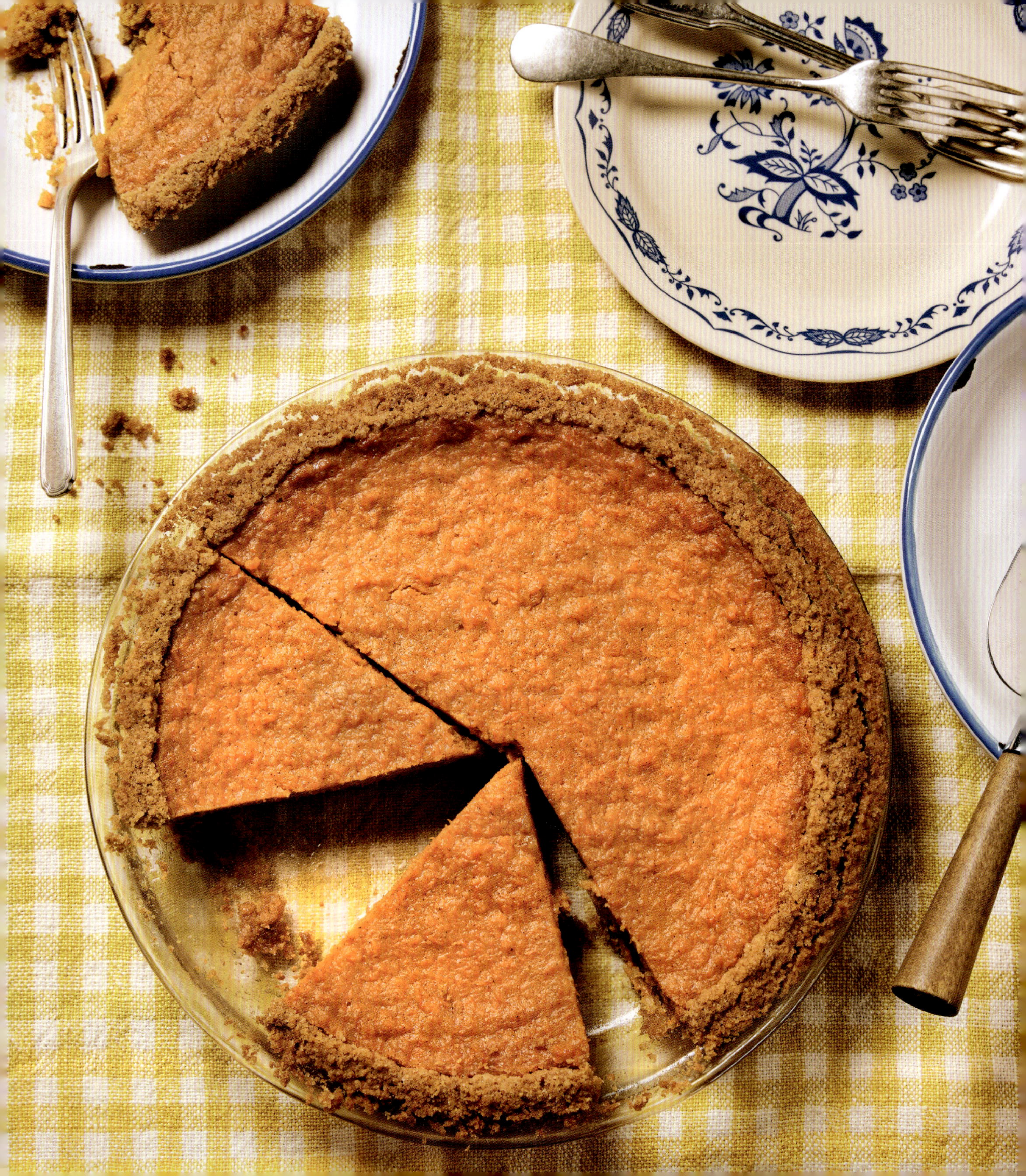

# Sweet T's Sweet Potato Pie

*Philadelphia*

Philadelphia has been a special place to me since I was a kid. I grew up in New York, and my first real trip was to the Franklin Institute in Philadelphia when I was in the fifth grade. And then, I met a girl who grew up right outside Philly, and she seemed pretty good, so I married her. I've been going there regularly for more than thirty years to visit Monica's family, but also because it's a great city that's steeped in civic pride. If you haven't been, I encourage you to go. And not just so your kids can learn about American history. There's a unique spirit that you can feel, a spirit that lives on in the community and especially in the local chefs, bakers, and food shop owners here.

One of the best places to experience that is Reading Terminal Market, which is where we went at the beginning of the "Philadelphia" episode in season six. It happens to be one of the oldest markets in the country, so if you've got kids, it counts as a very delicious history lesson. The one rule is that you need to go very, very hungry. I always start with a soft, hot pretzel from Miller's Twist (I like mine plain, with mustard), and you're gonna want a pastrami Reuben from Hershel's East Side Deli. You can't miss DiNic's, either. They make a great roast pork sandwich (get it with everything). But I could only pick one recipe for this book, and it had to be Sweet T's sweet potato pie.

"Sweet T" is Tia El. When we were there for the show, her bakery had only been at the market a couple of years (it's not often that a space opens up). Tia and her husband, Mark, bake everything, and when you go, you're probably going to see one of them behind the counter. When I was there, even their daughter, Lamirah, was helping out. It's another true family business, one of the most special kinds of food businesses we have in this country and need to preserve. Her pie is so light and creamy, not at all heavy like some. It's going to change the way you think of sweet potato pie.

## TIPS

*The velvety texture and lemon extract, which lends a citrusy flavor that balances the sweetness of the potatoes, is what makes this easy-to-make sweet potato pie special. To get that light, creamy texture, first mash the potatoes by hand, then mix the filling in a stand mixer or with a handheld mixer. (A food processor will make the potatoes dense and gummy.)*

*A higher-end extract (Nielsen Massey, Pendery's, or similar) is excellent in this pie, but an everyday version is also very good (Tia uses McCormick). Don't use lemon oil; it's much stronger than the extract.*

*If you're not using the standard large rectangular graham cracker sheets, check the package, as the smaller square cookies vary in size and weight.*

**MAKES 1 PIE; FEEDS 8**

2 large orange flesh sweet potatoes (1¼ to 1½ pounds/about 625g)

1 cup (200g) granulated sugar

1 teaspoon ground cinnamon

½ teaspoon ground nutmeg

½ cup (1 stick/115g) salted butter, or unsalted butter plus ¼ teaspoon fine salt, cut into cubes

1 teaspoon lemon extract

½ cup (240ml) sweetened condensed milk (about ½ 14-ounce/400g can)

2 large eggs

1 unbaked Graham Cracker Crust (recipe follows), pressed into a 9-inch (23cm) standard pie pan

**Prep:** Put a baking rack in the center of the oven and preheat the oven to 350°F (175°C).

Peel the sweet potatoes and cut them into roughly 1-inch (2.5cm) thick rounds. Set aside 4 cups (1 pound/455g) for the pie.

**Make the filling:** In a medium pot, cover the sweet potatoes with about 1 inch (2.5cm) of water and bring to a boil. Reduce to a simmer and cook until the potatoes are very tender and begin to fall apart when pierced with a fork, about 10 minutes, depending on their size. Drain the potatoes and return them to the pot.

In a small bowl, mix together the sugar, cinnamon, and nutmeg.

To the pot with the hot (drained) potatoes, add the butter, sugar mixture, and lemon extract. Use a potato masher or the back of a large spoon to mash the potatoes until broken down into small pieces; the mashed potatoes should still have some texture but no large lumps.

Transfer the warm potatoes to a stand mixer fitted with a paddle attachment (or use a large bowl with a hand mixer), add the condensed milk and eggs, and mix on medium speed until the mixture is smooth with only small lumps of potatoes, about 30 seconds.

Pour the filling into the graham cracker crust. Stop when the filling is almost at the level of the pie crust; you may have a few extra tablespoons.

**Bake the pie:** Carefully transfer the pie to a rimmed sheet pan and bake, rotating the sheet pan front to back halfway through, until the edges of the pie are golden brown and firm to the touch and the center is set but still slightly soft, 50 to 55 minutes; in a metal pan, the edges will be a darker golden brown and the pie will set more quickly than in a glass pan.

**Cool the pie and serve:** Transfer the pie to a baking rack or stovetop grate to cool for at least 1 hour before cutting into slices and serving. Or, if not serving right away, let the pie cool completely, cover tightly with plastic wrap, and store at room temperature for up to 5 days.

> *When you come to our bakery, we like to say, "You don't just get a pie, you get an experience," and this sweet potato pie is a very special part of that story (and our best seller). The recipe is from my late grandmother Delores Truitt, who passed it down to me. (I added my own twist to the graham cracker crust, but you'll have to come to the bakery to try it!) The potatoes need to be tender enough where you can mash them by hand along with the butter, sugar, and spices. The key is the mashed potatoes have to be warm while you make the filling. I hope any time of year you sit down to eat a Sweet T's sweet potato pie, it will remind you of the holidays, filled with love and laughter with family and friends. And that you will remember Sweet T's Bakery and my grandma every time, because each pie is made with love and sweetness, like her!* —TIA

## GRAHAM CRACKER CRUST

In a medium saucepan or in a large microwave-safe bowl, melt the butter over medium-low heat. Remove the pan from the burner.

In a food processor, process the graham crackers on high speed until ground into very fine crumbs. If you don't have a food processor, crumble the graham crackers with your fingers into small pieces, put them in a large food storage bag, and press down with the bottom of a bowl to smash the crackers as finely as possible.

Add the sugar and 2 to 3 pinches of salt to the saucepan or bowl with the melted butter and stir to combine. Add the graham cracker crumbs and stir until the mixture is well combined; it will be very crumbly.

Press the crust firmly into the bottom and up the sides of a standard 9-inch (23cm) metal or glass pie pan. (Don't use a deep-dish pan.) The crust will be very loose feeling in texture but the filling will bind it together.

**5 tablespoons unsalted butter**

**5 ounces (140g) graham crackers (9 full-size rectangular sheets; more if smaller squares)**

**2 tablespoons granulated sugar**

**Fine salt**

SWEETENED
RED BEAN
ゆであずき
NET WT.15.16 OZ.(430 G)
COCONUT SPORT
CONDENSED

# Marie Mercado's Halo Halo with Vegan Halaya

📍 *Sampaguita, Orlando*

Going to a local ice cream shop is one of my favorite things to do when I'm traveling. No matter how much you've eaten, you can always find room for a scoop of gelato, ice cream, or some soft serve. And if you're hungry, you can get a milkshake or sundae, and you'll be good until dinner. When you're in Orlando, you need to go to Sampaguita, a Filipino-style ice cream shop run by Marie Mercado and Mo Hassan. The flavors are like nothing I'd had before: guava creamsicle, soy sauce–butterscotch, jackfruit–chili nut, and buko pandan (a milk jelly with lychee fruit), their house flavor. I was in Orlando before we shot that episode for season seven, and I got this halo halo, which means "mix mix." I told Richard we had to go there for the show. It's one of the best sundaes in the world. Marie makes her own halaya, which is a sweet paste made from ube, which are a specific variety of purple yams (her recipe is on page 332), and they make their own soft serve at the shop, so you'll have to go there to have hers. (I recommend you get the halo halo with their ube soft serve.) At home, you can get everything at your local Filipino market. It's a fun thing to make with the family. This is part of the real magic kingdom, the real Orlando.

> *Filipino flan is very thick, so you can slice it easily once it's chilled. If you don't have a Filipino market, check your local Latin supermarket if you don't want to make it from scratch. (We make a regular and vegan version.) And for the red mung beans (also sweetened in syrup), you are either team beans, or not . . . it's your halo halo, so make it any way you like! The one rule is to serve it with an extra-long spoon.* —MARIE

**MAKES 1 HALO HALO; FEEDS 1 GENEROUSLY, 2 TO SHARE**

**BASE**

2 generous spoonfuls (3 to 4 tablespoons) Sampaguita's Vegan Halaya (page 332), divided

Plenty of shave ice

Evaporated milk, heavy cream, or vegan coconut milk, as needed

**MIX-INS (GENEROUS SPOONFUL EACH, YOUR CHOICE)**

Nata de coco (coconut jellies), plain or the green pandan leaf-flavored

Macapuno (coconut shreds with a jelly-like center)

Kaong (palm fruit in syrup)

Red mung beans sweetened in syrup (optional)

*(ingredients continue)*

*If you don't have a small shave ice machine, even crushed ice ground up in a blender works. The more finely ground the ice, the better, and make plenty! To build our halo halo, we make most of the components from scratch, including all of our ice creams, but you can buy most of the prepared ingredients in glass jars (packed in sugar syrup) at Filipino markets. With jackfruit, you know the fruit is ripe when it turns yellow; instead of fresh, you can substitute jackfruit in syrup (not the one in salty brine).* —MARIE

### ICE CREAM

2 generous scoops ube, vanilla, or mango ice cream

### TOPPINGS

2 to 3 slices fresh jackfruit (or canned in syrup)

1 slice chilled leche flan

Corn flakes

Puffed rice cereal

Sweetened condensed milk (dairy or coconut), for drizzling

**Assemble the halo halo:** Smear all but a spoonful (about 1 tablespoon) of Sampaguita's Vegan Halaya in the bottom of a very large, tall glass. Fill the glass about halfway with shave ice and add enough evaporated milk to completely cover the ice like you're pouring syrup over a snow cone.

Top the shave ice with the nata de coco, macapuno, kaong, and candied red mung beans (if using), then the remaining spoonful of halaya and the ice cream. Tuck the sliced jackfruit and leche flan on the side of the glass, sprinkle the corn flakes and puffed rice cereal lightly on top, and finish with a drizzle of sweetened condensed milk. Serve with an extra-long spoon.

# Somebody Scoop Phil

**Vanilla Bean Ice Cream, Chocolate Chunks,
Rivers of Hot Fudge and Peanut Butter, and Twix**

📍 *Caffè Panna, New York*

One weekend when I was in New York, Hallie Meyer, the genius pastry chef behind Caffè Panna in Gramercy Park, invited me to her shop to create my own sundae for the menu. The texture of her ice cream is unlike any I've ever had—more of a cross between a creamy gelato and fluffy soft serve. (Her shop's fantastic vanilla bean ice cream recipe is on page 334.) Ice cream, chocolate, peanut butter, caramel, and coffee are some of my favorite things, so I did an affogato sundae with chocolate ice cream, Hallie's homemade fudge, a peanut butter sauce, mini Twix bars (so you get the caramel filling and crunchy cookies), and panna, which is whipped cream made from cream that Hallie imports from Italy. When you pour hot espresso over everything, the ice cream starts to melt, and you get all those flavors in one bite.

This is the ice cream flavor we made based on that sundae. You can still get a scoop or buy a pint at certain times of year at Caffè Panna. (Hallie rotates the ice cream flavors regularly.) The only difference is there's no espresso (doesn't need it), and we used vanilla ice cream instead of chocolate (the fudge sauce is already so rich, the vanilla is perfect). One thing you need to get is a really good dark chocolate fudge sauce. Hallie keeps her recipe a secret, but she recommends Coop's, which you can get online. Like hers, it's a really thick, bittersweet chocolate sauce and isn't too sweet. If I could come back in another life as ice cream, this would be the flavor.

> *Layering in the ingredients adds new textures that bring out the creaminess of the ice cream base, and you're left with a perfect flavor and texture symphony!* —HALLIE

**MAKES ABOUT 1½ QUARTS (1.2L); FEEDS PHIL**

1 3.5-ounce (100g) 65% or higher dark chocolate bar (Lindt, Ghirardelli)

1 cup (260g) creamy peanut butter (not natural peanut butter)

1 cup (260g) Coop's hot fudge sauce (about ¾ of a 10-ounce/280g jar)

Hallie's Vanilla Bean Ice Cream (page 334), well chilled

12 mini ("fun size") Twix, preferred, or 2 packages full-size Twix (4 cookie sticks)

## TIPS

*It works best to layer up the mix-ins and ice cream in a wide, deep food storage container (or if you don't have one, a 2 quart/ 2L baking dish) so you can get each of the mix-ins in every scoop. The warm peanut butter and fudge sauces partially melt the ice cream, so allow time for the ice cream mixture to firm back up for at least 2 to 3 hours in the freezer after you layer in the mix-ins.*

*Coop's hot fudge sauce is almost like soft dark chocolate fudge at room temperature, so it freezes into thick chocolatey chunks. The mass-produced hot fudge "toppings" available at most grocery stores are too sweet for this ice cream.*

**Prep:** Break the chocolate bar into bite-size pieces.

Put the peanut butter in a microwave-safe bowl, microwave for 30 seconds, and stir until smooth. Microwave the hot fudge sauce in the jar (remove the lid) in 15-second bursts; it should be easy to stir but not hot and still very thick. Or, on the stovetop, heat the peanut butter in a small saucepan over low heat just until easy to stir. For the hot fudge sauce, put the jar in a small saucepan filled with 2 to 3 inches (5 to 7.5cm) of water and heat over medium heat just until you can stir the sauce.

**Assemble the ice cream:** Scoop about three-quarters of Hallie's Vanilla Bean Ice Cream into a bowl.

Working quickly, scatter about a third of the chocolate chunks on top of the ice cream that's left in the container. Drizzle about half of the peanut butter sauce and dollop about half of the fudge sauce over the chocolate. Don't spread the sauces out; you want chunky hills and valleys of ice cream and mix-ins. Top the mix-ins with about half of the ice cream in the bowl and spread it out.

**Repeat the layers:** Add a third of the chocolate chunks and the remaining half of the peanut butter and fudge sauces, then spread the rest of the ice cream on top. Scatter the last of the chocolate chunks on top of the ice cream, and press plastic wrap onto the surface of the ice cream.

Cover the container and freeze the ice cream in the back of the freezer until it firms up again, 2 to 3 hours or overnight.

**Serve:** If using full-size Twix, use your fingers to break the candy bars into thirds (don't use a knife to cut them as the cookie will shatter). Leave the "fun size" Twix whole.

As you scoop the ice cream, dig deep into the container so you get a generous amount of every mix-in. Top each ice cream serving with 2 "fun size" Twix or candy bar pieces.

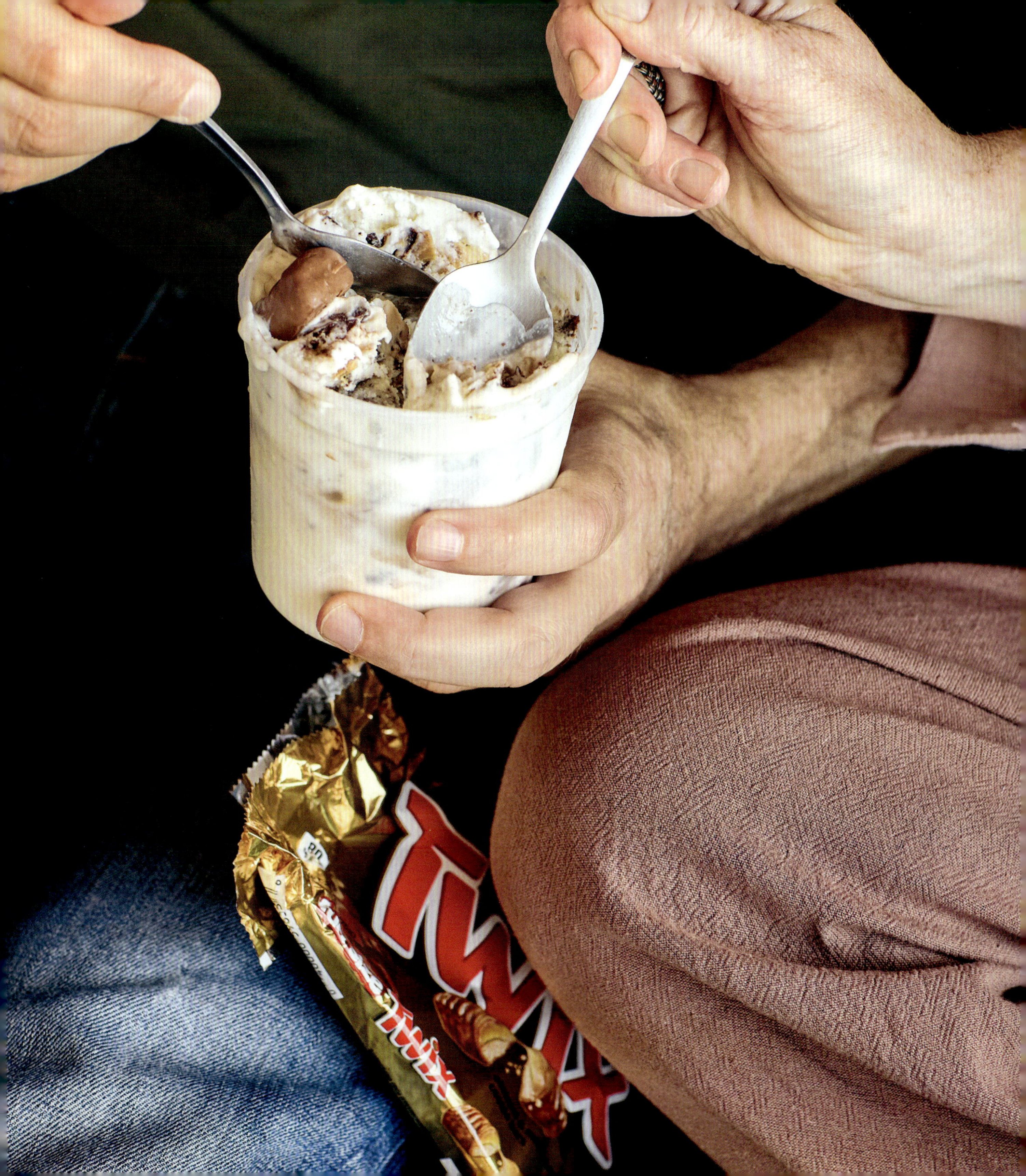
TWIX

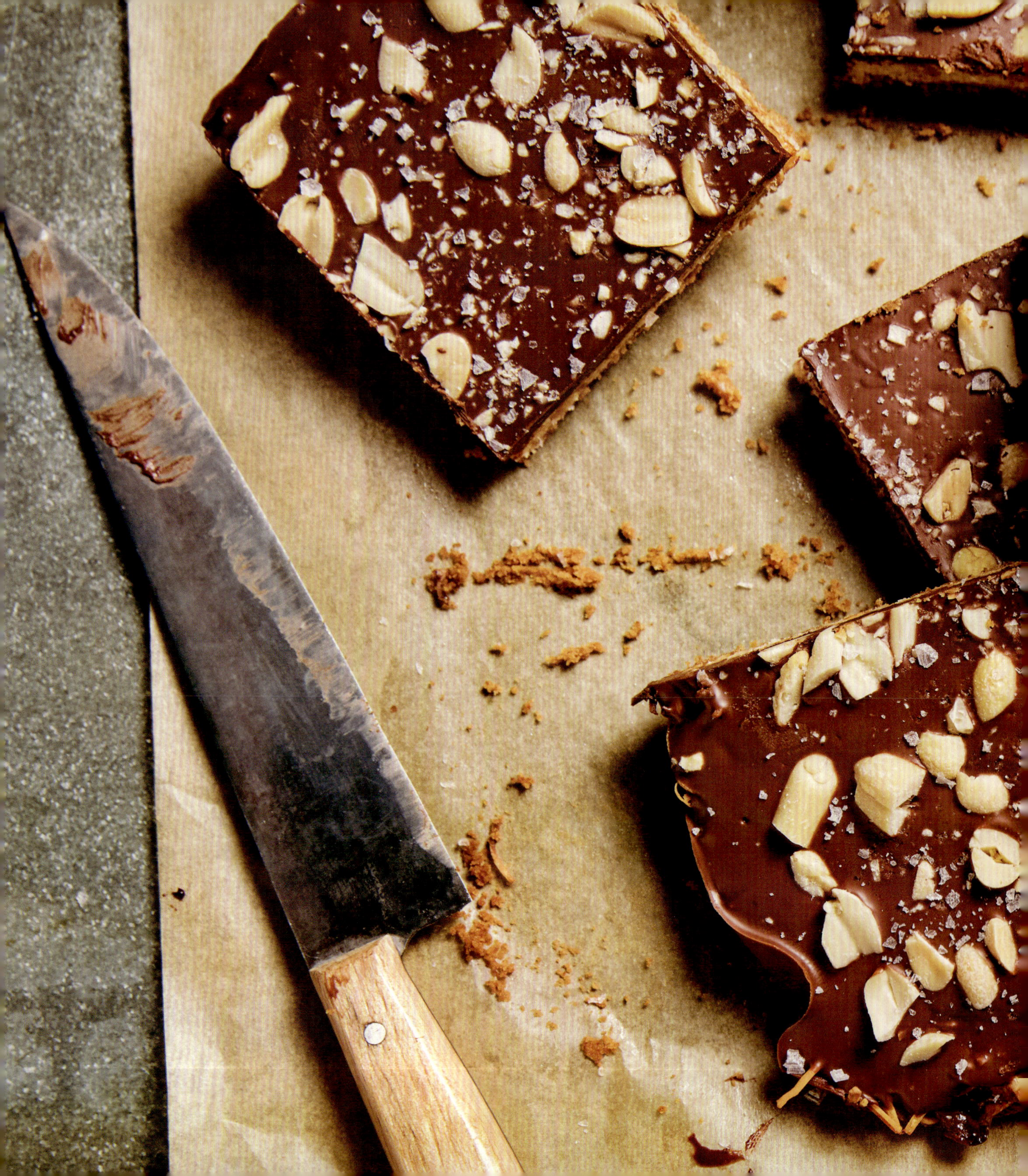

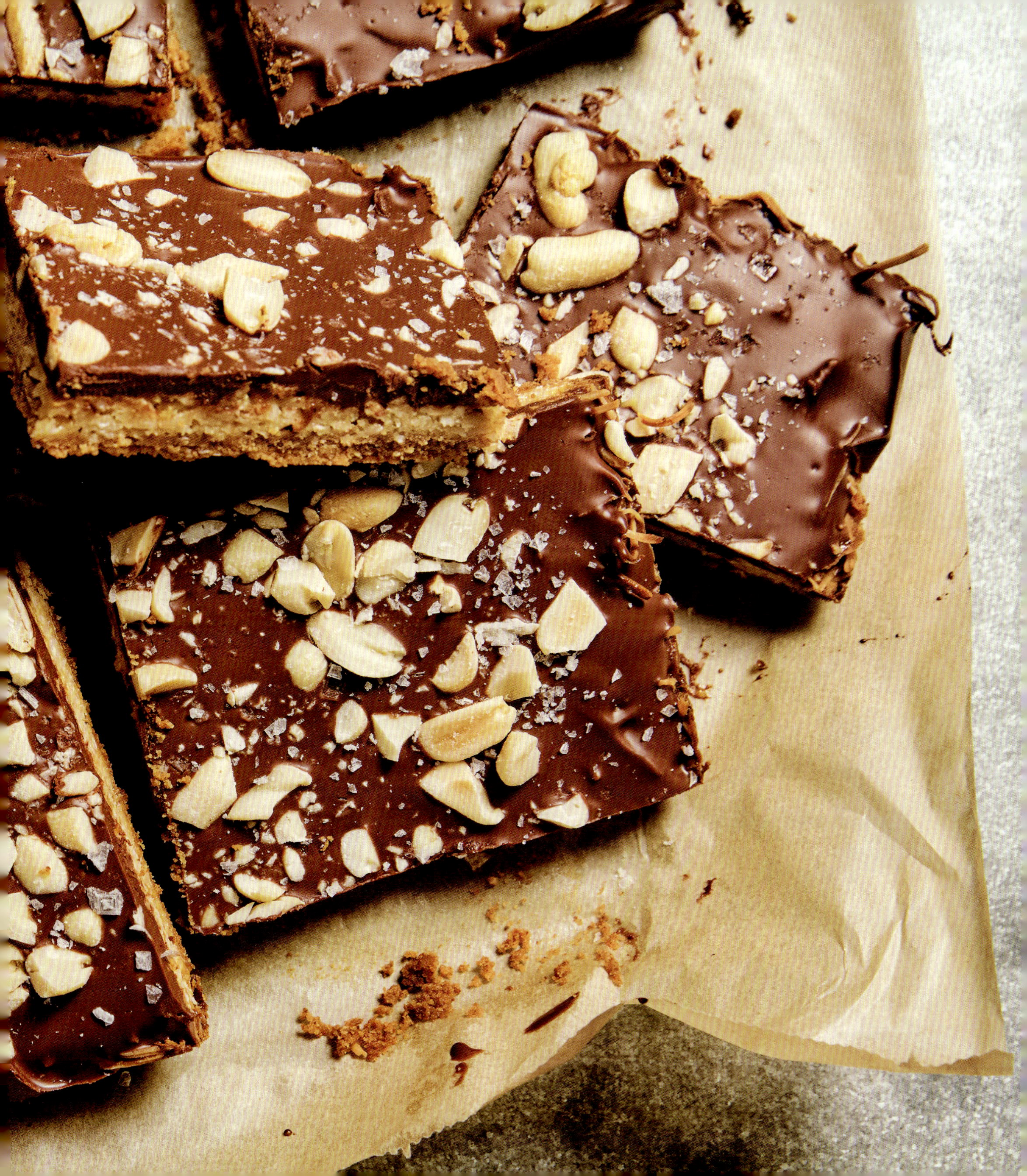

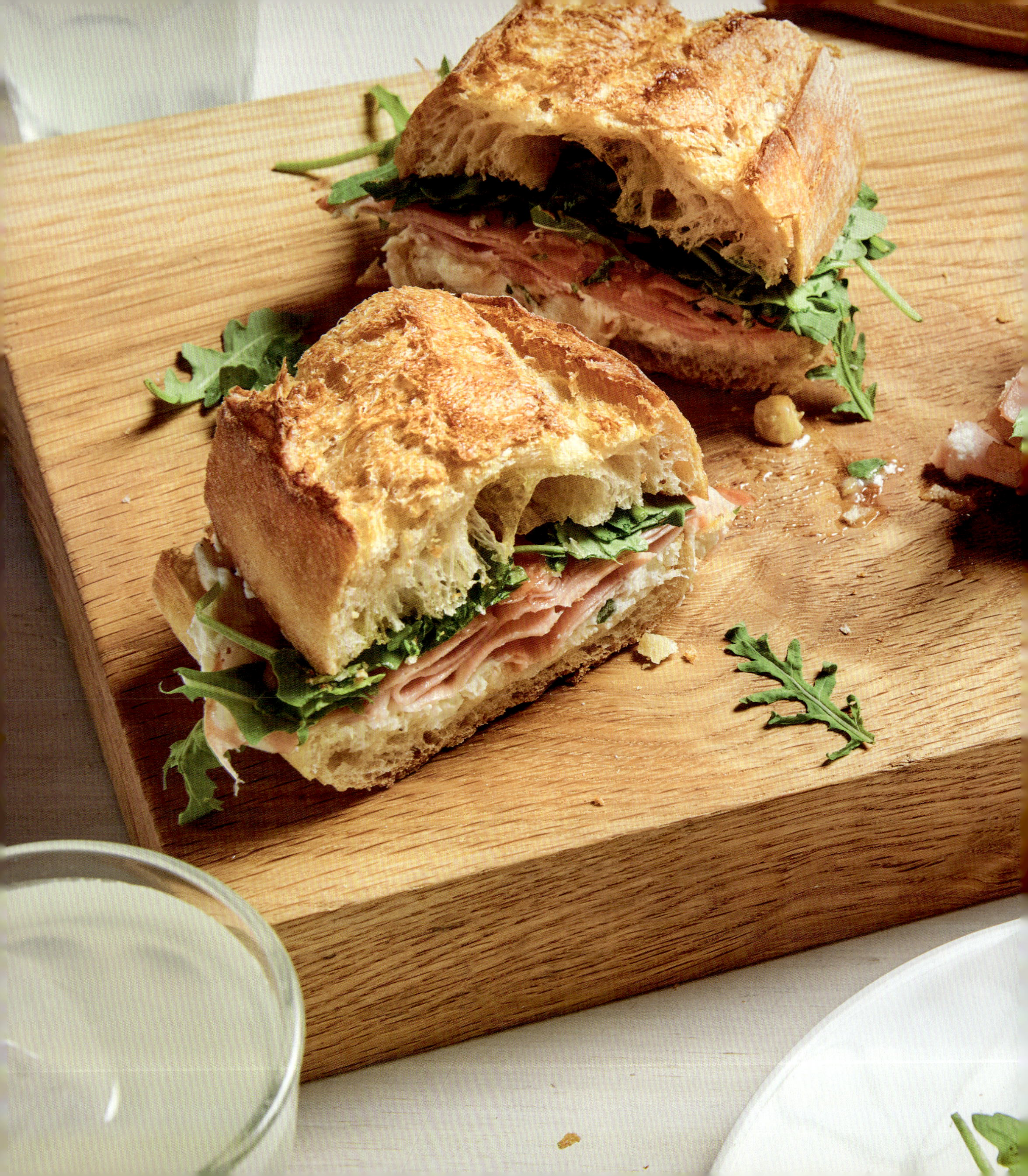

# OTHER THINGS YOU'LL WANT TO HAVE AROUND

If I cooked, I'd keep everything in this chapter in my kitchen.

## Chad's Bread-and-Butter Pickle Chips

*Palace Diner, Biddeford*

**MAKES ABOUT 1½ QUARTS (1.4L), DRAINED, ENOUGH FOR 6 TUNA SANDWICHES**

- 1½ pounds (680g) large cucumbers (2 large English Hothouse or 3 American)
- 1 habanero chili or 2 small jalapeños, halved
- 3 leafy sprigs dill
- 1½ cups (360ml) distilled white vinegar
- ¾ cup (150g) granulated sugar
- 1½ tablespoons kosher salt
- 1½ teaspoons crushed red pepper flakes
- 1 teaspoon whole yellow mustard seeds
- ¾ teaspoon celery salt
- ¾ teaspoon ground coriander
- ½ teaspoon ground turmeric

> *A batch of pickles doesn't last very long at the diner, so we leave the jalapeños in the brine after we make the pickles. You could take the peppers out after a few days if you want. It's best to use a mandoline to slice the cucumbers so the pickles are thin enough to be heavily shingled on the tuna melt (see page 69).* —**CHAD CONLEY**

Trim one end off the cucumbers and use a mandoline to shave them into very thin rounds (or use a sharp knife).

Pack the cucumber slices, habanero pepper, and dill into a large 2-quart (2L) glass or heat-proof plastic food storage container or medium stainless steel bowl.

In a medium saucepan, bring the vinegar, sugar, salt, red pepper flakes, mustard seeds, celery salt, coriander, turmeric, and ¾ cup (180ml) of water to a simmer and stir until the sugar has dissolved. Pour the hot brine over the cucumbers, cover the container or bowl with the lid or plastic wrap, and let it cool completely.

Refrigerate the pickles overnight or up to 3 weeks; the flavor will intensify the longer they are in the brine. If you transfer the pickles to smaller jars, divide the habanero pepper and dill sprigs among the jars.

### TIP

*When you've polished off the pickles, a little of the brine is delicious stirred into mayonnaise to make a tangy potato salad or coleslaw dressing.*

**CONDIMENTS AND SANDWICH SPREADS**

# Mohamad's Brown Butter Caramelized Onions

*Orfali Bros, Dubai*

Preheat the oven to 275°F (135°C).

Arrange the thyme sprigs in a single layer on a baking sheet and roast until the leaves are fully dried, about 20 minutes; check the leaves frequently toward the end of the baking time so they don't burn. When cool, run your fingers down the stems to remove the leaves.

While the thyme roasts, cut off the top ends of the onions (keep the root ends intact) and use a mandoline to slice them into thin rings (or use a sharp knife).

In a Dutch oven, melt the butter over medium heat and toast, swirling the pan occasionally, until the butter smells nutty and dark toasted bits have accumulated on the bottom of the pan, 4 to 5 minutes. Add the onions and bacon, stir to combine, and slowly cook, stirring and scraping the bottom of the pan occasionally with a wooden spoon, until the onions are a rich golden brown, 30 to 45 minutes, depending on the size of the pot.

Add 1 tablespoon of water and the white balsamic vinegar and scrape up the brown bits on the bottom of the pan. Turn off the heat, stir in the honey and 1 scant tablespoon roasted thyme leaves, and season the onions with salt and pepper.

If not using the caramelized onions within an hour or two, cool completely, cover, and refrigerate for up to 1 week; rewarm over low heat. Store any extra roasted thyme leaves at room temperature for up to 1 week.

**MAKES ABOUT 1½ CUPS (375G), ENOUGH FOR 6 BURGERS**

4 to 5 leafy thyme sprigs

1¾ pounds (800g) white or yellow onions (3 to 4 medium)

3 tablespoons (40g) unsalted butter

6 ounces (170g) bacon, roughly chopped

1 tablespoon white balsamic vinegar, or 1 tablespoon white wine vinegar mixed with ½ teaspoon honey

1 tablespoon plus 1 teaspoon honey

Kosher or coarse sea salt and freshly ground black pepper

### TIP

*Freshly roasted thyme leaves are more intensely flavored than conventionally dried leaves. Use any leftovers in sauces or on eggs, poultry and meats, and roasted vegetables.*

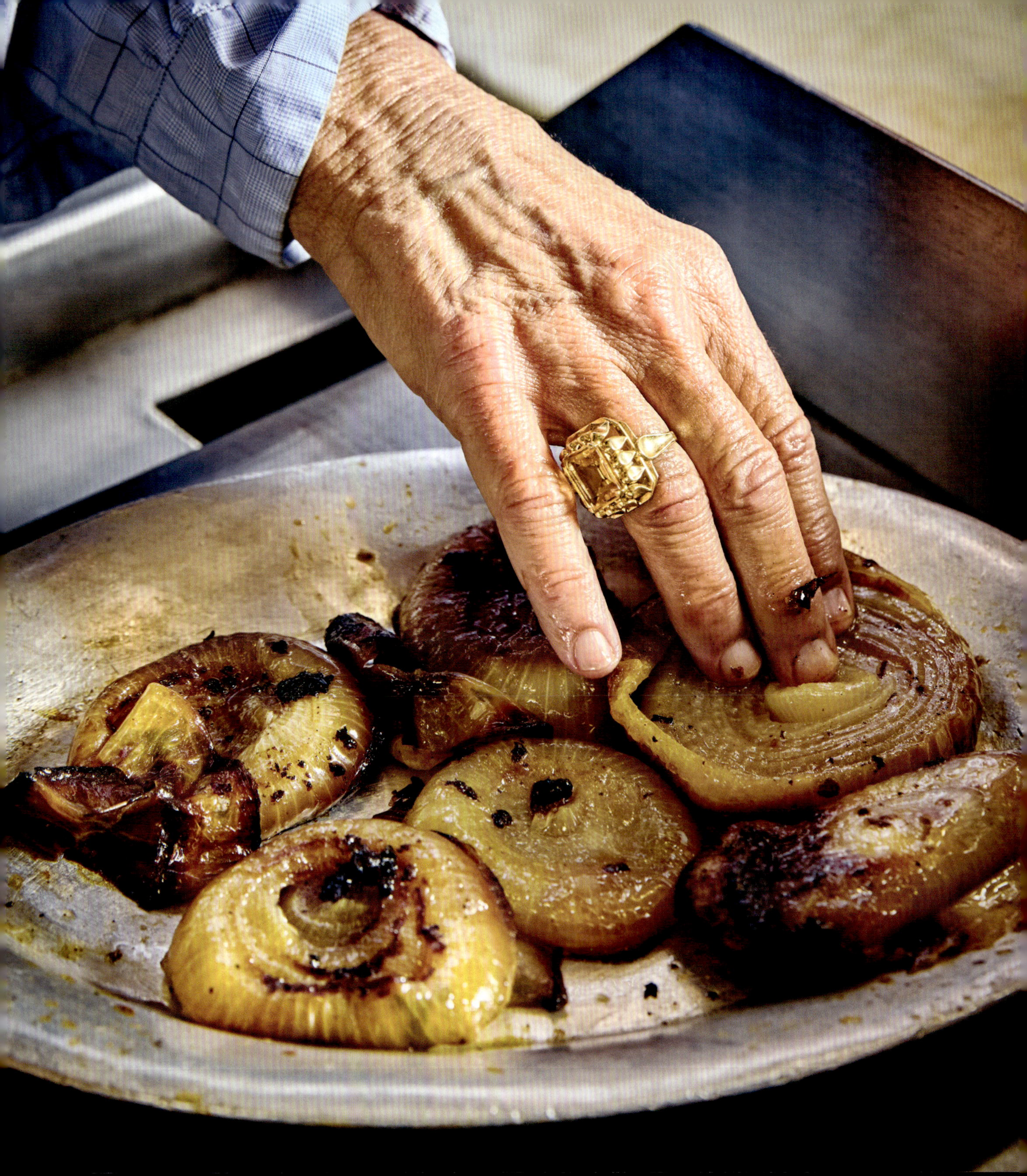

# Nancy's Ultimate Hamburger Onions

📍 *Chi SPACCA, Los Angeles*

Preheat the oven to 350°F (175°C).

Trim about 1 inch (2.5cm) off the top ends of the onions, peel, and slice each into large ¾-inch (2cm) thick rounds, keeping the rings intact. You'll only get 2 to 3 thick center slices out of each onion (save the scraps for stock).

Drizzle enough olive oil over a rimmed sheet pan to lightly coat the bottom and arrange the 6 largest onion slices on the pan in a single layer. Drizzle 3 tablespoons of the olive oil over the onions, sprinkle 1 tablespoon salt evenly over each, flip, and repeat with the remaining 3 tablespoons of oil and 1 tablespoon of salt.

Pour ½ cup (120ml) of water along the sides of the sheet pan, being careful not to pour it directly onto the onion slices.

Bake the onions for 30 minutes and use a large metal spatula to carefully flip the onions so they stay intact; reassemble any onions that separate. Return the onions to the oven, rotating the pan front to back, and roast until the onions are caramelized around the edges and soft in the middle, 35 to 40 minutes. Check the onions often during the last 5 to 10 minutes and carefully remove any from the pan that have already caramelized.

If not using right away, let the onions cool completely, cover, and refrigerate for up to 3 days. Gently rewarm the onions in a low oven (250°F/120°C) for about 10 minutes.

**MAKES 6 THICK SLICES, ENOUGH FOR 6 BURGERS**

**3 large yellow onions**

**6 tablespoons extra-virgin olive oil, divided, plus more for the pan**

**Kosher or coarse sea salt**

CONDIMENTS AND SANDWICH SPREADS

# Nancy's Calabrian Chili-Mint Aioli

*Chi SPACCA, Los Angeles*

**MAKES ABOUT 1 2/3 CUPS (360G), ENOUGH FOR 6 BURGERS**

1 cup (240ml) mayonnaise, preferably Best Foods

1 tablespoon roughly chopped mint

2 to 3 medium garlic cloves

½ cup (115g) Calabrian chili pepper paste (Tutto Calabria crushed peppers or paste)

2 tablespoons freshly squeezed lemon juice

Kosher or coarse sea salt

> *Like the onions, this is the aioli on our burgers (page 93) at Chi SPACCA. You can use it on almost everything.*
> —NANCY SILVERTON

In a bowl, combine the mayonnaise and mint. Use a fine Microplane zester to grate 2 garlic cloves over the mayonnaise, then add the Calabrian chili pepper paste, lemon juice, and a pinch of salt, and stir to combine. Season the aioli with more garlic and salt, if needed.

Cover and refrigerate the aioli for up to 3 days.

# Joe's Anchovy-Caper Aioli

*Pizzeria Beddia, Philadelphia*

> *We use this on our tuna and smoked sardine hoagie (see page 73), but it's good on sandwiches, salads, everything. You want enough anchovies for the salt and flavor.*
> —JOE BEDDIA

**MAKES ABOUT 1¼ CUPS (290G), ENOUGH FOR 6 HOAGIES**

2 large egg yolks, at room temperature

3 to 4 good-quality oil-packed anchovy fillets (Agostino Recca, chili pepper–spiced or regular)

1 medium garlic clove

1 large lemon

Kosher or coarse sea salt

1 cup (240ml) extra-virgin olive oil

2 tablespoons capers plus 2 tablespoons of the brine

In a blender, combine the egg yolks, 2 anchovy fillets, garlic, the juice of half the lemon (about 1 tablespoon), and a pinch of salt and mix on medium-low speed to combine. With the blender running, slowly pour in the olive oil in a very thin stream; the aioli will gradually begin to thicken. Transfer the aioli to a bowl and stir in the capers and brine.

Cover and refrigerate the aioli for up to 3 days.

### TIPS

*To make a quick version of Joe's aioli with mayonnaise, omit the eggs and olive oil. Smash the anchovies, garlic, and salt in a mortar with a pestle, then mix the anchovy mixture, lemon juice, capers, and caper brine with 1 cup (240ml) mayonnaise.*

*Agostino Recca anchovies are larger and meatier than most; if you use another brand, use 6 anchovies.*

## CONDIMENTS AND SANDWICH SPREADS

# Jace's Basil Pesto Sandwich Spread

*Fried Egg I'm In Love, Portland (Oregon)*

**MAKES ABOUT 1 CUP (240ML), ENOUGH FOR 6 SANDWICHES**

1 cup (28g) tightly packed basil leaves

2 ounces (1 cup/55g) fresh, coarsely grated parmesan cheese

½ cup (60g) pine nuts

4 to 5 garlic cloves, roughly chopped

Kosher or coarse sea salt and finely ground black pepper

⅔ cup (160ml) extra-virgin olive oil, plus more as needed

*Because this is going on a sandwich, you want to taste a nice, strong balance between the basil, olive oil, and salt in this pesto. You're also looking for a smooth texture, which makes it easier to spread onto the bread for the Yolko Ono (page 39).* —JACE KRAUSE

**In a food processor (easiest method):** Pack the basil into the processor first, then the parmesan, pine nuts, garlic, ½ teaspoon salt, and 2 pinches pepper. Add the olive oil and blend for about 30 seconds. Scrape any pesto off the sides of the processor and blend until well combined, about 30 seconds. Let the pesto rest for about 1 minute, scrape the sides of the processor again, and blend until very smooth.

**In a blender:** Start with the olive oil, then add all the other ingredients. Blend for about 15 seconds, stir to incorporate any basil leaves sitting on top of the pesto, if needed, and blend for about 15 seconds longer until smooth; if the pesto becomes too thick to blend, stir again and add a splash or two more olive oil.

**With a mortar:** Pound the pine nuts with a pestle to a paste, add the garlic, and grind until smooth. Add the salt, then tear any large basil leaves in half or thirds and add them to the mortar (in a small mortar, do this in batches). Grind the basil leaves until broken down into a paste; be patient, they will eventually break down. Mix in the parmesan and olive oil.

**Finish the pesto:** Season the pesto with salt and thin with a little more olive oil, if needed; the flavor should be stronger than pesto for pasta and the texture very spreadable.

If not using the pesto within a few hours, cover and refrigerate for up to 3 days. (Unlike most pesto, you don't need to top it off with more oil to store; there's already plenty of olive oil that will separate and rise to the top.) Serve at room temperature and stir well.

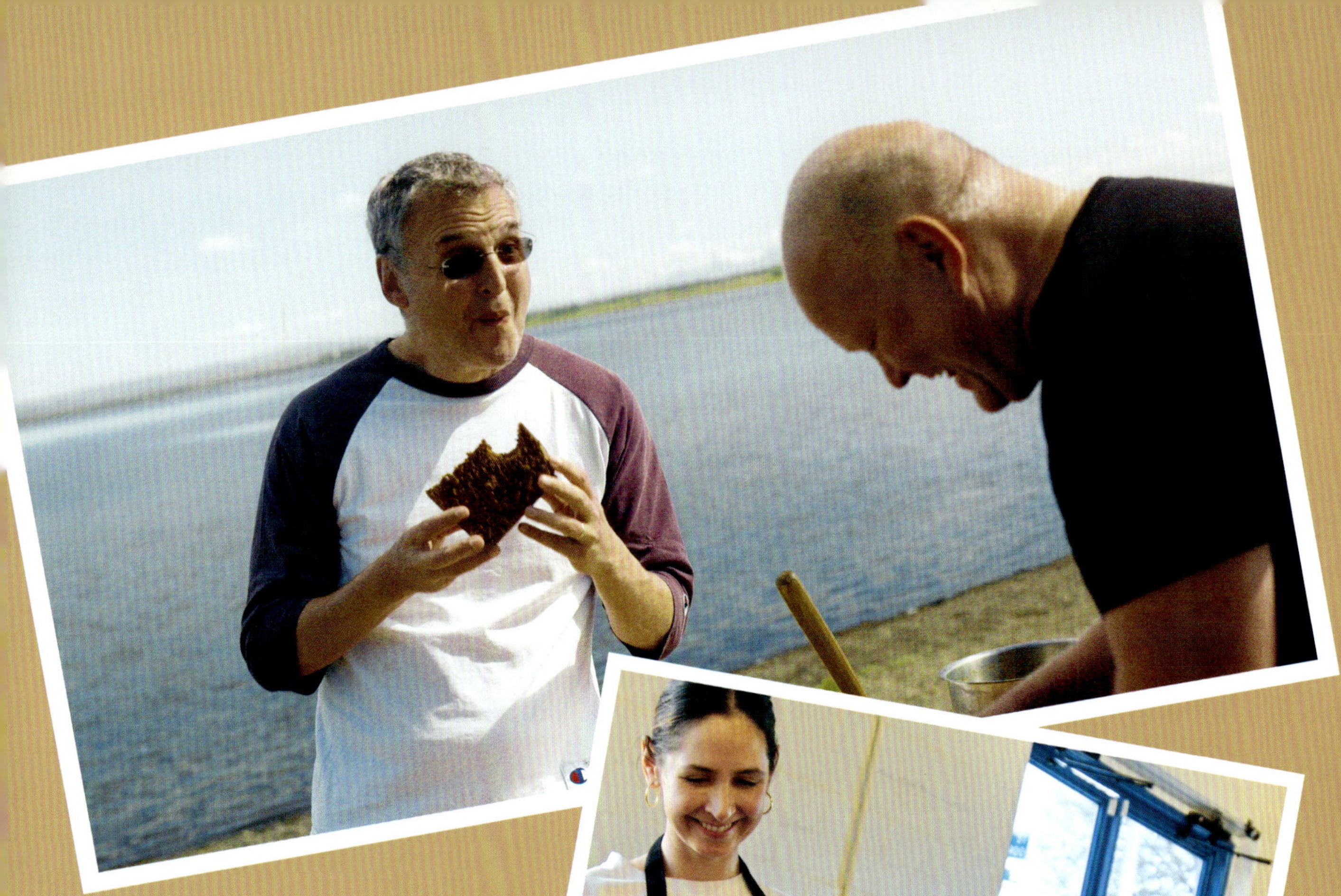
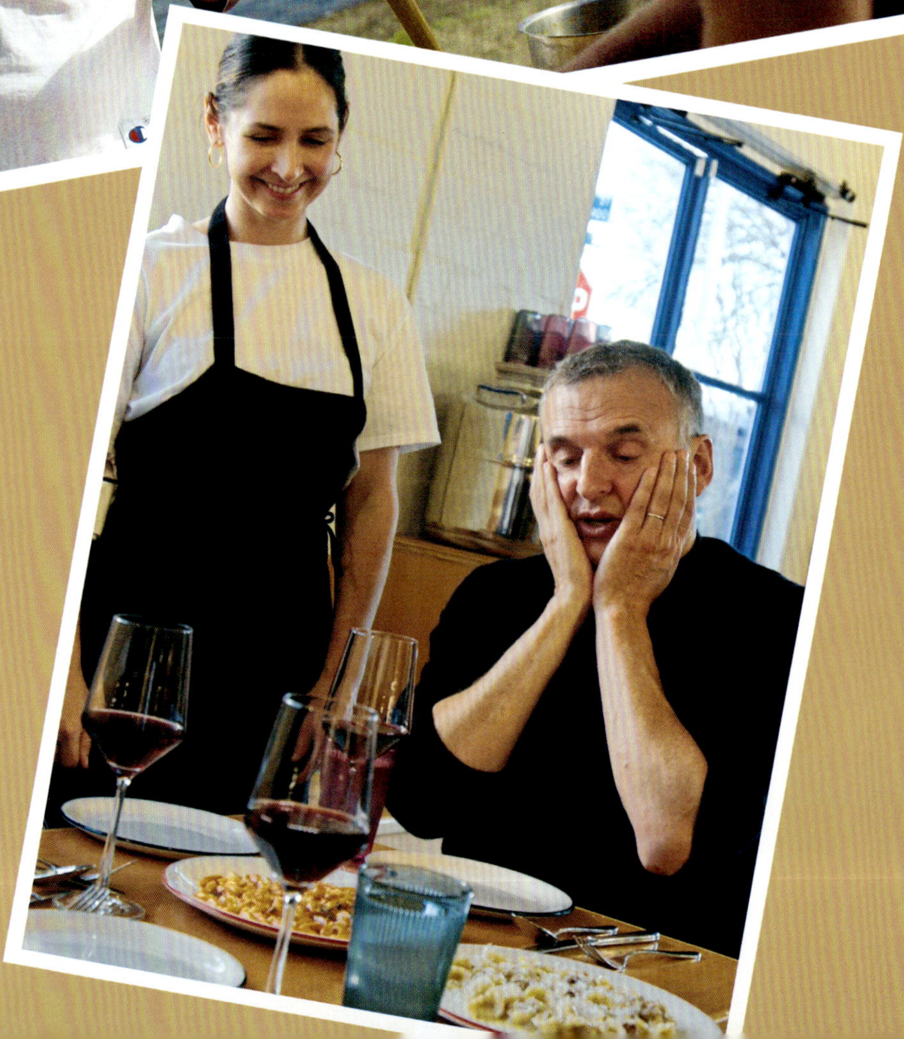

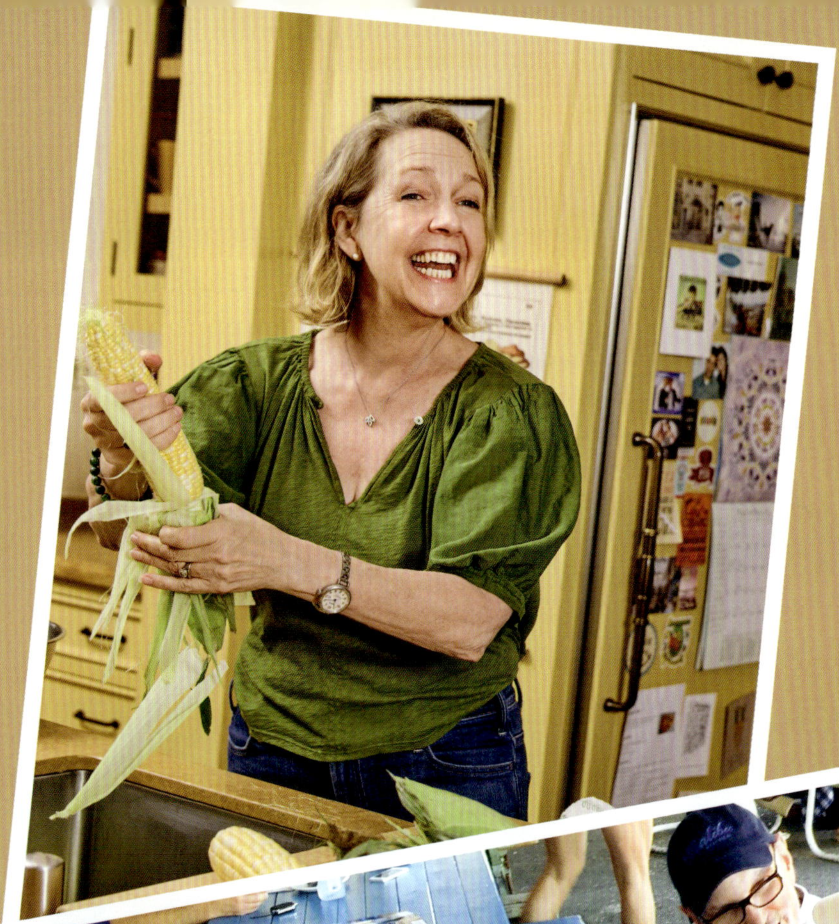

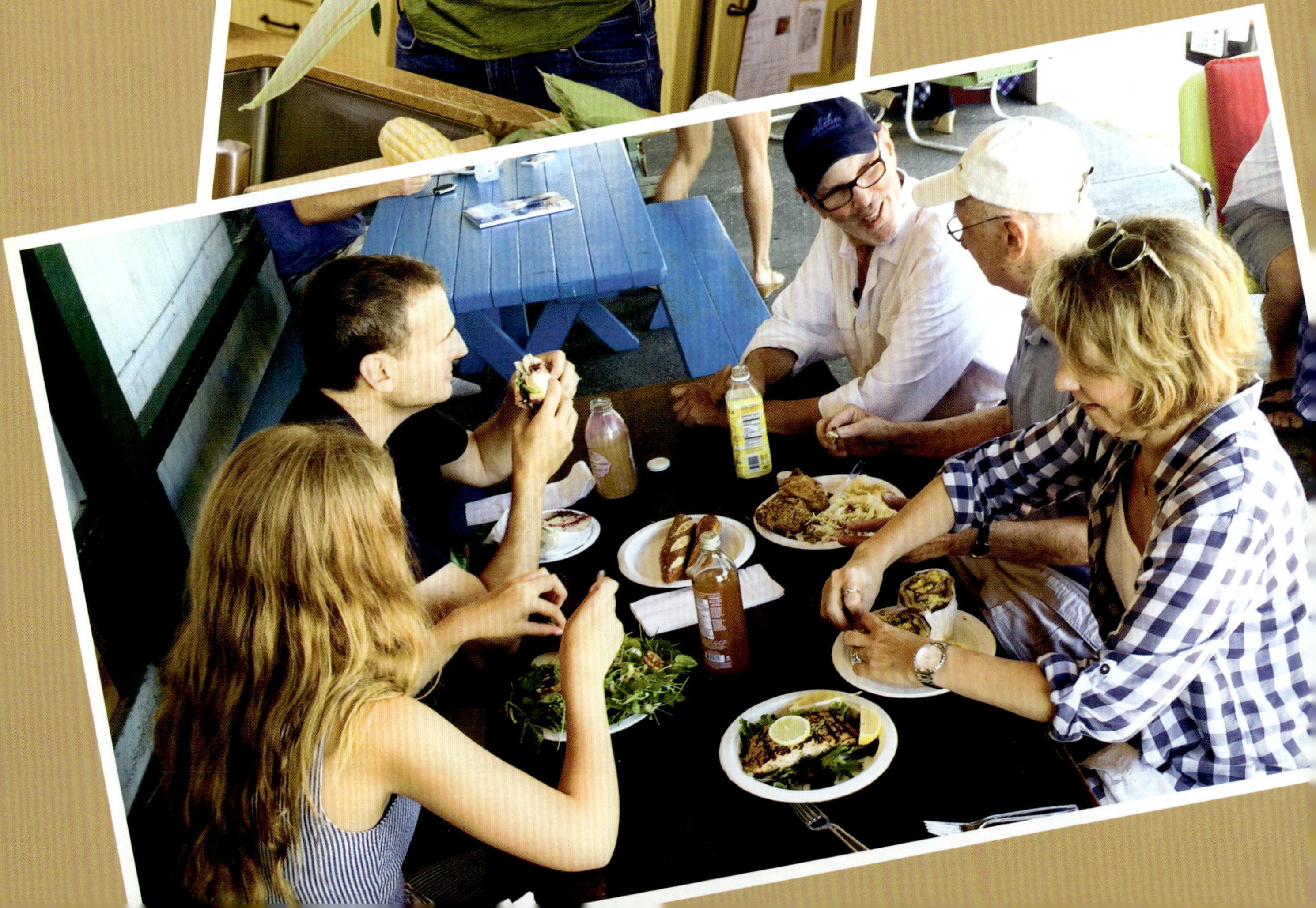

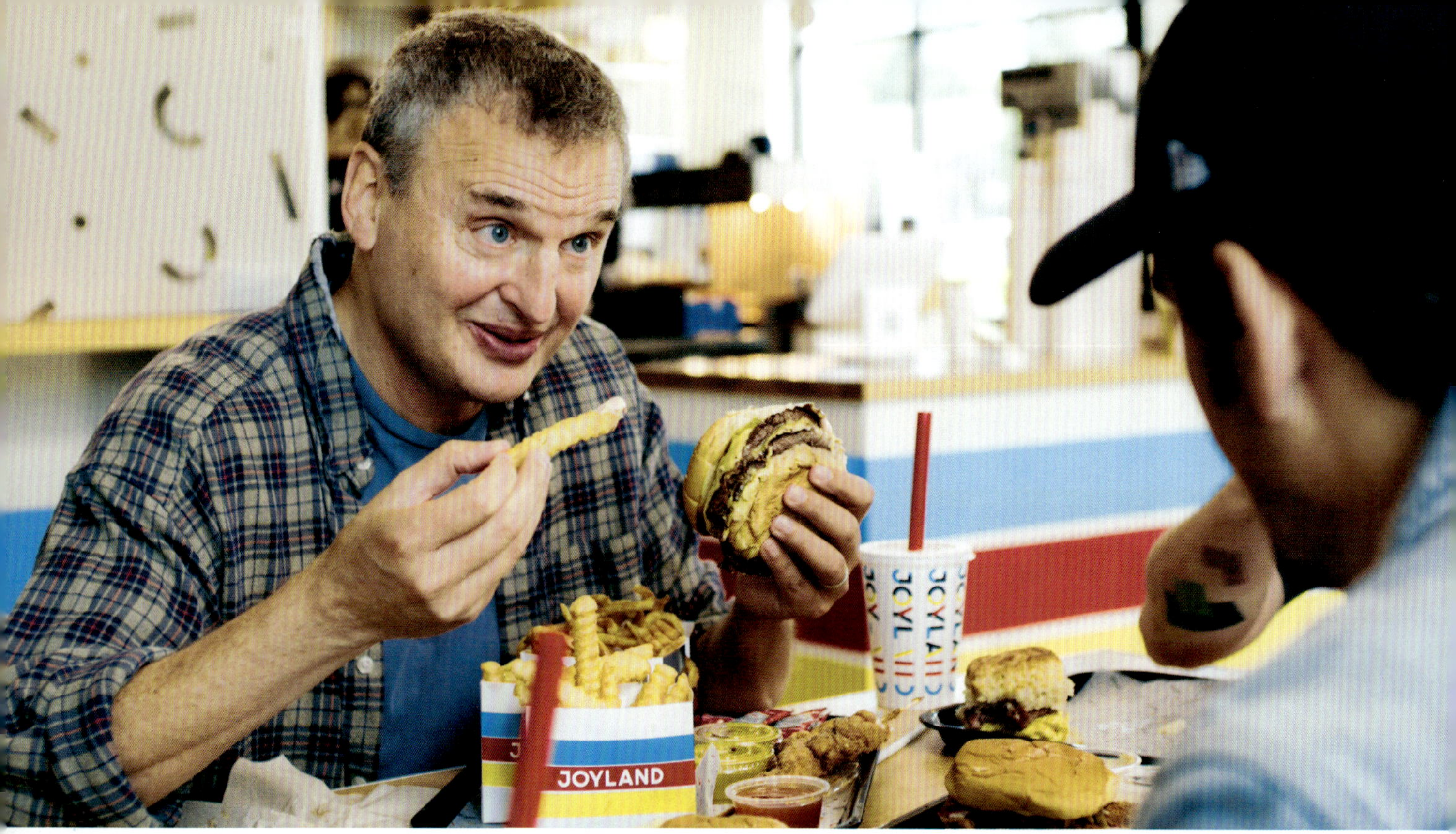
JOYLAND

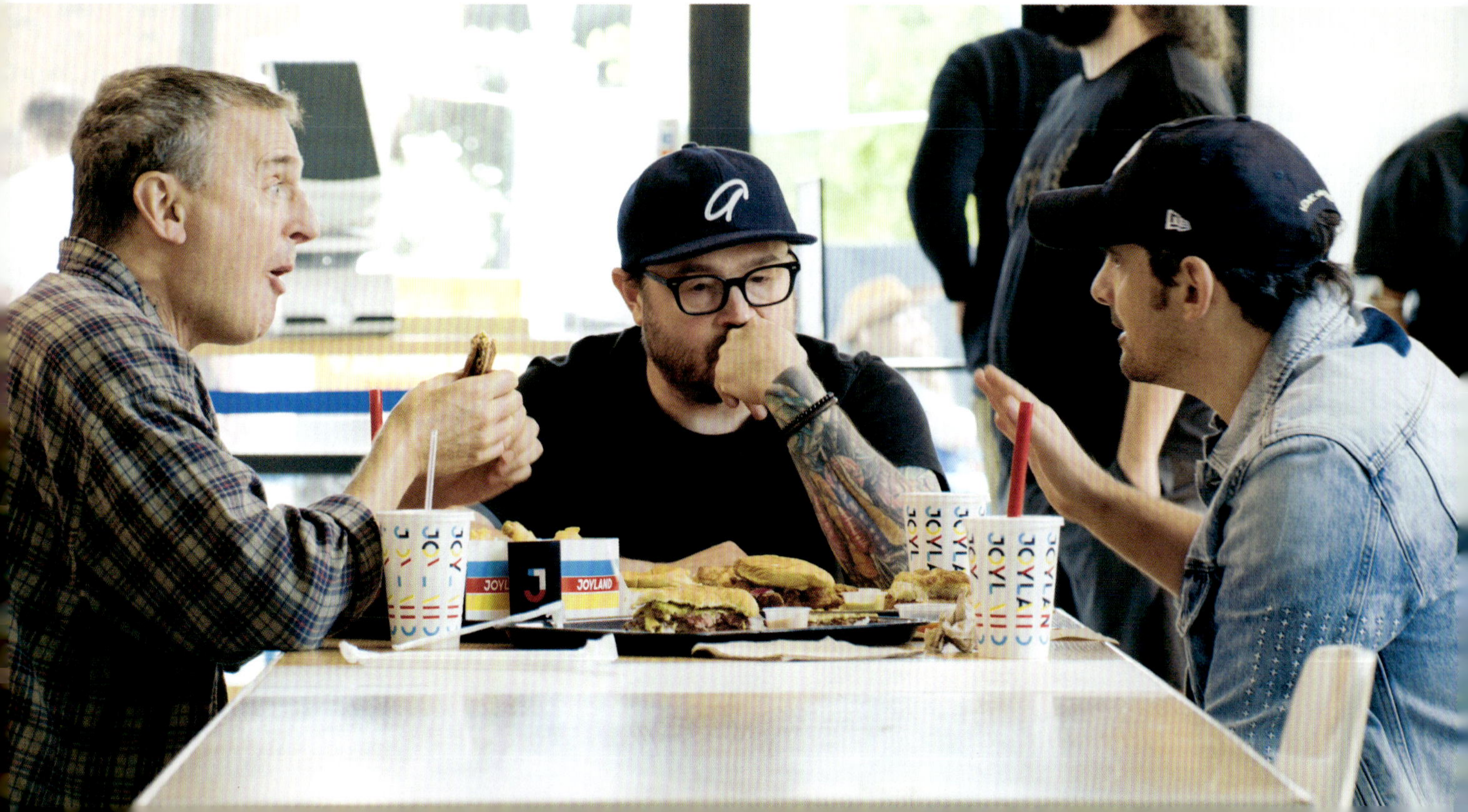
JOYLAND

# Sean's Fancy Burger Sauce

*Joyland, Nashville*

> *We sneak a little Red Boat Fish Sauce into this sauce that we serve with the Crustburger (page 99) for the occasional burger dip. You're also going to want it for fries. Always serve the sauce at room temperature. That goes for ketchup, too.* —**SEAN BROCK**

In a medium bowl, whisk together the mayonnaise, ketchup, hot sauce, and fish sauce. Season the sauce with salt.

Cover and refrigerate the sauce for up to 1 week. Serve at room temperature.

**MAKES ABOUT 1¼ GENEROUS CUPS (300ML), ENOUGH FOR 6 BURGERS**

¾ cup (180ml) mayonnaise

⅓ cup (80ml) ketchup

2 teaspoons vinegar-based hot sauce (Frank's RedHot)

Scant ¾ teaspoon Vietnamese-style fish sauce (Red Boat)

Kosher or coarse sea salt

OTHER THINGS YOU'LL WANT TO HAVE AROUND • 309

# Ludo's Dijon Vinaigrette

*Petit Trois, Los Angeles*

**MAKES ABOUT ⅔ CUP (165ML)**

2 tablespoons plus 1 teaspoon (35ml) Dijon mustard

1 tablespoon plus 2 teaspoons (25ml) white wine vinegar

½ cup (120ml) grapeseed or other mild oil

2 tablespoons (16g) finely minced shallot (½ medium)

2 generous pinches fleur de sel

*Make the dressing ahead and have some tender butter lettuce (Boston or Bibb) chilled and ready. A good French omelette (see page 29) does not wait.* —LUDO LEFEBVRE

In a medium bowl, whisk together the mustard and vinegar. Very slowly pour in the oil in a slow, steady stream, whisking constantly. The oil will integrate into the mustard and vinegar but will not emulsify. Add the shallot, fleur de sel, and 1 teaspoon of room-temperature or cold water (not hot) and whisk vigorously until the vinaigrette emulsifies.

Cover and refrigerate the vinaigrette for at least 1 hour or up to 3 days.

# Sieger's Vegan Soya Crema

📍 *Here's Looking At You, Los Angeles*

> *Other than our golden beets (see page 167), this crema goes well with any roasted or grilled vegetable, or use it as a sub for aioli or mayo when making your next batch of potato salad. For grilled fish, blend in some dill.*
> **—SIEGER BAYER**

**MAKES 1 GENEROUS CUP (275ML), ENOUGH FOR 6 SERVINGS OF BEETS**

8 ounces (225g) firm tofu, drained

2 medium garlic cloves, minced

2 teaspoons finely grated ginger

Finely grated zest of 1 medium lemon

¼ cup (60ml) extra-virgin olive oil

2 tablespoons champagne vinegar

1 tablespoon plus 1 teaspoon tamari, preferably, or good-quality soy sauce

½ teaspoon white peppercorns, or ¼ teaspoon finely ground white pepper

Kosher or coarse sea salt

Crumble the tofu into a blender, preferably, or food processor. Add the garlic, ginger, lemon zest, olive oil, vinegar, tamari, white peppercorns, and 1 teaspoon salt and blend until combined. Scrape down the sides of the blender or processor bowl and blend until very smooth and creamy, about 45 seconds; the crema should look like aioli.

Cover and refrigerate the crema for at least 2 hours to allow the flavors to develop, or up to 3 days.

### TIP

*A blender whips the most air into the tofu for the silkiest crema, but a food processor also works. Be sure to process the ingredients long enough so the tofu is completely smooth.*

# Angel's Gochujang Wing Sauce

*Anju, Washington, DC*

**MAKES ABOUT 2 CUPS (480ML)**

1 cup (240ml) light corn syrup

½ cup (145g) gochujang chili paste

⅓ cup (80ml) white vinegar

3 tablespoons ketchup

3 tablespoons stock (vegetable or chicken) or water

1 tablespoon toasted sesame oil

2½ to 3 tablespoons Everyday Garlic-Ginger Paste (page 314)

*You need a lot of sauce to fully coat the wings. We go through a ton.* —**ANGEL BARRETO III**

In a bowl or measuring cup, combine the corn syrup, gochujang, vinegar, ketchup, and stock.

In a medium saucepan, heat the sesame oil over medium heat. Add the garlic-ginger paste and cook, stirring constantly with a rubber spatula or wooden spoon, until aromatic but not browned, about 1½ minutes. Add the gochujang mixture, scrape the paste off the bottom of the pan with a wooden spoon, and stir to dissolve the chili paste. Bring the sauce to a vigorous simmer, stir a few times, then remove the pan from the heat and let cool.

If not using within a few hours, cover and refrigerate the sauce for up to 5 days.

# Angel's White Barbecue Sauce

*Anju, Washington, DC*

> *We drizzle this sauce on our fried chikin wings (see page 141), but you can also use it as a marinade for grilled chicken: marinate the chicken overnight, shake off the marinade, and grill it up.* —ANGEL BARRETO III

**MAKES ABOUT 1 CUP (240ML), PLENTY FOR THE WINGS**

¾ cup (180ml) mayonnaise

2½ to 3 tablespoons Everyday Garlic-Ginger Paste (page 314)

3 tablespoons unseasoned rice vinegar

2 teaspoons toasted sesame oil

2 teaspoons yellow (ballpark) mustard

1 teaspoon granulated sugar

Kosher or coarse sea salt and freshly ground black pepper

In a bowl or jar, mix together the mayonnaise, garlic-ginger paste, rice vinegar, sesame oil, mustard, sugar, 1 teaspoon salt, and 1 teaspoon pepper. Set aside for at least 30 minutes to allow the flavors to meld. If not using within a few hours, cover and refrigerate for up to 5 days. Serve at room temperature.

### TIP

*To use the white barbecue sauce as a marinade for grilled chicken, rub about half the sauce over 1 large, whole chicken (spatchcock it if you'd like), season the chicken lightly with salt and pepper, cover, and refrigerate overnight. Shake off the excess marinade before grilling the chicken, and serve with extra sauce on the side. The white barbecue sauce also works well as a tangy, creamy salad dressing.*

# Everyday Garlic-Ginger Paste

**MAKES ABOUT 6 TABLESPOONS**

½ cup (60g) roughly chopped ginger (peeled), packed

8 medium garlic cloves, smashed

1 tablespoon neutral oil (vegetable, grapeseed, or similar)

In a blender, combine the ginger, garlic, and vegetable oil and blend, stopping to scrape down the sides of the blender a few times, until thick and paste-like. Press a piece of plastic wrap on top of the paste and refrigerate for up to 1 week.

### TIP

*For both Angel's Gochujang Wing Sauce (page 312) and his White Barbecue Sauce (page 313), you'll need the full amount of the Everyday Garlic-Ginger Paste to make the sauces for his chikin wings on page 141. For Saw Naing's Pe Hainn (page 121) and Chintan's Goat (or Lamb) Curry with Fried Onions (page 218), you can cut the paste in half and smash the garlic and ginger in a mortar with a pestle (the smaller quantity doesn't mix as well in a large blender), or use the leftover paste in a sauce or dressing.*

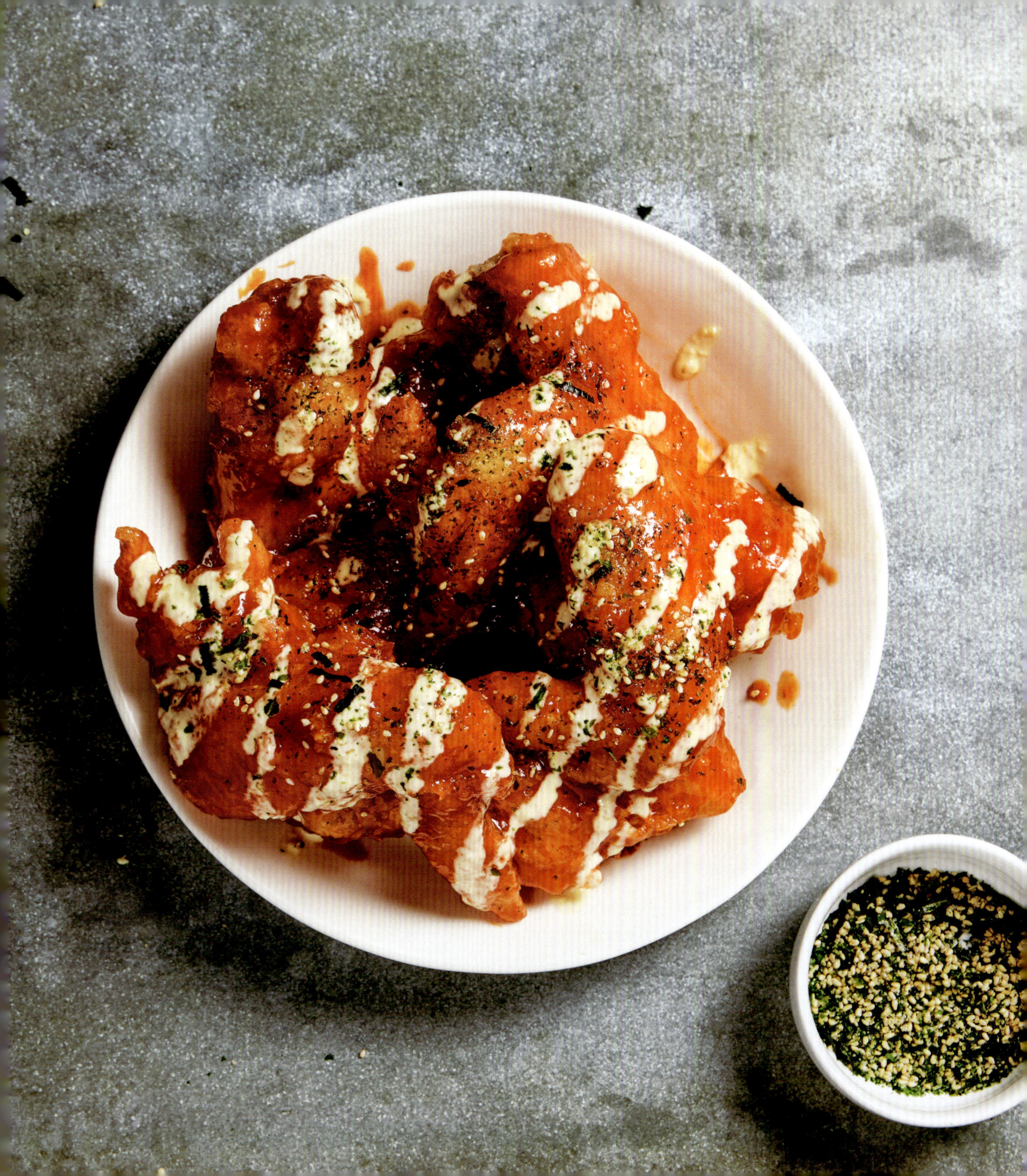

DRESSINGS, SALSAS, AND SAUCES

# Hussain's Butter-Garlic Sauce

*The Bombay Canteen, Mumbai*

**MAKES ABOUT 2 CUPS (480ML), ENOUGH FOR THE CRAB KULCHA**

2 jwala peppers or 1 medium serrano pepper

1 2-inch (5cm) piece ginger, peeled

15 medium garlic cloves, finely chopped

2½ teaspoons cornstarch

1 teaspoon coconut or apple cider vinegar

1½ cups (3 sticks/340g) unsalted butter, well chilled, divided

1½ teaspoons dashi granules (Ajinomoto Hon-Dashi)

Finely ground black pepper

*This sauce for the crab kulcha (see page 153) starts like a sofrito by gently cooking the aromatics (only without browning them), and ends like a beurre blanc, with cold butter slowly added at the end to emulsify it.*

—HUSSAIN SHAHZAD

**Prep:** For a less spicy sauce, devein and remove the seeds from the jawala or serrano peppers, if you'd like, and finely chop them. Use a fine Microplane zester to grate the ginger over the peppers and set them aside with the garlic.

In a small dish, combine the cornstarch, coconut vinegar, and 1 teaspoon of water and mix together with your finger until the cornstarch is completely dissolved.

Put ½ cup (1 stick/115g) butter in a medium saucepan and cut the remaining 1 cup (2 sticks/225g) into small cubes.

**Make the sauce:** Have a wooden spoon or heat-proof spatula and a whisk near the stove.

Melt the ½ cup (1 stick/115g) butter in the saucepan over medium heat. Add the peppers, ginger, and garlic, and when the butter begins to simmer, reduce the heat to medium-low (it will still be bubbling). Cook the aromatics, stirring occasionally with the wooden spoon, until the garlic has completely softened but has not browned, 5 to 6 minutes. Add ¾ cup (180ml) water, stir, and bring to a low boil.

Stir the cornstarch slurry with your finger to loosen it up and add it to the pan, whisking constantly and vigorously until the sauce thickens, about 1 minute. Immediately reduce the heat to low and stir in the dashi granules and ¼ teaspoon black pepper.

Add 3 to 4 cubes of the remaining 1 cup (2 sticks/225g) of cold butter to the pan, whisking constantly and vigorously as when emulsifying an aioli. When the butter has almost fully melted, add a few more cubes, still whisking constantly so the sauce doesn't break. After about half the butter has been added, the sauce should look very creamy; you can now add a few more cubes at a time, whisking all the while. When all of the butter has been added and has melted, take the pan off the heat.

If not using right away, let the sauce cool completely in the pan for up to 2 hours. Do not refrigerate the sauce.

To serve, gently rewarm over low heat, stirring constantly, just until warm.

### TIPS

*Like any beurre blanc, you need to watch this sauce closely as you make it, but the cornstarch in this umami-packed version makes it less prone to breaking. It doesn't take well to tinkering; even reducing the overall quantity by more than one-third will likely cause the sauce to break.*

*You can find Ajinomoto Hon-Dashi (dried dashi granules) at Japanese markets and online.*

# Jimmy's Salsa de Chile Morita

*Lotería Grill, Los Angeles*

**MAKES ABOUT 5 CUPS (ABOUT 1.2L), ENOUGH FOR 6 SERVINGS OF HUEVOS RANCHEROS**

1¼ pounds (570g) tomatillos (about 16 small and medium)

1 pound (455g) Roma tomatoes (4 to 5 large), quartered

Vegetable oil, for frying

1⅓ ounces (38g/about ¾ cup, loosely packed) dried chile moritas (12 to 15), plus a few extras (in case some burn)

½ large white onion, sliced into 2 or 3 sections

4 medium garlic cloves, peeled (not smashed)

1 tablespoon dried oregano leaves, or ¾ teaspoon ground oregano

1 tablespoon dried thyme leaves, or ¾ teaspoon ground thyme

½ dried bay leaf

Kosher or coarse sea salt

1⅔ cups (400ml) chicken or vegetable stock

*This is one of my favorite salsas, not just for its flavor and versatility but, especially, for the wonderful memories it brings back and how it's truly a family creation. When I opened Lotería in 2002, we tamed the heat in our salsas just a bit for north-of-the-border palates. Still, many guests were asking for something spicier. The idea to make a salsa with chile moritas came from my brother Andy, who, like me and all my siblings, caught the kitchen bug from our mother. On a visit to Cuernavaca to see my parents, we spent some days cooking together in our mama's kitchen, playing with combinations of ingredients and preparations to design this beautiful salsa. It's spicy, smoky, and absolutely wonderful. Best of all, it always reminds me of my dear mama and my brother. I hope you enjoy it as much as we do. Beyond the huevos rancheros (see page 43), the salsa goes well with any seared fish, a great steak, chicken, or some local carnitas, and makes the best shrimp tacos. When you toast the chiles in the hot oil to release their flavor, be extra careful not to burn them, as it will make the sauce bitter.* —JIMMY SHAW

**Roast the tomatoes and tomatillos:** Preheat the oven to 450°F (230°C).

Remove the papery husks from the tomatillos, rinse well, strain, and spread them out on a large, rimmed sheet pan. Arrange the quartered tomatoes, skin side facing down, on the same sheet pan and roast until the tomatillo skins are blackened and the tomato skins are nicely charred in spots, about 30 minutes. Set aside until cool enough to handle, then scrape the tomatillos, tomatoes, and their blackened bits and accumulated juices into a bowl.

**Fry the chiles and aromatics:** Set a rack over a heat-proof plate or line with paper bags or towels.

Meanwhile, in a medium high-sided saucepan or small Dutch oven, heat about 1 inch (2.5cm) vegetable oil over medium-high heat until very hot, 3 to 4 minutes. Have a slotted spoon, spider, or small metal sieve near the stove.

Add 1 chile to the oil; it should sizzle. (If not, remove the chile and continue to heat the oil.) Flash-fry 3 to 4 dried chiles at a time, constantly flipping each by lifting them in and out of the hot oil to fry all sides, until they puff up and turn reddish-brown in spots, about 10 seconds. Transfer the chiles to the rack or paper-lined plate and fry the remaining chiles in batches.

### TIPS

*This salsa is a true "sauce" with big flavors. It makes a large batch, enough for six generous plates of huevos rancheros (see page 43), or use it to slather over quickly seared shrimp (Jimmy's favorite), leftover roasted chicken, pork, or potatoes to make tacos. The salsa also freezes well.*

*Frying the chile moritas, also called morita chipotles (dried and smoked fully mature jalapeños), at high heat until they are deeply colored releases their flavor. Have a few extra on hand, as they can go from toasted to burnt quickly.*

Reduce the heat to medium, add the sectioned onion to the hot oil (be careful, the oil will sizzle and pop), and fry until lightly caramelized on the edges and the flesh has blistered, about 5 minutes. Transfer the onions to the plate with the chiles.

Fry the garlic until light golden brown, about 3 minutes, and transfer to the plate.

If any toasted chiles are completely black and have hardened, discard them (they will make the salsa bitter) and fry a few fresh dried chiles to replace them.

**Finish the salsa:** In a blender, preferably, or food processor, combine the fried chiles, onion, garlic, oregano, thyme, bay leaf, 1 teaspoon salt, and about half of the chicken stock and blend on high speed until the sauce is very smooth, about 1 minute. Add a little more stock, if needed, to make a smooth sauce. If using a food processor, stop to scrape down the sides of the bowl occasionally as you process the mixture to fully grind the fried chiles.

Add the remaining stock, tomatillos, tomatoes, and any accumulated juices and blend or pulse a few times on low speed until the tomatoes and tomatillos are almost smooth. Taste and season with salt, if needed.

Cover and refrigerate the salsa for up to 5 days (the flavor will intensify over time). You can use the sauce in this fresher, thinner consistency, or reduce the salsa on the stovetop for a few minutes to thicken it up, as Jimmy does to make the huevos rancheros (see page 43).

# Big Daddy's Slaw Sauwce

📍 *Daddy's Dogs, Nashville*

> *Keep this spicy-sweet sauce around to mix with your cabbage and carrot slaw (see page 104), and you'll have the tastiest treat at the barbecue!* —SEAN PORTER

**MAKES ABOUT 1⅓ CUPS (315ML), PLENTY FOR THE SLAW**

⅓ cup (80ml) apple cider vinegar

⅓ cup (65g) granulated sugar

⅓ cup (80ml) sour cream

3 tablespoons mayonnaise

1½ tablespoons yellow (ballpark) mustard

1 teaspoon cayenne pepper

Kosher salt and finely ground black pepper

In a medium bowl, whisk together the apple cider vinegar, sugar, sour cream, mayonnaise, mustard, cayenne pepper, 1 teaspoon salt, and 1 teaspoon black pepper until smooth. Cover and refrigerate the dressing for up to 5 days.

**DRESSINGS, SALSAS, AND SAUCES**

# Mohamad's Tarator

*Orfali Bros, Dubai*

**MAKES 2 SCANT CUPS (450ML), ENOUGH FOR THE EGGPLANT BAYILDI**

1¼ cups (300ml) full-fat Greek or Icelandic yogurt

1½ tablespoons fresh lemon juice

1½ tablespoons fresh lime juice

6 tablespoons (90g) good-quality unsalted tahini, slightly warmed if stiff

Kosher or coarse sea salt

In a medium bowl, whisk together the yogurt, lemon and lime juices, and 2 tablespoons cold water. Add the tahini and ¼ teaspoon of salt and whisk until very smooth.

Cover and refrigerate the tarator for up to 3 days.

### TIPS

*This thick, balanced tarator that Mohamad Orfali spreads over his eggplant bayildi and Salam Dakkak's lemon and garlic are great on sandwiches (falafel, schwarma), or served with hummus, roasted vegetables, and grilled meats and chicken.*

*For both, very fresh tahini from a good producer (Soom, SoCo, Har Bracha) makes a difference. When you open a jar, it should be light in color and after a gentle (not stiff) stir, easily pourable, with no bitterness.*

# Salam's Fatet (Fatteh) Sauce

*Bait Maryam, Dubai*

> *We use this tangy sauce for our fatet muskhan (see page 229) and many other dishes; it goes well with kebabs and can be used as a dip for almost any other meat dish. We also use it like a salad dressing on a rocca (arugula) salad with cooked beets and walnuts.*
> —SALAM DAKKAK

**MAKES ABOUT 2¼ CUPS (540ML), ENOUGH FOR THE FATET MUSKHAN**

1 to 2 small lemons

2 cups (480ml) full-fat Greek or Icelandic yogurt

6 tablespoons (90g) good-quality unsalted tahini, well stirred

2 medium garlic cloves

Kosher or coarse sea salt

Finely zest 1 lemon over a blender. Juice both lemons and add 2 tablespoons of lemon juice, the yogurt, tahini, garlic, and 1½ teaspoons salt to the blender and blend until smooth. If the mixture is too thick to blend, add a splash of water. Season the sauce with more lemon juice, if needed (it should be tangy), and cover and refrigerate for up to 5 days.

DRESSINGS, SALSAS, AND SAUCES

# Bombay Canteen Kulcha

*Mumbai*

> *Instead of a tandoor, these can be cooked in a pizza oven (something like an Ooni works well), or even a regular oven. They're good on their own, even if you're not making the crab kulcha (see page 153).* —HUSSAIN SHAHZAD

**MAKES 8 KULCHA**

¾ teaspoon instant or dry-active yeast

2 teaspoons granulated sugar

1⅓ cups (315ml) whole milk, slightly warm if using dry-active yeast, plus more as needed

3 cups (360g) all-purpose flour, plus more for the work surface

1 cup (120g) bread or 00 flour

1 teaspoon baking powder

2 tablespoons vegetable or other neutral oil

Kosher or coarse sea salt

**TO SERVE**

1 to 2 pats (1 to 2 tablespoons) ghee or unsalted butter, at room temperature or melted

Sea salt

**Make the dough:** In a stand mixer bowl fitted with a dough hook attachment, combine the yeast, sugar, and milk. If using dry-active yeast, set aside for 5 minutes to bloom the yeast; for instant, there's no need to wait.

Add the all-purpose flour, bread flour, baking powder, vegetable oil, and 2 teaspoons salt and mix on medium-low speed until a shaggy dough forms. Increase the speed to medium-high and mix until the dough is fairly smooth but still a little sticky, 2 to 3 minutes. Don't overmix or the dough will become stiff; if the dough is difficult to shape, add up to ¼ cup (60ml) of additional milk and mix well. Shape the dough into a round, let rest for 1 to 2 minutes, and press it with your finger. The indentation should spring back slowly (if not, mix for another minute). Put the dough in a medium bowl, cover with plastic wrap, and let rise until almost doubled, about 1½ hours.

**Shape the dough:** Dust a work surface with flour and lightly flour your hands.

Divide the dough into 8 pieces (about 3½ ounces/100g each). Flatten each and shape into a ball by pinching the bottom of the dough ball closed like you're sealing a balloon. Roll each ball around on the work surface to smooth out the bottom and space 1 inch (2.5cm) apart on the work surface, or transfer to a flour-dusted baking sheet. Loosely cover the dough rounds with plastic wrap and let rise until doubled, about 1 hour, depending on the temperature of the room.

**Shape and bake the dough:** Heat a tandoor or pizza oven as instructed by the manufacturer (to about 725°F/400°C). Or, put a rack in the middle of a conventional oven (remove any rack above it) and put a pizza stone or upside-down rimmed sheet pan on the rack. Preheat the oven to 500°F (260°C).

Meanwhile, lightly re-flour the work surface and peel the dough off the plastic wrap. Lightly flour your hands and flatten each dough round with your palm, then shape it into a 5- to 6-inch (12 to 15cm) circle. Let the dough rest for about 5 minutes and re-flatten the dough rounds again with your hands. Don't pick the dough up like you would with pizza dough; it will overly stretch.

Just before baking the flatbread, use your hands (or a bench scraper or knife) to lift the dough off the work surface. (If you've never made kulcha, pick one up dough round and pass it back and forth between the palms of your hands a few times to get the hang of transferring it quickly to the oven so it lays flat.)

In a tandoor or pizza oven, slap as many dough rounds as will fit on the walls of the tandoor or on the surface of the pizza oven. Cook the kulcha until charred in spots on the bottom and puffy; check the bread after 1 to 1½ minutes. Use tongs to flip the kulcha and bake until charred on the opposite side, 1 to 2 minutes longer.

Or, in a conventional oven, slide out the oven rack with the hot pizza stone or sheet pan, drop 3 to 4 dough rounds on top, and bake for 3 minutes; it will puff up but likely will only be lightly browned on the bottom. Use tongs to flip the kulcha and bake until crispy on the opposite side, about 2 minutes.

### TIP

*The trick to making this flatbread is to transfer the dough rounds to the cooking surface quickly to avoid crumpling up the edges so the kulcha lay flat. Failed attempts will still bake up well and make excellent sopping-up utensils for things like Saw Naing's Pe Hainn (page 121) and Salam Dakkak's Fatet Muskhan (page 229). Though best eaten the day they are made, the flatbreads will keep for a day or two in a well-sealed container, or you can freeze them; rewarm before serving.*

Transfer the kulcha to a baking sheet or large plate and bake the remaining kulcha; you may need to loosen them up from the work surface again with the bench scraper.

**Serve:** While still warm, rub the butter on both sides of each kulcha, sprinkle a little sea salt on top, and serve.

To rewarm, toast up the kulcha for a few seconds on each side in a very hot iron skillet or comal.

# GGET's Toasted Almond-Macadamia Milk

📍 *Go Get Em Tiger, Los Angeles*

> *This is the nut milk we use in our iced latte (see page 23). Most recipes have you discard the soaking water, but because we use toasted, blanched nuts, we find we get a much deeper flavor in the final product when we use the soaking water in our final liquid. The macadamias add a richness that almonds alone just can't emulate.*
>
> **—KYLE GLANVILLE**

**MAKES ABOUT 5 CUPS (1.2L), ENOUGH FOR ABOUT 7 ICED LATTES**

- 8 ounces (225g) whole raw almonds (1⅔ cups), blanched (technique follows) or 2 cups blanched slivered almonds
- 2 ounces (generous ⅓ cup/55g) raw macadamia nuts
- 6 cups (1.4L) filtered water, divided
- 2 tablespoons granulated sugar, divided
- Finely ground salt

### DAY 1

**Toast and soak the nuts:** Preheat the oven to 350°F (175°C) and put a rack in the top third of the oven.

Spread out the almonds in a single layer on one side of a rimmed sheet pan. Spread out the macadamia nuts in a small metal baking pan (a cake or brownie pan works well) and put it on the sheet pan.

Toast the nuts, stirring occasionally to evenly toast, just until light golden brown on the edges, 6 to 7 minutes for the macadamia nuts and 8 to 10 minutes for the almonds. Watch the nuts closely toward the end of the baking time so they don't overly toast.

Transfer the nuts to a medium bowl or storage container, add 2 cups (480ml) filtered water, cover, and refrigerate for 18 to 24 hours. Don't strain the soaked nuts.

## TIPS

*A high-speed blender is best for pulverizing the nuts completely and to extract the most liquid, but a standard blender can be used (the final milk yield may be slightly less). And get good, fresh nuts from a specialty grocery store with bulk nut bins or a nut vendor that sells unsalted macadamias (most pre-packaged macadamias are salted).*

*To blanch whole almonds, put as many whole, unsalted almonds as you want to peel in a saucepan, cover with water, and bring to a boil. Boil for 1 minute (no longer or the flesh will start to "cook"), strain, and rinse the almonds under cold running water. Squeeze the almonds between your thumb and forefinger until they pop out of their skins. It helps to do this over a large bowl, as they pop out of their skins like little torpedoes (a fun project for kids).*

### DAY 2

**Finish the nut milk:** In a small dish, stir together the sugar, a generous pinch of salt, and 2 tablespoons of warm tap water until the sugar has completely dissolved.

In a blender, combine the nuts, the nut soaking water, and 1 cup (240ml) filtered water and blend on high until the nuts are finely ground, 1 to 1½ minutes; even if the mixture looks smooth, keep blending for the full time. Add 2 cups (480ml) filtered water and blend again for 1 minute, then add the remaining 1 cup (240ml) filtered water and blend until well combined. (If the blender is at capacity, transfer the nut milk back to the container you used to soak the nuts before stirring in the remaining filtered water.)

Strain the nut mixture through a nut milk bag into a large bowl, and squeeze and massage the bag firmly to get out every last drop of the liquid. Or, line a fine-mesh strainer with two pieces of cheesecloth large enough so the overhanging fabric can be gathered together at the top. In batches, pour the nut milk mixture into the cheesecloth and use the back of a spoon to push down on the solids to release the excess liquid. Gather up the edges of the cheesecloth to enclose the nut solids and very firmly squeeze out all of the milk. Discard the solids.

Stir about two-thirds of the sugar water into the nut milk and taste; add the remaining sugar water, if you'd like.

Cover and refrigerate the nut milk for up to 5 days; shake or stir well before using.

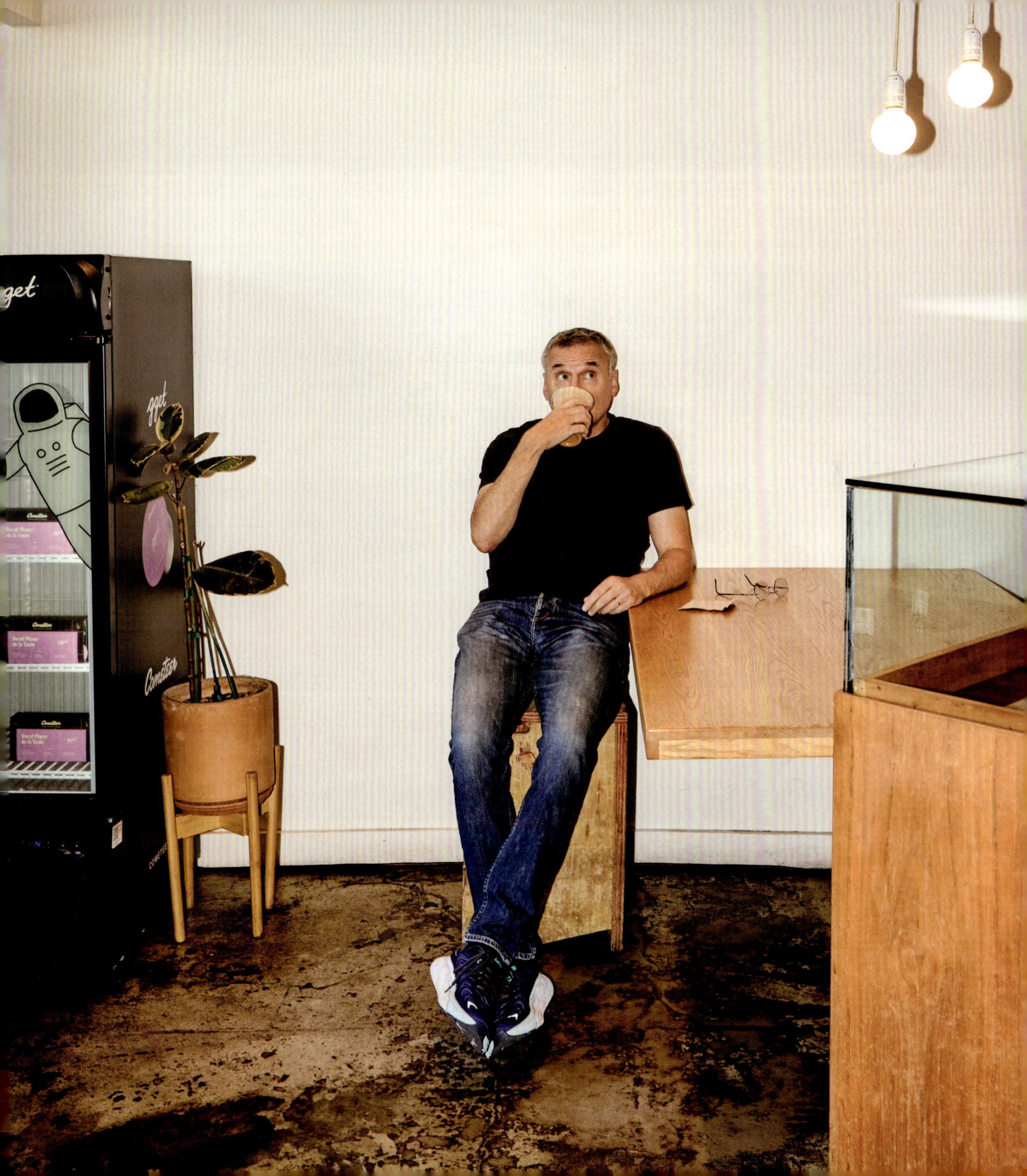
Cometeer

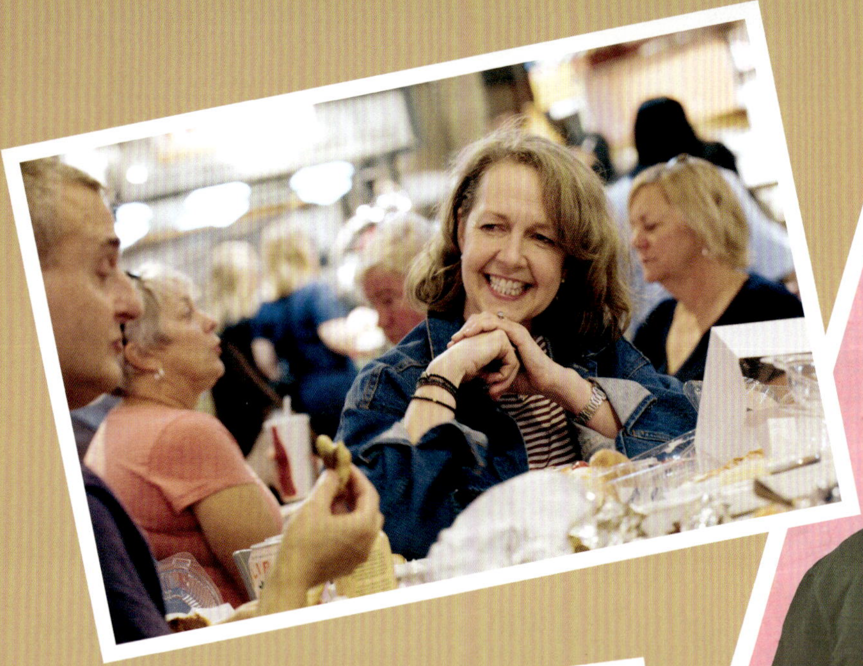

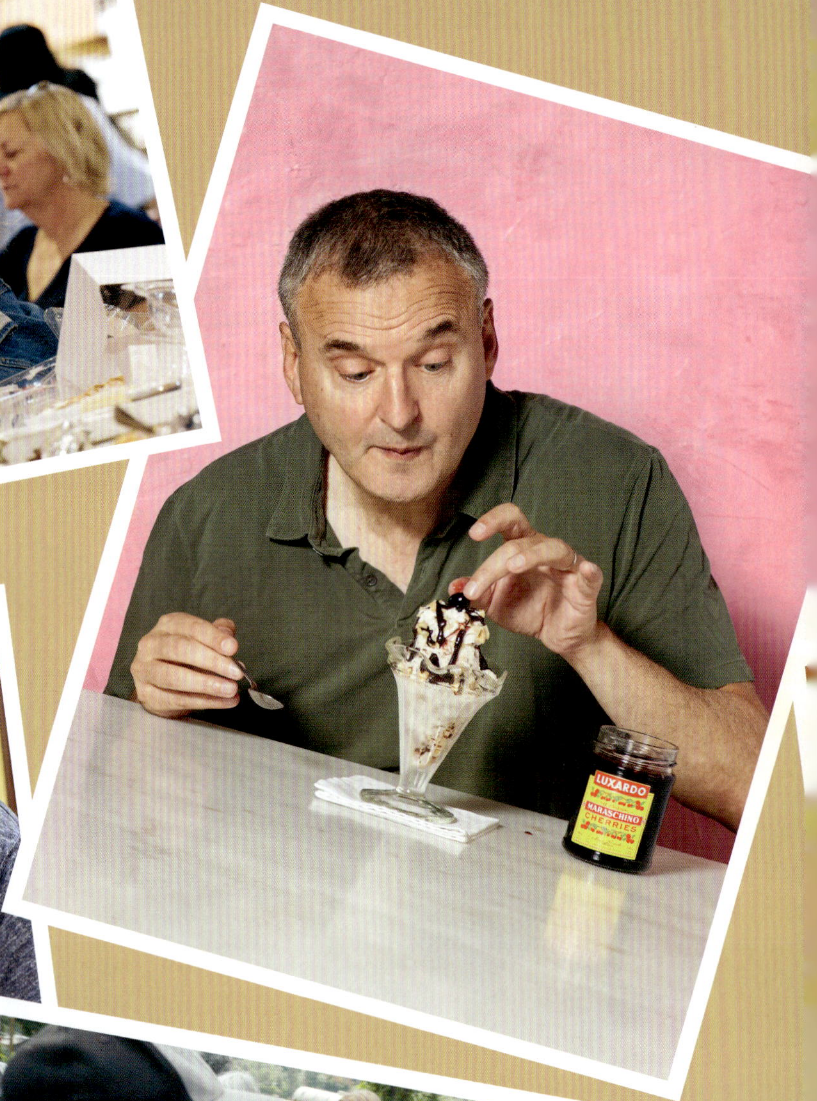
LUXARDO
MARASCHINO
CHERRIES

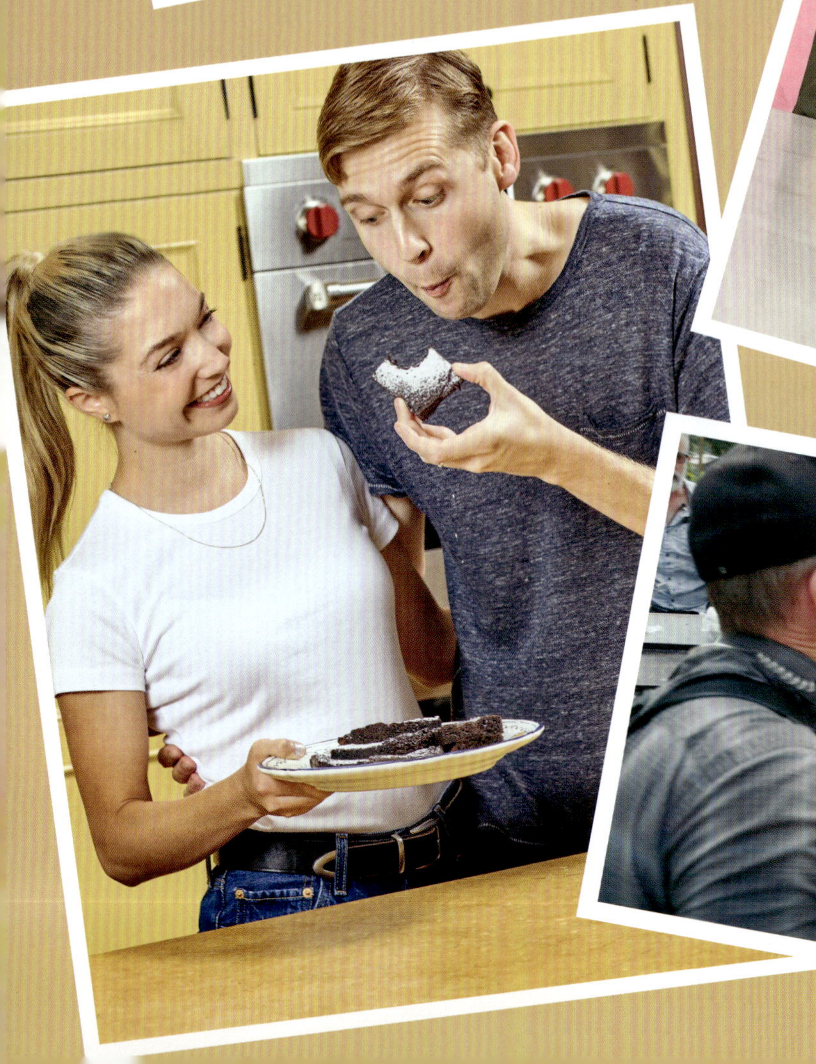

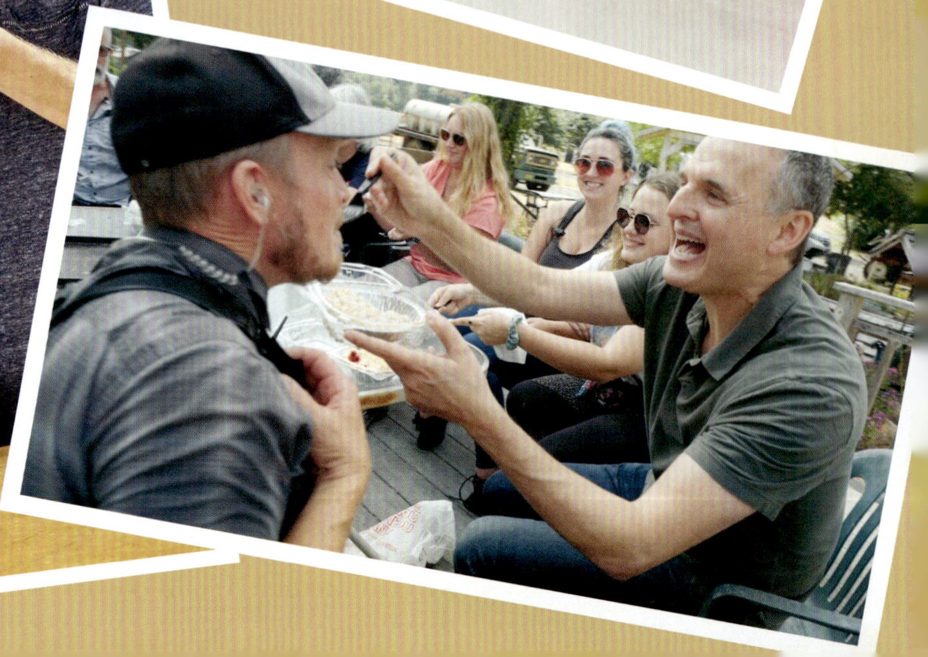

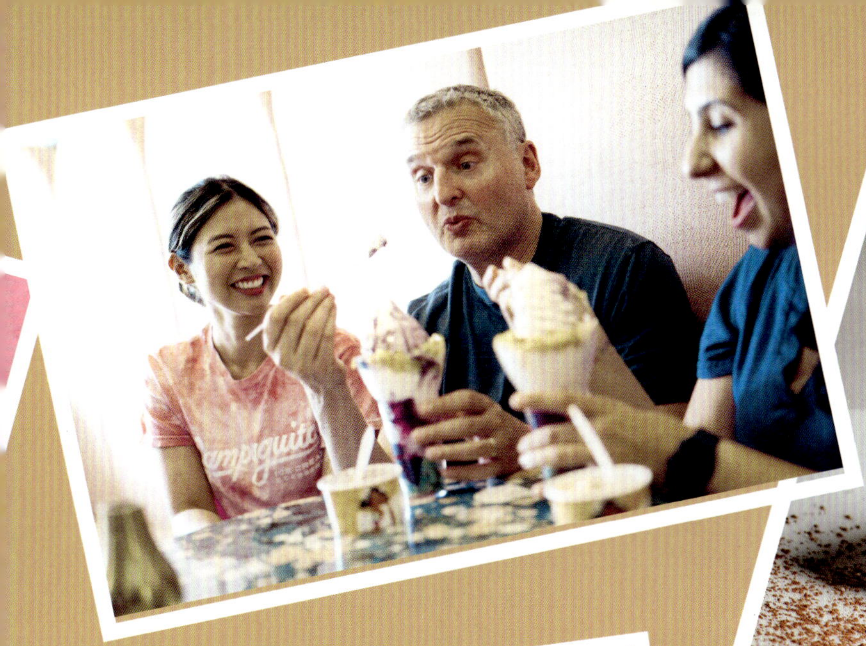
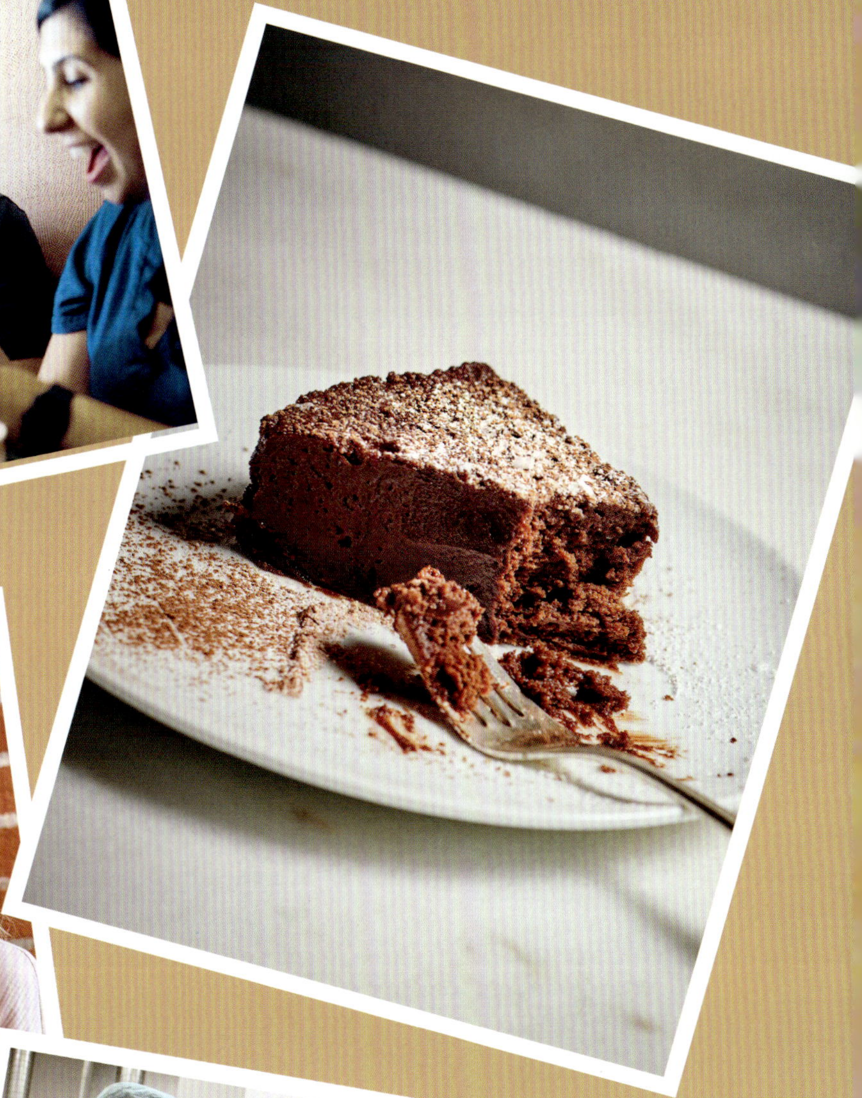
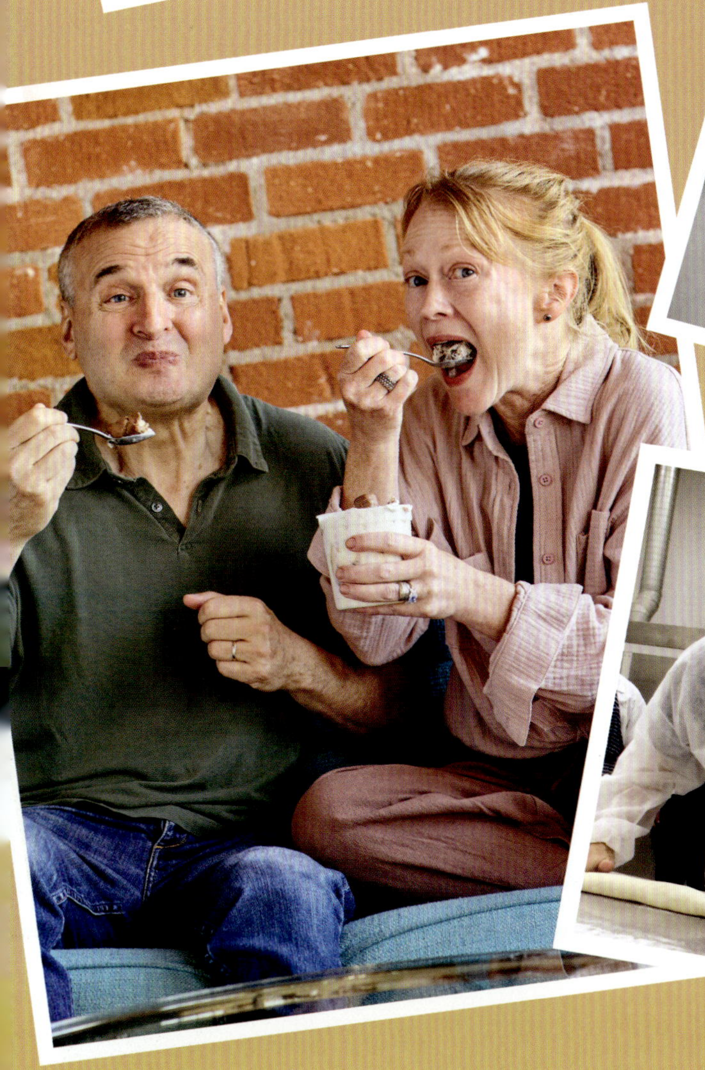
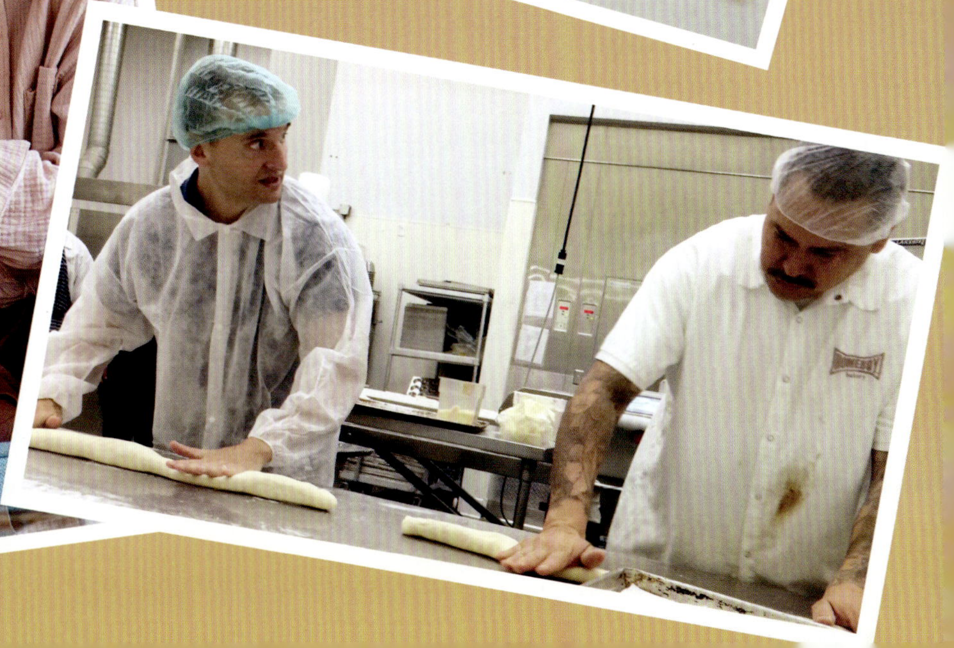

# Sampaguita's Vegan Halaya

*Orlando*

**MAKES ABOUT 2½ CUPS (750G), ENOUGH FOR 10 TO 12 HALO HALO**

1 16-ounce (455g) package frozen grated ube (see Tips), thawed

⅔ cup (160ml) full-fat coconut milk, well stirred or briefly warmed if solidified

½ cup (120ml) sweetened condensed coconut milk, well-stirred

½ teaspoon ube extract

½ cup plus 2 tablespoons (125g) granulated sugar

5 tablespoons vegan butter (salted or unsalted), cubed

½ teaspoon vanilla extract

Fine salt

*We make this vegan halaya for our halo halo (see page 289). It isn't hard to make, but you have to babysit it more with vegan ingredients. You need to blend everything until it's incredibly smooth (otherwise the halaya will be chunky like potato salad) and cook the yams long enough—stirring, so they don't burn—so the coconut fat doesn't seep out when it's chilled. Frozen ube loses some of its punch, so the ube extract helps give back that yam-y flavor and purple color (most contain food coloring), but you can leave it out if you want to go all natural.* —MARIE MERCADO

**Mix the ube base:** In a blender, combine the thawed ube, coconut milk, sweetened condensed coconut milk, and ube extract and blend until combined. Add the sugar and blend on medium-high for 30 seconds; scrape down the sides of the container. Blend again until completely smooth, about 1 minute; the mixture should look like a cream sauce with no visible specks of sugar.

**Cook the halaya:** Scrape the yam mixture into a large nonstick skillet and cook over medium heat, stirring every 30 to 45 seconds with a large heat-proof rubber spatula or wooden spoon, just until beginning to lightly bubble. Reduce the heat to low and cook, stirring and scraping the bottom and sides of the skillet every minute or two, until the paste thickens and begins to pull away from the sides of the skillet, about 15 minutes; if it starts to smell toasty, reduce the heat. Continue to cook the halaya, now stirring every 45 seconds or so, until very thick, satiny smooth, and deep purple, 10 to 12 minutes. Remove the skillet from the heat, add the butter, vanilla extract, and a generous pinch of salt, and stir until the butter is melted and fully incorporated. Season the halaya with salt and let it cool completely in the pan.

**Chill the halaya:** Pack the halaya into a storage container or measuring cup (1 quart/about 1L), smooth out the top, lay a piece of plastic wrap on the surface, and refrigerate until well chilled, 3 to 4 hours or up to 5 days.

Use your hands to massage any visible white streaks of coconut fat back into the halaya before serving.

### TIPS

*When thawed, grated ube (available at Filipino markets in the freezer aisle) is soft enough to easily blend into a smooth sauce-like consistency without boiling (a necessary step with fresh ube and frozen whole ube). Some bags of grated ube are a deep purple color (the natural interior color of the yam ranges from creamy purple to a deep lavender), but if it's more brownish, the food coloring in the ube extract will give the halaya that classic bright purple color. Don't use purple sweet potatoes; the flavor and texture are very different.*

*Unlike the other ingredients, vegan sweetened condensed coconut milk (Nature's Charm and similar) and vegan butter are more specialty grocery store finds. For a non-vegan version, dairy butter and sweetened condensed milk (along with the canned coconut milk, all available at Filipino markets) work in this recipe.*

OTHER THINGS YOU'LL WANT TO HAVE AROUND • 333

# Hallie's Vanilla Bean Ice Cream

*Caffè Panna, New York*

**MAKES 1 GENEROUS QUART (1L)**

1½ cups (360ml) whole milk

1½ cups (360ml) heavy cream

¾ cup (150g) granulated sugar

½ teaspoon kosher salt

3 tablespoons tapioca syrup or light corn syrup

3 ounces (85g) brick cream cheese

¾ teaspoon vanilla extract

½ teaspoon vanilla bean paste

> *This ice cream is the base for many of our flavors, including Somebody Scoop Phil (page 291). The cream cheese and tapioca syrup in the ice cream base help keep your ice crystals super small, resulting in a creamier mouthfeel. Sometimes ice cream churned at home can be a bit more icy than what you'd get in a shop with an Italian gelato machine, so these two ingredients really help.* —HALLIE MEYER

In a medium saucepan, heat the milk, heavy cream, and sugar over medium-high heat, stirring occasionally, just until the sugar has dissolved, 2 to 3 minutes. (Don't boil or the cream will curdle.) Remove the pan from the heat and stir in the salt and tapioca syrup.

In a blender, combine the cream cheese and about a third of the warm cream mixture and blend until very smooth, about 15 seconds. Add the vanilla extract, vanilla bean paste, and the rest of the cream mixture and blend again until well combined. Pour the custard into a heat-proof bowl or food storage container, let cool completely, cover, and refrigerate at least 6 hours or overnight.

Freeze the cream mixture in an ice cream maker according to the manufacturer's instructions. Put the freezer bowl insert (with the ice cream inside) in the freezer for at least 30 minutes to firm up.

Transfer the ice cream to a food storage container, press a piece of plastic wrap or parchment paper directly onto the surface of the ice cream, and freeze in the very back of the freezer until firm, 4 to 5 hours or overnight.

### TIPS

*Teetering between homemade ice cream and soft serve, this ice cream is much softer than most when it comes out of the machine. Freezing the finished ice cream in the machine's freezer bowl insert for about an hour before transferring it to a storage container helps it firm up more quickly, so it can be layered without melting and helps prevent ice crystals from forming.*

*A compressor-style ice cream maker that incorporates a lot of air will produce a texture closest to the ice cream at Caffé Panna, but a freezer bowl ice cream maker also works.*

# The Pie Guy's Pie Crust

📍 *North Plains*

**MAKES 1 (9-INCH) PIE CRUST**

¾ cup (1½ sticks/170g) salted or unsalted butter, at warm room temperature

2 cups (240g) all-purpose flour, divided, plus more for the work surface

2 tablespoons granulated sugar

Kosher salt

Equipment: 1 9-inch (23cm) deep-dish pie pan, preferably metal (see Tips)

> *The dough I use for my pies (see page 277) is best to use immediately, without any wait time, when it's very soft and easy to roll out. If the kitchen is cold or the dough sits for too many hours in ball form (be sure it's wrapped in plastic), it can firm up. I'll put it in the microwave to warm it very briefly, just a few seconds. Be careful not to leave it in the microwave too long, or it will overly soften.*
>
> **—BART VANDOMELEN**

**Make the dough:** In a stand mixer fitted with the paddle attachment, lightly smash the softened butter with your hands or the paddle. Sift 1 cup (120g) all-purpose flour over the butter (or press the flour through a fine-mesh sieve), and add the sugar and a generous pinch of salt (2 to 3 pinches if using unsalted butter). Cover the stand mixer with a kitchen towel (to catch the flour). Mix on low speed until the flour is incorporated, 10 to 15 seconds. Remove the kitchen towel, increase the speed to medium-high, and mix until creamy and fluffy and the color has lightened, about 1½ minutes.

Remove the bowl from the stand mixer (put the paddle attachment off to the side of the bowl). Sift the remaining 1 cup (120g) all-purpose flour into the bowl and drizzle 3 tablespoons water (cold or room temperature) over the flour. Scrape the batter off the paddle attachment, then use the paddle to firmly swipe the bottom and sides of the bowl five to six times, just until the dough begins to come together.

Sift a light coating of flour on a work surface and lightly flour your hands. Scrape the dough onto the work surface and fold the dough two to three times, re-flouring your hands or the work surface as needed, to create a soft, smooth dough that no longer sticks. Add as little flour as possible, ideally no more than 2 to 3 tablespoons. Shape the dough into a disc.

It's best to roll out the dough for the pie crust right away (if you're using the crust for the marionberry pie on page 277, you can wipe out the stand mixer bowl and use it to mix the butter crumb topping). If you're making several pies, you can wrap the disc in plastic wrap and set it aside for 2 to 3 hours at room temperature.

**Roll out the crust:** Generously flour a work surface. You need a standard 9-inch (23cm) (not deep-dish) pie pan (see Tips).

Roll out the dough, very lightly flouring the top if needed, into roughly a 12-inch (30.5cm) circle. (No need to trim the edges of the crust.) Use a bench scraper or very large spatula to test the dough to make sure you can lift it off the work surface; if it sticks, reshape the dough into a ball, add a little more flour to the work surface, and re-roll the dough. (Unlike most pie crust dough, this is much softer, like a cookie dough, and more forgiving; you can re-roll it and patch up the crust in the pie pan.)

Transfer the dough to the pie pan. Patch up any holes in the dough and even out the edges at roughly the same height as the pie pan; you can also crimp the edges, but too much crust above the height of the pie tends to overcook and dry out.

Fill and bake the pie as directed.

## TIPS

*Throw out everything you know about making a pie crust. There are no pebbly bits of chilled butter to maintain, ice water quantities to guess, or chill hours required. Here, a set amount of water is drizzled over a creamy, cookie-like batter, then a few tablespoons of flour are added as you lightly shape the dough until it's no longer sticky to create more of a cross between a pie crust and a very delicate shortbread. (Take the time to sift the flour; it creates the softer texture you're after.) It's a very forgiving dough to roll out (and re-roll or patch holes in the crust directly in the pie pan, if needed), but it benefits from being rolled out immediately. If you're making the crust ahead, it can be stored, tightly wrapped, for a few hours at room temperature; it tends to dry out when refrigerated.*

*You can use any pie pan (glass, ceramic, or metal) with this dough, though the bottom will brown slightly better in metal pans, which conduct heat the most quickly. Standard-height pans (not deep-dish) work best for Bart's marionberry pie, unless you're using disposable foil pans, as Bart does. In that case, get a deep-dish foil pan (they are not as deep as most standard pie pans).*

OTHER THINGS YOU'LL WANT TO HAVE AROUND • 337

LIVE & COOKED
LOBSTERS
CASHIER
JOHN YI FISH MARKET
EAT FISH LIVE LONGER

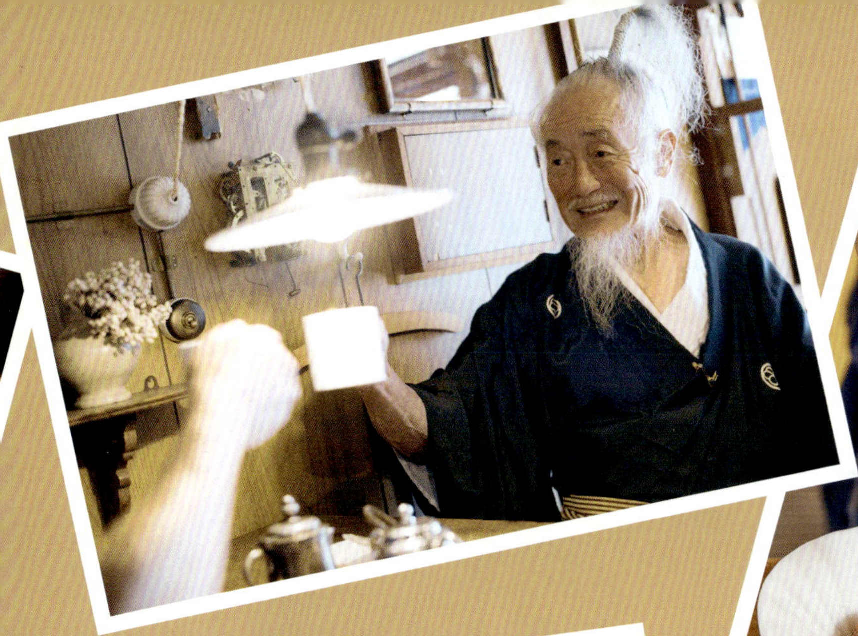

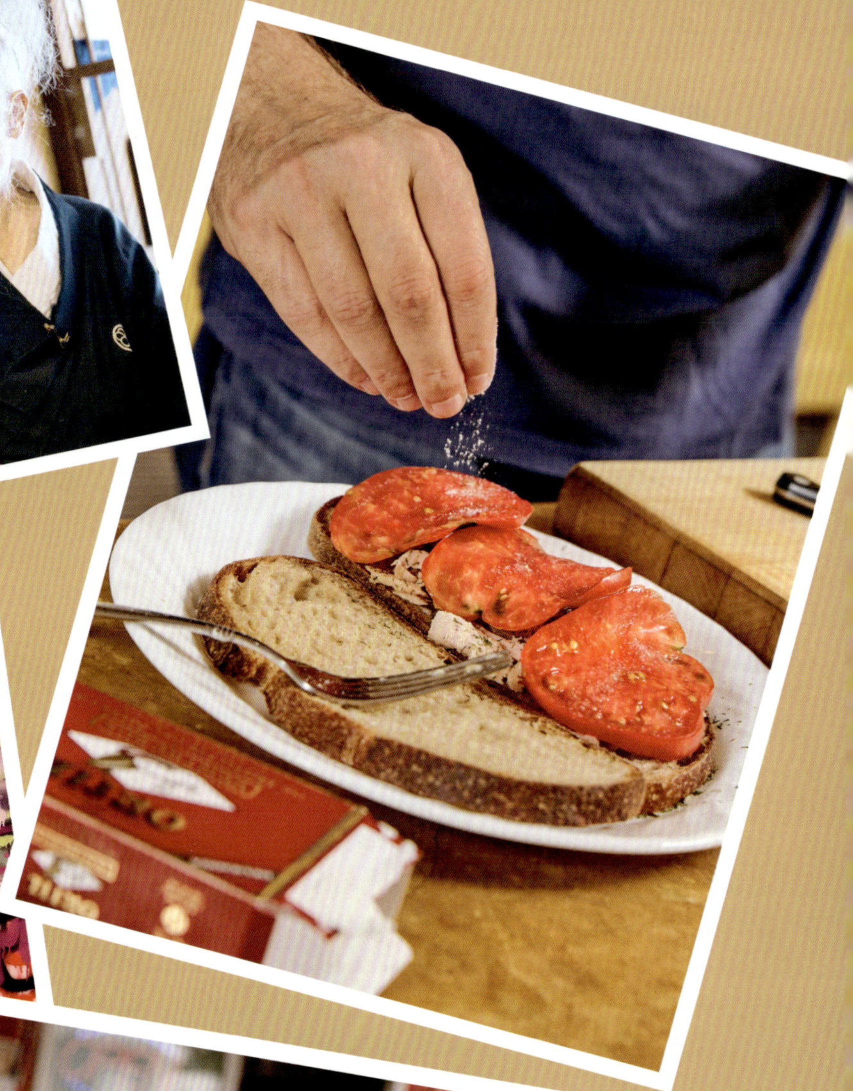

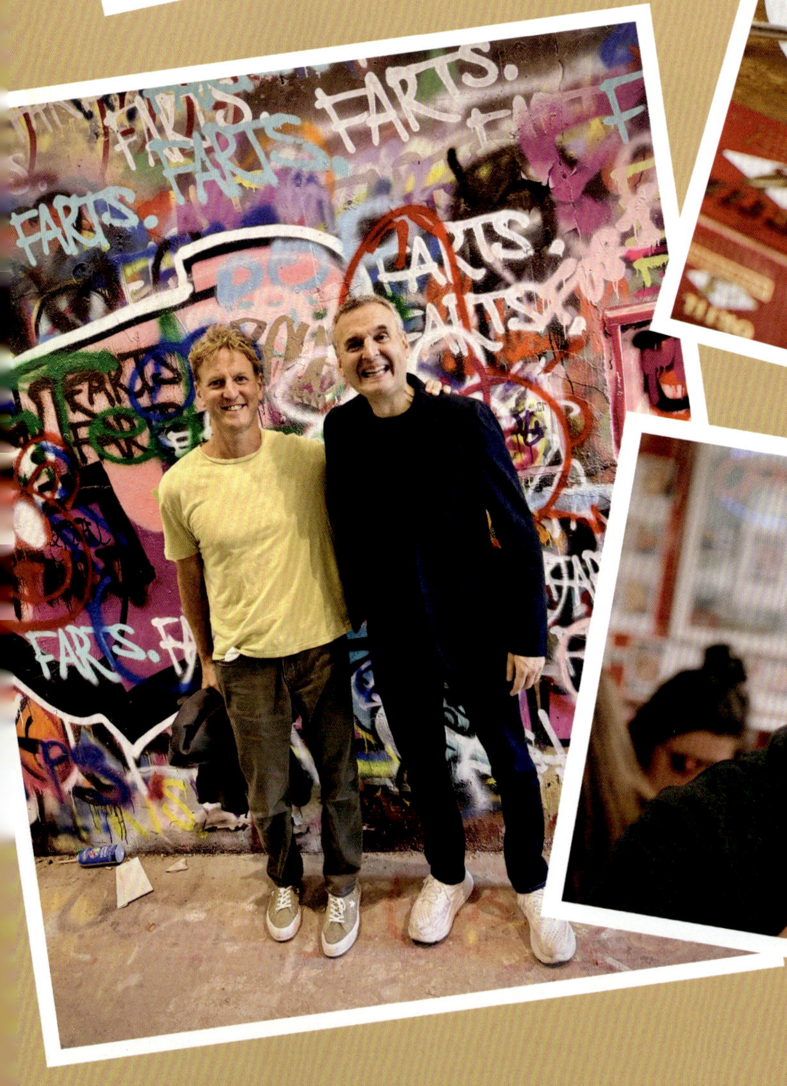
FARTS.

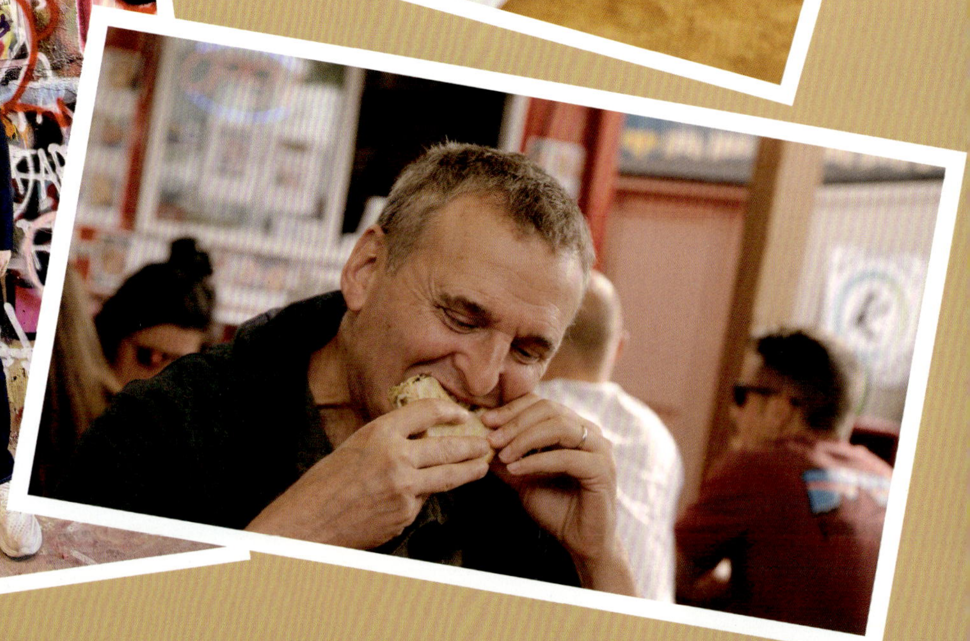

# Acknowledgments

**A special thanks to everybody I thanked in the first book, because you were all just as important in making this book happen:**

Zero Point Zero and everyone at Netflix who works on *Somebody Feed Phil,* and every single one of you who watches those episodes.

Erin Champion, my assistant (you're going to want to make her Chocolate Peanut Butter Triple Layer Bars on pages 265–67).

Brandi Bowles at UTA and the team at Simon & Schuster, especially executive editor Justin Schwartz and editorial assistant Gina Navaroli; senior production editor Benjamin Holmes; publicity director Jessica Preeg; marketing director Elizabeth Breeden; publisher Richard Rhorer; and the designer who put the whole book together, Catherine Casalino.

Every single home cook and chef who shared their recipes and helped make what I think is another great book, and I hope you agree.

The creative team: Other than Richard's great behind-the-scenes photography, the incredible photos of food, family, and friends on these pages are the work of Andrea D'Agosto. She is such a talented photographer, and I only wish we had room in this book to include more of her photos.

Most of the recipe photos were shot at Historic Hudson Studios, but when you opened the book, you might have recognized the guy eating a tuna sandwich in front of his refrigerator on the title page. All of those family photos were taken at my house because that's where we all eat, and some of us actually cook together. Andrea and I also went to a couple of restaurants in LA that I really like, plus my favorite coffee shop, which is why there are recipes from them in the book.

Just like the show, none of this would have happened without all the people behind the scenes: our lead stylists, Alicia Buszczak on props and Caroline Hwang for food; Andrea's assistants, Ashli Buts and Tyler Ferguson; prop assistants Aubrey Devin and Katie Iannitello; and food assistants Daniela Swamp, Jessica Darakjian, and Diana Kim. And our set dog, Dashi (who belongs to Caroline).

My friend and two-time collaborator, the great Jenn Garbee. Her partnership has been invaluable on these books, and I'd recommend working with her to anyone who has a cookbook to write and no idea how to write one. Jenn is the hero here and has done all the heavy lifting, including home testing every single recipe so that it will work for you in your home.

My family: Monica, Ben, and Lily, and our newest additions: Ben's wife, DeLaney, and Lily's husband, Mason. I remain the luckiest person in the world. **—Phil**

*Clockwise from top left: Daniela Swamp, me, Jenn Garbee, Alicia Buszczak, Aubrey Devin, Andrea D'Agosto, Jessica Darakjian, Caroline Hwang, Ashli Buts, and Katie Iannitello. Not pictured: Tyler Ferguson, Diana Kim, and Dashi.*

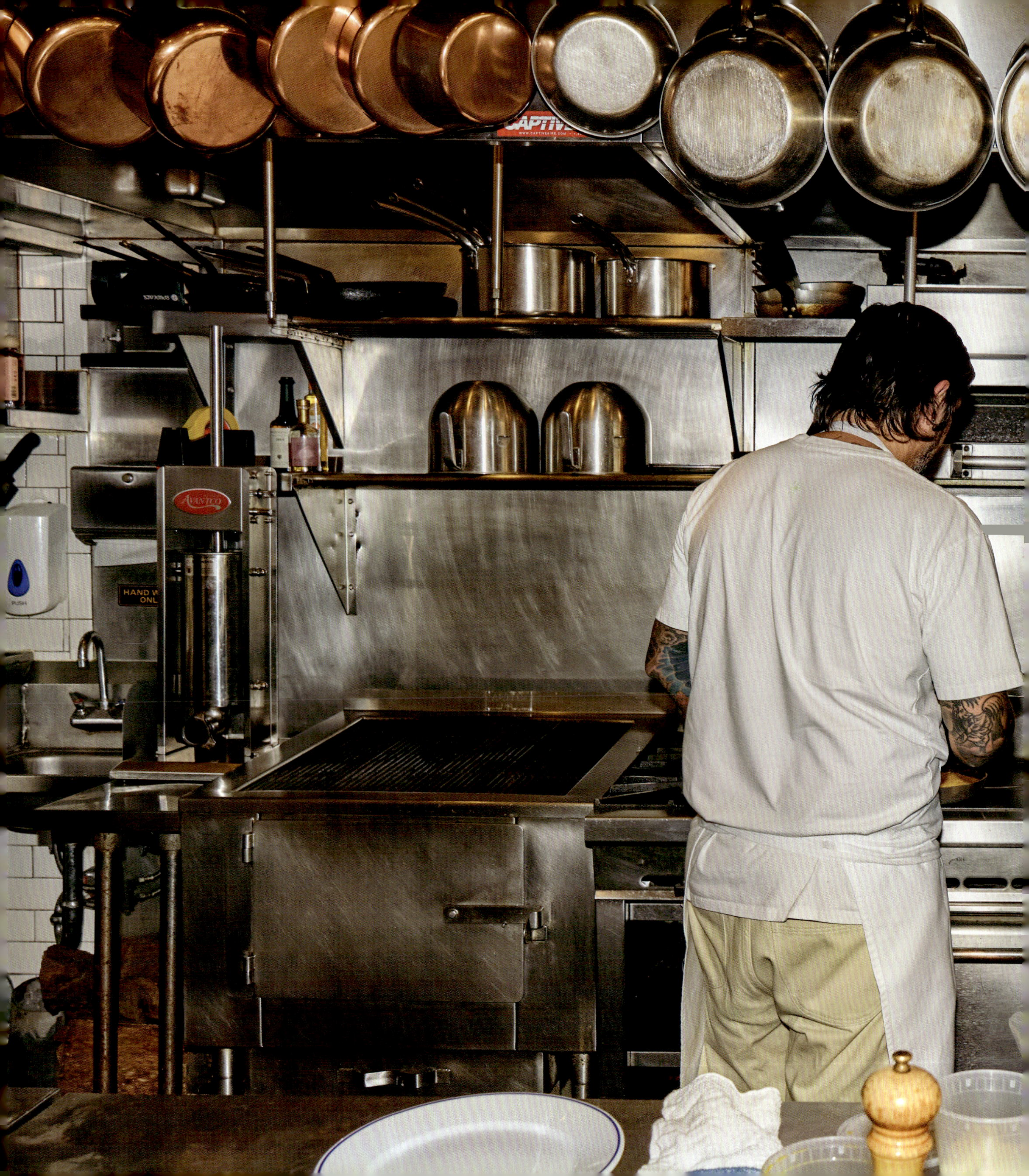
Avantco

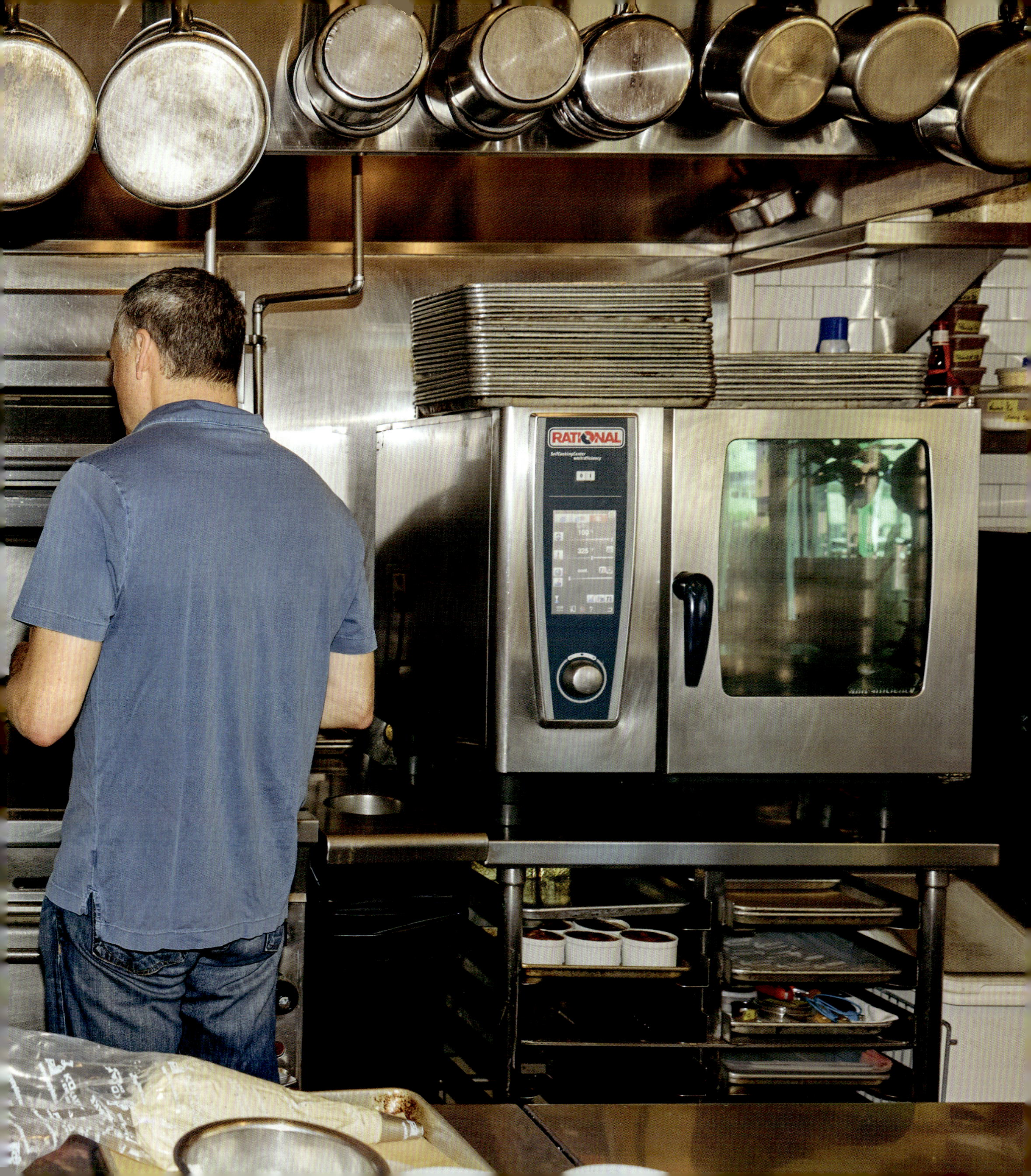
RATIONAL

# Index

## A

aioli
   Joe's Anchovy-Caper Aioli, 303
   Nancy's Calabrian Chili-Mint Aioli, 302
Ajay Sahgal's Peanut Butter and Pickle Sandwich, 85
Akimowicz, Joanna, 61
Aleppo, Syria, 163
Alex's Lemonade Stand Foundation for Childhood Cancer, 79
almonds
   Carolina Bazán's White Gazpacho, 109–12
   GGET's Toasted Almond-Macadamia Milk, 327–28
   Salam Dakkak's Fatet Muskhan, 229–32
Ambrosia Bistró, Santiago, 109
American cheese
   The Crustburger, 99–100
   Orfali Bros' Cheeseburger, 95–96
anchovy fillets
   Daniele Uditi's Spaghetti alla Puttanesca, 183–84
   Joe's Anchovy-Caper Aioli, 303
   Mason Royal's Lemony Chicken with Garlic-Anchovy Sauce, 191–92
   Tracy Malachek's Cavatelli with Tomatoes, Anchovies, and Garlic Bread Crumbs, 187–90
Angel's Gochujang Wing Sauce
   Angel Barreto's Korean Fried Chikin Wings, 141–44
   recipe, 312
Angel's White Barbecue Sauce
   Angel Barreto's Korean Fried Chikin Wings, 141–44
   recipe, 313
Anju, Washington, DC, 141, 312, 313
Antico Forno Giglio, Florence, 257
arborio rice, in Gverović-Orsan's Black Risotto, 251
Arbroath smokies fillets, in Roseleaf's Cullen Skink (Scottish Smoked Fish Chowder), 125–26
arugula
   Bill Miller's Turkey-Brie Sandwich, 81–82
   Marc Vetri's Mortadella and Ricotta Sandwich, 79–80

## B

bacon
   The Carolina, 103
   Max's Fluffy Eggs with Slab Bacon and Toast, 35–37
   Mohamad's Brown Butter Caramelized Onions, 299
   The Music City, 103
baguettes
   Joe Beddia's Tuna and Smoked Sardine Hoagie, 73–74
   Marc Vetri's Mortadella and Ricotta Sandwich, 79–80
Baharat (Seven Spice Blend)
   recipe, 232
   Salam Dakkak's Fatet Muskhan, 229–32
Bait Maryam, Dubai, 229, 323
bakeries
   Antico Forno Giglio, Florence, 257
   Homeboy Bakery, Los Angeles, 57
   Laugarvatn Fontana bakery, Iceland, 49
   Sweet T's Bakery, Philadelphia, 285
Balasubramanian, Rupa, 153
banana leaves, in Seng Luangrath's Moak Paa (Steamed Fish in Sticky Rice Marinade), 205–7
bananas, in Lily's Chocolate Chip–Streusel Banana Bread, 55–56
barbecue sauce
   Angel's White Barbecue Sauce, 313
   The Carolina (Big Daddy's Hot Dog), 103
   The Music City (Big Daddy's Hot Dog), 103
barberries, in Bonnie Morales's Duck Plov, 221–23
Barcelona, Spain, 145
Barreto, Angel III, 141, 312, 313
Bars, Bob Champion's Chocolate Peanut Butter Triple Layer, 265–67
Bavel, Los Angeles, 235
Bayer, Sieger, 167
Bayildi, Mohamad Orfali's Charred Eggplant, 163–64
Bazán, Carolina, 109
beans, in Frijoles Negros, 121–22. *See also* garbanzo beans
Beddia, Joe, 73
beef. *See also* ground beef
   Debra Barone's Braciole, 247–50
   Sholo Olunloyo's Charred Steak with Olive Oil, 197–98
   The SPACCA Burger, 93–94
beets. *See* Roasted Golden Beets with Verjus Marinade
Ben and Jeremy's Seafood Boil, 239–44
Benjamin, Jeff, 79
Bergsson, Jón, 61
berries
   Buckwheat Blossom Farm's Wild Blueberry Pie, 283
   The Pie Guy's Marionberry Pie, 277–81
   Rob Weiner's Poppy Seed Cake, 275–76

Bhanage, Yash, 153
Big Daddy's Grilled Onions, 102
Big Daddy's Hot Dogs, 101–3
Big Daddy's Slaw, 104
Big Daddy's Slaw Sauwce
   The Big Daddy, 102
   Big Daddy's Slaw, 104
   recipe, 321
Big Daddy's Spicy Mayo
   The Big Daddy, 102
   The Carolina, 103
   recipe, 104
Big Sky Bread, Portland, Maine, 69
Bill Miller's Turkey-Brie Sandwich, 81–82
Bill's Red Onion Cranberry Sauce
   Bill Miller's Turkey-Brie Sandwich, 81–82
   recipe, 82
Birdie's, Austin, 187
Biryani, Chintan Pandya's Lucknow Dum, 215–17
Biryani Dough
   Chintan Pandya's Lucknow Dum Biryani, 215–17
   recipe, 219
Bisquick, in Steve Horan's Fried Chicken Livers, 151–52
Bite into Maine (food truck), 87
Bite into Maine's Curry Lobster Roll, 87–88
black cocoa powder, in DeLaney Harter Rosenthal's One-Bowl Black Brownies, 261–62
blood oranges, in Richard's Staten Island, 179
blue cheese, in Wife & Husband's Honey Cheese Toast, 25–26
Bob Champion's Chocolate Peanut Butter Triple Layer Bars, 265–67
Bombay Canteen Kulcha
   recipe, 324–26
   Saw Naing's Pe Hainn (Coconut Chickpea Curry with Greens), 121–22
The Bombay Canteen, Mumbai, 153, 316
The Bombay Canteen's Butter Garlic Crab Kulcha, 153–54
Bonnie Morales's Duck Plov, 221–25
bourbon, in Richard's Staten Island, 179
Boursin cheese, in Ludo Lefebvre's French Omelette, 29–31
Boyle, Father Greg, 57
Braciole, Debra Barone's, 247–50
Brau∂ & Co.'s Cinnamon Rolls, 61–65
bread(s). *See also* baguettes; brioche bread/buns; buns; challah; ciabatta rolls; sandwiches; sandwich rolls
   Lily's Chocolate Chip–Streusel Banana Bread, 55–56
   Max's Fluffy Eggs with Slab Bacon and Toast, 35–37

Siggi Hilmarsson's Geothermal Lava
   Bread, 49–51
Wife & Husband's Honey Cheese Toast,
   25–26
The Yolko Ono (Fried Egg, Sausage, and
   Basil Pesto on Sourdough), 39–41
bread crumbs
   Debra Barone's Braciole, 247–50
   Garlic Bread Crumbs, 190
   Oma's Stuffed Cabbage Rolls, 211–13
Brie cheese, in Bill Miller's Turkey-Brie
   Sandwich, 81–82
brioche bread/buns
   Bite into Maine's Curry Lobster Roll, 87–88
   Chad Conley and Greg Mitchell's Tuna
      Melt, 69–70
   Orfali Bros' Cheeseburger, 95–96
   Wife & Husband's Honey Cheese Toast,
      25–26
brisket, in The SPACCA Burger, 93–94
broccoli, in The Only Way Ray Will Eat
   Broccoli, 119–20
Brock, Sean, 99
Brownies, DeLaney Harter Rosenthal's One-
   Bowl Black Brownies, 261–62
Brown Trading Company, 126
Buckwheat Blossom Farm's Wild Blueberry
   Pie, 283
buns
   Big Daddy's Hot Dogs, 101–3
   Bite into Maine's Curry Lobster Roll, 87–88
   The Crustburger, 99–100
   Orfali Bros' Cheeseburger, 95–96
   The SPACCA Burger, 93–94
Burchstead, Jeff and Amy, 283
burgers
   The Crustburger, 99–100
   Orfali Bros' Cheeseburger, 95–96
   The SPACCA Burger, 93–94
burger sauce. *See* Sean's Fancy Burger Sauce

## C

cabbage
   Big Daddy's Slaw, 104
   Korean-Style Cabbage and Carrot Salad,
      227–28
   Oma's Stuffed Cabbage Rolls, 211–13
Caffé Panna, New York, 291, 334
cakes
   Rob Weiner's Poppy Seed Cake, 275–76
   Scott Linder's Flourless Chocolate Cake,
      269–73
Calabrian chili peppers and pepper paste
   Daniele Uditi's Spaghetti alla Puttanesca,
      183–84
   Nancy's Calabrian Chili–Mint Aioli, 302

The Only Way Ray Will Eat Broccoli,
   119–20
Candied Orange Peels
   Dario Landi and Dania Nuti's Cavallucci
      Cookies, 257–59
   recipe, 260
Cardoz, Floyd, 153
The Carolina, Big Daddy's Hot Dogs, 103
carrots
   Ben and Jeremy's Seafood Boil, 239–44
   Big Daddy's Slaw, 104
   Duck Stock and Confit, 224–26
   Fish Stock, 131
   Judy Gold's Carrot Kugel, 173–75
   Korean-Style Cabbage and Carrot Salad,
      227–28
   Monica's Chicken Corn Soup, 113–14
   Salam Dakkak's Fatet Muskhan, 229–32
cashews, in San Xi Lou's Sichuan Spicy
   Chicken, 157–59
cavatelli, in Tracy Malachek's Cavatelli with
   Tomatoes, Anchovies, and Garlic Bread
   Crumbs, 187–89
Chad Conley and Greg Mitchell's Tuna Melt,
   69–70
Chad's Bread-and-Butter Pickle Chips, 298
challah
   Chad Conley and Greg Mitchell's Tuna
      Melt, 69–70
   Jennifer Heftler's Chopped Liver, 147–49
Champion, Erin and Bob, 265
Charred and Cured Eggplant and Red
   Peppers
   Mohamad Orfali's Charred Eggplant
      Bayildi, 163–64
   recipe, 165–66
Charred Spaghetti
   Daniele Uditi's Spaghetti alla Puttanesca,
      183–84
   recipe, 185–86
cheddar cheese
   Chad Conley and Greg Mitchell's Tuna
      Melt, 69–70
   The Music City, Big Daddy's Hot Dogs, 103
   The SPACCA Burger, 93–94
cheese. *See also* cheddar cheese; parmesan
   cheese
   Bill Miller's Turkey-Brie Sandwich, 81–82
   The Crustburger, 99–100
   Debra Barone's Braciole, 247–50
   Homemade Suzma, 228
   Ludo Lefebvre's French Omelette, 29–31
   Orfali Bros' Cheeseburger, 95–96
   Wife & Husband's Honey Cheese Toast,
      25–26
Chi SPACCA, Los Angeles, 93, 301, 302
chicken

Angel Barreto's Korean Fried Chikin
   Wings, 141–44
Mason Royal's Lemony Chicken with
   Garlic-Anchovy Sauce, 191–92
Monica's Chicken Corn Soup, 113–14
Salam Dakkak's Fatet Muskhan, 229–32
San Xi Lou's Sichuan Spicy Chicken,
   157–59
chicken andouille sausage, in Ben and Jere-
   my's Seafood Boil, 239–44
chicken livers
   Jennifer Heftler's Chopped Liver, 147–49
   Steve Horan's Fried Chicken Livers, 151–52
chickpeas. *See* garbanzo beans
Chikin Wings, Angel Barreto's Korean Fried,
   141–44
chile moritas, in Jimmy's Salsa de Chile
   Morita, 318–20
Chintan Pandya's Lucknow Dum Biryani,
   215–17
Chintan's Goat (or Lamb) Curry with Fried
   Onions
   Chintan Pandya's Lucknow Dum Biryani,
      215–17
   recipe, 218–19
Chi SPACCA, Los Angeles, 93, 301, 302
chocolate and chocolate chips
   Bob Champion's Chocolate Peanut Butter
      Triple Layer Bars, 265–67
   DeLaney Harter Rosenthal's One-Bowl
      Black Brownies, 261–62
   Lily's Chocolate Chip–Streusel Banana
      Bread, 55–56
   Scott Linder's Flourless Chocolate Cake,
      269–73
   Somebody Scoop Phil, 291–92
Chowder, Scottish Smoked Fish (Roseleaf's
   Cullen Skink), 125–26
Chuk, Stanley, 157
ciabatta rolls
   Bill Miller's Turkey-Brie Sandwich, 81–82
   La Casa del Abuelo's Gambas al Ajillo
      (Garlic Shrimp), 139–40
Cinnamon Coffee Cake, Homeboy Bakery's,
   57–59
Cinnamon Rolls, Brau∂ & Co.'s, 61–65
clams, in Ben and Jeremy's Seafood Boil,
   239–44
Clarified Butter
   Ben and Jeremy's Seafood Boil, 239–44
   recipe, 244
coconut, in Bob Champion's Chocolate Pea-
   nut Butter Triple Layer Bars, 265–67
coconut milk
   Marie Mercado's Halo Halo with Vegan
      Halaya, 289–90
   Sampaguita's Vegan Halaya, 332–33

INDEX • 345

coconut milk (*cont.*)
    Saw Naing's Pe Hainn (Coconut Chickpea Curry with Greens), 121–22
    Sticky Rice Marinade, 209
    vegan, in Marie Mercado's Halo Halo with Vegan Halaya, 289–90
coffee
    Cold Brew Concentrate, 24
    GGET's Iced Almond-Macadamia Latte, 23–24
Cookies, Dario Landi and Dania Nuti's Cavallucci, 257–59
corn
    Ben and Jeremy's Seafood Boil, 239–44
    Monica's Chicken Corn Soup, 113–14
corn flakes, in Marie Mercado's Halo Halo with Vegan Halaya, 289–90
cornichons, Jennifer Heftler's Chopped Liver served with, 147–49
corn tortillas, in Jimmy Shaw's Huevos Rancheros, 43–45
crab, in The Bombay Canteen's Butter Garlic Crab Kulcha, 153–54
cranberries, in Bonnie Morales's Duck Plov, 221–23
cranberry sauce, in Bill's Red Onion Cranberry Sauce, 82
cream cheese
    The Big Daddy, Big Daddy's Hot Dogs, 102
    Hallie's Vanilla Bean Ice Cream, 334–35
cream sherry, Steve Horan's Fried Chicken Livers with, 151–52
Croatia, 251
Crocante, Orlando, 201
The Crustburger, 99–100
cucumber(s)
    Carolina Bazán's White Gazpacho, 109–12
    Chad Conley and Greg Mitchell's Tuna Melt, 69–71
    Chad's Bread-and-Butter Pickle Chips, 298
Cullen Skink (Scottish Smoked Fish Chowder), 125–26
currants, in Debra Barone's Braciole, 247–50
curries
    Chintan Pandya's Lucknow Dum Biryani, 215–19
    Saw Naing's Pe Hainn (Coconut Chickpea Curry with Greens), 121–22
Curry Lobster Roll, 87–88
Curry Mayonnaise, Zesty, 88
curry paste, in Sticky Rice Marinade, 209
cuttlefish, in Gverović-Orsan's Black Risotto, 251

# D

Daddy's Dogs, Nashville, 101, 321
Dakkak, Salam, 229
Daniele Uditi's Spaghetti alla Puttanesca, 183–84
Danish blue cheese, in Wife & Husband's Honey Cheese Toast, 25–26
Dario Landi and Dania Nuti's Cavallucci Cookies, 257–59
Debra Barone's Braciole, 247–50
DeLaney Harter Rosenthal's One-Bowl Black Brownies, 261–62
Dominican oregano, in Yamuel Bigio's Puerto Rican Porchetta, 201–4
dry-aged beef fat, in The SPACCA Burger, 93–94
dry vermouth, in Richard's Staten Island, 179
Dubai, 95, 163, 229, 322, 323
Dubrovnik, Croatia, 251
duck fat
    Bonnie Morales's Duck Plov, 221–23
    Duck Stock and Confit, 224–26
    Jennifer Heftler's Chopped Liver, 147–49
Duck Stock and Confit
    Bonnie Morales's Duck Plov, 221–23
    recipe, 224–26
The Dutchess, Ojai, 121

# E

eggplant
    Charred and Cured Eggplant and Red Peppers, 165–66
    Mohamad Orfali's Charred Eggplant Bayildi, 163–64
eggs. *See also* hard-boiled eggs
    The Bombay Canteen's Butter Garlic Crab Kulcha, 153–54
    Jimmy Shaw's Huevos Rancheros, 44–45
    Joe's Anchovy-Caper Aioli, 303
    Judy Gold's Carrot Kugel, 173–75
    Ludo Lefebvre's French Omelette, 29–31
    Max's Fluffy Eggs with Slab Bacon and Toast, 35–37
    Scott Linder's Flourless Chocolate Cake, 269–73
    Soft-Boiled Pickled Eggs, 75–76
    The Yolko Ono (Fried Egg, Sausage, and Basil Pesto on Sourdough), 39–41
El, Tia and Mark, 285
espresso, in GGET's Iced Almond-Macadamia Latte, 23–24
*Everybody Loves Raymond*, 119, 247
Everyday Garlic-Ginger Paste
    Angel's Gochujang Wing Sauce, 312
    recipe, 314
    Saw Naing's Pe Hainn (Coconut Chickpea Curry with Greens), 121–22
Ezekiel, Arjav, 187

# F

Fatet Muskhan, Salam Dakkak's, 229–32
fennel bulb
    Fish Stock, 131
    Red Onion–Fennel Salad, 75
finnan haddie, in Roseleaf's Cullen Skink (Scottish Smoked Fish Chowder), 125–26
Fiorella, Philadelphia, 79
fish and seafood. *See also* salmon; shrimp; tuna
    Ben and Jeremy's Seafood Boil, 239–44
    Bite into Maine's Curry Lobster Roll, 87–88
    The Bombay Canteen's Butter Garlic Crab Kulcha, 153–54
    Gverović-Orsan's Black Risotto, 251
    Jasper Pääkkönen's Lohikeitto (Finnish Smoked Fish Soup), 129–31
    Roseleaf's Cullen Skink (Scottish Smoked Fish Chowder), 125–26
    Siggi Hilmarsson's Geothermal Lava Bread with, 49–51
Fish Stock
    Gverović-Orsan's Black Risotto, 251
    Jasper Pääkkönen's Lohikeitto (Finnish Smoked Fish Soup), 129–31
    recipe, 131
flatbread
    Bombay Canteen Kulcha, 324–26
    The Bombay Canteen's Butter Garlic Crab Kulcha, 153–54
    Bonnie Morales's Duck Plov, 221–23
    Mike Solomonov and Andrew Henshaw's Lamb and Beef Koobideh, 235–38
    Salam Dakkak's Fatet Muskhan, 229–32
    Saw Naing's Pe Hainn (Coconut Chickpea Curry with Greens), 121–22
Florence, Italy, 257
Fort Williams Park, Cape Elizabeth, 87
Fried Egg I'm In Love (food truck), Portland, Oregon, 39, 304
Frijoles Negros
    Jimmy Shaw's Huevos Rancheros with Salsa de Chile Morita and, 43–45
    recipe, 45

# G

Gagnon, Debbie, 89
garbanzo beans
    Bonnie Morales's Duck Plov, 221–23
    Saw Naing's Pe Hainn (Coconut Chickpea Curry with Greens), 121–22
García, Thalía Barrios, 133
Garlic Bread Crumbs
    recipe, 190
    Tracy Malachek's Cavatelli with Toma-

toes, Anchovies, and Garlic Bread Crumbs, 187–90
Gazpacho, Carolina Bazán's White, 109–12
GGET's Iced Almond-Macadamia Latte (The "New York"), 23–24
GGET's Toasted Almond-Macadamia Milk
  GGET's Iced Almond-Macadamia Latte, 23–24
  recipe, 327–28
Glanville, Kyle, 23
goat cheese, in Homemade Suzma, 228
gochugaru, in Korean-Style Cabbage and Carrot Salad, 227–28
Gochujang Wing Sauce, Angel's
  Angel Barreto's Korean Fried Chikin Wings, 141–44
  recipe, 312
Go Get Em Tiger (GGET), Los Angeles, 23, 327
goji berries, in Bonnie Morales's Duck Plov, 221–23
Graham Cracker Crust
  recipe, 287
  Sweet T's Sweet Potato Pie, 285–87
graham crackers, in Bob Champion's Chocolate Peanut Butter Triple Layer Bars, 265–67
Great Chefs Event, Philadelphia, 79
ground beef
  The Crustburger, 99–100
  Mike Solomonov and Andrew Henshaw's Lamb and Beef Koobideh, 235–38
  Oma's Stuffed Cabbage Rolls, 211–13
  Orfali Bros' Cheeseburger, 95–96
  The SPACCA Burger, 93–94
ground lamb
  Mike Solomonov and Andrew Henshaw's Lamb and Beef Koobideh, 235–38
  Salam Dakkak's Fatet Muskhan, 229
Guzmán, Rodolfo, 109
Gverović, Igor, Eta, and Nea, 251

# H

habanero chili, in Chad's Bread-and-Butter Pickle Chips, 298
haddock, in Roseleaf's Cullen Skink (Scottish Smoked Fish Chowder), 125–26
halaya. *See* Sampaguita's Vegan Halaya
Hallie's Vanilla Bean Ice Cream
  recipe, 334
  Somebody Scoop Phil, 291–92
hard-boiled eggs
  Bonnie Morales's Duck Plov, 221–23
  Jennifer Heftler's Chopped Liver, 147–49
  Monica's Chicken Corn Soup, 113–14
  Siggi Hilmarsson's Geothermal Lava Bread, 49–51

hazelnuts, in Marc Vetri's Mortadella and Ricotta Sandwich, 79–80
Heftler, Jennifer, 142
Helsinki, Finland, 129
Henshaw, Andrew, 235
Here's Looking At You, Los Angeles, 167, 311
Hilmarsson, Siggi, 49
Hoagie, Joe Beddia's Tuna and Smoked Sardine, 73–74
Homeboy Bakery, Los Angeles, 57
Homeboy Bakery's Cinnamon Coffee Cake, 57–59
Homeboy Industries, 57
Homemade Suzma, 228
Hong Kong, 157
Horan, Steve, 151
Hot Dogs, Big Daddy's, 101–3
Huckleberry (bakery), Santa Monica, 47
Hussain's Butter-Garlic Sauce
  The Bombay Canteen's Butter Garlic Crab Kulcha, 153–54
  recipe, 316–17

# I

Ibérico ham, 145
iceberg lettuce
  Iceberg Steaks, 71
  The SPACCA Burger, 93–94
Iceberg Steaks
  Chad Conley and Greg Mitchell's Tuna Melt, 69–71
  recipe, 71
ice cream
  Hallie's Vanilla Bean Ice Cream, 334–35
  Marie Mercado's Halo Halo with Vegan Halaya, 289–90
  Somebody Scoop Phil, 291–92
Iced Almond-Macadamia Latte, 23–24
Iceland, 49, 61

# J

Jace's Basil Pesto Sandwich Spread
  recipe, 304–5
  The Yolko Ono (Fried Egg, Sausage, and Basil Pesto on Sourdough), 39–41
jackfruit, in Marie Mercado's Halo Halo with Vegan Halaya, 289–90
jalapeño(s)
  Chad's Bread-and-Butter Pickle Chips, 298
  pickled, in The Big Daddy, Big Daddy's Hot Dogs, 102
  Thalía Barrios García's Mushroom-Tomatillo Soup, 133–35
Japan, 25
Jasper Pääkkönen's Lohikeitto (Finnish

Smoked Fish Soup), 129–31
Jennifer Heftler's Chopped Liver, 147–49
Jimmy Shaw's Huevos Rancheros, 43–45
Jimmy's Salsa de Chile Morita
  Jimmy Shaw's Huevos Rancheros, 43–45
  recipe, 318–20
Joe Beddia's Tuna and Smoked Sardine Hoagie, 73–74
Joe's Anchovy-Caper Aioli
  Joe Beddia's Tuna and Smoked Sardine Hoagie, 73–74
  recipe, 303
Joyland, Nashville, 99, 309
Judy Gold's Carrot Kugel, 173–75
jwala peppers
  Chintan Pandya's Lucknow Dum Biryani, 215–17
  Hussain's Butter-Garlic Sauce, 316–17
  Picked Red Onions, 154

# K

Kachka, Portland, Oregon, 221
kaffir lime leaf, in Sticky Rice Marinade, 209
kale, in Saw Naing's Pe Hainn (Coconut Chickpea Curry with Greens), 121–22
Kane, Jonny, 125
kewra water, in Chintan Pandya's Lucknow Dum Biryani, 215–17
khao niew sticky rice
  Seng Luangrath's Moak Paa (Steamed Fish in Sticky Rice Marinade), 205–7
  Sticky Rice Marinade, 209
kibbeh nayyeh, 229
Koobideh, Mike Solomonov and Andrew Henshaw's Lamb and Beef, 235–38
Korean Fried Chikin Wings, Angel Barreto's, 141–44
Korean-Style Cabbage and Carrot Salad, 227–28
Kosher pickles, in The SPACCA Burger, 93–94
Krause, Jace, 39
Kugel, Judy Gold's Carrot, 173–75
Kyoto, Japan, 25

# L

labneh, in Homemade Suzma, 228
La Casa del Abuelo, Madrid, 139
La Casa del Abuelo's Gambas al Ajillo (Garlic Shrimp), 139–40
La Cocina de Humo at Levadura de Olla, Oaxaca, 133
LA Loves Alex's Lemonade event, 79
lamb. *See also* ground lamb
  Chintan's Goat (or Lamb) Curry with Fried Onions, 218–19

lamb (cont.)
	kibbeh nayyeh, 229
		Mike Solomonov and Andrew Henshaw's Lamb and Beef Koobideh, 235–38
Landi, Dario, 257
Laser Wolf, Philadelphia, 235
Latte, GGET's Iced Almond-Macadamia, 23–24
Laugarvatn Fontana (spa), Iceland, 49
leafy greens, in Saw Naing's Pe Hainn (Coconut Chickpea Curry with Greens), 121–22
leche flan, in Marie Mercado's Halo Halo with Vegan Halaya, 289–90
Lee, Danny, 141
Lefebvre, Ludo, 29
Leith, Scotland, 125, 129
lemongrass
	Saw Naing's Pe Hainn (Coconut Chickpea Curry with Greens), 121–22
	Sticky Rice Marinade, 209
Levadura de Olla, Oaxaca, 133
Lily's Chocolate Chip–Streusel Banana Bread, 55–56
lobster meat/lobster rolls
	Ben and Jeremy's Seafood Boil, 239–44
	Bite into Maine's Curry Lobster Roll, 87–88
	Carolina Bazán's White Gazpacho, 109–12
	at Red's Eats, Wiscasset, Maine, 89
Los Angeles, California
	Chi SPACCA, 93, 301, 302
	Go Get Em Tiger, 23, 327
	Here's Looking At You, 167, 311
	Homeboy Bakery, 57
	LA Loves Alex's Lemonade, 79
	Lotería Grill, 43, 318
	Matū, 269
	Max & Helen's, 35
	Petit Trois, 29, 310
	Pizzana, 183
Lotería Grill, Los Angeles, 43, 318
Löyly, Helsinki, 129
Ludo Lefebvre's French Omelette, 29–31
Ludo's Dijon Vinaigrette, 310
lump crab meat, in The Bombay Canteen's Butter Garlic Crab Kulcha, 153–54

# M

macadamia nuts, in GGET's Toasted Almond-Macadamia Milk, 327–28
Madrid, Spain, 139
makdous muhammara, in Mohamad Orfali's Charred Eggplant Bayildi, 163–64
Malachek, Tracy, 187
Malibu Kitchen, 81
Marc Vetri's Mortadella and Ricotta Sandwich, 79–80

Marie Mercado's Halo Halo with Vegan Halaya, 289–90
marinara sauce, in Daniele Uditi's Spaghetti alla Puttanesca, 183–84
marionberries, in The Pie Guy's Marionberry Pie, 277–81
Martinez, Vidal, 57
marzipan, in Brau∂ & Co.'s Cinnamon Rolls, 61–65
Mason Royal's Lemony Chicken with Garlic-Anchovy Sauce, 191–92
Matū, Beverly Hills, 269
matzoh meal
	Debra Barone's Braciole, 247–50
	Judy Gold's Carrot Kugel, 173–75
	Oma's Stuffed Cabbage Rolls, 211–13
Max & Helen's, Los Angeles, 35, 93
Max's Fluffy Eggs with Slab Bacon and Toast, 35–37
McDougal, Anna, 283
meerrettich, in Oma's Stuffed Cabbage Rolls, 211–13
Menashe, Ori, 235
Mercado, Marie, 289, 332
Mexican crema, in Jimmy Shaw's Huevos Rancheros, 43–45
Mexico, 133
Mike Solomonov and Andrew Henshaw's Lamb and Beef Koobideh, 235–38
milk. See also coconut milk
	Bombay Canteen Kucha, 324–25
	GGET's Toasted Almond-Macadamia Milk, 327–28
	Hallie's Vanilla Bean Ice Cream, 334–35
	Rob Weiner's Poppy Seed Cake, 275–76
	Roseleaf's Cullen Skink (Scottish Smoked Fish Chowder), 125–26
	Siggi Hilmarsson's Geothermal Lava Bread, 49–51
	Steve Nathan's Vanilla Pancakes, 47–48
	White Gazpacho, 111–12
mixed greens, in Bill Miller's Turkey-Brie Sandwich, 81–82
Moak Paa (Steamed Fish in Sticky Rice Marinade), Seng Luangrath's, 205–7
Mohamad Orfali's Charred Eggplant Bayildi, 163–64
Mohamad's Brown Butter Caramelized Onions
	Orfali Bros' Cheeseburger, 95–96
	recipe, 299
Mohamad's Tarator
	Mohamad Orfali's Charred Eggplant Bayildi, 163–64
	recipe, 322
Monica's Chicken Corn Soup, 113–14

Morales, Bonnie and Israel, 221
mortadella, in Marc Vetri's Mortadella and Ricotta Sandwich, 79–80
mozzarella, in Wife & Husband's Honey Cheese Toast, 25–26
MSG substitute, in San Xi Lou's Sichuan Spicy Chicken, 157–59
Mumbai, India, 153, 215, 316, 324
mushrooms
	Seng Luangrath's Moak Paa (Steamed Fish in Sticky Rice Marinade), 205–7
	Thalía Barrios García's Mushroom-Tomatillo Soup, 133–35
The Music City, Big Daddy's Hot Dogs, 103

# N

Nancy's Calabrian Chili–Mint Aioli
	recipe, 302
	The SPACCA Burger, 93–94
Nancy's Ultimate Hamburger Onions
	recipe, 301
	The SPACCA Burger, 93–94
Nashville, Tennessee
	Daddy's Dogs, 101, 321
	Joyland, 99, 309
nasturtiums, in Mohamad Orfali's Charred Eggplant Bayildi, 163–64
Nathan, Steve, 47, 121
Nathan, Zoe, 47, 121
New York, 173, 215, 291, 334
*The New York Times*, 23
North Plains, Oregon, 277, 336
Nuti, Dania, 257
Nuti, Lorenzo, 257

# O

Oaxaca, Mexico, 133
Odam, Matthew, 187
Ojai, California, 121
olives
	Daniele Uditi's Spaghetti alla Puttanesca, 183–84
	Mason Royal's Lemony Chicken with Garlic-Anchovy Sauce, 191–92
	Red Onion–Fennel Salad, 75
Olunloyo, Shola, 197
Oma's Stuffed Cabbage Rolls, 211–13
Omelette, Ludo Lefebvre's French, 29–31
Onetto, Rosario, 109
onions
	Mohamad's Brown Butter Caramelized Onions, 299
	Nancy's Ultimate Hamburger Onions, 301
	Pickled Red Onions, 154
	Red Onion–Fennel Salad, 75

The Only Way Ray Will Eat Broccoli, 119–20
orange(s)
    Candied Orange Peels, 260
    Richard's Staten Island, 179
    Roasted Golden Beets with Verjus Marinade, 167–68
Orfali Bros' Cheeseburger, 95–96
Orfali Bros, Dubai, 95, 163, 299, 322
Orfali, Mohamad, 95, 163
Orlando, Florida, 201, 289, 332

## P

Paisley, Brad, 99
Palace Diner, Biddeford, Maine, 69, 298
The Palace Diner's Tuna Salad
    Chad Conley and Greg Mitchell's Tuna Melt, 69–70
    recipe, 71
Pancakes, Steve Nathan's Vanilla, 47–48
Pandya, Chintan, 215
panecillo tetiña, in La Casa del Abuelo's Gambas al Ajillo (Garlic Shrimp), 139–40
panko bread crumbs, in Garlic Bread Crumbs, 190
parmesan cheese
    Debra Barone's Braciole, 247–50
    Jace's Basil Pesto Sandwich Spread, 304–5
    The Yolko Ono (Fried Egg, Sausage, and Basil Pesto on Sourdough), 39–41
passata
    about, 186
    Daniele Uditi's Spaghetti alla Puttanesca, 183–84
pasta
    Charred Spaghetti, 185–86
    Daniele Uditi's Spaghetti alla Puttanesca, 183–84
    The Only Way Ray Will Eat Broccoli, 119–20
    Tracy Malachek's Cavatelli with Tomatoes, Anchovies, and Garlic Bread Crumbs, 187-90
peanut butter
    Ajay Sahgal's Peanut Butter and Pickle Sandwich, 85
    Bob Champion's Chocolate Peanut Butter Triple Layer Bars, 265–67
    Somebody Scoop Phil, 291–92
peanuts, in Bob Champion's Chocolate Peanut Butter Triple Layer Bars, 265–67
pea shoots, in Roseleaf's Cullen Skink (Scottish Smoked Fish Chowder), 125–26
Pecorino Romano
    Debra Barone's Braciole, 247–50
    Homemade Suzma, 228
    Tracy Malachek's Cavatelli with Tomatoes, Anchovies, and Garlic Bread Crumbs, 187–90
pepitas, in Toasted Pepita Crumble, 171
Pesto Sandwich Spread. *See* Jace's Basil Pesto Sandwich Spread
Petit Trois, Los Angeles, 29, 310
Philadelphia, Pennsylvania
    Fiorela, 79
    home of Shola Olunloyo, 197
    Laser Wolf, 235
    Pizzeria Beddia, 73, 303
    Reading Terminal, 285
Pickle Chips, Chad's Bread-and-Butter, 298
Pickled Cucumber Salad, 110
Pickled Red Onions
    The Bombay Canteen's Butter Garlic Crab Kulcha, 153–54
    recipe, 154
pickles
    Ajay Sahgal's Peanut Butter and Pickle Sandwich, 85
    The Big Daddy, Big Daddy's Hot Dogs, 102
    Secret Sauce, 96
    The SPACCA Burger, 93–94
Pickle Skewers, in Chad Conley and Greg Mitchell's Tuna Melt, 69–71
The Pie Guy, Oregon, 277
The Pie Guy's Marionberry Pie, 277–81
The Pie Guy's Pie Crust, 336
pies
    Buckwheat Blossom Farm's Wild Blueberry Pie, 283
    The Pie Guy's Marionberry Pie, 277–81
    Sweet T's Sweet Potato Pie, 285–87
pineapple, in Judy Gold's Carrot Kugel, 173–75
pine nuts
    Debra Barone's Braciole, 247–50
    Jace's Basil Pesto Sandwich Spread, 304–5
*Pizza Camp* (Beddia), 73
Pizzana, Los Angeles, 183
Pizzeria Beddia, Philadelphia, 73, 303
Plov, Bonnie Morales's Duck, 221–25
poleo leaves, in Thalía Barrios García's Mushroom-Tomatillo Soup, 133–35
Poppy Seed Cake, 275–76
Porchetta, Yamuel Bigio's Puerto Rican, 201–4
pork
    Spiced Breakfast Sausage, 41
    Yamuel Bigio's Puerto Rican Porchetta, 201–4
pork sausage, in Spiced Breakfast Sausage, 41
Portland, Oregon, 39, 221, 277, 304
potato buns, in The SPACCA Burger, 93–94
potatoes
    Ben and Jeremy's Seafood Boil, 239–44
    Jasper Pääkkönen's Lohikeitto (Finnish Smoked Fish Soup), 129–31
    Roseleaf's Cullen Skink (Scottish Smoked Fish Chowder), 125–26
    Thalía Barrios García's Mushroom-Tomatillo Soup, 133–35
potato starch, in Angel Barreto's Korean Fried Chikin Wings, 141–44
prosciutto, in Debra Barone's Braciole, 247–50
provolone cheese, in Debra Barone's Braciole, 247–50

## Q

queso fresco, in Jimmy Shaw's Huevos Rancheros, 43–45
Quintero, Ana, 133

## R

rainbow trout, in Jasper Pääkkönen's Lohikeitto (Finnish Smoked Fish Soup), 129–31
raisins
    Bonnie Morales's Duck Plov, 221–23
    Debra Barone's Braciole, 247–50
Raye's mustard, Eastport, Maine, 69
Reading Terminal Market, Philadelphia, 285
Red Onion–Fennel Salad
    Joe Beddia's Tuna and Smoked Sardine Hoagie, 73–74
    recipe, 75
Red Onions, Pickled. *See* Pickled Red Onions
Red's Eats, Wiscasset, Maine, 89
restaurants and eateries. *See also* bakeries
    Adda, Queens, 215
    Ambrosia Bistró, Santiago, 109
    Anju, Washington, DC, 141, 312, 313
    Bait Maryam, Dubai, 229, 323
    Birdie's, Austin, 187
    Bite into Maine (food truck), 87
    The Bombay Canteen, Mumbai, 153, 316, 324
    Brauð & Co., Reykjavík, 61
    Caffé Panna, New York, 291, 334
    Chi SPACCA, Los Angeles, 93, 301, 302
    Crocante, Orlando, 201
    Daddy's Dogs, Nashville, 101, 321
    The Dutchess, Ojai, 121
    Fiorella, Philadelphia, 79
    Fort Williams Park, Cape Elizabeth, 87
    Fried Egg I'm In Love, Portland, Oregon, 39, 304
    Go Get Em Tiger, Los Angeles, 23, 327
    Gverović-Orsan, Dubrovnik, 251
    Here's Looking At You, Los Angeles, 167, 311
    Huckleberry, Santa Monica, 47
    Joyland, Nashville, 99, 309

restaurants and eateries (cont.)
    Kachka, Portland, Oregon, 221
    La Casa del Abuelo, Madrid, 139
    La Cocina de Humo at Levadura de Olla, Oaxaca, 133
    LA Loves Alex's Lemonade, 79
    Laser Wolf, Philadelphia, 235
    Lotería Grill, Los Angeles, 43, 318
    Löyly, Helsinki, 129
    Malibu Kitchen, 81
    Matū, Beverly Hills, 269
    Max & Helen's Los Angeles, 35
    Orfali Bros, Dubai, 95, 163, 299, 322
    Palace Diner, Biddeford, 69, 298
    Petit Trois, Los Angeles, 29, 310
    The Pie Guy, North Plains, 277
    Pizzana, Los Angeles, 183
    Pizzeria Beddia, Philadelphia, 73, 303
    Reading Terminal Market, Philadelphia, 285
    Red's Eats, Wiscasset, 89
    Roseleaf, Edinburgh, 125
    Sampaguita, Orlando, 289
    San Xi Lou, Hong Kong, 157
    Thip Khao, Washington, DC, 205
    Tony Packo's, Toledo, Ohio, 85
Reykjavík, Iceland, 61
rice
    Bonnie Morales's Duck Plov, 221–23
    Chintan Pandya's Lucknow Dum Biryani, 215–17
    Gverović-Orsan's Black Risotto, 251
    Saw Naing's Pe Hainn (Coconut Chickpea Curry with Greens), 121–22
    Seng Luangrath's Moak Paa (Steamed Fish in Sticky Rice Marinade), 205–7
    Sticky Rice Marinade, 209
Richard's Staten Island, 179
ricotta (hand-dipped), in Marc Vetri's Mortadella and Ricotta Sandwich, 79–80
Risotto, Gverović-Orsan's Black, 251
Roasted Golden Beets with Verjus Marinade
    recipe, 168–69
    Sieger Bayer's Golden Beets with Tofu Crema and Verjus, 167–68
Rob Weiner's Poppy Seed Cake, 275–76
rolls. See ciabatta rolls; sandwich rolls
Romano, Ray and Anna, 43, 119
Roseleaf, Edinburgh, 125
Roseleaf's Cullen Skink (Scottish Smoked Fish Chowder), 125–26
Rosenthal, Ben, 239, 261
Rosenthal, DeLaney Harter, 261
Rosenthal, Lily, 55
rye flour, in Siggi Hilmarsson's Geothermal Lava Bread, 49–51
rye, in Richard's Staten Island, 179

# S

Saffron-Cardamom Cream, in Chintan Pandya's Lucknow Dum Biryani, 215–17
Sahgal, Ajay, 85
Salam Dakkak's Fatet Muskhan, 229–32
Salam's Fatet (Fatteh) Sauce
    recipe, 323
    Salam Dakkak's Fatet Muskhan with, 231
salmon
    Jasper Pääkkönen's Lohikeitto (Finnish Smoked Fish Soup), 129–31
    Seng Luangrath's Moak Paa (Steamed Fish in Sticky Rice Marinade), 205–9
    Siggi Hilmarsson's Geothermal Lava Bread, 49–51
Sampaguita, Orlando, 289
Sampaguita's Vegan Halaya
    Marie Mercado's Halo Halo with Vegan Halaya, 289–90
    recipe, 332–33
sandwiches. See also burgers
    Ajay Sahgal's Peanut Butter and Pickle Sandwich, 85
    The Best Classic Maine Lobster Roll, 89
    Bill Miller's Turkey-Brie Sandwich, 81–82
    Bite into Maine's Curry Lobster Roll, 87–88
    Chad Conley and Greg Mitchell's Tuna Melt, 69–71
    Joe Beddia's Tuna and Smoked Sardine Hoagie, 73–74
    Marc Vetri's Mortadella and Ricotta Sandwich, 79–80
    My Tuna Sandwich, 77
    The Yolko Ono (Fried Egg, Sausage, and Basil Pesto on Sourdough), 39–41
sandwich rolls
    Bill Miller's Turkey-Brie Sandwich, 81–82
    Bite into Maine's Curry Lobster Roll, 87–88
    La Casa del Abuelo's Gambas al Ajillo (Garlic Shrimp), 139–40
Sanghvi, Vir, 153
San Xi Lou, Hong Kong, 157
San Xi Lou's Sichuan Spicy Chicken, 157–59
sardines, in Joe Beddia's Tuna and Smoked Sardine Hoagie, 73–74
sausage
    Ben & Jeremy's Seafood Boil, 239–44
    Spiced Breakfast Sausage, 41
    The Yolko Ono (Fried Egg, Sausage, and Basil Pesto on Sourdough), 39–41
*Savoring Italy* (Scicolone), 247
Saw Naing's Pe Hainn (Coconut Chickpea Curry with Greens), 121–22
schmaltz, in Jennifer Heftler's Chopped Liver, 147–49
Schneider, Rhonda, 247

Scicolone, Michele, 247
Scotland, 125, 129
Scott Linder's Flourless Chocolate Cake, 269–73
Sean's Fancy Burger Sauce
    The Crustburger, 99–100
    recipe, 309
Seasoned Salt, 152
Secret Sauce
    Orfali Bros' Cheeseburger, 95–96
    recipe, 96
Seng Luangrath's Moak Paa (Steamed Fish in Sticky Rice Marinade), 205–9
serrano peppers
    Chintan Pandya's Lucknow Dum Biryani, 215–17
    Hussain's Butter-Garlic Sauce, 316–17
    Pickled Red Onions, 154
Seth, Sameer, 153
Shahzad, Hussain, 153, 316, 324
Shartar, Jeremy, 239
Shaw, Jimmy, 43, 318
Shaya, Alon, 235
sheep's milk, in Homemade Suzma, 228
shokupan, in Wife & Husband's Honey Cheese Toast, 25–26
Sholo Olunloyo's Charred Steak with Olive Oil, 197–98
shrimp
    Ben and Jeremy's Seafood Boil, 239–44
    Carolina Bazán's White Gazpacho, 109–12
    La Casa del Abuelo's Gambas al Ajillo (Garlic Shrimp), 139–40
Sichuan chili peppers, in San Xi Lou's Sichuan Spicy Chicken, 157–59
Sieger Bayer's Golden Beets with Tofu Crema and Verjus, 167–68
Sieger's Vegan Soya Crema
    recipe, 311
    Sieger Bayer's Golden Beets with Tofu Crema and Verjus, 167–68
Siggi Hilmarsson's Geothermal Lava Bread, 49–51
Silverton, Nancy, 35, 93, 119
Soft-Boiled Pickled Eggs
    Joe Beddia's Tuna and Smoked Sardine Hoagie, 73–74
    recipe, 75–76
Solomonov, Mike, 235
*Somebody Feed Phil* (television program), 17, 133, 235
*Somebody Feed Phil the Book* (Rosenthal and Garbee), 17, 119, 257
Somebody Scoop Phil, 291–92
soups
    Carolina Bazán's White Gazpacho, 109–12
    Jasper Pääkkönen's Lohikeitto (Finnish Smoked Fish Soup), 129–31

350 • INDEX

Monica's Chicken Corn Soup, 113–14
The Only Way Ray Will Eat Broccoli, 119–20
Roseleaf's Cullen Skink (Scottish Smoked Fish Chowder), 125–26
Thalía Barrios García's Mushroom-Tomatillo Soup, 133–35
sour grape juice, in Roasted Golden Beets with Verjus Marinade, 168–69
spaghetti
Charred Spaghetti, 185–86
Daniele Uditi's Spaghetti alla Puttanesca, 183–84
Spain, 139, 145
Spiced Breakfast Sausage
recipe, 41
The Yolko Ono (Fried Egg, Sausage, and Basil Pesto on Sourdough), 39–41
Spicy Mayo
The Big Daddy (hot dog), 102
recipe, 104
spindleworks.independenceassociation.org, 283
steak(s)
Debra Barone's Braciole, 247–50
Sholo Olunloyo's Charred Steak with Olive Oil, 197–98
Steve Horan's Fried Chicken Livers, 151–52
Steve Nathan's Vanilla Pancakes, 47–48
Sticky Rice Marinade
recipe, 209
Seng Luangrath's Moak Paa (Steamed Fish in Sticky Rice Marinade), 205–7
strained tomatoes, in Daniele Uditi's Spaghetti alla Puttanesca, 183–84
sushi rice
Seng Luangrath's Moak Paa (Steamed Fish in Sticky Rice Marinade), 205–7
Sticky Rice Marinade, 209
suzma
Bonnie Morales's Duck Plov, 221–23
Homemade Suzma, 228
sweetened condensed milk
Bob Champion's Chocolate Peanut Butter Triple Layer Bars, 265–67
Marie Mercado's Halo Halo with Vegan Halaya, 289–90
Sweet T's Sweet Potato Pie, 285–87
sweet potatoes, in Sweet T's Sweet Potato Pie, 285–87
Sweet T's Sweet Potato Pie, 285–87
Swiss chard, in Saw Naing's Pe Hainn (Coconut Chickpea Curry with Greens), 121–22
Syrian chili pepper paste, in Mohamad Orfali's Charred Eggplant Bayildi, 163–64

# T

Thalía Barrios García's Mushroom-Tomatillo Soup, 133–35
Toasted Pepita Crumble
recipe, 171
Sieger Bayer's Golden Beets with Tofu Crema and Verjus, 167–68
tofu
Sieger's Vegan Soya Crema, 311
Tofu Moak Paa, 206
Toledo, Ohio, 85
tomatillos
Jimmy's Salsa de Chile Morita, 318–20
Thalía Barrios García's Mushroom-Tomatillo Soup, 133–35
tomato(es)
Debra Barone's Braciole, 247–50
Frijoles Negros, 45
Jimmy's Salsa de Chile Morita, 318–20
Mike Solomonov and Andrew Henshaw's Lamb and Beef Koobideh, 235–38
My Tuna Sandwich, 77
The SPACCA Burger, 93–94
Tracy Malachek's Cavatelli with Tomatoes, Anchovies, and Garlic Bread Crumbs, 187–90
tomato broth, in Daniele Uditi's Spaghetti alla Puttanesca, 183–86
tomatoes, canned
Debra Barone's Braciole, 247–50
The Only Way Ray Will Eat Broccoli, 119–20
tomato puree, in Daniele Uditi's Spaghetti alla Puttanesca, 183–84
tomato sauce
Debra Barone's Braciole, 247–50
Oma's Stuffed Cabbage Rolls, 211–13
Tony Packo's Sweet Hots pickle slices, in Ajay Sahgal's Peanut Butter and Pickle Sandwich, 85
Tony Packo's, Toledo, Ohio, 85
Tracy Malachek's Cavatelli with Tomatoes, Anchovies, and Garlic Bread Crumbs, 187–90
tuna
Chad Conley and Greg Mitchell's Tuna Melt, 69–70
Joe Beddia's Tuna and Smoked Sardine Hoagie, 73–74
My Tuna Sandwich, 77
The Palace Diner's Tuna Salad, 71
turkey, in Bill Miller's Turkey-Brie Sandwich, 81–82
Turkish chili pepper paste, in Mohamad Orfali's Charred Eggplant Bayildi, 163–64

Twix bars, in Somebody Scoop Phil, 291–92

# U

ube
Marie Mercado's Halo Halo with Vegan Halaya, 289–90
Sampaguita's Vegan Halaya, 332–33
Uditi, Daniele, 119, 183
Uzbekistan, 221, 227

# V

VanDomelen, Bart, 277, 336
Vetri, Marc, 79
Vida Nueva Women's Weaving Cooperative, 133
Vila Viniteca, Barcelona, Spain, 145
Vinaigrette, Ludo's Dijon, 310
Virginia-style peanuts, in Bob Champion's Chocolate Peanut Butter Triple Layer Bars, 265–67

# W

Wagyu beef, 269
Orfali Bros' Cheeseburger, 95–96
Walker, John, 73
walnuts
Dario Landi and Dania Nuti's Cavallucci Cookies, 257–59
Mohamad Orfali's Charred Eggplant Bayildi, 163–64
Washington, DC, 141, 205, 312, 313
Weiner, Rob, 275
Whitener, Jonathan, 167
Wife & Husband's Honey Cheese Toast, 25–26
Wiscasset, Maine, 89, 283

# Y

Yamuel Bigio's Puerto Rican Porchetta, 201–4
yogurt
Chintan Pandya's Lucknow Dum Biryani, 215–17
Homemade Suzma, 228
Mohamad's Tarator, 322
Salam's Fatet (Fatteh) Sauce, 323
The Yolko Ono (Fried Egg, Sausage, and Basil Pesto on Sourdough), 39–41

# Z

Zahav, Philadelphia, 235
Zesty Curry Mayo
Bite into Maine's Curry Lobster Roll, 87–88
recipe, 88